# IMMIGRATION AND FREEDOM

# Immigration and Freedom

Chandran Kukathas

PRINCETON UNIVERSITY PRESS

PRINCETON AND OXFORD

Published by Princeton University Press
41 William Street, Princeton, New Jersey 08540
6 Oxford Street, Woodstock, Oxfordshire OX20 1TR

press.princeton.edu

Library of Congress Cataloging-in-Publication Data

Names: Kukathas, Chandran, author.
Title: Immigration and freedom / Chandran Kukathas.
Description: Princeton : Princeton University Press, [2021] |
    Includes bibliographical references and index.
Identifiers: LCCN 2020026318 (print) | LCCN 2020026319 (ebook) |
    ISBN 9780691189680 (hardback) | ISBN 9780691215389 (ebook)
Subjects: LCSH: Emigration and immigration—Social aspects. |
    Emigration and immigration—Government policy. | Liberty.
Classification: LCC JV6225 .K84 2021 (print) | LCC JV6225 (ebook) |
    DDC 304.8–dc23
LC record available at https://lccn.loc.gov/2020026318
LC ebook record available at https://lccn.loc.gov/2020026319

British Library Cataloging-in-Publication Data is available

Editorial: Ben Tate and Josh Drake
Production Editorial: Kathleen Cioffi
Jacket Design: Karl Spurzem
Production: Danielle Amatucci
Publicity: Kate Hensley and Amy Stewart
Copyeditor: Tash Siddiqui

This book has been composed in Adobe Text and Gotham

Printed on acid-free paper. ∞

Printed in the United States of America

10 9 8 7 6 5 4 3 2 1

*For Christine*

It is seldom that liberty of any kind is lost all at once.

—DAVID HUME, 'OF THE LIBERTY OF THE PRESS'

I should have loved freedom, I believe, at all times, but in the time in which we live I am ready to worship it.

—ALEXIS DE TOCQUEVILLE, *DEMOCRACY IN AMERICA*

# CONTENTS

# PREFACE

Books, like nations, have their histories. Such histories, when given expression, serve the purposes of their authors, who write them with an eye to their audiences. Histories are exercises in persuasion.

The origins of this book lie in two of its author's concerns. The first is political. As someone sceptical about the pretensions of the modern state, I have long been troubled by its claims to control the movement of people, and even more bothered by the consequences of its exercise of the power to do so. The second is philosophical. As a political theorist, I have for some time been unsatisfied by the contributions of philosophers writing about immigration given their preoccupation with the question of whether states have the 'right to exclude', or with the obverse question of whether people have a 'right to move'.[1] The philosophical concern explains why this book addresses the question of immigration differently. The political concern accounts for the kind of answer it offers.

That answer is *not* an argument for 'open borders'—sympathetic though I am to that ideal. There are plenty of works putting such a case, whether by arguing for the rights of people to move freely or against the claims of states to exclude them. I share with many of these authors an interest in free movement; but my purpose in this book is to address the question of freedom as a more fundamental concern.

It is often said that immigration is something of which we should be wary, particularly in the countries of the liberal democratic west, because the movement of peoples from other parts of the world threatens to transform our society and to undermine its fundamental values. Pre-eminent among these values are *freedom* and *equality*. The argument of this book is that the threat to freedom comes not from immigration but from immigration control. The logic here is not difficult to grasp. Immigration control is not merely about restricting border-crossing but as much, if not more, about constraining what outsiders might do once they have crossed the border into a society. But it is difficult to control outsiders without also controlling insiders, since insiders are all too ready and willing to hire, teach, rent to, trade with, marry, and generally associate with outsiders. Moreover, insiders and outsiders are not readily distinguishable unless there are instruments of control in place to identify one or the other. Indeed, immigration control begins with the very process of distinguishing nationals from immigrants, natives from foreigners—insiders from outsiders. This means settling a philosophically unsettleable question: who, or what, is a native or a national—an insider or an outsider? In the end, the question tends to be answered not philosophically but politically, and the answer, almost invariably, is that the outsiders are those that political authorities wish to keep out—to define as (would-be or potential) *immigrants*. Immigration control is as much the means of determining who are nationals as it is a way of protecting them from those who are not. Immigration control is, in a more fundamental sense than is usually appreciated, entirely about identity politics.

Immigration control is usually defended by the proponents of the principle of nationality on the grounds that the interests of our fellow nationals should take precedence over the interests of foreigners. The trouble is, in reality, the politics of immigration control begins with the conflict over who are the nationals and who are the foreigners. And to the extent that political settlements are reached about whether and how many foreigners should be allowed to immigrate, they reveal nothing more than that *some* of the interests of *some* of our compatriots are served, despite the objections or reservations of others among them. The conflict over immigration, in the end, is a conflict not between the interests of insiders and outsiders—or nationals and foreigners—but between the various interests found within a society. This conflict has turned into a particularly destructive one because, as the immigration issue has been cast as an existential challenge to the integrity of states, so has the response been to develop solutions that threaten to do greater damage still to the institutions and values that make them hospitable places in which to live.

To show this requires a philosophical argument that builds both on a certain amount of necessary conceptual analysis, as well as a theoretical account of legal and political processes. This book differs from other studies of the political theory of immigration not only in its main line of argument but in another important respect. It approaches the immigration issue guided by a conviction that the philosophical question is best addressed on the basis of a deeper appreciation of the empirical reality of immigration—as a phenomenon to be understood in historical, institutional, and broadly legal and sociological terms. While there is an important place for purely philosophical investigations, that is not enough if immigration is really the subject. A philosophical examination of, for example, the question of whether immigration restrictions are 'coercive', might, if done well, tell us a great deal about how to understand 'coercion', but not very much about immigration restrictions unless it includes some consideration of the institutions and practice of immigration control. While I have engaged with philosophers and political theorists, I have drawn more extensively on the work of historians, political scientists, anthropologists, lawyers, and sociologists. The moral and political questions related to immigration cannot be addressed adequately without an acknowledgement of immigration's complexity and variability—and indeed of the difficulties that arise even when one tries to identify the phenomenon. Immigration is, after all, a concept we use to describe an aspect of the world of human affairs; but human beings do not always act with our concepts in mind. Sociologists and lawyers have grappled with this problem in work that has much to contribute to discussions of immigration in political theory,[2] just as political scientists and historians have helped us understand what immigration, and immigration control, look like. Taking this approach, drawing more freely on empirical social science than is usual in a work of political theory, has made this book longer than I originally intended. My hope is that this decision has paid off.

My aim in this inquiry, ultimately, is not to advance a set of solutions to the immigration questions we confront but rather to invite the reader to think through the issue in the way I have presented it. In essence, it draws out the implications of immigration control for values many people say they cherish, and asks that we consider whether the price of control is worth paying. It does not describe a possible world in which immigration controls have become negligible or insignificant—much less tell us how to get there—and it is, on the whole, less than sanguine about the immediate prospects of freedom.

David Hume, before finally publishing his *Treatise of Human Nature*, was criticized by Francis Hutcheson for his work's 'want of warmth in the cause of virtue'. He responded by insisting that he was a moral 'anatomist' and not a moral 'painter'. I have aimed in this work to be more of the former, though I hope the reader will also find in its pages some evidence of the latter. The epilogue to the book is a final effort to redress any imbalance.

# 1

# Panoptica

There was of course no way of knowing whether you were being watched at any given moment.
—GEORGE ORWELL, *NINETEEN EIGHTY-FOUR*

'Don't look at him!' he snapped, without noticing how odd it was to speak to free men in this way.
—FRANZ KAFKA, *THE TRIAL*

Borders have guards and guards have guns.
—JOSEPH CARENS, 'ALIENS AND CITIZENS'

## A Modern Panopticon

Immigration controls are restrictions on individual freedom. In debates about immigration, however, freedom is rarely mentioned. When it is raised it is usually indirectly, and the contending parties typically divide into those who question the wisdom or the morality of limiting the movement of would-be immigrants and others who think such restrictions warranted. The language of freedom does not make much of an appearance, perhaps because the liberty of foreigners or aliens does not really interest most people. Those who favour immigration commonly express a concern for the welfare of outsiders; others, who would rather such people did not immigrate, appeal to the welfare of natives and the integrity of the nation as the things that really matter. Freedom is never itself the issue.

The point of this book is to put freedom at the centre of the immigration question. At stake are the liberty of citizens and other residents of the free society, and therefore the free society itself. To put it simply, immigration controls are controls on people, and it is not possible to control some people without controlling others. More to the point, it is not possible to control outsiders (aliens, foreigners, would-be immigrants) without controlling insiders as well. Immigration controls are not merely border controls but controls on the freedom of the population residing within those borders. The purpose of this work is to show why this must be so, and to explain why it is significant. The conclusion it defends is that if we value freedom—as we should—we ought to be wary of immigration control.

This conclusion is unlikely to be a popular one. Even within the academy, which is on the whole sympathetic to freedom of movement, few find the idea of much more open immigration either attractive or plausible. Among the general population in modern liberal democracies, most think immigration should be limited, and significant numbers argue that it should be substantially reduced. To advocate a reduction, let alone the removal, of immigration controls in such circumstances would therefore seem to many a slightly quixotic, if not entirely preposterous, endeavour. Nonetheless, I think it is important to make the case. This work is not so much a defence of 'open borders' as an invitation to think through the implications of immigration control, even if it nonetheless recognizes that scepticism about immigration control has largely been expressed by advocates of open borders.[1] In the end, what I hope to show is that we have very good reason to take the idea of more open immigration seriously by bringing its detractors to acknowledge the heavy price we must pay to keep our borders controlled.

That price, I should say at the outset, is not an economic one. While economic considerations are not unimportant (and will be addressed in due course), the point here is not to advance the economic case for freedom of movement. It is rather to explore the relationship between open immigration and the free society. This is, in the end, an essay on the nature of a free society.

If there is a passage anywhere that captures the spirit of the argument that will unfold in these pages it is the funeral oration delivered by Pericles in Thucydides's *History of the Peloponnesian War*, reminding his fellow Athenians of what it means to live in a free society. There he said:

The freedom which we enjoy in our government extends also to our ordinary life. There, far from exercising a jealous surveillance over each other, we do not feel called upon to be angry with our neighbour for doing what he likes, or even to indulge in those injurious looks which cannot fail to be offensive, although they inflict no positive penalty. But all this *ease* in our private relations does not make us lawless as citizens.[2]

It is true, Pericles boasts, that 'the magnitude of our city draws the produce of the world into our harbour, so that to the Athenian the fruits of other countries are as familiar a luxury as those of his own'. But this is also possible because: 'We throw open our city to the world, and never by alien acts exclude foreigners from any opportunity of learning or observing, although the eyes of an enemy may occasionally profit by our liberality; trusting less in system and policy than to the native spirit of our citizens.'[3]

To draw inspiration from this passage is not to hold up the slave-dependent polis of ancient Athens as a model for modern society, or to buy uncritically into Pericles's rosy portrait of his city. Indeed, the historical Pericles was himself hardly an advocate of equality for immigrants and had been the architect of a system of restrictions on the rights and freedoms of non-Athenians. Plutarch recounts that upon being chosen once again by the Athenians to lead them as a general, Pericles asked that the law 'concerning base-born children, which he himself had formerly caused to be made, might be suspended; so that the name and race of his family might not, for want of a lawful heir to succeed, be wholly lost and extinguished.' That law, which Pericles had introduced in 451 BCE, provided that from then onward only children born of parents both of whom were Athenian could acquire citizenship.[4] Still, this does not change the fact that the Athens of the day stood in plain contrast to the outlook of Sparta, whose practice of *xenēlasia* (the arbitrary and deliberately violent expulsion of foreigners or immigrants) was criticized by Pericles as inconsistent with the Greek way of thinking.[5]

The funeral oration resonates with the thesis of this book because it offers a reflection on what it means for a society to be free. The freedom to be prized is in some ways a very ordinary thing, consisting in not being hindered or obstructed in the pursuit of our everyday ends, or watched as we go about our business, or prevented from associating with others from whom we can profit or to whom we wish to show our liberality. It means being able to live as we please under laws that recognize the freedom of all to go about their own business, and able to relate to one another not under the terms set by a system or policy but simply as people of the city. *It is to be at ease.* By implication, at least on this reading of Pericles, living freely means living in a society that is open to the world—from which others are not excluded—and not waking each day in trepidation of the risks that openness might bring.

In restricting the movement of people today we have been too little aware of what it means for the way we live. We have trained our focus on the immigrant and have dwelt on the perceived dangers of bringing foreigners into the state, but have not given much attention to what it means to create a society that tries to close itself off (if only to a degree) from the outside world. Even advocates of open borders have given relatively little consideration to this matter. Joseph Carens famously opened his defence of freedom of movement with the observation that 'borders have guards and guards have guns'.[6] His point was that violence is threatened or inflicted upon would-be immigrants, and that the power of the state when exercised to keep out 'ordinary, peaceful people seeking only the opportunity to build secure, decent lives for themselves and their families',[7] is a brutal and frightening thing. The presumption behind this observation, however, is that the guards sit at the border and that they and their guns face outwards. The truth of the matter is very different: the guns face *inwards* more often than they face out, and the guards are to be found not merely well within the boundaries of the state but in every part of society.[8] As we have tried to erect a fortress, so have we managed to build a prison. We have become used to living under surveillance, just as we are also getting used to monitoring each other in a panopticon[9] of the people. Whether or not we fully realize it, we are no longer at ease, and rely upon a policy and a system that threatens rather than secures our freedom. For some, it might mean living in fear, even as for others it means becoming complicit in a system of policing that contributes to this outcome.

The point of immigration controls is not simply to prevent entry into a state's territory, or to limit the numbers that come in, but to determine who may enter—and to restrict what people who enter may do. Few countries wish to reduce the volume of cross-border traffic, if only because most want to encourage tourism or to attract business.[10] In 2013, 69.8 million people entered the US as visitors, while more than 30 million entered the UK.[11] If citizens and residents are included, the numbers crossing American and British borders are even greater. While concerted efforts are indeed made to prevent people entering countries undetected by government authorities, the greater concern of governments is what those coming across the border do once 'inside'. Their worry is that they will seek employment, or enrol in a school or university to study, or try to reside for an indeterminate period of time, or marry, or set up businesses, or engage in any number of otherwise legal activities.[12] The problem is that visitors arriving in such large numbers cannot easily be monitored, and if they seek to work or remain for longer than permitted there is little authorities can do to keep track of their behaviour. This problem is exacerbated by the fact that citizens and residents are all too ready to cooperate with outsiders by hiring them, teaching them, buying their wares, and generally helping them to stay—either because they wish to take advantage of cheaper or more skilled labour some visitors can provide, or because they want to swell the ranks of their own groups with people of similar background, or because they have something to sell, or because they like their new-found friends, or because they fall in love. If visitors are to be kept from breaching the conditions of entry, it becomes necessary to monitor the behaviour of citizens and residents. For the restrictions under which visitors operate are largely restrictions on how they may cooperate with citizens and residents. If citizens and residents were disinclined to associate or cooperate with outsiders, the problem would never arise. Yet the propensity to truck and barter, and to collaborate in various (questionable as well as innocent) ways, is a deep feature of our nature, and foreigners will rarely find themselves welcome nowhere.

The only feasible way of monitoring and controlling would-be immigrants is to monitor and control the local population. It will be necessary to forbid among consenting adults not only capitalist acts, but also socialist, Christian, and more generally human ones—if one of those adults is a foreigner. Those in breach of laws forbidding such acts must be penalized—in the case of foreigners (and all too often, as we shall see, citizens) usually by deportation and the denial of any liberty to re-enter the country in the future—or punished, by fines, the rescinding of rights and privileges, or imprisonment.[13] Yet it is not just sins of commission that will attract the ire of the authorities. Citizens and residents will be expected to be vigilant in ensuring that they do not cooperate or associate inadvertently with foreigners—and to keep records to demonstrate that commitment. Employers will have to monitor their employees, teachers their students, international carriers their passengers, parents their nannies, doctors their patients, and Transportation Security Administration agents their fellow citizens. One nation under surveillance, its liberty diminished through unrelenting vigilance.

Now of course it remains to be established that the condition I am describing is one that should be cause for concern, let alone alarm. Every society places some restrictions on the freedom of its citizens and its residents, as well as on the movement and conduct of visitors. The question, it will be argued, is not whether there are restrictions in place but what limitations on freedom are warranted. And that is indeed the issue. The point of this book is to say that the loss of freedom is more significant than has been appreciated, and that the restrictions that make for that loss are not warranted. The gains, if they are in fact gains, are negligible, but the price is high. Immigration controls, more than many other instruments of governance, encourage the regulation of private and commercial life, the monitoring of social institutions—from schools and universities to professional organizations—and, at worst, the militarization of parts of society. So deeply can they intrude into the relations among people that make for civil life that they have the capacity to compromise a society's legal institutions as well as inflict serious harm on private citizens, their families and their communities. Unchecked, they encourage the replacement of the rule of law by regulations, of politics by police.

## The Apotheosis of Nationality

This brings us to a larger thesis that lies at the heart of this work. From the perspective of freedom, the root of the problem is a certain way of thinking about society, and the relationship between society and its inhabitants. Among political theorists, no less than among the rulers, civil servants, activists, and commentators who make up the political elite, society is imagined to be made up of *members*. That is to say, it is imagined that a society is some kind of unit comprised largely of people who *belong* together in some way, and whose belonging entitles them to determine who may or may not become a part of that unit, or indeed even enter the geographical space or territory it occupies. (The ambiguity in meaning of the word 'belong' ought not to go unremarked. People may wish to belong with others in their countries, but often states hold that their citizens belong to them whether or not those citizens wish it.[14]) The world is divided into territorial units occupied by members who have the right collectively to determine the participation or involvement in, and the membership, the character, and the future of, their particular units.

Yet the world was not always so divided,[15] and even today, societies are not made up entirely of members. They are made up of people: individuals, groups, and communities who pursue various ends or goals or purposes, most of which are independent of, or have no bearing upon, membership of their society. Some societies, such as Qatar, are made up predominantly of non-members: expatriates who have come to work to earn enough to make the move to a new place worthwhile. Others, like Singapore, have large expatriate populations living as residents for as long as their visas permit. The countries of the European Union are filled with non-citizens who have the right to reside in their chosen places because of their European identities, though business enterprises, universities, football clubs, orchestras, churches, and even state bureaucracies, all depend on and draw upon skilled people from all over the world. Even the numerous armies of the United States are sprinkled with soldiers, sailors, and airmen who are not American citizens and who, should they be killed in combat, would die not for their country but for their employer. In many parts of the world, there are entire peoples who remain unaware of their membership of the society that claims them: indigenous people in South America and large parts of Asia who have no idea of, or interest in, their citizen statuses.

In spite of these facts, philosophers and political leaders alike think of the world as (rightly) divided into territorial units that are (rightly) controlled by their members. Thus, Michael Walzer begins his reflections on justice by positing membership as the first issue any society must address,[16] while John Rawls, in describing the ideal society, asserts that it would be one in which immigration would have no place—for in an ideal world, why would anyone move?[17] In looking for employees, players, audiences, buyers, sellers, advisors, friends, lovers or computer gamers, people do not ask first, or even at all, about membership. Why then should political organization, and philosophical reflection on political society, begin with the premise that membership—political membership—is what matters, and matters above all else?

The thought running through this book is that membership is an ideal that is not only overrated but also dangerous from the perspective of freedom. It is at odds with the idea of people living together freely, for it subordinates that freedom to an altogether different ideal—one that elevates conformity and control over other, freer, ways of being. In the end, if we are to live freely, we must be able to relate to one another not as members but as humans. The point of immigration control is to separate us into members and interlopers, dividing us into groups of those whose legitimate place in a territory is beyond question and others who enjoy what entitlements they have as a matter of sufferance, and at the pleasure of the established residents. This is a bad thing not only for those whose status is uncertain but also for those who enjoy the benefits of membership, for in the end they too will have to sacrifice a portion of their freedom—even as they are led to regard as less than their equals those outsiders they are taught to see differently. Learning to be free means learning to live with others as equals, for without equality, freedom is nothing more than an advantage of power.

The general thesis of this book, then, is that immigration controls endanger freedom, for they threaten the freedom of residents and would-be immigrants alike. Immigration controls do so by transforming society into one in which control, and therefore the limiting of freedom, becomes necessary in order to preserve very different ideals. Those ideals, in the end, serve not so much human purposes as the ends or goals of a very different construction: an abstract entity whose interests will occlude and eventually subordinate the interests of the people it pretends to protect. That entity is the nation state. This work, in the end, also offers a critique of the ideal of nationality.

## The Structure of the Book

This work is divided into two parts. The first, comprising chapters 1 to 4, elaborates and refines the book's thesis by considering the nature of immigration, putting the case for being wary of immigration controls. Accordingly, chapter 2 begins with an account of the nature of *immigration*, and of what it might mean for borders to be open. Chapter 3 then presents an account of the ways in which attempts to *control* immigration pose a threat to the free society by increasing the extent to which individuals, groups, and communities are subject to surveillance, restriction, and sanction by the state, by its agents, and eventually, by each other. Chapter 4 turns to consider how this development undermines the institutions of a free society by looking at what it means for *equality* and the rule of law. The enforcement of immigration controls invariably requires the extension of arbitrary power, but also has a more deeply corrupting effect on social and political institutions generally, as must any policy whose purpose is to determine the shape and character of society as a whole. The elite will come to tyrannize over the majority until it brings the majority to tyrannize over itself.

The second part of the book asks whether this price is worth paying, for there are, after all, many advocates of immigration controls who think that such restrictions on freedom have important benefits. There are three main arguments that deserve serious examination: that immigration controls are economically beneficial, that they are necessary to preserve cultural integrity, and that they are warranted in the name of political self-determination. Chapter 5 takes up the arguments from *economy*, chapter 6 those from *culture*, and chapter 7 considers the political case for immigration controls in the name of the self-determination of the *state*. The purpose of each of these chapters is to show that the case for controls is without merit, for neither economics, nor culture, nor politics provide reasons for limiting the freedom of anyone, and certainly not of our fellow residents and citizens.

The conclusion of this book in chapter 8 brings us back to the fundamental moral and philosophical concerns that have prompted its writing. What, it asks, is a free society? And how do people in a free society relate to one another? The answer it offers is that such a society is one in which the spirit of liberality is at work, for the people are not dominated by a system but at ease in their relations with their fellows. Such a society, it concludes, can only be an open society. What this book offers then, along with a critique of nationality, is a theory of *freedom*.

# 2

# Immigration

*Immigrant*, n. An unenlightened person who thinks one country better than another.
—AMBROSE BIERCE, *THE DEVIL'S DICTIONARY*

In the popular imagination, immigration control is border control. This is evident in public discourse and this understanding is reinforced by political rhetoric and public policy, whether it is policy put into effect by governments or proposed by parties contending for power. The UK Border Agency, the US Border Patrol, and the Australian Border Force are just three examples of government agencies whose names suggest that immigration control is about policing a nation's borders. Even among political philosophers, discussion of immigration tends to begin with the assumption that the issue at stake is the claims of would-be immigrants against the rights or interests or natives or nationals: does one group have a claim to move freely, or does the other have a right to exclude? Yet further reflection suggests that immigration control begins not at the border, or even beyond the borders (where it extends, as we shall see), but with the definitions of immigration and immigrant—and so, by implication, of the notions of native and national. The first step in the exercise of control is to determine who is to be subject to control, and in the case of immigration it means establishing who is a native and who is a foreigner. One way of controlling the movement of people is by establishing through definition the number and type of people who need no permission to travel or to enter a territory or to exercise a variety of rights that are denied to others. Immigration control begins not with walls or fences but with *classification.*

Consider the example of Freddie Mercury, the lead singer of Queen, who was born Farokh Bulsara in Zanzibar (then a British protectorate) in 1946 to Parsi parents who had moved there from India. At the time of his birth he held no citizenship but was simply a British subject, until the British Nationality Act of 1948 created the status of 'Citizen of the United Kingdom and Colonies' (CUKC). There was no difference between the rights of CUKCs and other British subjects, and when the future rock star and his parents moved to Britain in 1964 it was as persons with the right to enter and live in the United Kingdom. Before the 1948 act, all British subjects in principle enjoyed freedom of movement and the right of abode within the empire—though in practice they enjoyed the right to move only to Britain and not to other countries such as Australia and New Zealand, which imposed their own immigration controls.[1] The earlier British Nationality and Status of Aliens Act of 1914 (which followed the 1911 Imperial Conference) had postulated that there was an equality of citizenship across the whole of the British Empire—without regard to race, ethnicity or religion. This meant that at the empire's height (around 1922) about 458 million people—a quarter of the world's population—shared a common nationality. Indeed, the figure here is a conservative one. According to Enoch Powell, 'by the end of the Second World War there were in the world some eight hundred million persons born outside the United Kingdom but endowed in the United Kingdom with all the rights of British subjects'. He added: 'In respect of British subjects . . . there neither was nor could be an immigration policy. All possessed under United Kingdom law the same unqualified right of entry and domicile.'[2]

But anxiety about the number of people from the Commonwealth moving to Britain led to the revision of British nationality law, which gradually restricted the freedom of British subjects outside Britain itself to move to the UK. The Immigration Act 1971 effectively divided CUKCs into two groups, distinguishing those who did from those who did not have the right of abode in the UK. By 1983 six different tiers of nationality had been created under the British Nationality Act 1981, and Commonwealth citizens ceased to be recognized as British subjects. Over the course of fifty years after the end of the Second World War Britain lost an empire, and millions of people lost a nationality even as they acquired new ones.[3] Immigration control was not the only purpose that lay behind these changes, but it was undoubtedly the most important. The more general point of principle to note, however, is that immigration control is not straightforwardly about protecting the interests of nationals from would-be immigrants, for immigration control plays a critical role in the establishment of nationality.

If immigration control begins with the act of defining and classifying persons, any investigation into the question of immigration should properly start by trying to understand what immigration could mean. This will require further investigation of related concepts, including nationality, citizenship, and borders. It is what we turn to now.

## The Problem of Definition

Though immigration and border controls are much discussed, definitions of these terms are hard to come by. Perhaps this is because it is assumed that they are words that are easily grasped and widely understood, making close investigation unnecessary. Nonetheless, the notions of immigration and border control deserve more careful conceptual and theoretical scrutiny, for it is far from obvious what (or who) is an immigrant, and what controlling immigration or borders means. Advocates of open borders, no less than the defenders of immigration restrictions, have not given sufficient attention to the question of what makes a border open or closed. Yet understanding the nature of immigration and border controls is vital if the moral and political issues surrounding immigration are to be properly addressed.

One reason why definition is a problem is that these terms do not identify 'natural kinds' but are, in fact, moral or normative notions.[4] An immigrant is not a person with particular characteristics (such as age or sex or race) but someone who is identified as such for reasons that are varied and contested. A border is also not something natural but political, and it is no less difficult to identify—since it too is variable and often contested. Immigration is not the movement of a natural kind (by an immigrant, or a person who becomes an immigrant by moving) across another fixed or natural physical entity or space, but the assuming or acquiring of a new status, or a new set of rights, or a new identity, by persons who may or may not move to do so.

Another reason the definitional question is complicated is that immigration and political borders are relatively recent phenomena. Human movement may be as old as humanity itself: there have been migrations of people stretching back to prehistoric times, and such movements continue even now, as changing physical landscapes, economic transformations, and natural and human-caused disasters prompt people to leave their homes for distant alternatives. Indeed, we are just beginning to appreciate the extent to which population movement has been a natural feature of life in many parts of the world, and was even before the advent of industrial society.[5] But migration is not immigration, for *migration is about demography, while immigration is about politics.* For immigration to become possible there must be political boundaries. More than that, there must be political agents (governments) who are capable of determining the location of these boundaries, who possess the technology and the resources to police their borders, and who are also sufficiently interested in monitoring both the movement of people across them and the behaviour of people within. Yet it was not until the rise of Napoleon that any ruler took the trouble to locate a country's borders with precision;[6] not until the First World War that serious efforts were made to control the movement of people between countries;[7] and not until the 1960s that the most prosperous countries in the world thought it necessary to distinguish legal from illegal migration.[8] Understanding the nature of immigration requires understanding the nature and development of the modern state. To date, comparatively little effort has been expended to try to understand these terms as interdependent notions.[9]

There is, however, a further aspect to this that has gone unremarked. Just as the term immigrant does not identify a natural kind, neither do the words 'native' or 'national'. What exactly is a native? More particularly, can an immigrant become a native or a national? (Personal experience tells me it is perfectly feasible.[10]) If such a transformation is possible, what does that tell us about how we should approach the issue of immigration control, especially if the arguments for control rest on assertions about the importance of protecting the claims and interests of natives over those of immigrants? If present immigrants are potential future natives or nationals, why should their interests be considered differently from those of current natives or nationals? On the other hand, if immigrants can never become natives or nationals, this might have important implications for our understanding of citizenship in a liberal democratic society committed to equality.

Definitions have consequences, though—as we shall see—they are also difficult to settle; but efforts to avoid them carry significant risks. In the matter of immigration control, the risk is that we lapse into incoherence, or fall into the trap of begging the question. If the point of immigration control is to protect the interests of nationals, but the laws governing immigration control do so by themselves defining the difference between immigrants and nationals, then the law cannot readily be defended on the grounds that its purpose is to uphold the claims of nationals when it can, at a stroke, turn an immigrant into a national. It would be entirely question-begging to defend the definition distinguishing national from immigrant on the ground that it serves to protect the interests of nationals.

The aim then of this chapter is, in the first instance, to offer an account of the meaning of immigration. I begin, in the section that follows, with the concepts of immigrant, native and national, before turning to the problem of understanding the nature of borders and border control—and, ultimately, of immigration and immigration control.

## Immigrants and Natives

According to the United Nations Department of Economic and Social Affairs, 272 million people or 3.5 per cent of the world's population lived outside of their country of origin in 2019,[11] representing more than a doubling of the numbers over the past twenty years.[12] Many, and possibly most, of these people are immigrants; but whether or not they are is hardly a straightforward matter.[13] Merely residing in a foreign country does not make one an immigrant, any more than does visiting a country as a tourist or a sportswoman or a guest lecturer or a delegate to a convention. Yet neither does one need to become (or even intend to become) a citizen of a country to which one has moved to be described as an immigrant. Equally, even a citizen might be re-classified as an immigrant if laws change, a border is moved, or rules once ignored are newly enforced.[14]

Consider the case of Mr Sikhou Camara, a Senegalese who was naturalized as a citizen of France in Rouen in 1966 after leaving the French colony for Bordeaux in the early 1960s. Twenty years later, on applying for citizenship for his wife, he was informed that she was ineligible because of an error in the naturalization process, which had seen him admitted to citizenship status at 20 rather than at the required legal age of 21. In 2012 Mr Camara was informed that he himself no longer held French citizenship and was officially an immigrant, though he would be granted a temporary residence permit.[15] This case is not a particularly unusual one: re-classifications of immigrant status are common. What it serves to highlight, however, is the problematic nature of any attempt to establish what or who is an immigrant. At what point did Sikhou Camara become an immigrant? Was it at the moment he arrived in Bordeaux? Or when he formulated an intention to stay in France indefinitely? Or when he decided to apply for naturalization as a French citizen? Or has he been an immigrant for his entire adult life? Do those who choose to live as permanent residents without taking up citizenship[16] remain immigrants—and more so than, say, people who have come only recently but take up citizenship at the first opportunity? When does one cease to be an immigrant?

Tempting though it is to say that immigration simply 'is the movement of a person or persons from one state into another for the purpose of temporary or permanent settlement',[17] the reality is more complicated, for neither political authorities nor scholars and advocates define immigration in the same way. There is no consensus on the definition of 'migrant' or the meaning of 'immigration'. In the UK, for example, there is no category or status of 'migrant' or 'immigrant' in law, only a distinction between those who do and those who do not have a 'right of abode' in Britain.[18] For some time, those who lacked the right of abode were regarded as more or less the same as 'Persons Subject to Immigration Control'—which is to say, persons who needed permission to enter or remain in the UK. Yet this implies that the large numbers of EU nationals who moved to Britain before Brexit, without being subject to restrictions on movement and already possessing the right of abode, were *not* immigrants.

There are various other ways of defining immigrants and immigration, but all are problematic to some degree. Migrants might be (and commonly are) defined as those who are foreign-born. The problem with relying on country of birth as the defining characteristic of migrants is that many citizens are born abroad, just as children born to parents temporarily resident in a country may not be entitled to citizenship, or even long-term residence, in their country of birth. Alternatively, migrants could be defined by nationality, taking immigrants to be those who reside outside their countries of citizenship.[19] Here several complications might arise. Many people who hold more than one nationality could move between some countries without ever immigrating. More problematically, people who were moved as children might find themselves in possession of a nationality of which they are unaware or to which they have no practical connection. There are numerous cases of adults classified as immigrants, despite having no memory of their official homelands, because they were born abroad and brought into the countries in which they were raised by parents who were not properly documented.[20] The children of fully documented foreign-born parents (or grandparents) might find themselves classified as foreign nationals in their countries of birth if their parents were never entitled to citizenship. In Malaya (later Malaysia), Indians, Sri Lankans, and Chinese residents were granted citizenship on the country's becoming independent on 31 August 1957. Until then, tens of thousands of people had no citizenship status in the country in which they were born and raised to adulthood.[21]

Even if the nationality issue were settled, however, there is a further complication arising out of the length of stay of any putative migrant. How long does one have to stay in order to be considered a migrant rather than a visitor? According to the UN, a 'long-term international immigrant' is 'a person who moves to a country other than that of his or her usual residence for a period of at least a year . . . so that the country of destination effectively becomes his or her new country of usual residence'.[22] In the UK the Office of National Statistics (ONS) uses this definition to measure migration flows, though it is not a universally recognized definition.[23] Indeed, within the UN itself, the international organization UNESCO offers a different understanding of migrant as 'any person who lives temporarily or permanently in a country where he or she was not born, and has acquired some significant social ties to this country', while also noting that 'this may be too narrow a definition when considering that, according to some states' policies, a person can be considered as a migrant even when s/he is born in the country'.[24] The problem with focusing on length of stay in the first instance is that in countries like the UK it is difficult to tell how long any individual will stay or has stayed when there is no mechanism for recording departures from the country—and no reliable way of assessing how many who report that they will stay for a particular length of time will remain longer or depart sooner than they indicated.

Migration data is counted in two ways following standard accounting principles: stocks and flows. It is difficult enough to establish the stock of immigrants given the problem of determining who is to count in the first place, though in principle it is a straightforward matter of adding up the numbers residing in a country at a given point in time. Measuring flows is more difficult still since the point is to calculate the rate of human movement over time.[25] Every year many people who move for specific purposes find their aims and interests changed by experience: would-be immigrants return home; sojourners or temporary workers settle for longer than they anticipated; some students may reside in a country for several years yet leave as soon as their degrees are completed, while others come for a semester abroad and find themselves wanting to remain indefinitely for personal or professional reasons. People become immigrants, but not always by design, sometimes unexpectedly; and they may also on occasion find themselves uncertain not only of their status but also of their plans.

Immigration is one aspect of the movement of people between states (just as movement is one aspect of immigration), but it is difficult to establish with precision who is an immigrant. In the end, governments, international organizations, and other interested agencies have adopted definitions of one sort or another in order to establish some kind of basis for policy. If the rights of immigrants are to be distinguished from those of visitors or residents or citizens, immigrants must be identified. If immigration targets are to be met, some measure must be found to establish how many people are coming and going. More particularly, if immigration is to be controlled, there needs to be some understanding of the subject of control. If precision and clarity cannot be achieved, policy can still be made and pursued, but the bearing of policy on individuals and societies more generally will be less certain.

This brings us back to the general point that has yet to be fully appreciated. The definition of immigrant and immigration is not a technical matter but a normative one. Indeed, it is a political matter. Immigration law does not determine what is to be done with immigrants as a natural kind but establishes (roughly but not always clearly or precisely) who is an immigrant and, in so doing, determines how certain kinds of people are to be treated. This point is all too little appreciated by political theorists as well as advocates and critics of immigration.[26] It is important not to overstate this. Some theorists have recognized that statuses like 'citizen', 'national' and 'immigrant' are normative constructs that are the products of the exercise of public power.[27] Nonetheless, the significance of this has been underplayed in discussions of immigration. That this is so is especially evident in discussions of 'illegal immigration', which is a notion that bears more careful scrutiny.[28]

The immediate point to note here is that immigration law varies from country to country, as does the extent to which immigration control is enforced. Moreover, the law is neither static—having changed (sometimes erratically) over time—nor consistent (or consistently applied), nor well understood by either would-be immigrants or employers or legislators or the general public other than immigration lawyers and similar professionals. There are a number of ways in which someone might run afoul of immigration law and be deemed an 'illegal', though as we shall see, whether violating such laws makes one an illegal *immigrant* is not always clear. An individual might act in violation of immigration law in some instances by crossing a political boundary without authorization—by failing to carry and present appropriate documents to the proper authorities at the border or port of entry, or by presenting fraudulent documents to gain entry. Alternatively, someone might gain entry by official channels (say by being admitted with a visa) but become an illegal by remaining in the country longer than officially permitted. Or someone might become an illegal by violating the terms of entry—say, by working or studying or setting up business or promoting a political cause or distributing samples of wares for sale or accepting remuneration of some sort or performing services rewarded in kind or simply by babysitting a grandchild without a work permit—even if the duration of a stay is limited.

Not all illegal 'immigrants' are illegal in the same way, since some transgressions of immigration law are *civil* violations, while others are deemed serious enough to warrant *criminal* prosecution. In the United States, remaining in the country without authorization is a civil violation remedied by voluntary departure or deportation, though this would become a criminal violation if the deported alien were to return unauthorized. This distinction is not as sharp as it might appear, however, since officials are reluctant to undertake criminal prosecutions in view of the higher standards of proof required by courts. Indeed, when would-be immigrants are apprehended attempting to enter unauthorized it is rare for either civil or criminal charges to be pressed in view of the costs to an immigration court system with a backlog of hundreds of thousands of cases.

An immigrant is not a person who can be identified by his or her legal status. In part, this is because immigration law is a political construction designed to serve a variety of ends, and as such one that depends on keeping the distinction between legality and illegality unclear. In the US case, legal scholars have noted, the notion of 'unlawful presence' in American immigration law is 'inconclusive by design'.[29] Many people live in a grey area between lawful and unlawful status while waiting (sometimes for years) for state officials to determine where they stand.[30] Immigration controls are thus not simply controls on the movement of 'immigrants' but more complex and not entirely clear or consistent mechanisms for defining who is and who is not an immigrant, and therefore also determining what that individual may or may not do within the borders of that country. The key to understanding the meaning of such notions as immigrant and immigration, then, is not population movement or entry into a country, but the standing or status people have when legal and political institutions define what they are free or unfree to do within the boundaries of the state.

Now, it might be objected at this point that a more common-sensical approach could surely be adopted. After all, even if there are some problems of definition, this is usual with most distinctions. We can distinguish an immigrant from a citizen just as we can separate the hirsute from the bald, despite the fact that no clear definition tells us precisely when the transition from one to the other is finally made. But the problem with defining immigration is not simply that there are a few grey areas or marginal cases where it is unclear into which category some people fit. The difficulty is that the definitional issue affects the way in which a great variety of people are categorized—and a great number of people as well. Proponents of immigration policy, and indeed states themselves, wish to limit and control the immigration of hundreds of thousands, if not millions, of people. Shifting from one understanding of 'immigrant' to another makes a significant difference to any assessment of what is actually accomplished by any particular policy or immigration regulation. Under UK and EU law before Brexit, people from Poland wishing to move to the UK enjoyed a right of abode anywhere in Great Britain and Northern Ireland, so Polish nationals who exercised that right were to that extent not immigrants.[31] This did not mean, however, that they were not subject to any controls on their movement. Deportations of EU citizens from the UK was made possible by a wide interpretation of Article 28 of Citizens' Directive 2004/38 which states that EU citizens can only be deported from another member state for reasons of public policy or public security. In 2017, the UK deported 5,301 EU citizens.[32]

A change of definition could raise or lower immigration figures by tens of thousands of people. Given that many have argued for a reduction of immigration—to Britain or the United States, or various European states, for example—the matter that needs to be clarified is what is being called for. Immigration control is not just about policing boundary crossing; it is in fact about managing, along with population movement, the rights, the status, and even the identities of people within as well as outside the borders of the state.

## Nationality: The Return of the Native

I must be the luckiest man in the world. Not only am I bisexual, I am also Welsh.

—JOHN OSBORNE, IN HERB GALEWITZ (ED.), *PATRIOTISM: QUOTATIONS FROM AROUND THE WORLD*

The definitional problem has a bearing not only on the status and claims of immigrants, however, but also on the status of natives—and indeed necessarily so. As was noted earlier, defining an immigrant has a bearing on the meaning or classification of native. We could use the terms national or nationality but that would not make matters any clearer. Establishing what is a native or a national is no easier, and is as much a normative (and political) enterprise as defining an immigrant. Consider the following options for holding someone to be a native or national.

> Definition 1: a native of a country is someone who was born in that country to parents both of whom are themselves natural-born citizens of that country—the definition sponsored by Pericles discussed in Chapter 1.
>
> Definition 2: a native of a country is someone who is born in that country to parents who are citizens of that country, the male partner being himself a natural-born citizen of that country and the female partner having been naturalized as a citizen of that country.
>
> Definition 3: a native of a country is someone who was born in that country to parents who are citizens of that country, provided one of those parents is a natural-born citizen of that country and the other has become a naturalized citizen of that country.
>
> Definition 4: a native of a country is someone who was born in that country to parents one of whom is a natural-born citizen, provided that the other parent has a legal right to reside in that country.

On these definitions, a native is someone whose ties to his or her native land are ties of blood and soil. A native must have been born in the country of nationality and must have parents who are natives. What makes these definitions demanding is that they require that the bloodline be unbroken—only the natural-born can pass on that status. Though no country today imposes so strict a test for the acquisition of nationality, it is not unheard of. Among the ancient Athenians, Metics struggled to acquire citizenship because the prevailing laws made it almost impossible for anyone to do so without ancestral ties to a citizen.[33] But this generated difficulties because claims of birth are notoriously complex. A part of the problem was that determining how thick blood ties needed to be was in the end a political matter and there was no obvious marker to distinguish legitimate from illegitimate lines of descent. While modern societies have placed less emphasis on tracing blood ties, vestiges of this preoccupation remain. Consider the following refinements in the definition of native or national.

> Definition 5: a native of a country is someone who was born in that country to parents both of whom are at least naturalized citizens of that country.
>
> Definition 6: a native of a country is someone who was born in that country to parents at least one of whom is a citizen (whether

natural-born or naturalized), provided the other has a legal right to reside in that country.

Definition 7: a native of a country is someone who was born in that country to parents who have a legal right to reside in that country and do not come from the wrong ethnic group.

Definition 8: a native of a country is someone who was born in that country to parents who have a legal right to reside in that country, regardless of ethnicity.

Definition 9: a native of a country is someone who was born in that country to parents at least one of whom has a legal right to reside in that country.

Under these definitions, a native is still identified by descent, but the bloodline does not need to descend 'all the way down'. A naturalized native can confer national status on his or her offspring; and by some definitions even legal residents might be able to do so. But now some mixture of territorial connection and blood is necessary. It is possible, however, for the basis of nationality to be moderated further. Consider the following definitions.

Definition 10: a native of a country is someone who was born in that country regardless of the legal status of the parents.

Definition 11: a native of a country is someone who was born anywhere to parents who are citizens of that country.

Definition 12: a native of a country is someone who was born anywhere to a father who is a citizen of that country.

Definition 13: a native of a country is someone who was born anywhere to parents either of whom is a citizen of that country.

Definition 14: a native of a country is someone who is a citizen (natural-born or naturalized) of that country.

Definition 15: a native of a country is someone who is a citizen (natural-born or naturalized) of that country and, if naturalized, has lived for at least ten years in that country.

On the first four of these definitions, nationality is determined by birth, and either by *jus soli* (the right by dint of birth on the soil) or *jus sanguinis* (the right by dint of bloodline) are equally acceptable bases for settling the matter. According to the following two (14 and 15), nationality can be acquired without any kinship ties or claims to birth on the territory— though definition 15 requires a period of residence before nationality can be claimed.

These requirements could, however, be weakened further still. Consider the following variants.

Definition 16: a native of a country can be someone who has a legal right to live in that country and has resided there for at least a specified number of years.

Definition 17: a native of a country is someone who has a legal right to reside in that country.

Definition 18: a native of a country can be someone who came to that country as a minor and has lived in that country for more than a certain number of years, even if without any legal right to do so.

Definition 19: a native of a country can be someone who has lived in that country for more than a certain number of years, even if without any legal right to do so.

Definition 20: a native of a country can be someone who considers himself or herself a native of that country and is so regarded by others in that country who are recognized as natives by other natives.

This list of definitions does not come close to exhausting the variations in immigration law defining the nationalities of persons today, let alone the different criteria that have been set and revised in the course of modern history. The logical possibilities are obviously more extensive still. The question is: who, or what, is a native or a national? Among the broadest understandings is one offered by Madame de Staël, for whom citizenship should have its basis in nationality, but nationality itself was the product of imagination, through which the *patrie* was created—since mere territory was insufficient to establish such a thing. Here nationality is understood normatively, and as something that appears inconsistent with tyrannical rule.[34]

Yet if we take the case of Mr Camara, who had lived in France for more than forty-five years when he was advised that he was never a citizen despite officially having been granted citizenship, according to definitions 1 to 15 he is not a native of the country he has considered home for most of his life. Were he to be acknowledged as a citizen, however, he would still not be a *native* according to definitions 1 to 13. On these definitions, an immigrant can never become a native. On definitions 14 to 20, however, it is perfectly possible for an immigrant to become a native—the only issue being what is necessary to make this possible.

The first thirteen definitions of 'native' put the emphasis on birth, as the etymological origin of the word anticipates. A native is someone born in the right place or born to the right person. Most criteria for determining birthright citizenship today thus invoke the principles of either *jus soli* or *jus sanguinis*. The question is, how deep-rooted must birthright be if someone is to count as a native? In the United States at present, for example, birth on American territory or to an American citizen confers citizenship immediately and without exception. In the late nineteenth and early twentieth century, however, there were many exceptions. Justice Roger B. Taney and the Supreme Court held in the 1857 *Dred Scott* case that no Blacks, slave or free, could be citizens because they were a 'subordinate and inferior class of beings'. Though this was invalidated by the 1866 Civil Rights Act, and while *jus soli* was later made into a part of the law of the land in 1868 by the Fourteenth Amendment to the US Constitution, in practice several racial minorities were denied the benefit of this principle. Not until the 1898 case of *U.S. v. Wong Kim Ark* did the Supreme Court rule that all native-born children of aliens were birthright citizens—including the children of permanently barred races. It was not until 1940 that Congress passed the Nationality Act which finally established that all Native Americans were citizens, as were all racial minorities born on American soil.

But being a citizen may not be sufficient to count one as a native, just as being a native (and who could be more native than a Native American?) was not always enough to secure citizenship. Indeed, it has been possible for native-born Americans to be stripped of their citizenship. When, for example, a non-citizen woman married a male American citizen she was, until 1922, held to acquire his citizenship—provided both were White. However, an American woman (of any colour) who married an alien was, by a practice validated in 1907 by an act of Congress, stripped of her citizenship. Though this aspect of that act was repealed in 1922, it still required that any woman who married a foreigner who was ineligible for citizenship on racial grounds be stripped of her citizenship and expatriated. In Britain, women were not able in their own right to pass their nationality on to their children until 1983. Indeed, until 1948, British women who married foreign men lost their nationality, while British men who married women from abroad were able to pass on British nationality.[35] Though it is no longer[36] legally possible for native-born American citizens to have their citizenship revoked against their will, there have been prominent calls for the repeal of sections of the Fourteenth Amendment to replace the citizenship clause with a provision declaring that only children born to mothers who are citizens or legal residents are citizens of the United States.[37] Were such a legal revision to come into effect, it would mean people who might be regarded as 'natives' because they were born in the country and have lived within its borders all their lives, would not legally be citizens. At the other extreme, British nationality law provides that anyone able to prove British or Irish (including the Republic of Ireland) ancestry through as little as a single grandparent is eligible for British residence and citizenship.

Table 1 illustrates the variable nature of the rules governing eligibility for nationality or citizenship. In the eighteen regimes listed from A to R, the nine criteria for eligibility, ranging from birth on the territory, to having one or more natural-born or naturalized ancestors, to having resident parents, might or might not, be sufficient to make a successful claim to hold a nationality or acquire citizenship. The variability holds not only between but also within countries, whose laws have changed from one period to the next.

It is also worth noting, however, that while the twentieth century saw countries like the United States expand their powers to control the movement of people, both by restricting entry (and increasingly through deportation) and by redefining or categorizing people as citizens, residents or aliens, this did not always square with the ways in which society more widely regarded the denizens of different communities. Indeed many communities took a much looser and less legalistic view of what made someone a native. Consider, for example, the public charge provision written into the Immigration Act by the United States Congress in 1891, designed to deport poor immigrants who used public hospitals or who had become dependent and incapable of supporting themselves. What the law ran up against was the fact that the public and private institutions in the various states, ranging from charitable hospitals to alms houses to facilities run by cities, counties, states, and churches, did not distinguish people on the basis of nationality or immigrant status. As facilities that 'emerged out of a long tradition of care of the poor dating from the colonial era', they considered that 'long-term residence in a state or county made one eligible for public care, irrespective of citizenship'.[38] States might view as immigrants or foreigners people who are viewed as natives by the cities, villages or communities in which they reside.

A curious example that nonetheless illuminates the complexity of the issue of native status comes from the Australian Rugby League. Since rugby is a sport that is strongest in two Australian states—New South Wales and Queensland—there has been for many years a rivalry expressed in yearly representative matches between teams from the two regions. However, since most of the best players joined teams playing in the much richer and stronger New South Wales Rugby League competition, the matches between the two states were lopsided. In 1981, however, the authorities initiated a

**TABLE 1.** Qualifying for Citizenship or Nationality

| Ancestry/ country | Born on territory | Born in colony | Grandparent native-born | Father native-born | Mother native-born | Father naturalized | Mother naturalized | Father resident non-national | Mother resident non-national | Citizen or national? |
|---|---|---|---|---|---|---|---|---|---|---|
| A | YES | NO | NO | NO | NO | NO | NO | NO | NO | YES |
| B | YES | NO | NO | NO | NO | NO | NO | NO | NO | NO |
| C | YES | NO | NO | NO | NO | NO | NO | YES | YES | NO |
| D | YES | NO | YES | YES | NO | NO | NO | NO | YES | NO |
| E | NO | YES | NO | NO | NO | NO | NO | NO | NO | YES |
| F | NO | YES | NO | NO | NO | NO | NO | NO | NO | NO |
| G | NO | NO | YES | NO | NO | NO | NO | NO | NO | YES |
| H | NO | NO | YES | NO | NO | NO | NO | NO | NO | NO |
| I | NO | NO | NO | YES | NO | NO | NO | NO | NO | YES |
| J | NO | NO | NO | YES | NO | NO | NO | NO | YES | NO |
| K | NO | NO | NO | NO | YES | NO | NO | NO | NO | YES |
| L | NO | NO | NO | NO | YES | NO | NO | YES | NO | NO |
| M | NO | NO | NO | NO | NO | YES | NO | NO | NO | YES |
| N | NO | NO | NO | NO | NO | YES | NO | NO | NO | NO |
| O | NO | NO | NO | NO | NO | NO | YES | NO | NO | YES |
| P | NO | NO | NO | NO | NO | NO | YES | NO | NO | NO |
| Q | YES | NO | NO | NO | NO | NO | NO | YES | NO | YES |
| R | YES | NO | NO | NO | NO | NO | NO | YES | YES | NO |

competition based on 'state of origin', so that natives of Queensland could play for their 'home' state rather than their state of residence. This levelled the playing field dramatically, and made the competition much more interesting, but raised the thorny question of who was a 'native' of New South Wales or Queensland, since many people born in one state moved to the other as children. Over the years, brothers found themselves eligible to represent opposing states, sons played for different states than their fathers, players born in Lebanon, Malta, and New Zealand, or coming from various Pacific nations, found themselves recruited by one state or another to play in the very competitive (and lucrative) matches. Of the eighteen series Queensland has won, fourteen were played with a greater percentage of non-Queensland-born players than the opposition, while of the thirteen series that New South Wales won, five were with a greater percentage of 'non-native' players than Queensland. There is, needless to say, a rich history of grumbling about the eligibility of players on the 'other' side.[39] Similar controversies dog the selection of players to represent teams in international football and, of course, the Olympic Games. It's not as easy for a native to become a winner as it is for a winner to become a native.

The purpose of this discussion is to establish a number of points. First, just as the term 'immigrant' does not identify a natural kind, neither does the term 'native'—both are legal categories and therefore ultimately political categories. The same goes for 'national', which is no less ambiguous than 'native'. Just as it is possible to deny that a native-born resident can be a citizen, so is it possible to identify someone who is a resident but not a citizen as a native, or as a national. It is worth noting that there are some countries that permit dual or multiple citizenship or nationality, others that prohibit it on pain of loss of citizenship for assuming a second nationality, a few that permit it on a selective basis (making it easier for celebrities), and fewer still like Spain and Pakistan that permit multiple nationality with a restricted number of countries. Nationality, as John Osborne seems to have appreciated, is a matter of luck.

Second, since the law can transform an immigrant into a citizen, as it can a citizen into an immigrant, these terms, and the statuses they describe, are entirely constructed, and indeed vague and not always easy to clarify. Immigration control is therefore, to a significant extent, as much about deciding about who counts as a native or national as it is about determining what is to be done to address the interests or concerns of natives. Immigration control is indeed substantially about identity, but the distinction between *defending* identity and *defining* identity is not an easy one to sustain. To the extent that immigration control is about exclusion, it might be fair to say that exclusion begins at home—as we shall see in the chapters to come.

Third, to the extent that so much of immigration control is mired in the politics of definition, it is a mistake to think that the most important form that the control of immigrants takes is to be found at the borders of the state. On the contrary, immigration control takes place well within those boundaries, and deep inside each society. Or, to put the matter differently, the borders of a country need to be seen differently if we are properly to understand the role they play in society's governance.

In order to gain a fuller appreciation of this we need to turn to look more closely at the nature of political borders and what it means to control them. It seems evident that we live in a world of closed rather than open borders, for there are few borders that are not subject to political control. Yet just as the notions of immigrant and immigration are not as straightforward as they initially appear to be, so are those of borders and border control similarly awkward—and poorly understood.

## Borders and Border Control

Borders are geographic boundaries demarcating or defining political entities or legal jurisdictions. They can be used to separate countries or states, but can also distinguish a variety of other entities including subnational administrative units such as provinces, counties, boroughs, townships, municipalities, Indian reservations (US), Indian reserves (Canada), cantons, territories, and parishes; and supranational entities such as empires, or superstates (for example, the EU). Borders today are generally regarded as clearly defined boundaries that are no more than imaginary lines that do not themselves occupy any space. In principle, they thus differ from the marchlands of earlier times, when political entities were separated by border regions or borderlands—spaces that were beyond the authority of the rulers on either side. There are remnants of this past practice in the modern world in the shape of demilitarized zones—such as that between North and South Korea—but these are rarities. Borders are considered notional rather than physical and can run not only across lands but also across waters, along rivers, through streets, and even through buildings.

Although borders can be delineated using physical objects or structures, this is uncommon. The Great Wall of China, the Maginot Line, the Berlin Wall, the Ceuta Border Fence between Spain and Morocco, and the physical barriers Churchill dubbed the 'iron curtain' are examples of structures used to draw the boundaries between different regions. But nowadays political boundaries are established by rules or laws rather than by fences and gates. This point is a significant one because it means that opening or closing borders is not a matter of adding or removing physical objects but of changing rules. Indeed, it could even be a matter of changing legal arrangements which have nothing to do—at least not directly—with movement across borders. Barriers, when they exist at all, come in the form of controls exercised at checkpoints when borders are crossed—controls that might involve the presentation of identity papers such as a passport, or visas or other entry permits.

The presence of a border signifies the existence of some authority that operates within the boundaries of a demarcated territory. One of the rights that authority may have is to exclude persons from its territory, but whether or not it does will depend on the kind of entity the authority represents. In international law, states have the right to determine whether, and under what conditions, persons may enter their territories. Provinces, parishes, and towns do not typically have such rights. Nonetheless, it is worth remarking that practice varies considerably. Although in international law countries can exclude persons from their territories, this is not always a straightforward matter. For example, under the Schengen Agreement concluded among European countries in 1985 and 1990, the twenty-five countries of the EU along with Iceland, Norway, Liechtenstein, and Switzerland adopted measures that have more or less done away with border controls. With the exception of Ireland and the United Kingdom, there are no border controls of any significance within this region of four hundred million people. The Schengen Agreement also provides for a common policy on the movement of temporary visitors, who may travel freely within the region for up to three months. At the other extreme, Sabah and Sarawak, the states of Malaysia on the island of Borneo, require even Malaysian citizens to obtain permission to enter their territories, and impose limits on the duration of visits and on what activities visitors can engage in. Within states, other entities may also have rights to exclude: Native American reservations, for example, may restrict entry onto their territories.

More often than not, however, the authorities within borders are responsible for attending to the interests of those within their jurisdiction rather than keeping others out. Provinces, cantons, counties, and towns may determine what rights and obligations residents have without having any power to determine who may become a resident. Even nation states might find their capacity to restrict entry to their territories limited by international and domestic law. For example, nations such as the United States, which have adopted the norm of *jus soli*, are obliged to admit anyone who was born in its territory as a citizen. Nations such as Germany, which have adopted the norm of *jus sanguinis*, cannot easily deny German residence or citizenship to someone with German ancestry. Countries that are signatories to the 1951 Refugee Convention cannot turn away those who have landed on their territory and asked for asylum—at least, not until such a claim is legally determined to be unfounded. Sometimes, simply crossing a border can give a person rights that the authorities have no power to ignore.

A border, in sum, is a complex notion. It does not merely impose a physical or even a notional barrier to forbid or permit entry from one region to another but specifies, and in some cases works to determine, the rights and obligations individuals and authorities have. Opening and closing borders is not a matter of opening or shutting gates but changing the working of a complex system of machinery. We should consider this machinery in more detail to try to understand what open borders could mean. Once we recognize this complexity, we may have to reconsider our understanding of borders, for while the lines of demarcation might be notional, they are not 'Euclidian'—that is, possessing length but not breadth. Borders are notional, but nonetheless thick, and heavy with sense.

The openness of borders is clearly a matter of degree. How do we determine whether a border is open or closed—or at least, how open a border might be? To answer this question we need to consider the variety of ways, and the different dimensions along which, borders operate to control the movement of persons. Indeed, we need to recognize that borders can be open in some respects and closed in others. Policy can therefore easily make borders more open and yet, at the same time, more closed. This is because policy can change the terms of entry in a number of different respects. It can vary the terms by specifying

i. what kinds of people may enter and what status they may hold on entering;
ii. how long they may stay;
iii. what qualifications or characteristics they must possess to enter;
iv. what procedures they must follow to remain within a territory;
v. the number of people admitted in various categories.

Nation states typically impose strict terms in all five of these respects while other kinds of jurisdictions do not, so most of the following discussion will focus on crossing national boundaries.

## I. ENTRY STATUS

Nation states admit people onto their territories in a variety of categories. It is easier to enter in some categories than in others. People move as tourists, students, diplomats, military personnel, journalists, pilgrims, seasonal workers, guest workers, resident scholars, sportsmen, performers, artists, and immigrants. Most countries make it easy to enter as a tourist, more difficult to enter as a would-be resident or worker, and even more difficult to enter as an immigrant.

In each of these categories entry may be more or less difficult. Entering as a tourist is easier in some countries than others. Consider these examples. For most people in North and South America, Australasia, and limited parts of Asia (Japan, South Korea, Malaysia and Singapore) entering Europe requires nothing more than turning up at a European port or airport. Everyone else must obtain a visa. Australia is one of a number of countries that requires everyone to obtain a visa, though Australia has loosened this requirement by allowing citizens of some countries to obtain their visas online or through travel agents. Brazil requires Australians, Americans, and Canadians—but not British and most EU citizens—to obtain visas to enter the country, and charges between fifty and two hundred dollars for one. Brazil, like many countries, also requires most visitors (including Britons and EU nationals) to have a return ticket and to show evidence of having sufficient funds for the duration of their stay. The United States exempts members of twenty-seven countries from the requirement to obtain a visa to enter as a tourist, though only three from Asia (Brunei, Japan and Singapore) and none from Africa or South America. It is possible to obtain a visa to travel to North Korea, but only as a part of a state-run tour—no independent travel is permitted.

Entering a country to take up employment is usually more difficult than entering as a tourist, though the regulations governing this vary widely. Most countries, and all developed countries, require visitors to obtain permission to work, and whether or not permission is granted will depend a range of factors, from seasonal demand for particular workers, to the worker's country of origin, to the status of the visitor (who might be eligible for a temporary work visa for holidaying youths). Work visas for professionals may be easy to obtain in some countries in some professions, but it is not always possible for accompanying spouses to secure work permits. For example, in the United States, Australia, and Canada it is necessary for employers applying to hire overseas professionals to demonstrate that no appointment could be made from the ranks of the domestic workforce—though the extent to which such claims are demonstrable is doubtful, and for the most part it is the assurance of the applying employer that settles the matter.

Entering a country as an 'immigrant' is invariably more difficult than entering as a tourist, though here it has to be noted that there are many kinds of 'immigrants' and many kinds of admission. Immigrants might enter the country with a view to staying temporarily but eventually returning to their homelands; or enter with a view to reuniting with family members who migrated earlier, but with no intention of working; or enter with a view to establishing a second home for a part of the year; or enter with a view to settling more permanently but never becoming a citizen; or enter with an intention of becoming a full citizen. Equally, immigration policy may encourage people to enter but discourage them from coming if they would only be dependents rather than workers (and taxpayers); it might encourage them to become residents but make it difficult to become citizens; and it might welcome new citizens but require that they repudiate their former citizenship.

## II. ENTRY DURATION

Most states control border crossing by limiting the duration of any visit. Tourists may usually enter a country only for a limited time, even in cases when they may re-enter without difficulty within hours of leaving it. Work permits and visas also expire. Even those who enter with long-term or permanent employment secured often find their visas expire and have to be renewed regularly. Many people have lived in countries for decades by renewing their visas every year. In particular cases, however, work visas can only be used for a fixed period before the entrant has to either change status or leave the country permanently.

## III. ENTRY QUALIFICATION

States also control border crossing by restricting entry to those with the right characteristics or qualifications. Restrictions can be based on any number of factors including ethnicity, nationality, religion, political affiliation, wealth, income, age, health, profession, and criminality. So, for example, Australia restricted entry by ethnicity in the many years that the White Australia Policy was in operation. Malaysia will not admit Israeli nationals except in special circumstances (and forbids its citizens to visit Israel). Every non-US citizen entering the United States or applying for a visa was until recently asked: 'Are you or have you ever been a member of the Communist party or any organization dedicated to the violent overthrow of the United States government?' Although it is not the case that membership of a communist party automatically disqualifies one from entry, it is something that has to be satisfactorily explained. A lack of substantial wealth or high income are not in themselves going to prevent anyone from gaining permission to enter a country, but many countries, including Canada and Singapore, will admit wealthy immigrants who can demonstrate an intention and capacity to invest in the country. People of advanced age can have their applications to immigrate to Australia turned down on the grounds that they will not live long enough to contribute enough in taxes to cover the costs they will impose on existing taxpayers. Australia has also turned away disabled would-be immigrants on the grounds that the costs of their care would outweigh the financial contribution they are likely to make over a lifetime. (There is no provision for those who wish to waive their right to public welfare in exchange for a right of entry.) Would-be visitors can be denied entry, or legal residents deported, if they are found guilty of criminal actions of varying degrees of seriousness. For example, Adam Crapser was deported to South Korea thirty-eight years after he was first adopted by American parents who had failed to secure his citizenship.[40]

## IV. ENTRANT RIGHTS AND OBLIGATIONS

States can shape the pattern of border crossing by restricting or limiting the rights of outsiders, or by imposing particular duties upon them. For example, those who have entered as residents may be forbidden to work in paid employment. Those with work permits may be restricted to work with the sponsoring employer and prohibited from changing jobs. Spouses of workers may be forbidden to work. Those free to work may find it impossible to work in their fields because their qualifications are not recognized. Those with or without qualifications may find it difficult to compete with the local labour force because labour laws, including minimum wage laws, do not allow them to offer their services at a lower price. In some countries non-citizens may not own certain forms of property—for example, Thailand restricts the rights of foreigners to buy land, or residential homes that are not apartments in multi-apartment buildings (with majority Thai ownership), while Switzerland has zones where foreign ownership is prohibited. For-eigners can also find they are limited by being ineligible for certain forms of employment (notably in government), ineligible for social security benefits, and ineligible to participate in the political process (for example, by voting in some or all elections). In some countries foreign residents are prohibited from commenting on local politics, on pain of deportation. Foreign nationals may also face reporting requirements, having to present themselves regularly to immigration officers, inform authorities of changes of address, and to register their arrivals and departures. Penalties for compliance failures can include deportation and loss of any right of re-entry.

## V. ENTRY QUOTAS

Most states employ some measures to restrict the numbers of people entering and leaving the country. Though tourist numbers are not typically limited, tourism is controlled by states for various reasons. For example, Nepal tries to limit the number of people trying to climb Mount Everest by imposing high fees on mountaineers. Countries where the volume of tourist traffic puts pressure on important sites have considered trying to limit entry. And western countries generally make it more difficult for people from poor countries to enter even as tourists because of the risk of overstaying, though by and large, tourism is too lucrative to be limited. Entry in other categories, however, is often substantially limited. The United States admits foreign workers in a variety of visa categories but has firm limits in most of them. It also admits many people as permanent residents through the Green Card Lottery, though again no more than fifty-five thousand are awarded each year. Australia has varied its intake of immigrants each year but tried to keep the numbers within firm limits. It also has special places for humanitarian cases and refugees, though again these are limited in number and each year many are turned away because the quota has been filled.

## Open and Closed Borders

In the light of these observations about the way in which border crossings and border crossers are dealt with, it should be clear that the openness or closedness of borders is a matter of degree. Borders can be more or less open in a variety of ways. People can enter countries with a view to visit, to visit and work, to study, to study and work, to reside, to reside and work, to perform, preach, or research, or to join the host society as a new citizen. State policy can open borders in one or more respects while closing it in others. It might make entry easier by granting more visas or removing visa requirements, by lowering visa costs, by widening the scope of visa waiver programmes, and even by ceasing negative advertising.[41] Yet at the same time it might make it more difficult to get work permits or permission to open businesses. It might increase the number of student visas but impose stronger requirements that students to return to their home countries or make it harder for students to work to support themselves. It might make it easier to enter the country to work but make it harder to renew a work permit. It might make it easier to become a resident but harder to become a citizen; or easier to become a citizen but harder to enter in the first place.

Since the border is such a variable thing, it would be useful to try to conceptualize the notion of a border understood in terms of its degree of openness—or closedness. For the sake of simplifying the problem let us say that there are three dimensions along which the issue can be considered: entry, participation, and membership. The first dimension, entry, covers the freedom of foreigners to enter and reside in a society. Participation covers foreigners' right to take up employment or to trade or open up a business. Membership covers the right of foreigners to become more closely involved in the society—perhaps acquiring the right to take government employment, or participate in elections, or even stand for public office. One way of acquiring membership might be by becoming a *citizen*, but citizenship is not always necessary for gaining significant membership rights. For example, in the UK, non-citizens from the Republic of Ireland and also Commonwealth countries like Australia and New Zealand can vote in both national and local elections—even before securing permanent resident status—and may stand for political office if they have resident status. Until Britain left the European Union, EU citizens, on the other hand, could vote only in EU and local UK elections and could not hold any political office. In Australia and the United States, to take two different cases again, only citizens may vote, though in the US it was common until the 1920s for states and territories to enfranchise non-citizen residents: western states to entice migrants to settle so that territories could meet the population requirements for admission to the Union, and southern states in the Reconstruction period to attract immigrants to replace slave labour.[42]

A society with fully open borders would be one in which entry, participation, and membership were all possible. A less open society would be one in which entry and participation were possible but membership not. A much less open society would make entry possible but not participation and membership. A society with completely closed borders would not permit entry, participation or membership. Table 2 presents the definitions that are

TABLE 2. Variations on the Openness of Borders

|  | Countries/States | | | | | | | |
|---|---|---|---|---|---|---|---|---|
|  | 1 | 2 | 3 | 4 | 5 | 6 | 7 | 8 |
| Entry | Yes | Yes | Yes | No | No | No | Yes | No |
| Participation | Yes | Yes | No | No | No | (Yes) | No | (Yes) |
| Membership | Yes | No | No | No | (Yes) | (Yes) | (Yes) | No |

(Yes) indicates that participation is permitted de facto through poor enforcement, or that membership is granted through amnesty.

conceivable. Along the three dimensions there are eight possible kinds of country distinguished by degree of openness of borders. Country 1 has the most open borders and country 4 the least. If we consider only legal immigration, countries 5, 6, 7 and 8 are not, in principle, feasible possibilities for participation or membership, but if the rules are poorly enforced they might be. Country 5 cannot offer membership to foreigners if it will not allow them to enter or participate—but it might periodically offer illegal immigrants amnesty and a path to citizenship. Country 6 cannot offer participation, let alone membership, if it will not allow entry, but it might in effect permit people to work without authorization because the consequences of enforcing the rules are economically damaging—and eventually offer amnesty and citizenship. Country 7 cannot really offer membership if it will not allow participation, even if it will allow entry—and is therefore no different from country 3—except that it offers amnesty, and eventually, citizenship, to those who have resided without permission. Country 8 forbids entry, enforces its restrictions on foreigners working and residing weakly or ineffectively, but never offers amnesty or a route to citizenship or any official status.

This presentation of the possibilities obviously simplifies matters considerably. After all, as has already been noted, entry, participation, and membership are all a matter of degree. Permitting entry is the first requirement for borders to be open at all, since participation is not possible without it; and the right to participate is the second requirement if we assume that membership, by its very nature, means having full rights to enter and participate. To lose the right to participate is to lose one's rights of membership.[43] Yet the value of the rights involved here is not always equal, and this too has a bearing on the openness of borders. The value of the right to participate by working, for example, might be affected by a number of factors. It might depend on whether or not an accompanying spouse is granted a corresponding

TABLE 3. Degrees of Openness of Borders

| | Countries/States | | |
| --- | --- | --- | --- |
| | Country A | Country B | Country C |
| Entry | Easy | Hard | Very hard |
| Participation | Hard | Very hard | Easy |
| Membership | Very hard | Easy | Hard |

entitlement to work, on the extent to which a work permit grants access to welfare services, on the laws governing re-entry on leaving the country (or limiting absences abroad without loss of residence status), and on laws controlling the right to sponsor relatives (notably children and elderly parents) to join the family. The value of the right to participate might also depend on the laws governing the process of becoming a citizen, since for many the difficulty of gaining citizenship might make it less attractive to move in the first place. (Australia and Canada require three years of residence before naturalization, the US and UK five years, Germany eight years and Austria ten years.) Whether or not a country permits dual citizenship also has a bearing on the accessibility of citizenship, and on the extent to which taking up the right to participate in the society is considered worthwhile.

Borders are more open as it becomes easier to enter, participate, and join. However, what is more difficult to determine is how to interpret an easing of restrictions in some respects but a tightening of restrictions in others. Consider, for example, the three countries A, B, and C, in table 3.

It's not clear which of the three has the most open borders. Country A is easy to enter but very hard to join as a citizen; B makes it easy to acquire citizenship but very hard to win the right to work; C is hard to enter but easy to gain working rights in (if you can get in, you can work), but still difficult to join as a citizen.

Or consider another presentation of the same problem in table 4, with a numerical weighting given to indicate the degree of difficulty of earning rights to enter, participate or become a member of a polity.

Would a move from A to B amount to a move to a regime with more or less open borders? Is C more or less open than B or A? To the extent that it is difficult to say, the extent of a border's openness is unclear or indeterminate.

There is a further complication that bears noting here. The openness or closedness of a border cannot be gauged simply by the regulations governing entry, participation or membership. Of crucial significance are the

TABLE 4. Degrees of Openness of Borders (numerical weighting)

| | Countries/States | | |
|---|---|---|---|
| | Country A | Country B | Country C |
| Entry | 5 | 2 | 8 |
| Participation | 5 | 7 | 2 |
| Membership | 5 | 9 | 2 |

1 = Easy
10 = Very Hard

nature and the effectiveness of the institutions that regulate the society. Laws that are not—or cannot be—enforced, do not regulate or control, and do not make borders less open. The capacity of states or governments to control how people move, what people do, and which identity or status people assume or acquire, is limited. It is constrained on the one hand by the resources the state has at its disposal to enforce its regulations, and on the other hand by the determination and ingenuity of the people looking for ways around the restrictions that laws nominally impose. Every year, tens of thousands of people enter countries, or choose to work or reside in them, or acquire citizenships of their chosen states, in defiance of laws that deny them the right to do so, and in spite of the efforts of governments to prevent these things from happening. Most obviously, people routinely evade detection to cross national borders, or are hired without authorization by employers willing to ignore the law, or unable to identify fraudulent documentation. But people are also able to acquire or exercise more extensive political rights despite attempts to limit this—partly through the use of fake documentation, but also because of institutional failures and, at times, political corruption. Passports and other official documents of identity can be forged,[44] public officials can be fooled or bribed; political parties can be manipulated; and governments can be tempted to make exemptions to secure re-election.[45]

The openness or closedness of a border is a matter of degree. Its determinants are not only the laws purporting to control the movement and the activity of foreigners or outsiders but also the effectiveness of the mechanisms of control. The effectiveness of institutional mechanisms is in turn dependent on the costs of establishing and sustaining them (which includes the cost of policing those responsible for their operation), and the resourcefulness of would-be immigrants ready to find ways around legal and bureaucratic obstacles to their pursuit of entry, participation and membership of their chosen countries. It also depends on the extent to which a society is open socially and economically to engagement with outsiders, and on the extent to which governments and states are ready to step up their efforts to control immigration by further efforts of regulation, monitoring, and enforcement.

This brings us to the crux of the issue. The openness of borders is a matter of the extent of control, and at the heart of this is the question of what has to be controlled. Though it might seem that it is movement of people that is the subject of control, this is only one aspect of the matter. What has to be controlled is not mere movement but also the conditions that make that movement possible and likely. This means controlling society more generally. What precisely this involves is the subject to which we will turn in chapter 3.

## Immigration

Political theorists who address the issue of immigration have been preoccupied with the questions of whether or not host societies or countries have the right to exclude outsiders, or whether other considerations trump any such right. Perhaps those who are fleeing persecution have stronger claims to be able to move freely. Maybe people who would otherwise live lives that are more precarious or simply poorer have a greater right to move than anyone has a right to prevent them. While some argue for open borders (without saying very much about what this might mean) and a few argue for substantial restrictions on immigration, most steer some sort of middle course, counselling that states have a right and indeed a duty to control immigration but also need to be mindful of a variety of practical and ethical considerations, including the need to manage labour markets, the obligation to respect citizens' interests in family migration and humanitarian responsibilities of aid to the unfortunate.[46] What is striking about all these discussions, however, is that the understanding of immigration and immigration control assumes a model of immigration as involving the movement of a distinct category of persons across borders separating clearly distinguishable jurisdictions. Yet this is not the world in which we live.

To some extent, of course, simplification is a necessary part of any philosophical or theoretical inquiry and it would not do to be too critical of efforts to sort out complex questions by modelling them in more tractable terms. Nonetheless, in the question of immigration, simplification carries significant costs if the process of abstraction takes us too far from reality. We have seen that the notion of the 'immigrant' is not a straightforward one because it is the product of legal and political contestation that has seen the definition changed and qualified as circumstances have demanded. The same can be said of nationality. And it should now be clear that the idea of a border as a boundary that enables us to distinguish clearly between the claims of insiders and outsiders or marks the limits of the powers of legal and political authorities is difficult to sustain. But there is a broader conclusion still to be reached. We have tended to view immigration from a perspective of a very particular kind: from the perspective of nationality. This model is of a world of independent nation states, made up of individuals many of whom (primarily from poorer regions) wish to move for motives that reflect their own individual or national circumstances, and whose movement is and must be managed by those states that would otherwise struggle to deal with an uncontrolled influx of people. Yet this model is seriously flawed because it assumes that the different variables in play are independent when in reality they are deeply interconnected. Borders, statuses, and rights are all equally changeable and have changed with startling frequency because the fact of immigration actually reflects not so much the separateness of people across the world but their continual interaction and their embeddedness in shared historical circumstances as well as shared political and institutional realities.

Immigration is not merely about the movement of individuals between distinct jurisdictions but rather involves a more complicated and subtler—and indeed, transformative—set of interactions between persons, institutions, and societies. We might see this more clearly if we return to the example of immigration to Britain after decolonization and the end of empire. Immigration control began with the redefinition of the status of former British subjects in territories in Asia and Africa once possessed and ruled by Britain—that point has already been made. But what also needs to be recognized is that, even with the curtailment of the rights of former subjects, what did not end was the complex economic network and institutional structure that had been built up over decades or centuries as a result of the interaction—through trade, government, and war—between Britain and her colonies. The outcome of this history was a set of substantial relations among peoples who came to share bonds that were thick enough to transform them and (all) their societies. When people from Malaya or Jamaica or India or New Zealand looked to move to Britain, it was for many less because a spirit of adventure made them want to travel to a foreign land than because such a move was to somewhere familiar and to which they had some connection. Even if some or many Britons might have considered the people from former colonies to be 'strangers in their midst', for many of the immigrants in question the move they made was to a place that was familiar and a meaningful destination.[47] The same might be said of the people of the former colonies of Portugal, France, the Netherlands, and the United States.

The more general point, however, holds not only for the societies and nations bound together by colonial histories. It holds also for the many places that have connections that were formed out of the deep engagements resulting from trade, political cooperation, and military conflict. In the case of the United States, for example, its ties to Mexico and parts of Latin America run deep as a result of a history of economic exchange (particular in the search for labour), warfare, and conquest—as well as political alliance in pursuit of strategic advantage. Its ties to Vietnam, Cambodia, Laos, Iran, Iraq, and Afghanistan—to take just a handful of examples—have also grown substantial as its military involvement in these regions have seen it build complex and deep relations with commercial interests and political actors as well as ordinary citizens who have been employed by American governments or agencies. At the end of the war, those who fled Vietnam headed for Australia and the United States—countries that had been thoroughly implicated in that conflict. No less surprisingly, in the period of the Cold War many Vietnamese also moved to communist eastern Europe (notably Czechoslovakia) because of shared political and economic connections. Immigration, as Sasskia Sassen notes, is an 'embedded' process in which people move across well-established bridges in both directions.[48] To think properly about the ethics and politics of immigration it is important to understand the nature of the phenomenon in question. It is a mistake to think about it from a perspective that takes the standpoint of nationality as a fixed, stable, and unquestionably appropriate standard from which address the question of the rights and wrongs of immigration control. While states make immigration policy and establish controls, it is no less true that immigration control creates—and shapes—states. As we shall see in the chapters to follow.

# 3

# Control

The prince who has more to fear from the people than from foreigners ought to build fortresses.
—MACHIAVELLI, *THE PRINCE*

Control in modern times requires more than force, more than law. It requires that a population dangerously concentrated in cities and factories, whose lives are filled with cause for rebellion, be taught that all is right as it is.
—HOWARD ZINN, *A PEOPLE'S HISTORY OF THE UNITED STATES*

Nobody controls me. I'm uncontrollable. The only one who controls me is me, and that's just barely possible.
—JOHN LENNON, *ALL WE ARE SAYING: THE LAST MAJOR INTERVIEW WITH JOHN LENNON AND YOKO ONO*

## Making Life Harder

On 30 July 2015, at the beginning of the 'Calais Crisis'[1] the then British Prime Minister, David Cameron, promised to address the problem of large 'swarms' of people, trying to enter the country, by getting tougher on would-be immigrants.[2] Not only was his government ready to strengthen deportation measures but it would also take steps to make certain Britain did not become a 'safe haven' for people who had crossed the Mediterranean. To be sure, the government intended to do more to prevent people coming over the border to enter the United Kingdom; but it also aimed through such measures as deportation to strengthen what the Prime Minister called Britain's 'internal borders'.

What is noteworthy here is the recognition that borders are not to be found at political boundaries or in geographic space but in laws and practical measures to control how people move and what people do. The Prime Minister was reported as saying that 'Britain's "internal borders" of a crackdown on housing entitlements and more removals' would make Britain less enticing to immigrants. Indeed he went on to indicate that there was a need for further domestic reforms to deter immigration. 'Frankly we also have to do more, and we are already passing legislation to do more, to make Britain a less easy place for illegal immigrants to stay.' In a particularly illuminating passage he said: 'Since I have become Prime Minister we have made it harder to get a driving licence, to get a bank account, to get a council house. We have removed more people. All of these actions—the internal border—matters, as it were, as well as the external border.'[3]

Though the opposition parties and other critics of government policy were quick to pounce on the Prime Minister's use of the word 'swarm' to describe the numbers of people trying to cross the ocean into Britain, no one commented on the notion of 'internal borders', or offered any reflection on what it would mean to make the country a 'less easy place for illegal immigrants to stay'. Given how difficult it is, as we saw in the previous chapter, to distinguish legal from illegal immigrants, and immigrants from residents and citizens, the obvious question to ask is: can one make life harder for illegal immigrants without also making it harder for everyone else? If the government makes it harder for 'illegal' immigrants to 'have a home, to get a car, to have a job, to get a bank account',[4] can it avoid making it harder for anyone to get these things? The answer to that question is plainly 'no'; but to understand why requires a more thorough examination of the matter. That is a main purpose of this chapter.

Immigration controls are controls on people, and it is difficult to control some people without also controlling others. Sometimes it is because it is not easy to distinguish those over whom control is sought from those who are considered exempt. At other times it may be because it is not possible to restrict particular persons save by co-opting others without whose cooperation success would be impossible. And on occasion, it may be necessary in order to control a few to put the liberty of almost everyone into abeyance. Immigration controls are not unique in this respect—the logic of human control is everywhere the same—but they have their own distinctive aspects, and these are worth investigating if we are to understand how the effort to shape and limit the movement of people also shapes and limits a society.

The subject matter of this chapter is the impact of immigration control on freedom. However, the fundamental thesis advanced here is a normative one: that the harm of immigration control to individual freedom is troubling, both in itself but also because what it betokens is the dereliction of the idea of a free society. The institutions and mechanisms of immigration control—most notably the practices of deportation and detention of unwanted persons—have begun to receive greater attention and it is important to understand the processes involved for their impact on those who are detained, incarcerated, forcibly removed, or returned to the countries from whence they came.[5] Nonetheless, it is not only the lives of migrants that are transformed by these practices: the lives and the society of others are also reshaped in the process, and the significance of this too needs to be grasped.

The argument of the chapter is developed over six further sections. The first begins with an elaboration of the most immediate ways in which immigration controls affect the freedom of the citizens and residents of a society. The second turns to the impact of the law in a number of areas—from labour markets to education—on individual freedom. The third considers the ways in which control of movement and legal regulation give rise to extended forms of policing, monitoring, and surveillance. The fourth looks at why successful social control also requires the development of forms of socialization to legitimize and make effective the institutions of regulation and surveillance. The fifth turns to the case of South Africa to discuss some illuminating parallels between freedom under its *internal* immigration policies and the kind of regime being built through immigration controls in other parts of the modern world. The final section concludes the chapter with a more general discussion of the nature of the trade-offs that must be made in the pursuit of greater control.

## Checkpoint Controls

Though immigration controls are frequently presented as restrictions placed on the entry and movement of outsiders, they require from the very outset limitations on the freedom of citizens and residents of a country, both at home and abroad. The logic of this is straightforward: if outsiders are to be controlled, even if only in their movements, mechanisms must be put in place to identify insiders—citizens and residents—so as to distinguish them from those others. In the modern state this means establishing an apparatus of documentation, but also checkpoints of various kinds so that identities might be verified. The more closely outsiders are to be controlled—whether by limiting the numbers entering the country or restricting the activities in which they engage—the more substantially will insiders have to be monitored. To put it simply, there will need to be more checkpoints.

We might usefully distinguish, at least at the outset, two kinds of checkpoints: *frontier* (or external) checkpoints and *domestic* (or internal) checkpoints. These are worth closer examination. However, as we shall also come to see, this distinction is not a sharp one, for the controlling of people is not a simple matter of patrolling a boundary and monitoring a few selected individuals but requires a complex institutional apparatus—one that involves the cooperation of domestic public services, private corporations (both national and transnational), international agencies, and foreign governments.[6] But let us begin by distinguishing the frontier from the domestic realm.

## FRONTIER CHECKPOINTS

Although the official geographical boundaries that demarcate the limits of territorial sovereignty formally constitute the borders of the state, the fact that borders have to be secured makes it difficult to maintain that they exist only where the lines on maps indicate. The frontiers of the state lie wherever its checkpoints exist—providing, of course, that the state is capable of securing them. These checkpoints may be moved as need dictates, even as some of them might remain very stable. They are found in domestic ports of entry, on borderlands in the form of patrols policing the official boundary with neighbouring states, in the seas in the form of coastguard or military vessels, and in foreign territories to the extent that governments arrange to monitor border crossing from within other countries. All of these checkpoints limit the freedom of citizens and residents—often in trivial, but from time to time in significant, ways.

The most obvious way in which frontier checkpoints restrict freedom is by requiring everyone, regardless of nationality, to present himself or herself before an official to show evidence of a right to enter the country. To be sure, this may not be anything more than a minor inconvenience for many. That the *Apollo 11* astronauts—Neil Armstrong, Buzz Aldrin, and Michael Collins—returning to earth after the first moon landing, were required to complete customs declarations and immigration forms is not worrying, just amusing.[7] Yet it remains the case that some freedom is taken away. Citizens wishing to travel abroad will have to spend time and money to obtain a passport; on returning they will have to queue (possibly for a brief time, but occasionally for long periods) to see an immigration official who will authorize entry; in some states they will have fingerprints taken or irises scanned; in general they will have to incur expenses, extend their travel time, and subject themselves to the scrutiny of a state official or member of the police. Residents traveling on foreign passports will usually have to undergo more time-consuming admission processes. Here it is worth noting that this can affect not only residents but also citizens. Those travelling with spouses, children or parents who are not citizens themselves will in effect have to endure the delays to which their partners or parents or offspring are subject. This is an important point to recognize: though citizens might enjoy rights mere residents do not, the fact is that people do not live in isolation but in community with others; and inequalities of rights can easily affect the liberty even of those with weightier rights. An American citizen travelling with a Canadian husband, or a British citizen travelling with a partner who is a Japanese national, in practice finds crossing the border of his or her own country as a citizen more burdensome than assumed.

It would not do to exaggerate the seriousness of this limitation. In a crowded world, queuing and registering are now a part of life. The reason for drawing attention to this example is to highlight the point that, even in trivial cases, rules and procedures designed to restrict only some almost invariably affect others, if not everyone. The more assiduously we try to control some people, the more substantially must we affect the freedom of others. A further reason for looking closely at frontier policing is that the diversity of types of checkpoints highlights another aspect of these institutions of control: the need to increase the reach of immigration authorities—which in turn has further implications for the freedom of citizens and residents everywhere. Since checkpoints at ports of entry are insufficient to control the movement of people, extraterritorial mechanisms have been established. These include the establishment of 'control zones' in foreign ports of departure,[8] patrol boats in international and national waters, and burden-sharing arrangements to monitor unwanted border crossings. All of these measures tend, and perhaps are designed, to push out the frontier—in an attempt to make it more difficult for unwanted persons to enter a country.[9]

Efforts to control the movement of would-be immigrants and asylum seekers from France to the UK by monitoring the movement of people through the port of Calais supply an illuminating example of such measures, and the difficulties they raise. In 2003 Britain and France cooperated to close the Sangatte refugee camp as a part of a plan to stop people coming into the UK to seek asylum, agreeing in the process to allow British border guards to check, on French soil, the passports of travellers on the Channel Tunnel and ferries bound for the English coast. Despite the removal of the original facility, new camps have sprung up as refugees from war zones in Africa and the Middle East have swelled the numbers of would-be immigrants, and prompted wrangling between British and French governments about who should accept responsibility for these people and who should foot the bill.[10] Affected parties included the residents of Calais, whose mayor called for the English border to be moved from his city back across the Channel to Dover,[11] and the residents of Kent and other parts of southeast Britain whose livelihoods were harmed by delays in the movement of goods and tourist traffic.

Another reason for extraterritorial immigration control that is worth noting is that it takes the decision-making process further away from public view. As Gina Clayton notes, the 'maintenance of decision-making away from public scrutiny is supported in the case of the UK by a belief in immigration control as a matter for the executive branch of government, and by practices that enact that belief'.[12]

While frontier checkpoints are often pushed outwards, however, it is important to recognize that they are frequently pushed inwards by extending border zones into the national territory. Thus, increasingly, travellers are stopped and questioned, or their persons and vehicles are inspected, a considerable time after and some distance from the borders they (might have) crossed. Following the creation of the Schengen Area in 1995 (five years after the 1990 Convention), the participating states shifted their internal border controls to a 30-kilometre inland zone known as the 'hinterland', within which mobile border guards could stop and question 'suspicious' travellers. Similarly, in the United States, there are thirty-two permanent interior checkpoints 25–100 miles (roughly 40–160 kilometres) inland where cars may be stopped and inspected by border patrol officers.[13]

The consequences of frontier checkpoint controls for citizens and residents range from the trivial—to the extent that they are merely inconvenienced for a brief period of time—to the more serious, as people who are settled, and perhaps even citizens, are denied entry because of inadequate or inaccurate documentation, clerical error, unfounded suspicion, or simply being seen by tired and frustrated (or hostile) border control officers. According to Jacqueline Stevens, in 2010 alone four thousand Americans were wrongfully deported or detained as aliens, and at any given time, 1 per cent of the people in American immigration detention are US citizens.[14]

This brings us to one further aspect of frontier checkpoints that needs now to be acknowledged. The frontier is not a fixed space or region (let alone identified by an imaginary boundary) at which checkpoints are established. To a significant degree, the checkpoints determine the frontier. This is because states, particularly powerful ones, look to control immigration not only by policing their boundaries but by taking proactive steps to prevent people from reaching them. In the case of the United States, for example, this means not only establishing immigration and customs checkpoints at selected foreign airports but also putting in place a range of measures to control movements between foreign countries. This might be accomplished in any of a number of ways. For example, not only does American law now require that third-country nationals who wish to enter the country supply biometric information to do so but US policy has moved to require other countries to issue biometric identity documents to their own citizens or lose preferential treatment, such as being allowed to participate in the US Visa Waiver Program.[15] Similar measures were introduced by the European Union in its own move towards greater securitization of immigration.[16] No less significantly, the United States has required that carriers to the US supply in advance Passenger Name Record (PNR) data for all travellers to the country. The initial reaction of the EU was to try to comply with US demands while respecting EU law (and its concerns with data protection), but over time this stance evolved into acceptance of the US model in principle. Eventually, the EU began working towards the development of a global system of passenger surveillance.[17]

Frontier checkpoints cannot, however, be viewed simply in terms of rules, or even of spaces manned by officials and inspectors. They have to be understood as a part of a broader strategy developed by states to control the movement of people—one that involves subtler forms of policing. Australia, for example, has for some time run 'scare campaigns' in an effort to deter potential refugees from trying to come to the country—including publishing a graphic novel depicting suffering asylum seekers held in Australian detention.[18] Similar strategies have been pursued by other countries, including Denmark, Hungary, the United States, and Canada (which has placed billboard advertisements in Hungarian villages to discourage the local Roma minority from applying for asylum in Canada).[19] On the advice of anthropologists, the US State Department decided to communicate its messages discouraging migration out of Afghanistan in *landays*—the two-line poems in Pashtun, most often written by anonymous Afghan women, known for their intense distillations of emotion as they reveal the struggles wives face once their husbands have been forced to migrate.[20]

Yet even this does not quite get capture the extent to which frontier checkpoints are more than just guards at the border, standing behind fences with guns facing outwards. What also has to be appreciated is the presence of guards and fences, as well as programmes and strategies, deployed in other countries to contain people lest they consider coming even close to the protected border. The reality is that border control for powerful states means systematic intrusion into the territories and the workings of other countries who are co-opted (however unwillingly) into the service of foreign masters. The United States, for example, has twenty-one Customs and Border Protection (CBP) attachés, in-house immigration control specialists who work under the ambassador, in diplomatic missions around the world. Immigration and Customs Enforcement (ICE) has forty-eight offices around the world. The agencies offer training and capacity-building programmes in countries whose internal borders are thought to be in need of more robust policing. This means providing support in the form of advisors, and equipment to build monitoring and surveillance systems as well as to train patrols. This assistance is supplied not only to adjoining countries like Mexico (to prevent the influx of immigrants on the southern border who might head for the US) or the Caribbean but also to states further away, from Kenya and Uganda to India and Pakistan to the Ukraine.[21] According to General John Kelly (then responsible for the US Southern Command and later Chief of White House Staff and Secretary of Homeland Security in the Trump administration), 'the defense of the Southwest border starts 1,500 miles to the south, with Peru'.[22] To this end, the United States not only deploys personnel but also exports the technology and, it must be emphasised, the ideology, of control.

It is also worth noting that frontier checkpoints sometimes take the form of direct outsourcing to foreign governments, not all of which are interested in or capable of managing the enforcement directives of, say, the United States or the European Union. In the case of European efforts to control the central Mediterranean route, for example, responsibility for enforcing immigration control was handed to Libya, 'a failed state torn between rival government forces and militia groups'.[23]

The notion of a frontier checkpoint reveals something important about immigration control. The standard assumption in discussions of immigration is that the borders of the state demarcate the limits of territorial jurisdiction and that the policing of those borders lies at the heart of the protection of a nation's integrity as a sovereign power. If the defence of sovereignty is the basis for immigration control, however, it would appear that sovereignty for some can only come at the expense of sovereignty for others. In this regard it is unsurprising to read among the conclusions of the *9/11 Commission Report*, discussing the basic assumptions of the US approach to counter-terrorism policy, that 'the American homeland is the planet'.[24] We shall turn to this issue more fully in chapter 7.

## DOMESTIC CHECKPOINTS

Controlling immigration is not only about controlling entry, since the point is to distinguish people not simply on the basis of their right of movement but, more importantly, on the basis of their rights to remain within a state and to undertake a range of possible activities, including working, studying, opening a business, buying property, voting, using public services (such as schools and medical facilities), and generally becoming an active participant in a society. Even with the most effective frontier checkpoint mechanisms, domestic checkpoints will be necessary if immigration is to be controlled, for people may fail to operate within their rights even after entering a country legitimately. Those who overstay or violate the terms of their visas cannot be identified at the frontier, any more than can those who cross borders undetected by immigration authorities.

Internal checkpoints affect the freedom of citizens and residents for much the same reason that external ones do: outsiders are not readily distinguishable from insiders, so everyone must be subject to some level of scrutiny if foreigners are to be restricted. If foreigners require documentation proving they have a right to reside, work, trade, or use public services, natives will need documentation confirming that they are not foreigners. It is for this reason that the gradual erosion of freedom of movement in the twentieth century has brought with it not only the reintroduction of the passport and other forms of travel documentation but also increased monitoring and surveillance of all citizens and residents.[25] But as the imperative to control immigration has grown, so have the number and types of internal checking mechanisms increased. Each mechanism has its own purpose, though not all are equally effective; and each has its own disadvantages from the point of view of the citizen and resident.

A particularly *in*effective mechanism was the UK Home Office's so-called 'Go Home Vans'. In a campaign to encourage illegal immigrants to surrender to the authorities or leave the country, the Home Office arranged for a number of vans bearing posters threatening illegal immigrants with arrest to patrol selected London boroughs.[26] Though the mechanism was a practical failure and quickly abandoned,[27] the larger problem it created was the anxiety provoked among sections of the communities through which the vans passed. Some ethnic minority groups simply did not believe that the vans were authorized by the Home Office but thought they were stunts designed by racist organizations like the English Defence League or the National Front to intimidate people like them. Others were made fearful that their own immigration status would be challenged even though they had secure resident rights, whether because they might get caught up in the investigation of other residents or because they simply did not consider that immigration officials could be relied upon to act justly or without making serious mistakes.[28]

A more robust form of internal monitoring is the 'sweep' of areas where it is suspected that unwanted migrants congregate. This practice has a notable history in Europe and the United States as well as in other parts of the world. The objective is to identify people who are not authorized to live or work in the country by conducting systematic searches and, sometimes, making mass arrests. The procedure might be deployed by national agencies or by officials in provincial or local districts, and the ultimate outcome is the deportation of those who are determined to be illegally resident or working unauthorized. For example, in the 1930s US federal immigration officials, along with local police, went systematically through predominantly Mexican or Mexican-American neighbourhoods in southern California demanding documentary evidence of the right to reside and work in the country—arresting and deporting hundreds of people who were unable to supply proof of immigrant status.[29] The disadvantage of this mechanism is that it is at once disruptive of the communities of residents and citizens and also liable to abuse by local and national authorities.

There are many ways in which this has impacted adversely on citizens and residents. First, even in cases where undocumented migrants are correctly identified, many are members of mixed households—mixed in the sense that different members of a family might hold different kinds of immigrant status. Arresting, detaining, or ultimately deporting, a family member bears seriously on the lives and freedoms of those with citizen or residence rights. The experience of the family of a Mrs Wang, deported for violating the terms of her visa, is a case in point. The UK Home Office determined that baby-sitting her niece while the child's parents were at work amounted to taking unauthorized unpaid employment, and warranted deportation and a ten-year prohibition on returning to Britain.[30] The loss here was incurred not only by Mrs Wang but also by her British sister, brother-in-law, and niece— leaving aside any other friends and relatives she might have had in the UK.

Second, the sweep is notoriously open to abuse in a variety of ways. For one thing, it tends to target minority communities and readily gives support to racist or other cultural prejudices.[31] Once again, this has harmful consequences not only for the unauthorized immigrant but also for the neighbourhoods and communities that bear the brunt of searches that are often conducted with force of arms and a disregard of the sensitivities of residents caught up in the process.

The sweeps may also be unfair to the extent that they demand the presentation of documentary evidence that people simply may not be able to produce. Ironically, this may be particularly problematic for residents and even more so for natural-born citizens, who have no reason to carry documentary evidence of national identity. Between 1930 and 2005 (the year the state of California officially apologized for immigration raids) two million people were forced to leave the country, including *one million American citizens*.[32] The 1954 programme, candidly named 'Operation Wetback', involved extensive sweeps planned and coordinated by the Immigration and Naturalization Service, with vehicle checks, workplace raids (especially in the agricultural sector), ID verifications of 'Mexican-looking' persons, and door-to-door home inspections. Sweeps beginning in California and Arizona were extended to Utah, Nevada, and Idaho, before moving east to Texas. This operation was exceptional for its military character and disregard for the basic rights of those caught up in it, and was also notable for its mistreatment of American citizens.[33] The unlawful detention and deportation of citizens remains a persistent feature of immigration control.[34]

The limitations of frontier as well as particular domestic checkpoint controls such as sweeps and raids may well be what lies behind the emergence of other kinds of internal checkpoint mechanisms. Over time, the strategy of immigration control enforcement has shifted in countries like the US and UK from a focus on preventing unwanted migrant entry to an emphasis on detection after entry. The strategy is to make detection after entry more probable and the point is to try to make it thus more difficult to secure work or access services, thereby at once encouraging people to self-deport or leave and discouraging others from entering. 'If the risks of detention or involuntary removal goes up, and the probability of being able to obtain unauthorized employment goes down, then at some point, the only rational decision is to go home.'[35] Thus states like Alabama started to require that police check the immigration status of people suspected of being in the country without authorization. The worry here is that such mechanisms expand the discretionary power of police, not least in areas where there is a history of race-based conflict between the authorities and the citizenry.

Finally, domestic checkpoints are being expanded by making more and more public and private organizations, as well as individual citizens, agents of immigration enforcement. In the UK, for example, legislation aiming to make it more difficult for unwanted immigrants to reside and work now requires landlords to check the immigration status of tenants, banks to ascertain the residency of people wishing to open accounts, and universities to obtain proof of visa status from students and faculty (as well as to monitor student classroom attendance and faculty presence at work).[36] In 2012 London Metropolitan University lost its right to recruit international students from outside the EU when the UK Border Agency determined that too many of its students did not have a legal right to be in the country, that a significant portion did not have a high enough standard of English, and that there was insufficient evidence that half of those enrolled were turning up to lectures. The revocation of its visa licence meant that the university faced a significant shortfall in its budget, as existing non-EU students had to transfer to other universities or leave the country, while no further international students could be admitted.

There are two respects in which this expansion of domestic checkpoints affects the freedom of citizens and residents. In the first instance, organizations and individuals are required to devote a portion of their time and resources (financial or otherwise) to comply with the law. To some extent, this is nothing new: individuals, businesses, and associations of all kinds have responsibilities to keep tax records, monitor their colleagues' and employees' personal and professional conduct, ensure that workplaces satisfy fire-safety regulations, and generally remain diligent in their dealings with each other, the public, and government agencies of various types. Nonetheless, it remains the case that compliance with immigration law imposes an additional burden. In the second instance, domestic checkpoints impose further burdens on citizens and residents who must now also find it more troublesome to open a bank account, rent a property, register a car, enrol at a university, or miss a lecture. If the point of legislatively imposed burdens is to deter the unwanted, those deterrents must also burden all others.

To appreciate the extent of this burden we should turn to look more closely at the nature of immigration control through the law. While the purpose of law in a free society might be to enhance individual liberty, its operation can also serve to limit it in significant ways.

## Immigration Law and Social Control

Law can be an instrument of social control in at least two ways. First, the law constrains behaviour by marking out the limits of permissible action—and enforcing those limits either by civil penalties or criminal sanctions. Second, the law might mandate certain forms of action, often to reinforce those regulations or codes whose objectives have not been met in the ordinary course of social practice. Immigration law typically, in the first instance, establishes the limits of what particular persons—immigrants and visitors—may do. It might, for instance, prohibit some persons from working, restrict the duration of employment for others,[37] specify where some people may reside,[38] or restrict the ability of particular individuals to travel in and out of the country.[39] However, in order to achieve a higher level of compliance with such regulations, the law might require employers, educational institutions, service providers, and even private citizens to take specified measures or face some form of punishment.

What bears noting here is that when the second type of social control is pursued the burden is borne, at least in the first instance, by citizens and residents—insiders—rather than by the outsiders who are the ultimate targets of that control. (I hasten to emphasize that this is only in the *first* instance. Outsiders who lose their jobs when an employer is forced to fire them are also clearly burdened by the law.) People who are not in the country, are not on the record books, or are not identified by being citizens or fully documented residents, are not easy to control directly, and therefore difficult to deter from acting in ways disapproved of by the authorities. Insiders are easier to control through the law.

It is for this reason that governments looking to control immigration have turned increasingly to the regulation of citizens and residents, and of domestic businesses and other organizations. This point deserves closer attention since it bears importantly on my thesis that immigration controls are ultimately limitations on the freedom of insiders as much as they are of the freedom of foreigners. But it is also worth careful exploration because some have argued that the real burden falls disproportionately, if not uniquely, on would-be immigrants or outsiders. To think this, however, is to fail to appreciate the domestic burden of immigration law.

There are several ways that immigration law limits the freedom of the citizens and residents of a society. First, it limits their freedom to associate, whether for economic, cultural, political, or simply personal reasons: employers cannot hire who, or as many as, they prefer; universities often cannot recruit the people they most want; and individuals and families cannot come together as they wish. Second, it limits people's autonomy of judgment, as they are compelled to yield to the determinations of the authorities (possibly with the support of the democratic majority) as to whether the people they hire, the students they admit, or the companions they choose are necessary or suitable for their own purposes. Third, it imposes not only compliance costs but also the risks that come with compliance failure—fines, loss of income, business collapse, institutional closure, separation from loved ones, or imprisonment. We should consider these limits upon freedom more closely by examining the way in which immigration law affects employers, educational institutions, and personal relations.

## EMPLOYERS AND IMMIGRATION LAW

It is often argued that employers are beneficiaries of immigration and that stricter measures need to be taken to discourage them from seeking foreign labour or hiring non-citizens. A particularly forthright statement of the argument for this is offered by Philip Cafaro, who asserts that, since jobs are the magnet attracting immigrants, making work unavailable will make most illegal immigration disappear—'without elaborate expense or intrusive policing'.[40] Two steps would be all that are needed: mandate the use of a national employment verification database for all new hires so employers can establish whether applicants hold US citizenship or certification to work; and 'strictly enforce existing civil and criminal sanctions against *employers* who hire illegal workers'.[41] What is lamentable, in Cafaro's judgment, is the failure of successive administrations to mete out high enough fines, or to 'seek jail time for employers'.[42]

There are many arguments offered to justify harsher treatment of employers. The most common is that that hiring foreign labour harms citizens, who are left unemployed or forced to accepted lower wages. (I will examine this claim more closely in chapter 5.) But it is also frequently alleged that unscrupulous employers are able to exploit their workers, both domestic and foreign, when an abundance of labour shifts the balance of power in their favour.[43] These claims lie at the heart of employer sanctions detailed in legislation in almost all EU countries, as well as in other nations like Australia, the US, and Canada.

Before considering the argument more closely it would be useful to look at the kinds of sanctions that have been proposed, enacted, and enforced. Australia's Migration Amendment (Reform of Employer Sanctions) Act 2013 is a good example. Proclaimed in September that year to further revise the

2007 Amendment to the Migration Act 1958, it introduced new non-fault civil penalties for employers, adjusted existing criminal penalties, expanded the liability of executive officers involved in employing 'illegal workers', and also established new investigative powers available to the Department of Immigration and Citizenship. Under the act, Australian employers wishing to avoid sanctions must be 'proactive in checking the immigration status and work rights of all workers'.[44] Penalties begin at 15,300 Australian dollars for an individual and five times that for a body corporate, and apply regardless of the state of mind of the employer—that is, the act makes no distinction between an employer who innocently allows someone to work unauthorized and one who knowingly disregards the law.[45] An employer who knowingly employs a foreign national to work illegally is also criminally liable to punishment by two years' imprisonment—or longer if there is evidence of worker exploitation, especially if it causes persons to enter into slavery, forced labour or debt bondage. A person who operates a service, whether for reward or otherwise,[46] referring other persons for work, would be guilty of a civil offence if a referred person is a foreign national not legally entitled to work, or is recommended for work outside the terms of his or her visa. The act also established new powers to search premises, operate electronic equipment, download materials, seize evidence, and ask questions. The purpose of the act was to address the problem posed by illegal workers, estimated by the Howells Report to number something less than 1 per cent of the Australian workforce.[47] The employer sanctions specified in this Australian act are not significantly different in character from those provided for in legislation by the EU, or by the US, or Canada.[48]

Is any of this warranted? Adam Smith addressed this issue, at least in part, as a matter of principle in *The Wealth of Nations* when he wrote:

> The patrimony of a poor man lies in the strength and dexterity of his hands; and to hinder him from employing this strength and dexterity in what manner he thinks proper without injury to his neighbor, is a plain violation of this most sacred property. It is *a manifest encroachment upon the just liberty both of the workman, and of those who might be disposed to employ him.* As it hinders the one from working at what he thinks proper, so it hinders the others from employing whom they think proper. To judge whether he is fit to be employed, may surely be trusted to the discretion of the employers whose interest it so much concerns. *The affected anxiety of the law-giver lest they should employ an improper person, is evidently as impertinent as it is oppressive.*[49]

*The Wealth of Nations* is a particularly appropriate point from which to begin to consider the arguments for employer sanctions, since Adam Smith's treatise was conceived as an attack on the 'spirit of monopoly' and the depredations of the mercantile class. No friend of the commercial establishment, which he saw as all too likely to favour regulations that served its own interests rather than the common good, he was nonetheless sceptical about many measures supposedly taken to protect workers and improve social welfare.[50] At the same time, however, he makes a point in this passage that is all too seldom made today, particularly in the context of debates on immigration. Why is it anyone's business who employers choose to hire; and what makes it anything less than an impertinence that the law interfere with their liberty to make that determination for themselves?

This is important not least because even those who argue for greater freedom of movement and defend the right to work tend to think that it is only immigrants or would-be immigrants who are harmed. 'Sanctions pretend to punish employers, but in reality, they punish workers.'[51] This is not to deny for a moment that significant harms are endured by those who lose their jobs as the result of laws that put pressure on employers to fire undocumented workers, or by those who fail to secure a job because willing employers must turn them away.[52] But the fact remains that employers, both in principle and in practice, can face civil and criminal penalties for nothing more remarkable than offering work to a job-seeker—albeit a job-seeker who is disapproved of by some section of the national population.

What also bears noting is that immigration laws preventing employers from hiring the people they wish put some citizens and residents in conflict with their fellows. Indeed, the conflict over immigration and its control is, in the end, much more a conflict among nationals than it is one between nationals and foreigners—as we shall see more clearly by the end of this book.

Though we will look more deeply into the question of whether there might be a broader consequentialist justification for controlling employers on either economic or cultural grounds (in chapters 5 and 6 respectively), there is on the face of it no good reason in principle for depriving anyone of the liberty to hire, whatever the preferences of other employers, workers, or the broader public happen to be. We might reinforce this point, even if not secure it completely, by drawing an analogy with the history of the regulated segregation of streetcars in the American South in the decades following Reconstruction. Significant numbers of streetcar companies were forced by state legislation and local ordinances to provide separate carriage sections for

Black and White patrons and to require that the two groups travelled apart. This was despite the fact that there was no significant appetite for this among customers, no history or custom of carriage segregation in practice, and a strong antipathy towards the idea on the part of streetcar companies—largely on grounds of cost.[53] The fact that some sections of the community might have a preference for segregation or exclusion of Blacks, and the ability to gain the support of legislatures or local governments, does not seem to be a compelling reason to force people to discriminate against one section of the population. The fact that Black people were required to suffer the indignity of exclusion adds insult and even greater injury to the original injury of deprivation of liberty of streetcar owners. The fact that some people might object to employers hiring foreigners seems like a very poor reason for depriving them of their freedom to decline to so discriminate—even if the employers' motives are entirely self-interested.

Much of the discussion of the obligation of employers to hire particular people (natives) and not others (foreigners) appears to operate on the assumption that the nation possesses something like a common stock of jobs, waiting to be justly distributed in accordance with ethical principles that favour fellow nationals. Yet there is, of course, no such stock. Jobs are created when people who set out to produce goods or services find that they need to employ others to contribute to parts of an enterprise that cannot succeed without more heads and hands. But those jobs would not exist but for someone embarking upon the enterprise that requires them. Except (possibly) in a world in which the freedom to be enterprising in this way was curtailed, there is no obligation upon anyone to set up a company or a business that required the creation of a single job. Should anyone do so, however, it does not mean that the job created is now somehow common property or a part of the stock of jobs to which all natives have first call.

The requirement that employers discriminate in favour of citizens and those with the official approval to work looks even less defensible when one considers how arbitrarily drawn is the line between those who have and those who are denied the right to accept employment. The legal right to work typically is held by all citizens above a minimum age, and also by most permanent residents, some temporary residents, some regular visitors, some transients, and sometimes by refugees and asylum seekers. Like all law, immigrant labour law abounds in exemptions and exceptions; but this is not the issue.

There are several points to consider. The first is that the distinction between a foreigner and a non-foreigner is itself an arbitrary distinction that is as much the creature of immigrant labour law as it is its subject. And while a more obvious distinction might be drawn between citizens and foreigners, almost no one—not even Philip Cafaro, who advocates both a dramatic reduction in immigration to the US and a long-term policy of domestic and global depopulation[54]—suggests denying employers the right to employ any non-citizens. A distinction is being drawn, therefore, between approved and non-approved non-citizens. The arbitrariness of this distinction is not resolved by distinguishing legal from illegal non-citizens, since illegal here means nothing more than 'non-approved'. Why are some people approved to work and others not?

This brings us to the second point. The arbitrariness of the distinction between legal and illegal workers is further in evidence in the variation we find in the definition of legality in different countries, provinces, and regions, and the rapid changes to the definition we see over time within single countries. Though governments and advocates of limits to immigration might imply that there is a stable basis for the distinction, the vagaries of immigration labour law suggest that it is the construction of very changeable factors, including economic interest and political advantage.

Thirdly, the attempt to sustain the distinction has given rise to a number of completely spurious claims about the rationale for making some non-citizens worthy of hire and others not. Perhaps the most absurd of these is that controls are needed to ensure that workers are only imported to take up positions that the domestic labour supply cannot fill. There are several reasons to be sceptical about such claims. To begin with, it is doubtful that any agency could reliably predict the occupational workforce needs of a country, although many routinely do so by specifying which professions will be looked upon favourably when immigration applications are considered— even if the idea of a country having needs is accepted uncritically.[55] It is also doubtful that we can meaningfully claim that a position cannot be filled by domestic labour without offering some judgment about the suitability of the available candidates or the skill standard necessary—yet it would be, in Smith's words, 'impertinent' to suggest that anyone is in a better position to make that judgment than the employer. But if the employer's word is taken—as it frequently is, going by the exemptions granted many enterprises by law—it has to be asked, what is the point of the immigration restriction?[56] The problem is that if the employers' views are ignored, jobs may remain unfilled, either because the wrong workers might be imported or no one is allowed in. If the employers' views are taken seriously, there is no need for immigration control—not, at least, on this basis.

None of this is to suggest that employers are to be assumed to be exemplars of selfless virtue. Indeed, it should be recognized that much of immigration control penalizes some employers precisely so as to benefit others. 'Operation Vanguard' conducted under the Clinton administration in 1998 offers an illustrative case. The enforcement of sanctions after federal agents sifted through the names of 24,310 workers in forty Nebraska meatpacking plants resulted in 3,500 workers being forced from their jobs. The director of the operation admitted that the purpose of the exercise was to put pressure on Congress and employer groups to support guest worker legislation. Since the US was dependent on foreign labour, he said, the best way to build up political support for guest workers was to reduce illegal immigration.[57] But what this means is that the gain to some employers is bought by sacrificing the interests of other employers—as well as of the workers who were ultimately displaced.[58]

One other justification offered for employer sanctions is that they are needed to protect workers from exploitation, and at the extreme from being trafficked or sold into slavery. The Australian Migration Amendment Act 2013, for example, makes very explicit the penalties for conduct that causes a person to enter into slavery, servitude, forced labour, forced marriage, or debt bondage. Immigration control is needed to shield the vulnerable from the forces of the market and from employers themselves. A number of observations are in order here.

It should be acknowledged at the outset that human trafficking is a serious problem everywhere, and people are to be found enslaved or forced into servitude all around the globe—including in the wealthy countries of the western world. However, the clandestine movement or transporting of people does not necessarily indicate trafficking. A distinction should be drawn between people trafficking and people smuggling.[59] Transporting people in secret, whether to rescue them from persecuting authorities or help them flee war zones or enable them to cross borders so they might find their way to make a living, may involve smuggling, but is not trafficking unless the persons transported are coerced into going, or pressed into servitude and traded like commodities. To be sure, the distinction is a fine one, and it would be too much to expect that people traffickers and people smugglers would always be separate groups distinguished by sharply differing ethical standards. But there is a difference; though it is one that is not always recognized or clearly drawn.[60]

The distinction between trafficking and smuggling is plainly acknowledged, for example, by US Immigration and Customs Enforcement (ICE), whose website has separate sections describing the different activities of 'Human Smuggling' and 'Human Trafficking'.[61] Nonetheless, the two activities are brought together in the agency's Human Trafficking and Smuggling Center (established in 2004 under the Intelligence Reform and Terrorism Prevention Act). This is because the ultimate purpose of this division of the Department of Homeland Security is 'Investigating the Illegal Movement of People and Goods'. Here, as with similar government agencies in the UK, Europe, and Australia, the mission of the immigration authorities is presented as one of protecting the vulnerable from exploitation at the hands of criminals. Ironically, however, what makes people more vulnerable is the fact that they are deprived of the protection of the law because the law makes it difficult for workers to move freely and openly across borders, and for employers to hire whomsoever they choose.

If the worry is that workers are being exploited, there is no need for anti-immigrant labour law, just anti-exploitation law.[62] The fact that the law assumes the employees are at risk when undocumented reveals that the exploitation is a result of their illegal status—which is an artefact of the very legislation purporting to protect them. This is made clearer still by the fact that employers with very good employment practices have been forced to fire foreign workers. Just as the criminalizing of the movement of goods turns that movement over to criminals, the criminalizing of the movement of people turns that movement into the hands of other criminals—and turns some employers into criminals in the process.

To the extent that restrictions on foreign labour encourage employers to hire illegal labour at reduced rates, it may appear that what is happening is straightforwardly exploitative behaviour by unscrupulous businesses. But here a few observations are in order. First, assuming comparable native labour is available at a higher price, it would make no sense for an employer to offer to pay the same wages when taking the risk of incurring criminal penalties for hiring illegally. If no native labour were available, an employer would still be unlikely to pay the minimum wage if it was above the market wage, since he would already be breaking the law in hiring people who are not authorized to work. There is no further penalty for hiring illegally *and* failing to pay the minimum wage. Making the hiring of unauthorized foreign labour illegal and subject to serious penalty sets up incentives to further encourage exploitation.

Second, the illegal status of foreign workers makes it not only difficult for them to negotiate with employers but also harder for domestic workers to protect their own interests by bringing foreign workers into their trade unions. This is not to deny that there are cases in which domestic workers might resent the competition from foreign workers, whose skills or lower costs might make them ready *substitutes* for local labour. Equally, however, there are also occasions when foreign workers *complement* the skills of domestic workers—or simply do not displace them because of shortages. In these circumstances, the restriction on foreign labour weakens the power of domestic labour to the extent that illegal workers cannot risk joining unions or speaking up with their domestic co-workers when important workplace issues are at stake. Now it might be argued that without illegal workers, trade unions would not be faced with employers able to ignore union demands because they could rely on an alternative source of labour. To the extent that this is true, however, it is as much the result of the law making it impossible for those foreign workers to become unionized.

Overall, if the concern is with reducing or eliminating the exploitation of people as a result of unauthorized or 'illegal' immigration, the most obvious answer is to increase the freedom of workers to work and employers to employ. The source of harm is not the exchange that takes place between worker and employer but the obstacles to such exchange that corrupt the process.[63]

In these times it is perhaps unusual to think about the interests or concerns of employers. Yet it is worth reflecting on the impact of immigration control on the way in which this very significant sector of society lives and operates. The responsibilities of employers have already been expanded under the law to include a range of obligations to their employees—often as a result of pressure from workers themselves. Yet some of the responsibilities set on the shoulders of employers have come not from workers but from governments or states looking to turn them into their agents—most notably for greater efficiency in the collection of taxes. A more recent responsibility laid at the door of employers is the obligation to serve as the state's agent in the monitoring and policing of society. To the extent that governments look to control immigration by restricting foreign entry into the labour force, it is employers who are asked to bear the burden of reporting on the origins and status of their imported workers. One further consequence of this, it is worth noting, is that employers increasingly have also to report on their native employees. We will consider this aspect of immigration control later in this chapter.

## IMMIGRATION LAW AND EDUCATION

Employers are not, however, the only sector of society on whom immigration law has placed a significant burden. Other parts of society have also felt its impact. One sector that is worth a closer look is the institutions in society responsible for education. To some extent, schools and universities face problems similar to those that affect employers, since they are employers themselves. But there are other issues that arise out of the distinctive purposes that educational institutions have. A part of this is because schools and universities not only recruit international faculty to teach and administer, but also admit students from different parts of the world. By 2015 there were more than five million foreign students in higher education worldwide. In the United States, by 2009, higher education was the country's fifth largest service export sector, with in-bound foreign students contributing 17.7 billion dollars to GDP.[64] But it is not only the colleges and universities that are welcoming international students. In 2013 about 73,000 foreign students enrolled in American high schools. By 2015 more than 450,000 American students—predominantly but not exclusively college students—were themselves studying abroad, encouraged to do so by state education authorities and schools as well as by universities. The world has also seen a dramatic increase in the number of international schools catering primarily to the needs of 'expatriates', but also to local populations interested in gaining more prestigious qualifications or acquiring an education in English. Students are a significant portion of the world's mobile population.

This mobility has, however, also produced a response from authorities concerned about the impact of the movement of students into their societies. The worries range from the burden that their numbers impose on social services (from transport to healthcare), to the competition they add to the labour market, to the danger that students will literally overstay their welcome and turn into long-term or permanent immigrants. If the point is to reduce immigration, students are a problem.[65]

The consequences for students of this view taken by governments have included rises in the cost of studying (in part because of higher fees for visas), increased scrutiny through more complex and time-consuming applications for admission, restrictions on rights to work, and a greater risk of exclusion or deportation for visa violations.[66] But it is the consequences for the education sector in the receiving societies that is the subject that merits further examination.

The most obvious consequence of stricter immigration controls is a rise in costs for schools and universities. Higher education institutions in particular have to devote a greater part of their human resources budgets to employing people whose job it is to ensure compliance with changing immigration laws.[67] This has meant not only recruiting staff to monitor students and faculty to ensure that they have secured and maintained the correct immigration status, and engaging firms specializing in immigration law to make sure that legislative and administrative changes are not missed, but also imposing additional responsibilities on faculty and other professional service staff who might be obliged to report on students. In Britain this has led one senior university official to observe that 'in effect, our universities are now acting in conjunction with the UK's Border Agency to manage immigration'.[68] The financial risk of not cooperating is being subject to fines or loss of sponsorship licences (which would make it impossible for the college or university to admit international students).[69]

No less significant a concern is the impact of immigration control on faculty recruitment. Universities and colleges, and increasingly schools, operate in a global market. Immigration controls not only impose financial costs but also burdens that are the result of delays or uncertainty—making planning more difficult and service provision more unreliable. Thus, for example, in the UK in 2016 there was a reported shortage of secondary school teachers in science, mathematics, computing, and selected languages that remained unaddressed in part because immigration regulations did not identify those specialisms on its Shortage Occupation List. Immigration law further required that foreign employees had to meet the minimum salary threshold of thirty-five thousand pounds, making it more difficult still to recruit.[70] The Shortage Occupation List is regularly revised on the recommendations made by the independent Migration Advisory Committee, but this information is not available until shortages have already emerged.

The same sort of problem arises wherever immigration restrictions prevent timely recruitment. For example, in the United States in the 1990s a rapid rise in demand for computer programmers went unmet because of the limited number of H1B visas available. The US government responded by increasing the number of visas, only for them to become available just at the time of the so-called 'dot-com crash' that led to a downturn in demand for programmers and a large number of unused H1B visas. The government responded by reducing the number of visas available, just in time to see demand increase again when the market recovered. The impact here was felt less by would-be immigrant programmers, whose skills were in demand everywhere, than domestically by individuals and industries whose freedom to recruit was curtailed by immigration controls.[71]

While these sorts of costs are significant, it is perhaps more troubling still that a necessary concomitant of immigration control is the increase in monitoring and surveillance of educational institutions by agencies of government, bringing about a decline in their autonomy as well as a transformation of their operations. It means governments requiring education professionals to conform to standards or comply with directives that have no bearing on the latter's own missions or judgments about how their purposes are best served. It also means turning these institutions into arms of government by requiring them to monitor and report on people for whom they have responsibility, establishing within schools, colleges and universities a norm of continual mutual surveillance. At the extreme, it threatens to bring about an active presence of the police as law enforcement agents—currently a live issue in American schools.[72] It may be for this reason that we have seen schools (as well as cities) declare themselves to be 'sanctuaries', and decline to cooperate with immigration enforcement agencies[73]—citing, among other things, harms to children and families, particularly in immigrant communities, traumatized by the fear of police action.[74]

The general point, however, is that immigration control in the sphere of education has wider implications. Aside from the direct costs it imposes on the institutions themselves, it has an impact on the constituencies that sustain them. This is true not only of the education sector but of civil society more generally.

## IMMIGRATION LAW AND CIVIL LIFE

Whether it is attempted through the control of employers or the control of institutions in civil society more generally, all efforts to control immigration must affect the personal lives of citizens and residents in that society, though some will be affected more profoundly than others. All must share in the economic cost,[75] but a number will face its implications less indirectly. To understand this point more fully, it would be useful to consider a sample of concrete cases.

Case 1: Paul and Gail Freahy, a native-born British man and his South African wife, sold everything and moved to Britain from South Africa after being the victims of violent crime, to open a small photography shop in Torquay. Despite having been married for thirteen years, they were refused a renewal of a spousal visa because, as shop-owners, they had not paid themselves salaries and failed to meet the eligibility criteria. They were given twenty-eight days for Gail Freahy, the non-British partner, to leave. There was no possibility of appeal from within the UK, and an application for a different visa would have to be made from South Africa. Deprived of the 55,000-pound annual income from their jointly-run business and faced with the cost of returning to South Africa as well as finding the funds to apply for a visa, the couple were financially ruined since separation was not economically viable. The burden of immigration control here has fallen as heavily on a native Briton as it has on his would-be-immigrant wife.[76]

**Case 2:** Patrick Thies, an American orthopaedic physician assistant, was recruited from Oregon at great expense by a Birmingham National Health Service hospital unable to find an equivalent specialist in the UK. He attempted to move to the UK with his British wife, their biological child and two adopted children but was advised on landing that the two adopted children were ineligible for admission to the UK and told to return them to the United States. (The family were detained at the airport and the two adopted children, aged 10 and 12, were issued one-way tickets to return to New York three days later. 'The officials were seriously insisting that these young children should be separated from their family and put on an airplane which would land in a strange city in the evening where we knew no one', said Thies.) The family found a lawyer who secured permission for the children to be released from detention and to be allowed to stay in the UK while the father applied for them to be permitted to remain as dependents of someone employed on a Tier 2 visa. The British mother was not eligible to apply for her adopted sons to remain with her in the UK because she was not British-born. After submitting the 1800-pound fee, the couple waited ten months only for their application to be turned down on the grounds that it had to be submitted from outside the UK. The Home Office's letter to the couple 'stated that while it was not their intention to separate the children from the rest of their family, one of the grounds for refusal was that one of the parents could return to the States with the boys and stay in touch with the rest of the family through email and Skype'.[77]

**Case 3:** Mrs Irene Clennell, married to her British husband for twenty-seven years, with two British sons and one British granddaughter, was held in detention for several weeks before being deported to Singapore in February 2017. She had long ago secured Indefinite Leave to Remain (ILR)[78] in the UK but had returned to Singapore to care for dying parents, during which time her ILR status expired. She applied for it to be renewed both from Singapore and within the UK, but the application was denied on the grounds that her husband, now in poor health and dependent on his wife as primary carer, did not meet the income threshold of 18,600 pounds to sponsor her to move (back) to Britain.[79]

**Case 4:** Johann 'Ace' Francis was born in Jamaica but grew up in mainly in the United States. Because his step-father was in the military the family moved regularly but settled in Washington state when he was 7 years old. His mother became a naturalized American citizen when Ace was 14, making him automatically an American citizen also. His biological father had never had custody of him and was not listed on his birth certificate. Shortly before he turned 18, Ace's mother moved to Georgia but he remained in Washington state to finish high school. During the spring break, before graduating, he visited the town of Seaside in Oregon, where he was caught up in a street fight. He was arrested and, having said he was born in Jamaica and being unable to prove his American citizenship, was deported after being moved first to Las Vegas and then to a detention centre in Arizona. After being deposited at Kingston airport, Ace lived on the beach and streets until he found his biological father in Jamaica some time later. His mother had no way of knowing that her American son had been wrongfully deported. His father contacted his mother but it was ten years before he was eventually returned to the United States. His mother wrongly assumed he must have been deported because he was not naturalized. When they figured out that he had been naturalized automatically, it took several years to find the necessary records, including birth certificates, to obtain the papers needed to get an American passport and bring their son home. Ace Francis died shortly after his return.[80]

Such stories can be multiplied a thousand-fold—indeed a million times over, given that more than a million American citizens have been wrongly deported since 1930. In the UK, the government estimated that its visa rules would *each year* prevent about eighteen thousand British citizens from being united or reunited with their spouses or families because of the income threshold that had to be met in order to sponsor a partner to enter the country[81]—to say nothing of those denied that freedom for other reasons. Since more than 40 per cent of those in employment, and 55 per cent of women in the workforce, do not meet the threshold there is a sad irony in these figures to the extent that one of the express purposes of immigration control is to protect the poor from the economic ill-effects of the influx of outsiders (about which more in chapter 5 below). It is generally the poorer citizens who find themselves bearing the harshest consequences of immigration control.[82]

The intrusion into personal life that is the effect of immigration control does not, however, end with the financial obstacles placed in the way of citizens who might chance to find themselves involved with an outsider.

Because of the fear that fraudulent marriages might be used as a means of entry, governments have set up tests of proof of varying degrees of strictness to examine the genuineness of relationships and put the onus on applicants to demonstrate the seriousness of their commitments to each other. This is a curious innovation in the history of marriage, which has generally been entered into for a variety of reasons, including only on occasion compatibility, or shared interests, or love.[83] Thus UK applicants looking to sponsor a partner have to prove their relationship is genuine by supplying, among other things, proof of address and length of time together, and an ability to speak the same language. More than this, they have to prove a continuing commitment to a relationship that must conform to state-determined notions of what constitutes a proper way for two people to share their intimate life.[84] One wonders what would have become of Tan Sri Eusoffe Abdoolcader, one of Malaysia's most distinguished judges, who fell in love with a young, uneducated Cantonese woman who spoke no English and little Malay. They married and lived happily until she passed away from cancer. Heartbroken, he became a recluse who every year took out full pages in various newspapers to post verses (mostly in Latin) to his departed wife, until he could bear the loss no longer and took his own life. He had graduated in 1950 with First Class Honours from University College, London, and that year was made a Freeman of the City of London. He rose to become a judge on the High Court and was known for his mastery of languages, especially Latin and English. From the standpoint of the state, bona fide relationships are all the same, and no sense could be made of the behaviour of this particular Freeman.

There are two arguments that might be offered to address the concerns raised here about the intrusions of the state into personal life, and the impact this has on the lives of citizens and residents. One is to say that the injustices to which the above cases draw attention are the disappointing but potentially avoidable consequences of a system of laws and bureaucratic processes that might benefit from reform. The other is that the intrusion into personal life is an unfortunate side-effect of procedures established to deter such things as sham marriages, or other relationships into which people enter in order fraudulently to gain rights of residence. We should consider these arguments more closely.

The idea that the law and the processes of administration that determine the shape of immigration control might be reformed to eliminate the injustices or the loss of freedom for citizens highlighted in the cases above is overly optimistic because the problems are inherent in the aspiration to control immigration. The more control is sought, the greater will be the loss of freedom. A part of this has to do with the politics not only of legislation but also of administration. Arguments for immigration control generally do not give much consideration to the question of state capacity to exercise control. While there is no doubt that legislation and executive action can have substantial effects, it is quite another matter to suggest that this amounts to control—at least, if control means securing determinate outcomes. Control has never been achieved if by this one means the reaching of pre-determined targets, but even by more modest standards that recognize that control is a matter of degree rather than an absolute measure, control has never been within reach—at least in liberal democracies. While the countries of the communist world before 1989, and a few continuing exceptions such as North Korea, have been able to seal their borders both to keep outsiders out and hold insiders in, liberal democratic states have enjoyed much more limited success. This is very readily evident, for example, in the presence of twelve million so-called 'illegal immigrants' in the United States despite continued efforts to reduce immigration and increase deportations; and in the failure of the UK government to reduce the net migration numbers below a hundred thousand per annum despite repeated promises to do so.

There are a number of reasons for this and other failures of immigration control. One is the continuing demand in both of these (and other) countries for cheap as well as high-skilled labour. This means that, even as political pressures for reductions in immigration pull governments in one direction, pressures to ease restrictions or to turn a blind eye to immigration violations pull them in another. Legislative measures therefore tend to be riddled with exemptions. At the same time, the management of control is compromised by the fact that there is a large gap between legislation and enforcement. Public interest advocacy organizations and private interest groups, whether independently or in collusion with each other, can work to block or slow down the enforcement of legislative or executive decrees—operating through the courts to invalidate regulations or decisions,[85] or by pressuring congressmen or parliamentarians to intercede in specific cases or bring in other legislation that works against existing laws. In federal systems such as the United States, the varying interests of different states or provinces again can lead to conflicting pressures. On top of all this, there is the fact that the interests of bureaucracies, and the contending pressures they face, will significantly determine whether and how policy is carried out at street-level.[86] Immigration issues are often the province of more than one agency, which may not see eye to eye, and which are also jealous of their territory.[87] The abuses of the freedoms of citizens (not to mention foreigners) as a consequence of government agencies acting without regard for basic human rights or even simple decency is worth noting because of the widespread and systemic nature of the problem.[88]

What this also means, however, is that efforts to reform immigration control to eliminate unfairness or to prevent the diminution of citizen freedom will run up against the same obstacles. Once policy targets are established, whether by executive decree or legislative enactment, the political pressure to achieve the stated goals will generate its own imperatives. If some groups gain exemptions that make it more difficult to achieve immigration targets, stricter enforcement will be pursued in other areas. The people who are most vulnerable in this process are those whose interests are too diffuse to enable them readily to form pressure groups or encourage public advocacy groups to take up their causes. The first, second, and third cases described above are examples of this problem.

The pressure to meet immigration targets, or be 'tough' on immigration, also inevitably gives rise to hasty action animated more by internal administrative imperatives than zealous attention to natural justice. Overworked officials are unlikely to expend much energy and time trying to ensure that people like Ace Francis, who appear to be 'illegal', are given the benefit of a thorough investigation. The risk of injustice as the result of the rigid enforcement of rules that do not fit every case cannot readily be remedied by granting discretion to those directed to enforce them, since that discretion might not be exercised to the benefit of citizens confronted by injustices, or simply might not be exercised at all.[89]

This brings us to the second argument that might be advanced to alleviate concerns about the intrusions of the state into personal life, and the impact this has on the lives of citizens and residents: that it is simply an unfortunate side-effect of efforts in good faith to deal with illegal activity, such as attempts to gain admission to a society through sham marriages. Every policy runs the risk of collateral damage, some policies more so than others, but the responsibility for this rests with those whose violations of the law necessitate such action. While all this is true enough as far as it goes, it is not enough to address the heart of the problem. The reason people resort to sham marriages as a means of immigrating is because other options have been closed. When other forms of movement are denied them, for example, many people choose the route of seeking asylum, if refugee status holds out some prospect of getting out of a bad situation and getting into a better one. This is not necessarily because they are 'economic migrants'—it may be because they are what E. F. Kunz called 'anticipatory refugees', people who flee before they are persecuted.[90] Erika Mann was precisely such an example.[91] But of course, many are economic migrants—people looking to move to improve their financial circumstances, or simply to seek their fortunes. Laws limiting or forbidding immigration will deter some from trying to enter a society, but there will always be some who are not put off, whether it is because they are by nature not easily deterred, or because their plight is desperate enough for them to put aside their scruples and try their luck. The higher the numbers with a strong incentive to move, the more extensive must be the immigration controls to prevent them from entering, and the more intrusive must those controls then become for citizens and aliens alike. But intrusion breeds resistance; and resistance necessitates more intrusion if the goals of policy are to be met.

There are other side-effects worth noting. In the UK, given the gender pay gap, the financial threshold to qualify to sponsor a spouse or partner makes it harder for women to sponsor would-be immigrant husbands than for husbands to sponsor wives, reinforcing women's dependency on men even as official policy declares its aim to be gender neutral and to discourage the importation of inegalitarian gender values.[92] To the extent that policy also aims to discourage immigration from countries in which arranged or non-voluntary marriage is normal, the penalty of deportation for immigrant spouses who divorce has the perverse consequences of, at once, encouraging people to stay in bad marriages, and strengthening the hand of abusive non-immigrant partners (predominantly men).[93]

Whatever the claims of legislators, the purpose of scrutinizing and controlling marriages between natives and foreigners is not so much to protect against poor-quality marriages as to ensure that the state does not admit poor-quality immigrants.[94] The consequences of this have been felt not just by the would-be immigrants—whether they end up admitted or excluded—but by the society and its institutions, including its institutions of marriage. When immigration status that could be claimed as a result of marriage becomes a central preoccupation of the state, the consequence must be that not only the rights that flow from marriage 'but also the marriage rites themselves are controlled in ways that would be regarded as unacceptably intrusive if they occurred in another context'.[95]

## Surveillance and the Socializing of Immigration Control

Immigration law brings with it important limitations on the freedom of citizens and residents insofar as it necessarily restricts what they may do: whom they may employ, whom they may teach or enrol, and even whom they may marry. But the search for immigration control also has a more subtle—if no less intrusive—impact on freedom. This is because, for immigration control to work, what is required is a continuous monitoring of the population. There needs, therefore, also to be a population that is ready to accept the necessary level of surveillance. This surveillance did not begin because of the move towards greater control of immigration; nor did it necessarily rise solely for that reason. The search for control everywhere brings with it an increase in surveillance, and immigration control is no exception. The point is to understand how immigration control extends the level of surveillance of citizens and residents in different ways.

The modern developed state has evolved to the point where it has sub-sumed and absorbed much of society. This is evident, first, in the sheer expansion of its budget and of the number of people in its employ, and conse-quently in the state's capacity to monitor every law-abiding citizen (and most others as well), and regulate every group or association within its borders. In the United States, for example, the Department of Homeland Security alone has 240,000 employees. This is second in size only to the Department of Defense, whose Terrorism Information Awareness Program[96] gathered information on every American citizen from databases of credit card trans-actions, ticket purchases, academic grades, and other forms of individual activity.[97] Not even the absolutist states of early modernity could establish a direct relationship with every individual within its borders in the way the developed states of today can. Now we take for granted something which once would have been considered astonishing: that states have the right 'to a monopoly of all the force within the community, to make war, to make peace, to conscript life, to tax, to establish and dis-establish property, to define crime, to punish disobedience, to control education, to supervise the family, to regulate personal habits, and to censor opinions'.[98]

One conclusion one might draw from this is that it is pointless, or perverse, or even faintly quixotic, to then be bothered about the further intrusion that immigration control might represent in our already highly controlled societies. Indeed, this is how the argument is so often presented. When, in 1987, the Australian government wanted to introduce a national identity card it argued that since everyone already carried credit cards, driving licences, and other forms of identification, one more would not prove to an inconvenience or amount to any great change. The most impor-tant step towards greater control is 'normalization'. (We shall return to this in the final chapter.) An alternative thought, however, is that this is precisely the outlook we should resist, beginning with a questioning of further extensions of control. At the very least, we should recognize that a tightening of immigration control through surveillance is an extension of control over citizens and residents, and not merely a means of monitoring the conduct of outsiders.

To see more clearly why this should be a matter of concern, we might consider the workings of the immigration surveillance apparatus at two extremes: from the explicit use of these instruments for political advantage to the low-level monitoring of citizens that raises more subtle questions. An arresting example of the use of the instruments of immigration control that amounts to the abuse of political power is supplied by the famous case of John Lennon, targeted for deportation by the administration of President Richard Nixon in a case the United States Immigration and Naturalization Service (INS)[99] eventually lost. Lennon was in the United States with his wife, Yoko Ono, a permanent resident who was trying to find her missing American-born daughter by her previous marriage. After participating at a peace rally at the University of Michigan in December 1971, in support of an imprisoned radical writer and musician, John Sinclair, Lennon came to the attention of undercover agents at the FBI, who reported his attendance to superiors in the agency—which then began a campaign to 'neutralize Lennon'. Subsequently, with the urging of Senator Strom Thurmond, the matter was sent up to John Mitchell, the Attorney-General (and therefore, head of the INS), who acted quickly to move to have Lennon's visa revoked and commence deportation proceedings.

At the root of these moves was a fear on the part of the American President and his advisors that Lennon was someone who was capable of inspiring the newly enfranchised 18-year-old voters who were protesting against their country's involvement in the Vietnam War. The complexities of the case, which lasted five years before Lennon was told he could stay and also apply for permanent residency, need not detain us.[100] The relevant point is that the powers of the immigration control bureaucracy, along with other agencies of government, were marshalled with the knowledge and connivance of senior officials, including the President of the United States, in an attempt to quell public opposition to an unpopular war. Leaving aside any injustice to John Lennon, the important concern is that his deportation proceedings were a part of a larger strategy aimed at the control of American opinion. That the case should have lasted so long is testimony to the determination of the government administration and its agencies to achieve specific political goals, which had absolutely nothing to do with any concern about immigration and its potential harm to American society.

At the other extreme, surveillance of the population takes place not through targeted investigations by such agencies as the FBI but in the every-day collection of data on travellers, employees, patients, asylum seekers and, in some countries, non-citizens more generally. Surveillance is increasingly conducted not through direct monitoring by officials but using biometric technology in systems deployed to verify and authenticate identity. If John Lennon was singled out as a unique individual, picked out for special treat-ment by virtue of his very public identity, others are now routinely identified as unique individuals by virtue of their file numbers that distinguish them using their names, places and dates of birth, nationality and fingerprints.[101]

While the harassment of John Lennon for political advantage looks clearly wrong, legally and morally speaking, the biometric surveillance of populations by states presents a trickier ethical problem. States, as well as the companies that supply the technology that make surveillance more effec-tive, consider it to be wholly justified and highly desirable. The arguments offered are worth reviewing.

Pre-eminent among them is the argument from *security*. There are two kinds of approaches to thinking about security and how to attain it. One is to consider the problem as one of dealing with or preventing breaches of security by people who can be identified as threats: responding to the exceptional, understood as the breakdown of security, ideally by prevent-ing those who might threaten it from acting. The other is to view security as a problem of management, which aims at reducing the risk of a security breach in a world in which it is not always easy to identify those people who are potential threats to security. In this latter model, the search for the exception is replaced by the method of continual monitoring. The rise of global mobility presents challenges for both of these approaches. The case for biometric surveillance reflects a growing preference for the latter, as a population that is on the move (not just globally but also domestically), from different ethnic, linguistic, and even political backgrounds—in some cases in possession of multiple citizenships—or working for more than one organization, becomes more difficult to identify and individuate without resort to increasingly sophisticated tracking tools. The dangers such people could present range from the threat of political subversion to engaging in criminal activity. Perpetual surveillance seems like the obvious tool to use to protect the state from subversion and the population from threats ranging from terrorist attacks to identify theft.

A subsequent reason offered for biometric surveillance is then that it offers *convenience*—for travellers in particular. The need to monitor the movement and behaviour of people creates costs and delays for innocent travellers, but a system of biometric management makes it possible to distinguish legitimate or 'trusted' travellers from other travellers who require closer scrutiny.[102]

Yet another reason proffered for increased surveillance is the *protection* of the innocent from those seeking to exploit them. People smugglers entice the unwary with promises of safe passage to the west in unseaworthy vessels, leaving them to become victims of nature and the elements. Better surveillance would enable governments to find out in advance about people looking to make bad choices, and also make possible the capture and punishment of those criminals trafficking in human misery. The EU says it is working to eliminate these criminal activities to save lives. Australia makes a similar claim to justify the detention of asylum seekers on Nauru and Manus Island: it is trying to save the lives of people who would have set out into dangerous waters. By preventing asylum seekers from making landfall in Australia and denying them the opportunity to make claims to refugee status (as they would be eligible to do under the terms of the 1951 Refugee Convention to which Australia is a signatory), the detention policy serves as a deterrent to future asylum seekers and smugglers, and thereby as a life-saving measure.

Ultimately, the argument for immigration control offered by these and other states is that the objective is not the prevention but the facilitation of immigration through effective management. Most people do not want to move permanently but wish nonetheless to be mobile: to be able to travel, to work, and to return home. Monitoring and surveillance is simply a part of a larger constructive effort to manage the flow of people to ensure that the interests of all parties are duly taken into account. These interests include those of domestic employers, domestic workers, foreign workers, and those countries sending foreign workers (and which might suffer serious losses if talent drains away to the wealthy west). The purpose of immigration control is not to stop immigration but to promote a form of 'circular migration'—to use a term adopted by the EU.

All of these arguments for increasing political and administrative control need to be viewed with some caution, if not outright scepticism. That scepticism should be firmly in place most particularly when security is invoked as a justification for restrictions on freedom of any kind, since it is the oldest and most widely invoked reason offered for controlling human beings— possibly excepting religious ones. It is especially appropriate when increased surveillance and data collection are held up as necessary for the collection of intelligence on subversive or terrorist activity.

So spake the fiend, and with necessity,
The tyrant's plea, excused his devilish deeds.[103]

The obvious but typically unaddressed problem here is that increasing the volume of data collected and retained makes it more difficult to sort through the noise to find information that is of any relevance or use. Increasing the size of the haystack makes it more difficult to find the needle.[104] If everyone becomes a person of interest, no one will be very interesting—unless some other means is found to distinguish those who are *really* interesting.

A more substantial worry, however, is that the expansion of 'securitization' we have witnessed reflects a very different narrative to the one that is generally offered: that securitization tracks developments in the world that call for an expansion of control. In fact, the expansion of security checks also reflects the emergence of powerful interests—both private and governmental—that profit from the growth of the security industry. Didier Bigo puts the matter more starkly: 'Securitization of immigration is the result and not the cause of the development of technologies of control and surveillance. It is linked to computerization, risk profiling, visa policy, the remote control of borders, the creation of international or nonterritorial zones in airports.'[105] The argument here is not that there are no security concerns modern societies face. It is rather that 'securitization' should not be viewed uncritically as the necessary outcome of the existence of some objective security threat rather than as a strategy pursued by agencies with a direct interest in the development and deployment of security systems. Indeed, looking at the matter more broadly still, the state through its various agents and agencies has an interest at stake. It therefore has a tendency to present itself as the structure through which security is made possible, and therefore to portray every intrusion into its realm as a potential threat to security. Thus, defending the security of the state against all threats, wherever they might appear—domestically or in remote parts of the world—is represented as coterminous with the defence of society itself. The loss of freedom in all this is viewed by the state and its agents as a small price to pay, but the gain in security is illusory when the threats are manufactured.

This is certainly the case with the securitization of immigration, which all too often presents the movement of people as a danger. An obvious case here is the representation of refugees as a security threat when they pose no such risk. The Australian response to the refugee question since 2001 is especially instructive. For purposes of *external* border control it has stepped up the patrolling of its territorial waters (having asserted a reduction of

the extent of those waters for the purpose of asserting a right to asylum),
it has declined to allow people coming by boat to make landfall—shipping
them off, at vast expense, to other destinations for 'processing'—and it has
kept people in detention camps without access to the outside world while
restricting the freedom of Australian and other journalists to visit or review
conditions there. The narrative offered to the public has been consistent:
national security demanded that the government 'stop the boats'. This is
despite the absence of any evidence that the bedraggled asylum seekers
(particularly children who were also subject to detention for months or
years) were a security threat—and despite plenty of evidence that governments also sought to capitalize on the public anxiety generated by repeated
insistence on the dangers posed by refugees. (One important Liberal Party
strategist was reported in 2009 as admitting that the party, then in opposition, thought that the issue was 'fantastic' and that 'the more boats that
come the better'—even as it was excoriating the government for putting
Australian lives at risk by not stopping boats from coming.[106]) For the purpose of *internal* security, the Australian Border Force (ABF) in August 2015
initiated 'Operation Fortitude', a programme it announced as one in keeping
with its 'mission of promoting a secure and cohesive society'. The plan was
to have ABF officers stationed at various locations around the city of Melbourne, ready to speak to any individuals who crossed their path to remind
them that they needed to be aware of the conditions of their visas, and that
if they committed visa fraud they would be caught. On this occasion, the
public reacted with horror at the prospect of being stopped at random, or
as a result of some form of racial profiling, and 'Operation Border Farce', as
it was promptly dubbed, was hastily cancelled.[107]

These cases are instructive in part because they reveal how readily security
is manipulated for political purposes—and indeed partisan advantage. For
this reason, among others, claims that mass surveillance must be extended
for the increased convenience of travellers should also be taken with a grain
of salt. Similarly, claims that the motivating concern is the protection of the
innocent, including immigrant victims of smugglers and traffickers, should
be viewed sceptically given that neither the logic of the measures proposed
nor the practices through which they are implemented show any evidence
of genuine care for the harm that might befall the people moving. In the case
of refugees, European and Australian insistence that by deterring smugglers
they are preventing deaths at sea carries little weight when the reason so
many take to boats is to escape circumstances so grim that they are willing to
risk their lives—and when the result of policy is simply to ensure that those

people do not die in European or Australian coastal waters but elsewhere. This calculating logic aside, the fact also remains that neither European nor Australian policy towards those who survive and are deposited in refugee or detention camps show much concern for their wellbeing.[108]

As to the claim that the purpose of surveillance is to facilitate rather than prevent immigration, the point to note is that the aim is not to render immigration *per se* easier but to make it possible for some to move more readily and others not to move at all, and everyone to move at a time and a rate that suits the interests of particular parties, whether in host or sending countries. It is certainly not about freeing movement, any more than it is about treating people equally (about which more in chapter 4 below). There is also the concern that the instruments of surveillance established for one purpose could quickly be turned to use for others. Thus, while some advocates have pressed for the extension of employment monitoring systems such as E-Verify in the United States, others have warned against it for fear that it might be a significant step towards more intrusive forms of surveillance of other citizens, from landlords to healthcare providers.[109]

Questionable though these reasons for surveillance might be, however, they do also reveal something significant about the process of immigration management by the state and its agencies. This is the importance of controlling not only movement but also the narrative of immigration management. The story that has to be told is that immigration control is needed to protect the population, who are bound together by a shared identity, from threats posed by outsiders. The population ought therefore to be fearful of potential harm to them individually and to the society more generally. Those who are the source of harm are people whose actions are not law-abiding, and whose actions or even status are 'illegal'. The narrative relies upon creating a hierarchy of acceptable people, while presenting the agencies of the state as operating with nothing but the interests of the population in mind, and in accordance with the values the community itself embraces—for it is the legitimate representative of the community. The idea that private security companies, IT providers, government agencies, and political leaders might have interests of their own that shape immigration management is not, and cannot be, a part of that narrative. Equally, the narrative depends upon the promotion of a variety of confusions, or even falsehoods. For example, asylum seekers who arrive by boat or by clandestine means are described as 'queue jumpers', when that term has no legal meaning and no practical sense to the extent that no 'queue' exists.[110] Similarly, those who facilitate the movement of refugees—'people smugglers'—are reviled in the official narrative as traffickers in human misery when the actual, more complex, story reveals a network of people, many of them refugees and former refugees themselves, collaborating to make possible the escape of people trying to avoid war zones or persecution.[111]

The way in which the immigration control narrative arises is not, however, a straightforward matter. It is bound up, in the end, with a larger story or set of stories in which the place of political authority or the state is set out in relation to the life of the people, as well as the wider world of states and other people. Though this narrative might be dominated by various elites who have a bigger role—and stake—in its construction, it is also kept alive by the mass of people who embrace and perpetuate it.[112] To understand this a little better, it would be useful to turn to examine a society whose history offers an instructive case study of the logic and character of immigration control. The policy of the South African government in the period between 1948 and 1994 supplies us with an analogy through which to understand the impact of the aspiration to control on a society's freedom. Like all analogies, it has its limitations; but that need not diminish its usefulness if considered carefully.

## South Africa and the Control of (Internal) Migration

> A man cannot go with his wife and children and his goods and chattels on to the labour market. He must have a dumping ground. Every rabbit must have a warren where he can live and burrow and breed, and every native must have a warren too.
> —SIR GODFREY LAGDEN, CHAIRMAN OF THE NATIVE AFFAIRS COMMISSION IN THE TRANSVAAL, QUOTED IN NANCY L. CLARK AND WILLIAM H. WORGER, SOUTH AFRICA: THE RISE AND FALL OF APARTHEID[113]

In order to control the internal movement of people, South Africa developed a very particular system of immigration control. Apartheid was both an ideology and a system of laws that emerged to give expression to and further entrench an 'intensified form of segregation' in South Africa.[114] Though as policy it officially came into existence in 1948, in practice it was an extension of the country's long history of racial discrimination—and according to some, one that represented a regressive turn even given South Africa's brutal past treatment of its Black population.[115] What is often remarked upon but perhaps insufficiently appreciated (at least outside South Africa) is the way in which apartheid emerged as an institution of immigration control. Its purpose was to control the movement and the integration of people—primarily of Black Africans, but ultimately of Blacks and Whites alike. The rationale for this was much the same as the reasons offered by the defenders of immigration control everywhere: cultural survival, economic advancement, and national security. The fundamental dilemma it confronted was the same one facing other regimes that have been troubled by the movement of people: it wanted workers, not people, but struggled to figure out how to get one without the other, for not only were workers people themselves but they also came with other people attached: spouses, children, parents, friends. Apartheid was literally a philosophy of 'apartness' (which is what the word means in Dutch and Afrikaans), and the policy was one of keeping different races separate. Achieving this, however, necessitated other forms of separation: of Black husbands and wives from each other and from their families, of the mixed races from other races, and eventually of some Whites from others.

The need for labour that lies at the heart of the matter bears fuller recounting.[116] The National Party that was the force behind the introduction of apartheid was, according to Gwendolen Carter, the author of the first comprehensive study of apartheid, driven by two concerns. One was to control the desire of Black Africans to secure more power as well as a better return for their labour. The other was to maintain European supremacy in all spheres of life, and to advance the industrial development of South Africa so as to make it independent of outside forces.[117] But these two aspirations were always in tension with one another, because industrial advancement in a capitalist economy required labour, and as the demand for labour grew so did the threat not only of a rise in Black African wages but also of a rise in Black influence. The most obvious solution to emerging Black influence was to exclude Black Africans from White society altogether, but such a policy had its costs. For one thing, it would deprive White society of a source of cheap labour; for another it threatened to establish economic competitors on the outskirts of White society if Black Africans established their own enterprises.

That pure exclusion was not a viable strategy was already evident to the country's rulers before the establishment of the Union of South Africa in 1910. Earlier policies of segregation, combined with native labour legislation that set limits to Black wages, made participation in the workforce less and less attractive to Black Africans, who attempted to avoid employment by returning to farming and setting up their own enterprises in competition with Whites. The British rulers responded with a variety of measures to limit the ability of Black Africans to secure their own livelihood and thus force them back into the workforce. These included heavy taxes on African farmers (on everything from huts to dogs) to try to force them into employment in mines or on White farms. When Black Africans responded by increasing agricultural production and selling their crops in competition with White farmers, the South African government reacted in 1913 by passing the Natives' Land Act (No. 27), restricting Black African ownership to 7 per cent of the nation's total land area. Successive governments increased the pressure through legislation and heavier taxation until Black Africans were forced onto White farms and into factories. But a consequence of all this was also a drift of the Black population into the cities as people went in search of work—and as many, who tired of trekking back and forth, opted to remain in the cities rather than to live far from their places of work.

The influx of poorly paid Black Africans into the cities put pressure on White municipalities that needed to supply housing and social services, with the result that policies of segregation were tightened—forcing more and more workers to live in segregated townships or to return to their distant homes and families each day. In effect, Black Africans were 'forced into a system of migrant labour'.[118] From the point of view of the White government, the problem was how to maintain the supply of cheap labour without any loss of convenience, and also without the establishment of a firm Black foothold—economically, culturally, or politically—in European society.[119] The policy and ideology of apartheid were designed to solve that problem. Apartheid was South Africa's internal immigration policy.

The enforcement of this immigration policy required laws. Besides legislation to control the employment of workers, the South African government also introduced measures to control other aspects of life that might threaten segregation: the Prohibition of Mixed Marriages Act (1949), and the Immorality Act (1949) outlawing sexual relations across racial groups, were early examples. These acts, however, meant that there was now a need to pass the Population Registration Act (1950), which classified South Africans into four racial types—Black, White, Coloured, and Indian, the latter two groups being further divided into sub-classifications. (This was a source of endless difficulty since racial classification by descent would compromise the claims of Whites, too many of whom had some Black African ancestry, but classification by appearance was open to question—and abuse.[120]) Yet maintaining control required more than the passing of laws. It also necessitated the forcible movement of populations, and thus the removal from their homes of 3.5 million non-White South Africans between 1960 and 1983—many of them 'deported' to designated tribal 'homelands' or Bantustans and declared not (or no longer) to be South African citizens. It necessitated the introduction of 'passbooks', which Black Africans moving through the country, but especially through cities, needed to produce for inspection on demand by White authorities, in particular by the police.

It should be noted that although the vast majority of White South Africans before the end of apartheid favoured racial segregation, not everyone wanted apartheid. Many in fact wanted complete racial separation from the beginning, with the deportation of all Black Africans to live in tribal 'homelands'. The prospect of being 'swamped' by Africans meant that only 'the removal of all Africans from the economy in order to protect the jobs, wages, and "dignity" of white labour'[121] was a plausible policy. Thus, one wing of the HNP (the predecessor of the National Party that introduced apartheid) proposed a scheme of forced removals of Black Africans to homelands and a scheme under which only male 'migrant' workers would be allowed into the cities to do only the most menial jobs—with all women and children barred from entry. The party as a whole was not, however, persuaded that the resulting labour shortage could be overcome through greater White immigration from abroad and the mechanization of industry, and the alternative proposed was that, instead of barring Black Africans from all jobs in White areas, the government should directly supervise their movement.[122] The Sauer report, which recommended the establishment of government agencies to direct Black African workers into specific White businesses, came as a welcome proposal from the point of view of Afrikaner farmers and other White businesses that had been struggling during the postwar labour shortage, and were hoping that apartheid would help not only by keeping the races separate but also by directing African workers their way. *Volkshandel*, the Afrikaner industrialists' newsletter, was quite candid about the matter, editorializing in June 1948:

> It must be acknowledged that the non-white worker already constitutes an integral part of our economic structure, that he is now so enmeshed in the spheres of our economic life that, for the first fifty to one hundred years (if not longer), total segregation is pure wishful thinking. Any government which disregards this irrefutable fact will soon discover that it is no longer in a position to govern.[123]

The aspiration of the National Party at this time was a conception of White rule that saw total segregation as the ultimate objective, with a slow move towards the elimination of Africans from industry until Blacks came to be no more than visitors to cities to meet occasional labour needs. The labour of Africans would be managed by government bureaucracies, with the Black population able to move about the country only under government supervision.

Turning this vision into reality, however, was another matter altogether. First of all, it required the compliance of the Black African population, which had little incentive to embrace either the laws or a way of thinking that ran so clearly against their interests. Thus, a good part of the policy of apartheid, as Gwendolen Carter argued, was about identity transformation: trying to 'make the African the different kind of person that theory says he is',[124] the 'theory' being the theory of apartheid. It was this aspect of apartheid against which the South African activist Steve Biko struggled, arguing that it sought a transformation of consciousness—to make Black Africans see themselves only as the system viewed them and never as free and independent human beings.[125] But a transformation of the African consciousness was never going to be enough if the ideology of apartheid was not secure within the White South African population, so an equally important condition of its preservation was the control of society more broadly. That meant control of any recalcitrant elements of the White population.

The brutality of apartheid as a system of social control is most readily visible in its treatment of the Black population. Aside from the systematic injustice they suffered under laws that limited their rights and freedoms, Black South Africans were the victims of repeated acts of physical violence perpetrated by the police and the military arms of government. But apartheid also required the gradual escalation of control of—and violence against—the White population whenever it showed any sign of wavering in its support for government policy, and for the policy of apartheid in particular. Under the Native Laws Amendment Act (No. 54) and the Abolition of Passes and Coordination of Documents Act (No. 67) in 1952, regional passbooks were abolished and replaced with 'reference books' that contained vital information, including taxation and employment records, and Black Africans travelling without their reference books were subject to criminal punishment, including imprisonment. Around 1970 the Department of Interior initiated a registration project for all other South Africans (including Whites, Indians, and Coloureds)—creating what was known as the 'Book of Life', a document that would itself include all material information about every individual.[126] White employers were already forbidden to hire people who were not appropriately vetted by the government. Increasingly, however, authorities clamped down on any form of dissent that appeared in the press, in popular culture (which was highly censored), and in the courts.[127] By common consensus,

South Africa developed into a police state,[128] but one that exercised its power both over its Black majority population and the minority of Whites who might have threatened the stability of the regime.[129] It depended for its survival on the acquiescence of all those subject to its laws, and that required enough people buying into the ideology that sustained it. Members of the White population who dissented in public thus had to be silenced. Indeed, not only were such people forbidden to speak out in South Africa, they were also prevented from travelling abroad in case they spoke out against the government and criticized the policy or the ideology of apartheid.

There is an instructive parallel to be drawn here between twentieth-century South Africa and the American antebellum South, which was above all a slave society. Over the course of the early nineteenth century, as more of the northern states abolished slavery, the southern states began to feel the pressure to end it everywhere. Though the events that led to the Civil War in 1861 suggest a mixture of motives on the northern side of the conflict—predominantly a concern to preserve the Union threatened by southern secession rather to emancipate slaves—the southern states were motivated primarily by a commitment to preserving slavery, tied as it was to what they saw as their own way of life. But in a century in which the practice of slavery was unravelling, this was becoming increasingly difficult to manage, given the steady stream of attacks on the institution. One response to this in the South was to develop what might be called the ideology of slavery—a doctrine upholding the moral rightness of slavery, and of the enslavement of Africans in particular. This required the elaboration of a sophisticated theory of the morality of slavery, but it also demanded that those within the South who wavered from a commitment to this view be challenged, criticized or punished. As slavery as a global practice waned in the first half of the century, so did the intellectual defence of it in the South intensify between 1830 and 1860. Southern governments, as well as the leading figures among the political elites, were fully aware that a population without ideological conviction would never be able to resist an assault on its institutions.[130] The governments of South Africa were no less aware of the importance of not losing the hearts and minds of the White population as a part of a broader strategy to control the thinking of Black and White alike—the Whites to persuade them that their oppression of the Black African was justified, and the Blacks to convince them that their inferior status was entirely warranted.

The human victims of apartheid were overwhelmingly Black South Africans. The institutional victims were the freedom of the press, the independence of the courts, and more broadly the rule of law. The South African immigration strategy is instructive because it supplies, in its ambition and rationale, a model of immigration policy in the west, and in the extremes into which it fell, a portent of what might come if the aspiration to control is left unchecked.

Like twentieth-century South Africa's, western immigration policy has been shaped by two imperatives: to sustain a reliable supply of labour to economies that are subject to the normal vicissitudes of the market, and to limit the movement into its societies of people who might either out-compete natives in the workplace or out-number natives in the public square. Though some advocates have favoured very restrictive measures to cut out immigration altogether, or reduce it to a trickle, the pressures exerted by those who need the workers, those demanding family reunion, and other institutions and organizations wanting students and sports stars and actors, have meant that there are limits to the limiting of movement. The answer everywhere, therefore, has not been a *stop* to immigration but *controlled* immigration.

The challenge facing western immigration controllers has been the same as that confronting the immigration controllers of South Africa in the last century: how to find that balance between supplying industry with labour and keeping would-be immigrants in their own warrens so that they don't end up burrowing too deeply into the host societies. The tools of immigration control have thus turned out to be substantially the same as those used in South Africa: the careful categorization of workers and the creation of a hierarchy of desirable people, the monitoring of movement and surveillance of the population, the selective deportation of undesirables, the discouraging of relationships between foreigners and natives, and the development of a rationale or ideology that has stressed the importance of control for reasons of security, economic protection, and cultural preservation. The stresses imposed on society also bear important similarities to those brought about by apartheid. The control of society and its citizens in itself means a loss of freedom. It also puts a strain on its institutions: the courts, the press, and the rule of law. More broadly still, it means creating a climate of opinion that emphasizes the dangers posed by immigration, which is presented as a threat to security that requires careful management and justifies harsh measures of control.

The parallel between western policy and apartheid might be extended even further. White South Africa found itself not only wanting Black labour but also unable to stop the drift of Africans to the cities because its policies made it difficult or impossible for Black people to make a living through farming and trade. Western policy on trade has carved out a similar path, restricting the free movement of goods and services in order to protect the living standards of selected elements of its population, but thereby adding to the hardships of farmers and other enterprises in parts of Africa and Asia and contributing to the pressure to move to seek opportunities for work and advancement where the pastures are greener.[131]

There are, of course, limitations to the analogy drawn here between apartheid and western policies of immigration control. South Africa is a country with its own distinctive history, stretching back to the settlements created in the seventeenth century, and encompassing deep conflicts not only between Black Africans and Europeans but also between British and Dutch, and then British and Afrikaner. Most importantly, however, apartheid was a policy that was not only brutal in its implementation but also one that came to be reviled throughout the world and criticized by most of the nations of Europe and the west more generally for its explicit endorsement and defence of racial inequality. Europe, North America, Australia, and New Zealand, as the main immigrant-receiving liberal democracies, have repeatedly and vigorously repudiated race as a relevant consideration in the treatment of people. In this regard, it seems unfair and misleading to use an analogy that threatens to discolour serious analysis. And yet, race is perhaps one issue that ought to be more carefully examined in discussions of immigration, since it remains a suppressed or hidden feature of the policies of control with which we have been concerned. This is a matter for the next chapter.

## Taking Back and Giving Up

The language of immigration policy everywhere is the language of control. The condition to be feared is 'uncontrolled' immigration, and the borders must be closed and movement restricted if we are to 'take back control'. What has always been obscure in these calls, however, it precisely what is to be understood by establishing or taking back control. The image governments and the advocates of greater control have wished to conjure up is one of a population or its representatives somehow exercising a benign form of power to keep undesirable outsiders at bay, while enabling the people with legitimate claims to a presence in the land to go peacefully about their business. The reality, however, is not so benign.

Immigration control—like all forms of government control—means giving some people the power to control others, and those others include not just outsiders but also insiders. It means giving some people the power to determine who is and who is not an insider. It means telling insiders when and how they may relate to outsiders.[132] It means control taken back—or taken up—by some and relinquished by the great majority of others. It means creating a society in which monitoring and surveillance are extended more deeply into everyday forms of life, an expansion of powers of police, and the subjection of citizens and foreigners alike to a form of what Alexis de Tocqueville identified as 'soft despotism'.

Ultimately, what immigration control is about is the reshaping of the denizens of a society to ensure that they are not only compliant but also committed to and invested in the institutions of that society. The intrusion of outsiders is a challenge to the control of natives because it is a disruptive force that disturbs the existing order and threatens to take it in unpredictable directions. That people, and the future, are ultimately uncontrollable—in the sense of determinable by concerted human action—makes no difference to the longing for control by those who see the opportunity to take it.

There is a trade-off that is at stake in the matter of immigration policy, and the question of control lies at its heart. The trade-off is not, however, between the freedom of natives and the freedom of foreigners. It is between the freedom of society's members and the freedom—the power—of its rulers and their hangers-on. Greater control over society can only be won by individuals relinquishing more control over their own lives. That may, of course, be a trade-off that some are willing to make. But it is a trade-off that has further consequences, not only for freedom but also for other important values, as we shall see in the chapter to come.

# 4

# Equality

The great aim of the struggle for liberty has been equality before the law.
—FRIEDRICH HAYEK, *THE CONSTITUTION OF LIBERTY*[1]

The rule of law refers, in good part, to the right of citizens to be free
from abuses by the state. It is not enhanced by the expanded use of
policing as an instrument to maintain control over immigration. . . .
When the objects of stronger police action include an ever-expanding
spectrum of people—immigrant women, men and children—sooner or
later the state will get caught in the expanding web of civil and human
rights. It will then violate those rights, interfering with the functioning
of civil society.
—SASKIA SASSEN, *GUESTS AND ALIENS*

One is not a racist; after all, it is a tradition that one is not a racist.
—MAX FRISCH, FOREWORD TO ALEXANDER J. SEILER, *SIAMO
ITALIANI—DIE ITALIENER. GESPRÄCHE MIT ITALIENISCHEN
ARBEITERN IN DER SCHWEIZ*

## Uncompromising Equality

A free society in the modern world must be a society of equals. The equality
that all must share is equality before the law, but what is to be understood by
this is not self-evident, for individuals who come before the law can be equal
or unequal in a variety of relevantly important ways. It seems unlikely that

we will find a society all of whose members are perfectly equal along any, let alone most, of a number of dimensions: income, wealth, leisure, health, longevity, or happiness. Yet it is no less unlikely that we will find people who are truly equal before the law in a society marked by overwhelming inequalities along all other standards. The struggle for legal equality requires for its success not merely the formal establishment of a principle of equal treatment but a social transformation in which the least fortunate or powerful are protected by the law and can avail themselves of what is needed to secure that protection. In this regard, equality is vital for freedom, for if the less well-off are unable to protect their interests—or defend their persons— against the privileged, then freedom can be little more than an advantage of power and not a condition enjoyed by all inhabitants of a society. The crucial question here, of course, is: which equalities matter?[2]

No less important a question, however, is that of whose equality and, ultimately, whose freedom matters. For many—political theorists and political leaders no less than political activists and members of the general public— the answer is that it is the freedom and equality of the members of a society. How membership in society is to be delineated might be a significant and complex issue, and some wish to draw the boundaries more closely than others—perhaps by insisting that only citizens count as members of the political society that is the modern state. But however the line distinguishing insiders from outsiders is drawn, they argue, it is the freedom and equality of those within that matters. Indeed, one important reason for wanting immigration control is to protect the interests of society's members in freedom and equality.

Yet immigration control, far from being a means of securing the values of a free society, and of upholding equality in particular, is in fact highly problematic, if not positively threatening to these values. Indeed, the more vigorously immigration control is pursued, the more dangerous it becomes to equality within the free society. Distinguishing insiders from outsiders may serve the interests of some insiders, but there is no reason to expect it to do so in ways that diminish inequality, or make society freer, or benefit existing members more generally. This matters not only because the inequities created by immigration controls may be invidious in themselves, but also because they further serve to undermine the rule of law, which is an important cornerstone of a free society.

The point of this chapter is to show how immigration control compromises equality and the rule of law. This occurs despite the fact that the aim to treat everyone equally is a hallmark of a free society—since in such a society each individual's freedom matters as much as anyone else's. The effort to control everyone can lead only to unequal treatment, and the greater the extent of that effort, the more pronounced will be the inequality.

Most advocates of immigration control, particularly those who are liberals and democrats, are not defenders of inequality. While they favour limits on immigration, they typically do so on the basis of principles that take equality of consideration as a moral and legal requirement, and reject unequal treatment on the basis of race, or religion, or ethnicity, or gender as unacceptable.[3] Unfortunately, for as long as the extension of control remains the measure proposed, this can be little more than a pious hope—one that might be tenable in a theoretical realm in which perfect compliance with legal principle is assumed, but is implausible in a world where laws are made to direct, modify, or thwart actual human behaviour. In the world as it is, it is the aspiration to control that threatens equality. Without a measure of equality, there cannot be a free society; but as freedom is diminished through efforts of social control, so equality itself becomes less attainable. The enforcement of immigration controls invariably requires the extension of arbitrary power, but also has a more deeply corrupting effect on social and political institutions generally—as must any policy whose purpose is to determine the shape and character of society as a whole. There may be some hope of setting up a legal and administrative apparatus that is capable of controlling immigration without significant costs to equality and the rule of law, but the historical evidence suggests that it is a forlorn one. Deeper theoretical reflection should show why we ought not to be surprised.

To defend such a claim, this chapter is organized in the following way. The next section begins with a further examination of a question that, as we saw in chapter 2, is not always given sufficient attention: what is immigration control and how is it achieved? Controlling immigration requires the establishment of institutions that operate under law and make possible the implementation of policy. What kinds of institutions are needed will depend on the kind of control sought, and the circumstances under which the government or governments operate. Control might be desired in some respects but not in others. The section that follows then turns to the question of how immigration control poses a challenge to the rule of law. From here, the next two sections ask how this bears on equality, and consider the impact of immigration control on racial and sexual equality in particular. The final section concludes with a closer look at the relationship between equality and freedom.

## Understanding Immigration Control

As we've already seen, immigration control is a complex matter. Though there are many philosophical discussions of the desirability or otherwise of limits on immigration, too few recognize that control involves more than a simple determination of principle (of who to let in and how many) but requires a sophisticated and elaborate institutional framework—one that operates not merely within the confines of a single state but across international boundaries. Immigration law is domestic law that reaches deep into the workings of society, but much of it is also international law, manifest in agreements among states negotiating the terms that control the movement of their citizens and determine the rights they have when abroad, as well as in conventions governing the treatment of displaced people and asylum seekers. The institutions of immigration control are similarly to be found both within the social, legal, and political arrangements of domestic society (from government bureaucracies to educational establishments to financial centres to healthcare systems) and the organizations and regimes of the international order. Immigration is controlled by states, but also shaped by supranational organizations such as the European Union or the World Trade Organization, and affected by international human rights codes as well as by newly developed transnational regimes governing cross-border business transactions.[4] Immigration control is almost everywhere the outcome of the interaction of a variety of agents operating within a network of laws, organizations, and administrative rules, governed to some degree by authorities with the capacity to make policy that can influence and re-orient, even if not fully determine, the rights and freedom of people moving between states. Popular demand for immigration control is generally directed at national governments (although at times it has also led to intervention at the sub-state or provincial level), and it is national governments that claim the authority to exercise that control. But the capacity for control is limited by institutional and practical realities. Governments can produce effects; but securing desired or promised outcomes is another matter altogether. 'Ministers and bureaucrats still often see migration as something that can be turned on and off like a tap through laws and policies.'[5] Yet it is anything but that.

Those demanding or promising immigration control, and looking to see this goal pursued through policy, seek to control immigration in a number of respects. They wish to control *entry* to the state or broader supranational area (such as the Schengen region that covers most of the EU as well as Switzerland and Norway); to regulate the *terms of admission*, including determining the right to work, the length of stay, the conditions of legalization of unauthorized immigrants, and the qualifications for naturalization; to set the terms of *immigrant integration;* and to establish *enforcement policies* to deter or prevent entry as well as to remove unauthorized or undesired immigrants.[6] Control of these various aspects of immigration is difficult, in part because the different objectives are not always mutually consistent: for example, controlling the terms of admission may work against the objective of immigrant integration, as may enforcement policies designed to deter entry;[7] policies encouraging legalization of status can work against policies aimed at deterring unauthorized entry; and significant restrictions in the terms of admission may encourage unauthorized entry by people wishing to work and operate undetected by the authorities. At times the laws themselves are in tension with one another, as is often the case with asylum policy, to take one example.[8] The fact that immigration objectives are in tension with one another is revealed by the fact that all strategies of immigration control end up trying to strike a balance between securing the objectives of restricting immigration and protecting the rights and interests of citizens and residents. In the view of one scholar: 'The fundamental challenge of immigration control is that there is no reliable way to limit the effects of enforcement to deportable aliens without also imposing costs on legal immigrants and host-state citizens.'[9]

Control is also difficult for a number of other reasons. Most obviously, control is expensive, and the enforcement of immigration laws requires resources in the form of personnel as well as buildings, equipment, and specialist facilities. Efforts to hold down the costs of enforcement further limit the state's ability to 'get enforcement right'.[10] Even more important, however, is the existence of legal, administrative, and political constraints on state action. Particularly in liberal democracies, when the authority of the state is hemmed in by the independence of the judiciary, the freedom of the press, and the vagaries of public opinion, maintaining control over immigration can be highly problematic.

The slightly comical case of Mr Egon Kisch (1885–1948) supplies an instructive example that is worth recounting, since it draws attention to many of the complexities and inconveniences surrounding efforts to control immigration. Kisch was a Prague-born journalist imprisoned by the Nazis shortly after the Reichstag fire in 1933, who became a staunch opponent of war and fascism, and was vaguely associated with the Communist Party after being exiled to Czechoslovakia. His activities led the Movement Against War and Fascism to send him to an anti-war congress in Melbourne in November 1934. Learning of this, the Australian government declared that he was a 'prohibited immigrant', and denied him permission to set foot in the country when he finally arrived by sea, first in the port of Fremantle in Western Australia, and subsequently in Melbourne. Buoyed by the outrage and enthusiasm of well-wishers who visited him on the ship, and the notoriety he had begun to receive as a result of the legal efforts to enable him to enter the country, he jumped onto the Melbourne wharf, breaking his leg. He was returned to ship and taken to Sydney for treatment and was able to disembark there because Justice H. V. Evatt, sitting alone, found the prohibition order denying him the right to enter Australia to be illegal—albeit on a minor technicality. The authorities reacted by requiring Kisch to take a dictation test as prescribed by the Immigration Act. The test was in Scottish Gaelic (it was not uncommon for unwanted immigrants to be examined in unfamiliar tongues), which Kisch (though fluent in several European languages) promptly failed. He was therefore convicted on 28 November 1934 of being a prohibited immigrant and issued with deportation orders. That sentence was overturned on appeal to the High Court of Australia, which ruled on 19 December that Scottish Gaelic was not a European language within the meaning of the Immigration Act. Now able to move freely in Australia, Kisch was nevertheless pursued by the Australian government, who eventually managed to convict him of being a 'prohibited immigrant'. By this time, however, the publicity generated by the Kisch affair, and the popularity earned by this likable, witty, gallant, and good-humoured man, made the government appear clumsy and unfair—and to many, undemocratic. Though upon conviction Kisch had been sentenced to three months imprisonment, the government bowed to public opinion and offered not only to remit the sentence but also to pay his costs if he left Australia—which he did at the end of a series of public appearances, culminating in a torchlight procession in Melbourne to commemorate the Reichstag fire.[11]

The Kisch affair offers a sharp illustration of the problems of immigration control. The issue arose when the White Australia Policy was firmly in place, having been established de facto by the Immigration Restriction Act of 1901—the first act passed by the Parliament of the newly established Federation of Australia—and national governments were mindful of the need to control who came into the country, for reasons of economic and cultural protection as well as national security. In the interwar period, the threat posed by communism was already a staple of political discourse, and there was little appetite amongst Australians for the ideology, despite its influence in parts of the labour movement. Keeping out a communist sympathizer should not have been a problem. The obstacles to controlling Mr Kisch's entry and subsequent political activity were, in the first instance, legal. Unable to pass a bill of attainder[12] aimed directly at Kisch, the government was obliged to act within the terms of the law, which afforded him and his supporters a number of protections. Though able to issue prohibitions on his entering the country, it was unable to prevent their being reviewed and overturned by the courts—in one case because of the discretion exercised by a single judge, and in another because of a determination of the High Court; and even when it finally managed to secure a conviction, it was loath to enforce it when it looked foolish in the eyes of public opinion and there remained the threat of continued legal and political agitation on the foreign visitor's behalf. The government was also unable to prevent news of these events circulating through the press. The bad publicity its action generated was of serious concern: unfavourable reports abroad would prove embarrassing, and within Australia Kisch's plight lifted the spirits and profile of anti-war campaigners, provoking the formation of the Australian Writers' League, dedicated to challenging government censorship.

Immigration control is a complicated matter, for it involves not only the establishment of mechanisms and facilities to deal with foreign persons who have entered or intend to enter the country, but also the development of institutions to deal with domestic and international challenges to that control. Domestically, governments have to address the complaints of residents who want their foreign relatives to be allowed to enter, the interests of employers who want to hire foreign labour, the protests of activists who agitate on behalf of refugees and the foreign poor, and the disaffection of those who consider the government to be too lenient with foreigners and not doing enough to keep them out. Immigration control is a management problem—one that involves the management not merely of would-be immigrants, and foreigners more generally, but also of citizens and residents.

Two aspects of the institutions of immigration control serve as useful illustrations. The first is the existence of legalization programmes, whose purpose is to turn unauthorized immigrants into legitimate residents and—ultimately—citizens. In the United States, the primary purpose of these programmes is to reduce the number of unauthorized immigrants more cheaply than is possible through deportation and other enforcement measures. Though not every immigrant is as costly to remove as was Mr Kisch, in 2010 it cost the American government 2.5 billion dollars to deport four hundred thousand people. Legalization is less expensive: immigrants tend to identify themselves voluntarily, pay fees and fines, remain in work and

continue to pay taxes without burdening their employers, who would otherwise have to replace them. Nonetheless, legalization creates a significant
management issue. Criteria must be established to determine who is eligible
for legalization, migration histories and identity checks taken, tests applied,
and legal hearings scheduled. Then the concerns of those who object that
such programmes reward bad behaviour and encourage further unauthorized immigration will have to be addressed and managed. Not everyone
will be convinced by the arguments, or sympathetic to the government's
plight given the cost of deportation, so the disquiet and anger of citizens
will have to be assuaged—perhaps with additional or alternative measures
that address particular grievances. Indeed, deportation is so ineffective a
measure—because of the expense, its limited capacity to deter future migration (whether by the deported themselves or by others), and the distress it
causes not just to the deported but the families and communities from which
they are taken—that its only purpose in many instances is to show those
who are worried about immigration levels that 'something' is being done.[13]

A second aspect of immigration control that illustrates the nature of the
management problem is the extent of international collaboration. One problem faced by a government seeking to limit immigration is that deporting
people, or turning them away at the borders, does not ensure that they will
not simply try and try again. Imprisonment is costly, and it only postpones
the decisions that will have to be taken when those detained are eventually
released. In order to exercise any sort of control over immigration flows,
governments must seek the cooperation of other governments, not least of
governments from sending countries.[14] Managing migration is thus often a
process built on bilateral, or even multilateral, agreements. But this also creates difficulties of its own. It is complicated enough when agreements have to
made about such matters as the management and upkeep of refugee camps,
or sharing information and intelligence about criminal operations, including
smuggling and trafficking in people. Once other migration issues come into
play, including how to classify people, where to send them, and who should
take final responsibility, collaboration becomes more problematic still.

One reason collaboration is difficult is that other governments are often
beholden to their domestic constituencies, which may not favour agreements
that assure the movement of people, even if they also restrict movement.
Should agreements be made, they are often compromised by defections or
poor management by one party or the other. Sending nations, particularly
when they are poor, may claim to be ready to cooperate in principle by
agreeing to reduce the outflow of migrants, but unable or unwilling to take

the measures needed to do so. If people are looking to leave because their lives are in danger, or if they cannot find work, or if they aspire to a better standard of living than they can achieve by remaining where they are, there may be little that governments can do to keep them from emigrating, and even less incentive for governments to try if the result would be having to manage a substantial population of unemployed and disaffected citizens.

For these and other reasons, deportation also becomes problematic as a solution to immigration management. Deportation very clearly requires international cooperation, since the deporting country will have to secure the agreement of the receiving country to accept those being sent back. At the very least, the receiving country will require proof that the deportees they are accepting are their own citizens, and that may not always be possible to provide. Indeed, receiving countries would need to supply the people to be deported with travel documents such as passports—at some expense to themselves, since they would need to establish the identities and eligibility of those being returned. This gives countries of origin an effective veto power over repatriation, which they can exercise simply by refusing to issue travel documents—as has often happened with countries of origin declining to grant travel documents to unsuccessful asylum applicants in Europe.[15] The price of extracting agreements, and cooperation, from other states may be concessions on other matters at issue or under negotiation between their governments. Depending on the foreign-policy agendas of the different parties, such a price may be too high—further complicating the problem of cooperation in the management of immigration.

The upshot of all this is that immigration control is something that is much sought after and is achieved to a certain degree—but not necessarily in the ways and to the extent that its proponents might wish. It is certainly possible for policies to be announced, legislation to be passed, and administrative agencies to be established, and for such steps to have significant consequences. But whether or not the outcomes of immigration control measures are the ones intended—or more generally desired—is an entirely different matter. The failure of the British government to meet its own immigration target supplies an instructive example. Shortly after taking office in 2010, the Conservative administration under Prime Minister David Cameron announced plans to reduce 'net migration'[16] to below one hundred thousand a year. In 2016, while maintaining its intention to reduce immigration, it conceded that it would no longer be guided by a numerical target. By its own accounting, net migration had been closer to three hundred thousand a year.[17] This was despite all of the government's best efforts, including those designed to get around problems posed by the fact that many of the obstacles to reducing immigration were legal in nature.

## Immigration Control and the Rule of Law

It is not unusual for advocates of immigration control to invoke the rule of law in demanding action to limit entry, prosecute people who have entered illegally or violated the conditions of entry, or deport undesirable visitors.[18] The failure to enforce statutes prohibiting unauthorized entry or undocumented employment is bad enough; but to decline to deport or, worse, to open a path to legalization, appears to be letting administrative or political discretion undermine the operation of the law. On this view, the source of the problem is the reluctance of public officials, including political leaders, to uphold the law, and the rule of law is diminished by inaction, wilful ignorance, incompetence, or sabotage.

Yet once one understands the nature of immigration control, and the difficulties that accompany the management of immigration in general, it becomes less obvious that the problem is one of enforcement failure. On the contrary, it is the rule of law that tends to check and moderate attempts to control immigration, and more extensive or energetic efforts of immigration control that tend to weaken and perhaps undermine the rule of law.

To see this, we should begin by taking a more careful look at the idea of the rule of law. This is a term that is often invoked—and for that reason, sometimes derided[19]—but not always well understood. For many, its meaning is straightforward: that the law as it stands should be applied, without the use of discretion to favour particular parties or to secure outcomes different than those that a disinterested application of legal rules would produce. It means the 'government of law and not men'. While this understanding is not off the mark, however, it slides over important difficulties—and subtleties—that should be brought out more explicitly if the ideal of the rule of law, and the idea of law itself, is to make sense.

To grasp the idea of the rule of law we need to understand it under three aspects: formal, institutional, and sociological. In formal terms, the rule of law obtains when the law and its application satisfy a number of desiderata. In Lon Fuller's well-known formulation, the law should be *general* in character, *publicly known* rather than concealed or known only to a few, *prospective* rather than retrospective, *intelligible, practical, stable, consistent,* and *congruent*.[20] These criteria—elucidated in similar though not identical ways by a number of legal philosophers[21]—reveal the nature of the ideal of law as a set of norms whose point is to make possible the interactions among, and the government of, people of a particular kind: people who are free and not simply ruled arbitrarily by others.[22] The rule of law therefore demands not simply that 'the law' be applied or enforced but that the law itself satisfy certain requirements. In a country ruled by a despot who each day makes a decree at his whim, the rule of law cannot be served by applying 'the law' thus created, for a jumble of commands issued by authorities cannot establish law. Indeed, to understand rightly the idea of the rule of law is to understand what can properly count as law.[23]

This brings us to the second aspect under which the rule of law has to be understood: its institutional setting. For the rule of law to prevail, it is necessary not only that law is made or declared but also that there exist mechanisms and procedures by which law can be given proper expression. In any complex society that is governed by norms more sophisticated than custom, it is important that there are procedures by which law is established; bodies capable of promulgating the law, as well as people capable of finding their way through its complexities to interpret it and to defend their interpretations of its meaning; and courts or tribunals ready to hear reasoned argument and adjudicate disputes about what the law demands. Since law is a living thing, it needs living institutions to sustain it and to enable it to serve its purpose. The rule of law can have an existence only when this is so.

The third aspect under which the rule of law should be understood is perhaps the least appreciated, but no less important than the first two. We might call it the sociological aspect, but another way to put it would be to talk about the circumstances of the rule of law. For law to serve its purpose, it must not only conform to certain formal requirements that are given institutional expression but also be capable of eliciting compliance by the people to whom it applies—people who understand and accept the substance of the law. Should the law be out of step with customs or mores—or more broadly, with the way people live—it is unlikely to command assent or obedience, and lawmakers will find themselves trying to enforce rules that are not widely accepted, or are honoured only in the breach. This is an old insight, first explored comprehensively by Montesquieu[24] and then, more fully, by Tocqueville.[25] This is not to say that laws that go against the grain cannot change and re-shape society, helping to bring about a deeper social transformation. But even then, any social reformer would have to be wary of the risks, since a recalcitrant population will resist change that goes too sharply against the prevailing understanding, and the law itself may lose some of its authority as a result.

It is this third aspect of the rule of law that draws us immediately to the problem that arises out of the attempt to control immigration. Once the search for control produces policies that are significantly—or radically— inconsistent with the way in which society functions, the institutions of law will come under strain. And there is something about the way in which modern, liberal democratic societies in particular work that makes immigration control especially problematic.

Contemporary liberal democratic societies are, by and large, open societies, shaped and governed by the ceaseless flow of goods and services across national borders, and the constant interaction of people who live and operate in different political jurisdictions. They are also marked by a perpetual movement of individuals, who enter and leave countries in order to work, to holiday, to study, to visit relatives, to research, and to entertain. In the United States in 2013, for example, the federal government processed more than 362 million travellers entering through land, air or sea borders—not including the 412,000 people apprehended attempting to come into the country outside these official entry points or the many thousands who entered undetected. At the same time, more than 12 million shipping containers enter each year by sea, and hundreds of thousands of trucks by land, with less than 2 per cent of all cargo inspected because of the sheer volume of goods moving across the border. The way of life of people in liberal democracies—to a greater extent than in authoritarian states or in less developed countries—is thoroughly shaped by their openness to the outside world. This interdependence is not entirely new, since trade is as old as human civilization, but the extent of the international division of labour makes independence, whether at the national or local level, now all but impossible without causing serious disruption and distress.

In these circumstances, law must recognize and work within the norms already adopted by the society it governs. Liberal democratic states are societies in which the norms that have developed are ones that have adapted to the presence of foreign goods, services provided by foreign enterprises, and people visiting, working, or settling from foreign countries. These are not welcome developments everywhere, and there are great differences among residents and citizens on the benefits and desirability of the transformation that greater interdependence has wrought. Workers in the declining automobile and mining industries in Michigan and Pennsylvania do not welcome competition from foreign cars or lower-priced steel, though American companies supplying repairs and spare parts to Japanese vehicles, and manufacturers (including car-makers) wanting cheaper inputs, do. Agricultural labourers in Britain do not want the competition from seasonal workers from eastern Europe, whom they fear will drive down wages, but urban populations are more likely to look favourably on foreigners in the workforce and the neighbourhoods. There are many who do not like finding 'strangers in their midst', but equally there are others who are ready to tolerate it, or who welcome it, and yet others who, because of the integration of all things foreign into their social circumstances, do not consider those whom some regard as outsiders to be strangers at all.

The upshot of this integration of the outside world into society—whether because of the movement of tourists and students, or the penetration of foreign goods into local markets, or the mobility of international labour—is that society's practices and norms have become geared to its presence. This means that efforts to disrupt or close off movement or activity, whether at the borders or within them, will be met with resistance, or noncompliance, or efforts to work around or 'game' the rules so as to continue as before. Immigration controls are efforts of this nature when they become extensive enough to provoke resentment or disdain or contempt. At this point, immigration laws may no longer be regarded as means to make social life easier to manage, and come to be seen as obstacles to be overcome. When law is out of step with the way people live, it is almost always the law that will have to yield, or cease to command respect, or even to be law.

To understand this point it would be helpful to look more closely at the arguments of those asserting that the rule of law requires the enforcement of immigration law, and that the problem lies in the failure of governments, courts, and public officials to exercise their power to do so. There are three types of arguments that need to be considered. The first is an argument that the rule of law requires that *procedures* be followed, without the exercise of discretion or intrusion in favour of particular parties—in this case, usually immigrants, but also employers or other agents who have ongoing relationships with immigrants. If immigrants are in the country 'illegally', the argument goes, the rule of law requires that they feel the full force of the law's disapproval. To fail to follow procedure is to disregard the rule of law. The second argument is an argument from *fairness*. Any failure to enforce immigration controls is unfair to citizens and legal residents, since it advantages immigrants by allowing them to gain access to benefits that ought to be reserved to citizens, or to avoid penalties for transgressions, or to be granted the benefits of membership despite their having evaded the law. The third argument is an *incentives* argument: that a failure to enforce immigration controls undermines the rule of law because it diminishes respect for the law—particularly when it becomes apparent that many of those who break the law are rewarded with amnesty or paths to legalization rather than with deportation.

These arguments are important because they point to frequently expressed concerns. In the end, however, they do not hold up because the complex institutional structures of immigration control in liberal democratic societies make the problem a more subtle and difficult one than the advocates of these views have recognized. A part of the problem here is that immigration control and immigration law have always been difficult to reconcile with the rule of law, since the management of immigration has been marked by rules, measures, and practices that sit uneasily with that political ideal. This is so whether one looks at the history of immigration control, at current practice, or at proposals for the future.

First, if one looks at the history of immigration control, it is difficult not to be struck by the extent to which policy has been shaped by fears and anxieties that have given rise to legislation that would not satisfy all the requirements of the rule of law, and administrative practice that is marked by arbitrariness and discretion without accountability. If one considers the United States over the course of the nineteenth and twentieth centuries, a number of legislative measures stand out. Though the Page Act of 1875 was the first federal immigration law, and the first act to prohibit the entry of 'undesirables' to the United States, the 1882 Chinese Exclusion Act was the first significant step in the development of the idea of illegal immigration—in this case, focusing on the undesirability of Chinese labourers in particular.[26] The Immigration Act of 1903 (Anarchist Exclusion Act) added anarchists, beggars, epileptics, and the importers of prostitutes to the list of undesirable immigrants, and the Immigration Act of 1917 (Barred Zone Act) restricted immigration from Asia. In 1924, the Johnson-Reid Immigration Act established the first numerical limit on immigration into the US, and also set up the first quota system for nationals from selected countries. It was revised by the Immigration and Nationality Act of 1952 (the McCarran-Walter Act) that abolished the category of 'alien ineligible for citizenship' but still capped immigration from Asia. In the era of civil rights, the pathbreaking Immigration Act of 1965 repealed the system of national quotas—though it established hemispheric quotas, indicating that the explicit intention of the act was to redress the wrongs done to southern and eastern Europeans by the 1924 and 1952 acts—and was pushed through Congress after members of the Johnson administration had testified that few Asians would enter the US for the foreseeable future.[27] An unintended and entirely unforeseen consequence of this act was a steep rise in Asian and Mexican immigration, leading to the 1986 Immigration Reform and Control Act (IRCA), which introduced penalties for knowingly hiring illegal aliens and made so doing a criminal offence. Subsequent acts, including the 2002 Enhanced Border Security and Visa Reform Act and the 2005 Real ID Act, added a range of further controls, including requiring schools to report on foreign student attendance, further restricting eligibility for political asylum, and reducing the rights of immigrants to make appeals of *habeas corpus*.

Even on the face of it, these legislative enactments look like they run contrary to the spirit of the rule of law. Though cast as general laws, they are in many cases crafted so as to apply to specific classes of people, and while they may have been internally consistent, they were much less consistent over time, and too often were amended to suit short-term concerns about particular policy outcomes. Those subject to the law were not considered equally but discriminated against on the basis of health, disability, nationality, and race—sometimes explicitly, but often implicitly by design. Institutionally, the rule of law was compromised to the extent that the right of appeal and access to courts was limited. In practice, it was further disregarded insofar as the law was not applied equally but used to target particular groups while sparing others. Under the terms of the 1986 IRCA, for example, the Immigration and Naturalization Service (INS) was bound to look for and deport people working illegally. But the terms of the act specified that its officers could not enter the premises of an *outdoor* or agricultural enterprise without a warrant. The consequence of this limitation was that illegal Mexican labour hired by large and politically powerful agricultural businesses could not easily be targeted, but smaller, immigrant-owned, sweatshops hiring Mexican labour housed indoors could be, since the act did not prohibit entering *indoor* premises without warrants. The legislation was clearly established to serve particular interests. Moreover, even when Mexican agricultural labourers were found, they were not so much deported as issued with notices to leave, which they duly did (since their work was seasonal and they had planned to go back home anyway) with the aim of returning to their American employers the following year. The workings of the process, once again, did not harm the interests of the wealthy and politically powerful who relied on seasonal workers.[28] This was hardly in keeping with the spirit of the ideal of the rule of law.

Everywhere, the history of immigration control has not been one of the impartial and consistent application of general rules. In Britain, the laissez-faire approach to immigration came to an end with the passage of the Aliens Act of 1905, designed to keep out east European Jews. (It was also crafted to keep out the poor and included provisions for the Secretary of State to exercise discretion to exempt particular classes of passenger from its provisions.) Since then, policy has been dominated by the aim to control or keep out particular groups, whether Germans, or members of the Commonwealth, or West Indians, or refugees.[29] In the postwar years of the twentieth century, the problem Britain faced was the prospect of an increasing movement of British subjects from the colonies, many newly independent or on the road to becoming so. The 1948 British Nationality Act divided the world into six groups, which included the categories of Citizens of the United Kingdom and Colonies (CUKC) and Citizens of Independent Commonwealth Countries (CICC), who were all considered subjects of the Crown and entitled to travel freely to Britain. They could not be classified as immigrants if they moved because they had the right to remain if they wished. The 1962 Commonwealth Immigrants Act changed this by declaring some British subjects—those possessing passports not issued by the government of the United Kingdom—to be now subject to immigration controls and to no longer be guaranteed entry into the UK.[30] Subsequent legislative changes have reflected a continuing effort to shape and control the rights of people to enter, reside or work within the country, often without much regard for the arbitrariness of classifications and distinctions developed to meet the demands of policy, and reducing the access of people affected to courts or other avenues of appeal.

Australia's history of immigration control is no less compromised when it comes to the rule of law. For most of the twentieth century it was crafted in legislation and shaped by institutions designed to keep out people from different parts of the world. Many of its measures conformed superficially to the demands of the rule of law, but in practice they did not. The infamous Dictation Test was a case in point. Under the terms of the Immigration Restriction Act of 1901, only persons from a select few categories were permitted to enter Australia, but others could seek an exemption under the act. The granting of an exemption was dependent on successfully passing a fifty-word dictation test in a European language. The test was used to make it difficult for non-Europeans to immigrate to Australia. In the first years of the test, between 1902 and 1909, only 59 out of 1359 people passed the test, but this was largely due to some immigration officials not fully understanding the purpose of the test, and after 1909 no one passed it again—in Egon Kisch's case, because he was required to retake the test in a different language until he did fail. The test was used not only to control the composition of immigrants, however, and came to be deployed to single out particular individuals—such as Kisch—since the requirement that the test be taken was a matter of ministerial discretion. In 1932 amending legislation had made it possible for the test to be administered as many times as officially recommended for a period of up to five years—making the position of any visitor or immigrant precarious, if he or she had indeed been able to enter in the first place. The Dictation Test served the same broad purpose as literacy tests for Black voters in the Jim Crow South.[31]

The history of immigration control is replete with instances of questionable legislation and unfair institutional arrangements that bring into question the idea that the rule of law would be satisfied if the law were simply strictly enforced. Current practice does not change the picture to any great extent. Existing immigration law in many, if not most, liberal democracies, is full of rules, and is implemented by institutions, that make adherence to the ideal of the rule of law difficult. The generality requirement is always a problematic matter to assess, since every law will tend to select out or apply unevenly to particular categories or classes of people. Even so, it is often quite clear that law has been written to conceal, under the guise of general applicability, an intention to target surreptitiously certain kinds of groups. But if we leave this particular desideratum aside, it still remains clear that many other demands of the rule of law are not respected. The requirements of publicity, consistency, and stability, for example, are regularly breached both in the making of law and in the institutional enforcement.

A particularly striking example of this is presented by the approach taken by successive Australian governments since 2001 to deal with asylum seekers. As a signatory to the 1951 Refugee Convention, Australia is, along with 141 other countries, under a legal obligation to consider requests for asylum and to accept as refugees those people who can demonstrate that they are fleeing persecution. In order to get around the obligation to consider all such claims, the Australian government has decided to interdict vessels carrying asylum seekers to prevent them from making landfall and becoming eligible to have their claims heard. To ensure that no responsibility can be attributed to Australia, people so intercepted are now taken to a third country, Nauru, to be detained until some other state might be found willing to accept them. Australia recognises no official responsibility for them but funds the detention centres in which they are confined and offers generous forms of aid to the government that has formal responsibility. The fact that the people imprisoned are subject to indefinite detention is one respect in which the idea of the rule of law has been breached. A more direct challenge to it came with the attempt to invoke section 474(1)(b) of the 1958 Migration Act to argue that immigration officials could not 'be challenged, appealed against, reviewed, quashed or called in question in any court'. Though this particular attempt to get around the law was unsuccessful, it is merely one of many such examples, and calls into question the idea that the rule of law is served simply by leaving governments to enforce the laws that they themselves have made.[32]

The law being a complex institution, having an existence not only in statutes and mechanisms of interpretation and enforcement but also in a social and historical context that shapes the reading and assessment of legal judgments and formal statements, the rule of law cannot be satisfied by the demand that discretion be denied and that somehow the letter of the law be followed. So, for example, in the United States the proposed Immigration Rule of Law Act introduced on 23 February 2015 is misleading in suggesting that removing the discretion of the executive or other administrative bodies to make special provisions, or to fund particular programmes, or to determine how to allocate funds to manage the processing of claims of different kinds of immigrants including illegal aliens, would somehow be more consistent with the rule of law. Discretion is an inescapable part of the legal structure and of legal processes. The mere existence of discretionary authority is not the problem, and not something that brings the rule of law into question. The question is whether the exercise of discretion is consistent with the spirit of the rule of law.

The ambition to extend control over immigration, however, has tended to exacerbate the problem of maintaining adherence to the rule of law. Being more than simply an instrument of rule, law by its nature slows down the processes of government and checks the operation of policy by requiring that it conform to particular strictures and be subjected to tests for consistency as well as compliance with established norms. The imperative to control, and in particular to reduce the volume of immigration (both authorized and unauthorized), has increased the temptation to find ways around legal obstacles, as well as the incentives to change the law in order to make immigration management objectives easier to attain.

There are three ways in which the rule of law is compromised or eroded under pressure to further control immigration. First, changes are made to the content of the law to make it better suited to serve the ends of policy, whether or not that is consistent with the demands of legality in any higher sense. Second, the institutional arrangements that make law accessible and officials subject to scrutiny are (further) revised to reduce their capacity to slow or check the implementation of policy. Third, the pursuit of the objectives of policy is simply conducted in violation of the law, since even if some failures of compliance are brought to attention, many will go undetected, and the objectives of policy will be closer to being realized.

Illustrations of these different ways in which the rule of law is compromised are not difficult to find, but examples are most readily discoverable in refugee law. This is worth noting because refugee law, and the approach taken by states to asylum seekers more generally, offers an insight into the way in which immigration control has been transformed in the modern era. 'Refugee law is an exception to the general rule that states are free to decide who crosses their borders.'[33] As the imperative to control immigration has grown, so have states turned increasingly to refugee law as a source of international law governing human movement, and also in order to close off some of the opportunities that international law provided for people to enter those states.

Examples of changes to the content of law that compromise the rule of law may readily be found in the recent history of Australia's efforts to reduce the flow of asylum seekers to its shores. As we noted earlier, as a signatory to the 1951 Refugee Convention and the 1967 Protocols, Australia is obligated under international law to consider claims for asylum. In order to diminish the number of claims that could be made, the Australian government, beginning in 2001, took a number of measures that contravened the Convention. First, it began to interdict vessels containing potential refugees and send them to other destinations so as to prevent them from entering Australia's sovereign territory and claiming asylum—going not only against the spirit of the Convention but also against the letter, since Article 33 prohibits *refoulement* 'in any manner whatsoever'.[34] Second, the government brought in legislation declaring that some parts of Australia's territorial waters were not a part of its territory for the purpose of making refugee claims. As many legal scholars have noted, while such a move 'is within Australia's legislative competence, it is nonsensical from the perspective of international law'.[35] Third, the government legislated to 'modify' the definition of refugee by limiting interpretations of 'persecution'. As Dauvergne notes, the amending legislation departed from the accepted international principle that treaties are to be interpreted 'in good faith in accordance with the ordinary meaning'[36] by 'substituting a national parliamentary interpretation of the rules in the place of judicial interpretation and independence'.[37]

In all of these cases, the rule of law is compromised to the extent that the requirements of generality, stability, and consistency are violated. The generality requirement is violated most obviously when 'persecution' is redefined to exclude certain groups from consideration, but more broadly, the spirit of the rule of law is undermined by the crafting of the law to diminish the legal rights of particular people—indeed people whom the law had been especially concerned to protect. The stability requirement is violated by the perpetual changing of the law in response to successful appeals by individuals declared by the courts or review tribunals to have valid claims the government sought to deny. And consistency goes out the window with the selective application of the law defining the limits of Australia's territorial waters—to keep out the undesirable poor while maintaining a claim to the riches beneath the sea. But the crucial point here is that this diminishing of the rule of law has its source in the aspiration to control immigration. The reason why a government could get away with this most striking contradiction of international law is that governments around the world, seeking themselves to control the flow of immigrants, looked at Australian practice as something from which to learn.

This becomes all the clearer when we consider examples of the second and third ways in which the rule of law is compromised—by making the law less accessible and by straightforward official action in violation of the law. Australia is not the only government that has acted to limit the rights of asylum seekers or would-be immigrants to access the courts or acquire legal representation. Refugees everywhere have struggled with this difficulty as governments have looked to this as a way of reducing the number of claimants or to facilitate the deportation of others more rapidly and at lower cost.[38] Perhaps the most worrying aspect of this development is the growing assumption that entitlement to legal protection and redress is in some way tied to nationality, or at least residency, rather than a right available to anyone as a person. This is especially troubling when government officials routinely act in violation of the law, knowing that those who are the victims of the enforcement of illegal decisions or procedures are unable to defend themselves by going to the law.[39]

The deep source of the problem, however, is not the misbehaviour of particular officials, for one has to ask what it is that brings political leaders, and public servants, in liberal democracies to take steps that are so out of keeping with long-established traditions. The answer has to do with the aspiration to acquire and retain a measure of control over immigration that is, in the end, unattainable—at least if such societies are to retain ways of living in which the ideals of freedom and equality hold sway. The pursuit of the ideal of control means that every setback will have to be met with a search for other measures to secure it, and as the law reveals itself to be an obstacle to its achievement so will the law be changed, or worked around, or reinterpreted or ignored. If a government sets a target of one hundred thousand net immigrants a year and finds itself completely incapable of meeting it, the temptation to work around the law may become too great to resist. On every rung on the ladder of authority and responsibility, people will be under pressure to meet their own targets; and the more forceful the imperative, the greater the pressure, and the more likely the yielding to temptation to give short shrift to the spirit of the law.

What will make this even more difficult is that the population will prove to be recalcitrant to the extent that it is made up of people who do not all share the same concern that governments acquire a certain measure of control over the borders. Even in societies that are marked by strong anti-immigrant sentiment, there are large numbers of people whose general outlook cares little for such control, and whose particular interests are better served by their interaction with outsiders or foreigners. As the evidence of continued immigration, and the participation of immigrants in the workforce as well a society more generally, suggests, there are more than enough people ready to welcome foreigners to make moving—with or without authorization—worthwhile. Law that looks to prohibit this runs the risk of being ignored or broken, and of falling into disrepute. The rule of law cannot be sustained if the laws themselves have no practical legitimacy.

The dilemma faced by liberal democracies in this regard is that their societies are divided (though not always evenly) between those who wish to see immigration reduced and controlled, and those who welcome and depend upon immigration. To satisfy the former group, governments impose stricter controls and more comprehensive regulations, which members of the latter group try to find ways to work around or, at worst, ignore. The pursuit of control thus has the effect of discrediting the law (at least to some degree); abandoning the aspiration to control, however, would create disaffection among the anti-immigrant sections of the population (and more significantly, the electorate).

This problem cannot be resolved by the development of more extensive systems of control. The past century has seen a substantial 'legalization' of immigration, as countries in the liberal democratic west in particular have built up increasingly complex laws and institutions to govern the movement of people. This has included the criminalization of immigration as well as the expansion of the practice of deportation and the rollback of permanent immigration programmes. The growing harshness of immigration regimes has also produced more and more 'hard law'—and indeed, just more and more law. Early in the last century, immigration legislation provided the basic framework within which decisions were taken, with discretion being exercised by officials and courts to interpret the law and determine its application to the particular cases at hand. The rule of law obtained to the extent that general and public rules were established and the demands of fairness were served by the application of the law in a way that was consistent with the circumstances in question. The growth of the legislative approach, however, has seen discretion gradually removed from the courts and more and more detailed interpretive instruction specified in the legislation itself—making it difficult or impossible for judges to take particular circumstances into account.[40] To an extent, law has become less the broad framework within which immigration takes place than an instrument through which policy is made. One measure of this is the sheer volume of immigration legislation now passed. In Australia, there were more than twenty-five amendments to the Migration Act between 1990 and 2000 (with as many and more in the years since); in Canada, the Immigration and Refugee Protection Act was amended on fifteen separate occasions between 2010 and 2016; and in the UK and the US immigration reforms are being continually drafted and re-drafted.[41] The outcome of this has been not a decline in the volume of immigration but an increase in the amount of 'illegal' immigration, which is now a much greater proportion of overall migration in the world, and in liberal democracies in particular.

Perversely, immigration control has created illegal immigration and the term 'illegal immigrant' now has a currency that belies its non-existence only a few decades ago. It has also resulted in greater strain on the institutions designed to deal with people fleeing persecution and seeking protection or asylum, since they are not able to avail themselves of ordinary ways of migrating. Unsurprisingly, this has then provoked accusations that many asylum seekers are nothing other than 'economic migrants', as though the two categories were mutually exclusive and there are never differences in degree.

This may also be something that had to be expected because of another consequence of immigration control. The more closely immigration needs to be managed, the more carefully must distinctions be drawn between people, who therefore have to be classified, identified, and documented. To be permitted to move between one national jurisdiction and another, an individual needs documents—most commonly, a passport—that classifies him or her as a member of a particular eligible category, but at the same time as an individual. This individuality is not, however, given by anything but the marks and seals of the nation state, identifying a person's primary physical characteristics, circumstances of birth, and the numerical codes under which his or her particulars are filed.[42] And yet, ironically enough, the management of immigration will also be shaped by other markers of identity which, at least in liberal democracies, have no place in the assessment of the rights and claims of persons who are free and equal before the law. This brings us, then, to the matter of race.

## Race and Equality

The imperative to manage, control, and limit immigration, particularly in liberal democracies, is partly the result of the political pressure exerted by elements of the population that are wary of, if not altogether hostile to, the movement of strangers into their midst. For political leaders, the democratic aspect of this feature of social life is the source of one kind of pressure to bow to the demand for greater control; but for others too, the will of the people carries considerable weight. The point of immigration control, for many, is to preserve a certain way of life; and if that way of life is a liberal democratic one, it looks obvious that one should begin by respecting the will of the people. Respect for democracy (as reflected in popular opinion) and the rule of law supplies all the reason needed to control and limit immigration—indeed it seems to demand nothing less.

Understanding the nature of immigration management, however, suggests that the rule of law, far from being a justification for controlling immigration, is in fact an ideal that is all the more likely to suffer the more vigorously the objective of control is pursued. The deeper worry, however, is that the pursuit of control will not only compromise the rule of law but work against the more fundamental value that underpins it, and which is also of crucial importance in any democracy: equality.

The most important equality that is of concern here is equality before the law, for no liberal democracy can abide arrangements under which some are privileged while others enjoy fewer rights or have their interests less well protected because they labour under a lesser status. For this to hold, however, it is necessary that there be more than a mere formal legal entitlement to equal treatment, for unless the institutions of a free society make it possible for everyone to enjoy the equal protection of the law, that equality will be of little consequence. Beyond the existence of legal and political institutions that uphold equality, however, it is also necessary that there be a broader social outlook that is consistent with the egalitarian spirit: one that recognises the importance of equalities of race and gender, and that is unwilling to condone discrimination for reasons of religion or ethnicity, or income or wealth, or class, or sexuality—or indeed because of any of a number of characteristics that have been the source of disadvantage in the past.

Immigration control is a danger to equality because its pursuit threatens to undermine the egalitarian ethos of a free society, as well as to distort its institutions and ultimately make the sustaining of equality before the law attainable only inadequately, if at all. There are several reasons for this. Most obviously, immigration controls emphasize the importance of the differences among people, with a view to justifying the treatment of some more favourably than others. First, it means distinguishing insiders or natives from outsiders or foreigners—with a view to privileging the former over the latter. Second, it means distinguishing among foreigners, for immigration control invariably turns into selective immigration that prefers some kinds of people to others. Third, it means distinguishing among the citizens or residents of one's own society, and privileging some among their number over others. No less importantly, immigration controls encourage the development of institutions, both within government and in civil society more generally, that distinguish among people on the basis of their nationality, and the traits that make some persons likely to be granted the freedom to immigrate. Immigration controls encourage or give succour to those elements in society that look to protect the privileged standing of some sections of society. We should look more closely at why this is so.

To understand the inegalitarian spirit that underpins the imperative to control immigration it is easiest to begin by returning to its history. Any turn to the history of immigration control brings us rapidly to the matter of race and racism—a topic that has remained seriously under-discussed by political theorists and philosophers who have considered the issue of immigration,[43] but has been given much more attention by historians, lawyers and social scientists. Immigration control in the liberal democratic west has, to a significant extent, been about limiting the entry, or keeping out altogether, people of the wrong ethnicity, religion, colour or (more recently) culture.

The most striking example of this might be thought to be Australia, whose 'White Australia Policy' advertised its intentions with striking candour. Yet it was hardly alone in this regard. In some ways, the history of America's immigration policy is equally, if not more, instructive, since it reveals how debates over immigration shaped the country's racially inflected thinking about equality, the role of political institutions, and what it could mean to be an American. Similarly, the history of British policy, particularly in the twentieth century and in the years since decolonization and the loss of empire, reveals a tightening of immigration controls—controls that fall more heavily upon peoples from Asian and African countries. Even the European Union, despite its enthusiasm for freedom of movement within its own external borders, and indeed its formal commitment to human rights norms and conventions that proclaim the importance of racial equality, has hardened its resolve to resist the encroachment upon its territory of peoples to the south and east of its geographical boundaries.

Now the obvious questions—indeed, challenges—that must be considered here are, first, whether immigration control has been as racially shaped as is alleged and, second, whether this is necessarily so. We might begin with the second question first and ask whether race must be a factor in immigration control. There is certainly no logical reason why it must, and this may be the reason that so few theorists arguing the case for or against immigration control have touched upon this topic. Most liberal democratic writers today would take it as a given that immigration policy should not be biased in favour of one group or another because of race. Few who argue in favour of immigration restrictions put the case for exclusion that discriminates on racial grounds. Must immigration control become racially based immigration control?

Before addressing this question directly, we should make clear what is encompassed by the term 'race' in this context. In anthropological or biological terms, the notion of race has no meaning to the extent that it has no clear referent. There is no basis for distinguishing people by race, which is, in the end, a socially constructed notion that has its roots in discredited nineteenth-century scientific ideas[44]—albeit, as we shall see later, ideas that did much to underpin and justify twentieth-century immigration policies. Racially discriminatory immigration policy is so described to cover efforts to exclude or treat differently people distinguished by their appearance (notably colour), ethnicity, religion (particularly the Jewish people but increasingly Muslims), or nationality.

Can there be a non-racially inflected immigration policy? If we leave aside the extremes of immigration policies that are either completely restricted (permitting *no* entry into the state) or completely *un*restricted, it is very difficult for governments to leave race out of the equation. This is not to say that every immigration policy must be racially motivated or biased to the same degree. But for as long as immigration is *selective* rather than simply randomised[45] it is difficult for policy not to be racially biased to a certain degree since some kind of selection criteria will be applied. If the point is to distinguish, first, between insiders and outsiders and, second, among different outsiders, some reasons will need to be offered for choosing certain people and rejecting others. Race or ethnicity will turn out to be a salient marker for exclusion.

The historical record confirms this to the extent that immigration law and policy everywhere appear to have restricted the movement of outsiders, or to exclude them altogether, on the basis of some form of racial classification. Chinese immigration to Australia, beginning in the 1840s when the end of convict transportation led to a rise in demand for labour, and continuing through the gold rushes, led to various attempt at exclusion, starting in Victoria, with the government's Immigration Restriction Act of 1855. After other similar acts were passed in New South Wales, among the reasons advanced, by the end of the nineteenth century, for the creation of an Australian federation and a national government was the need to control the borders of the nation, with the large number of Chinese cited as a consequence of the absence of the necessary measures. The first act of the new Australian Parliament was the 1901 Immigration Restriction Act that formed the basis of the White Australia Policy. Hostility to Chinese immigration was also at the forefront of the development of American policy, beginning with the Chinese Exclusion Act 1882. Its failure either to control Chinese immigration or to satisfy anti-Chinese sentiment led to Chinese immigration being made illegal altogether in 1902 and spurred successful efforts to make other nationalities ineligible for admission to the United States, or for citizenship[46]—though the Naturalization Act 1790 had already established that only 'Whites' were eligible for naturalization as American citizens. The Immigration Act 1917 (Barred Zone Act) restricted immigration from Asia, and the Immigration Act 1924 (Johnson-Reed Act) created the National Origins Formula, which fixed the number of immigrants at 150,000 annually and divided the world into 'quota' and 'non-quota' nations for the purposes of immigration control (until repealed by the Hart-Celler Act of 1965). One of the consequences of this was the restriction of Jewish migration, since Jews, and particularly southern and eastern Jews, were considered less racially desirable. Although 123,000 Jewish refugees immigrated to the United States in the period between 1938 and 1941, several hundred thousand applicants were refused visas at American consulates in Europe when the Holocaust was in progress. The United States was not alone in turning away from Jewish refugees. Canada's officialdom fought to restrict Jewish migration—asserting that 'none is too many'—both before the war and after it,[47] as did successive Australian governments.[48]

Race has been a persistent factor in the making of immigration law and immigration policy. Britain in its years as an imperial power discriminated relatively little against other races to the extent that all peoples within the empire were granted the status of British subject under the British Nationality and Status of Aliens Act 1914, and with that gained the right of abode within the United Kingdom.[49] Nonetheless, it had with the Aliens Act 1905 aimed to exclude east European Jews, and in the 1920s responded to fears of Asian, African and Caribbean shipping crews from non-British colonies coming to the country by passing the Special Restriction (Coloured Alien Seamen) Order 1925. In the years since the end of World War II it has gradually tightened restrictions, most dramatically in passing the Commonwealth Immigrants Act 1968, which amended the Commonwealth Immigrants Act 1962 by substantially curtailing the rights of citizens of Commonwealth of Nations countries to migrate to Britain. Although it reduced the right of all such citizens, including those from Australia, Canada, and New Zealand, its purpose was to prevent Asian victims of Kenya's 'Africanization' policy from making their way to the United Kingdom.[50] While the legislation was opposed by some members of Parliament and the Liberal Party, it was passed in a few days by the Labour government with the support of the Conservative opposition. In the years that followed, further legislation made it more difficult for non-White members of the Commonwealth to seek abode in or enter the UK. The Immigration Act 1971 affirmed Britain's strong ties to Australia, New Zealand, and Canada while simultaneously tightening restrictions on the rights of other Commonwealth citizens to move to the UK by introducing the concepts of 'patrial and non-patrial' immigrants.[51] The British Nationality Act 1981 restricted immigration further by tightening eligibility for British nationality, abolishing the category of Citizen of the United Kingdom and Colonies. Now there were fewer British citizens, and only British citizens held the automatic right of abode and entry into the UK.

This very quick sketch serves no more than to offer a few illustrations of what is well understood: that immigration everywhere has been racially inflected. The point could be made even more forcefully with examples of racial bias at various stages of the immigration process.[52] But the problem of racial bias in immigration control is not the heart of the problem if the issue is the impact of immigration control on a society whose aspiration is to maintain a commitment to equality in general and therefore racial equality in particular. For the problem with immigration control is not only that it might be racially biased against some outsiders but that it makes it difficult to preserve racial equality within. Why should this be the case?

One reason might be of the sort advanced by Sir David Maxwell Fyfe in the discussion in Parliament during the Second Reading of the British Nationality Bill of 1948 when he expressed his concern that the creation of a different forms of citizenship within the British Empire. He said:

> we deprecate any tendency to differentiate between different types of British subjects in the United Kingdom. We feel that when they come to the United Kingdom there ought to be an open door and a reception for every type. If we create a distinctive citizenship for Britain and the Colonies, inevitably such differentiation will creep in. We must maintain our great metropolitan tradition of hospitality to everyone from every part of our Empire.[53]

Fyfe's argument was that any effort to distinguish between British and colonial citizens within the empire could only mean a kind of differentiation among British subjects that was inconsistent with the principles that had been established by the Imperial Conference of 1930—that all British subjects would hold British nationality, and that that nationality could not be taken away by the actions of any power. Differentiating citizenships, he feared, would not only reduce various protections and rights British nationals throughout the colonies enjoyed but would also mean treating them unequally.[54]

While Fyfe's concern was that differentiated citizenship would result in inequality among citizens throughout the *empire*, the broader point is that the effort of exclusion threatens to lead to differentiation among people within a society—and all the more so when exclusion is based on race. Let us consider whether this must be the case.

The most important reason to think that immigration control is a likely contributor to racial differentiation is that racial differences have no natural basis but are the product of needs or incentives to distinguish and classify persons for any of a variety of purposes. Controlling immigration has never been simply about limiting the numbers of persons entering a society but has always been about the kinds of person who are admitted, so the practice of immigration control is everywhere a practice of selection. Whenever purely numerical limits of immigration are set by governments, different groups invariably complain and petition for exemptions—employers because they want workers, communities because they have ties abroad, individuals because they want family reunification. Once selection is the name of the game, differentiation, classification, and comparison follow. No less importantly, once distinctions are made they have to be sustained, either by explicit defence of the categories created, or by more subtle means like using proxies for distinctions that cannot be drawn in the open. Immigration control—through immigration law and immigration enforcement—has contributed substantially to the creation of racial categories. It would be going too far to suggest that it is the only source of racial differentiation,[55] but its significance should not be underestimated.

To see this more clearly it would be useful to look at a particular historical case: the passage and implementation of the Johnson-Reed Act of 1924[56] in the United States. Also known as the National Origins Act, it was the product of the recommendations of the Dillingham Commission[57]—combined with a fear that postwar immigration would dilute the 'basic strain' of the American population because the formula for admitting people specified that a fixed percentage of foreign-born were to be permitted entry. This, nativists argued, discriminated again native-born Americans and north-western Europeans. Congress responded by passing an act that established national origin quotas. This required designing a system that was able 'to define the "national origins" of the American people and to calculate the proportion of each group to the total population'.[58] The problem facing the Quota Board charged with this task was that the concepts at hand—'national origin', 'native stock', and 'nationality'—could not readily serve as units of classification as they had no determinate meaning. The law as it stood defined 'nationality' according to country of birth, but that was shot through with qualifications that reflected a racial calculus. It excluded non-White people from the resident population by removing from the total all immigrants and their descendants from neighbouring regions in the Americas (such as Canada, the Caribbean, Central and South America), aliens ineligible for citizenship and their descendants, the descendants of slave immigrants, and the descendants of American aborigines. The Quota Board in the end embraced this understanding. It made its calculations using the race categories found in the 1920 census—'White', 'Black', 'mulatto', 'Indian', 'Chinese', 'Japanese' and 'Hindu'—counting mulattoes as Black, and ignoring the distinction between the descendants of free Blacks or voluntary immigrants from Africa. It also excluded from American nationality people from the territories of Hawaii, Puerto Rico and Alaska—even those who were US citizens.[59] It reinforced the restricted understanding of nationality and gave greater legitimacy to the racial biases behind it.

While the purpose of the new laws was to restrict southern and eastern European immigration, it also divided Europe from the rest of the world and ended up defining the world's nationalities in terms of race. 'The national origins quota system created categories of difference that turned on both national origins and race, reclassifying Americans as racialized subjects simultaneously on both axes.'[60] The Johnson-Reed Act also achieved an outcome that had eluded many nativists in completely excluding Asians from eligibility for citizenship—constituting 'Asian' as a distinct racial category in the process. Indeed, 'it codified the principle of racial exclusion into the main body of immigration and naturalization law'.[61]

At the root of the matter was the difficulty not only of distinguishing people according to nationality (what, for example, was the Quota Board to make of the descendants of intermarriage?) but also the problem of establishing who was White. In the three decades before the Johnson-Reed Act the federal courts had heard twenty-five cases in which the racial status of immigrants looking to take out citizenship was challenged. Supreme Court rulings in *Takao Ozawa v. U.S.* (1922) and *U.S. v. Bhagat Singh Thind* (1923) that Japanese and Asian Indians were ineligible for citizenship on racial grounds had helped establish the category 'Asian' and settled one aspect of the matter. But it left open the question of who (else) was an Asian.[62] In 1915 a Syrian, George Dow, appealed lower court rulings that he was ineligible for naturalization on the grounds that he was Asian and therefore not White. The Circuit Court, however, ruled that the people of some parts of Asia, including Syria, were according to received opinion classified as White.[63] In this period, lower courts ruled on seven separate occasions in favour of the naturalization of Syrians, Armenians, and Indians as Whites.[64] Though in most instances courts did not accept petitioners' claims to 'Whiteness', the history here illustrates the confusion surrounding the racialization that was wrought by immigration law.[65]

Interestingly, Mexicans were not excluded from eligibility for citizenship on racial grounds because they were deemed to be White (so the 1924 act exempted Mexico and other countries in the western hemisphere from numerical quotas). In the Mexican-American War of 1846–48 the opportunity to take all of Mexico was abandoned in part on the grounds that absorbing a mixed and Coloured race was undesirable, but to exercise sovereignty over the part of the country that was annexed required some determination of the status of Mexican citizens of Spanish, Native American, and mixed descent living there.[66] By according them US citizenship, the Treaty of Guadalupe Hidalgo (which ended the war) 'determined' that they were therefore also White. This did not prevent the Census Bureau in 1930 from classifying Mexicans as a separate race who were 'not definitely white, Negro, Indian, Chinese or Japanese'.[67]

Though the Johnson-Reed Act and its national origin quotas were over-turned by the Hart-Celler Act of 1965, and the US attempted to turn away from a racially based immigration law, the racialization wrought by efforts of immigration control could not be eliminated.[68] Here the treatment of Mexicans is especially instructive. Before 1920 the Mexican and Canadian borders had been 'soft', and it was not unusual for Europeans looking to move to the US to do so (both legally and illegally) via the countries on its northern and southern borders. Canadians and Mexicans also crossed the border relatively freely as seasonal workers. The introduction of Johnson-Reed changed much of this, not because the law imposed further restrictions on Mexicans, who were *not* subject to the quota system, but because the attitude to Mexican immigration changed. Though officially categorised as 'White', Mexicans were also increasingly viewed as culturally and racially different. The demand for Mexican labour and the long history of hiring seasonal workers meant that Mexicans continued to cross the border, but that movement was now controlled by an extensive system of visas—and checks by the newly formed Border Patrol, which came to see its role as one of protecting a cultural and racial boundary. The Federal Immigration Service instituted new inspection procedures at the border which included such measures as bathing, delousing, and medical testing (a superfluous procedure since a medical certificate was already a requirement for obtain-ing a work visa) as well as interrogation. Only Mexican immigrants were inspected naked, had their heads shorn, and saw their belongings fumigated.

The impact of the racialization of immigrant control was felt not only on Mexican immigrants. The Border Patrol concluded that while some would-be immigrants could be turned back at the border itself, many could only be apprehended by searching within the country. Consequently, immigra-tion enforcement went inland as officers took it upon themselves to stop and search travellers or intrude into businesses and families suspected of harbouring undocumented Mexicans. Given the large number of American citizens of Mexican descent, this meant that many Americans were subject to police intrusion because they fitted the racial profile of an illegal immigrant.

In the years of the depression, immigration authorities increased the number of deportations, and also began a programme of voluntary repatria-tion that saw nearly 20 per cent of the Mexican population return to Mexico in what has been described as the largest racial expulsion in the United States since the removal of Native Americans in the nineteenth century. A sub-stantial number of those repatriated were American-born children, as were many of those who were deported. Of course, not everyone was deported.

The continuing demand for labour led to many Mexicans being denied the opportunity to leave. In 1935 the California Relief Administration and the federal Works Progress Administration forced 75,000 Mexicans to remain to bring in harvests in southern California. In Sonoma County, state authorities forced men to pick hops for seventy-five cents a day while living in 'miserable impoverished shelters'.[69]

As was pointed out earlier, over the next seventy years more than a million Americans, mostly of Mexican descent or appearance, would be wrongly deported—largely as the result of the way in which Mexicans came to be viewed as racially distinct and likely to be 'illegal'.[70] It is worth noting again that the unlawful expulsion of citizens has not ceased, and Americans continue to be deported or detained (in some cases for years)[71] because their racial appearance[72] leads officials to suspect them of being illegal immigrants.

The broader conclusion to which all this points is the intimate relationship between immigration control and racialization. It is well established that immigration law, as well as enforcement practices, are significant forces in the construction of race—in the United States and elsewhere.[73] It should also be clear that this not only affects immigrants but also 'generates a host of *practices* that redound to the disadvantage of those citizens who share characteristics with immigrant communities'.[74]

To the extent that a society seeks to sustain norms and legal practices that repudiate racial discrimination or aspires to equality among its citizens and residents without regard to ethnic or cultural differences, immigration control poses a particular danger. Both theory and history suggest that racial discrimination turns out not merely to be a bug in the system but a fairly consistent feature of it.[75] The problem begins with the way in which 'the relaxed legal standards that apply to enforcement practices in this context migrate over time into the legal doctrines governing the policing of other racially subordinated groups'.[76] But it continues inasmuch as it has a corrupting effect on other legal and political institutions necessary to the health of the rule of law and the ideal of equality.

## Sex and Equality

Just as immigration control has in many countries aimed at controlling race, so has it no less importantly aimed at controlling gender and sexuality. Implicit in immigration control, though occasionally made explicit in official statements of policy, is a view of what kinds of personal relationships among people can be acknowledged, and therefore how individuals are to be identified and categorized. This is particularly evident, as we have already seen, in the way in which the imperative of immigration control has shaped the state's understanding of marriage. Citizens and residents might marry foreigners and wish to sponsor them to immigrate, and foreigners immigrating might wish to bring their spouses or partners. Assessing the legitimacy of their requests requires judgments of the 'authenticity' of their claims: are they really married, or are their marriages consistent with domestic norms (rather than, say, 'arranged')? To ascertain this, tests of one sort or another have to be devised, but these tests themselves end up articulating what counts as a marriage deserving of recognition. They also both depend upon and reinforce stereotypical understandings of the people and the relationships thus scrutinized.

An instructive example is the case of virginity testing in the UK. This practice was brought in after the 1971 Immigration Act because of the state's concern that female immigrants from the Indian subcontinent entering on fiancée visas might be abusing the fast-track scheme. Since, it was officially explained, unmarried South Asian women would be virgins, a physical examination would provide conclusive evidence[77] about whether or not the woman had ever engaged in sexual activity. African-Caribbean and other female immigrants were not subjected to this procedure, whose 'imposition was determined not only by gender but also by race, nationality, marital status, age and socio-economic status'.[78] When the practice was first reported by the *Guardian*, it was denied by the Home Secretary, then justified as necessary for public health reasons or to exclude immigrants requiring major medical treatment, and subsequently explained as a matter that involved only a few cases or as necessary for testing for communicable diseases—without any presentation of an entirely satisfactory account of how a visual examination of the hymen by an immigration official served this purpose. Ultimately, however, the Home Office simply conceded that discrimination was a necessary part of immigration control, stating: 'The whole system of immigration control is based on discrimination. It is the essence of the Immigration Act that people will be discriminated against on the grounds of race or nationality and it is the function of certain officials to ensure that discrimination is effective.'[79]

What is noteworthy here is that trying to ensure that only 'good' immigrants were admitted required assessing not just their economic or financial circumstances but also their capacity to conform to a particular understanding of the gender roles they would occupy. This assessment was in turn informed by stereotypes about the immigrant men and women from South

Asia. In essence, the government feared that South Asian men immigrating on their own would be a problem because of their 'excessive sexual desires', and that without enough South Asian women there would be mixed marriages and children—both legitimate and illegitimate—of mixed descent. Admitting South Asian women would solve the problem, both because the women would supply the men with wives and because the family would then moderate the tendencies of the men. 'South Asian women were therefore needed by the state to perform a specific function of ethnic containment.'[80] More importantly still, the case supplies an interesting example of the extent to which immigration control has to be understood not simply as a means of controlling the entry of outsiders but of shaping the society they enter— for they threaten to transform it by associating with the local population in ways considered undesirable by political authorities.

It is worth taking this analysis a little further still. Immigration controls involve an intervention by state authorities not only into the understanding of sex and marriage but also into the understanding of sexuality more generally.[81] For much of their histories, modern states have controlled immigration by restricting the movement of people considered unsuitable for one reason or another. Among the reasons they might not be regarded as fit for admission is sexual orientation. In the United States, for example, the 1917 Immigration Act excluded those who were deemed 'constitutional psychopathic inferiors', and others who possessed 'abnormal sexual instincts', from entering the country. Prior to the passage of the McCarran-Walter Act, which altered the language to target those with 'psychopathic personalities', a Senate Committee of the Judiciary suggested that 'classes of mental defects should be enlarged to include homosexuals and other sex perverts'. The Immigration and Nationality Act of 1965 still excluded such potential migrants, described now as 'sexual deviants'. Until the end of the twentieth century, American immigration laws used language that pathologized homosexuals as mentally ill.[82] Since the main purpose of immigration control has always been to shape society and its citizenry, this is hardly surprising. What is worth emphasizing, however, is not only the impact this had on excluded would-be immigrants but also the way in which immigration control continued to bear upon the construction of sexuality even after homosexuals could legally immigrate.

Once homosexuality ceased to be a reason for exclusion, it became possible for people to seek asylum on the grounds that they faced persecution on the basis of gender. The critical question for those looking for protection under the 1951 UN Convention relating to the Status of Refugees is whether they qualify as members of a 'particular social group'.[83] In the United States, the *Matter of Acosta* (1985) established the precedent for defining 'particular social group' so as to include sex or sexuality when it stated that it referred to

> a group of persons, all of whom share a common, immutable characteris-
> tic. i.e., a characteristic that either is beyond the power of the individual
> members of the group to change or is so fundamental to their identities
> or consciences that it ought not to be required to be changed.[84]

Thus, sex came to be viewed as a protected characteristic. Rather than set-tling the matter of who had claims to protection, however, this added further complications.[85] This issue now was what counted as persecution and, no less importantly, who was a homosexual—or perhaps more accurately, how was sexuality to be identified?

But it would be a mistake to think that the problem was how to determine a person's sexuality as an independent matter in order to establish his or her eligibility for immigration. While immigration regulations have at least since the nineteenth century considered sexuality, along with race, gender, class, and culture, as a grounds for controlling entry, they have not simply applied pre-existing understandings of these categories to persons but actively par-ticipated in producing these distinctions—all for the purpose of constructing nations and citizens.[86] Once it became possible for people to seek protec-tion on the basis of persecution for their sexual orientation, the question of establishing a person's sexuality came to the fore. The problem, however, is that sexuality or sexual identity is not something that is easily categorized, or identified by forms of behaviour, or even fixed to the extent that people often live in different worlds simultaneously or move between them. This does not sit well with the institutions of immigration control, whose officials must look for proof of sexual orientation from asylum seekers, much as they must search for evidence that a marriage is founded on a genuine relation-ship. Thus someone seeking asylum as a male person persecuted for his sexuality might be asked to prove it by demonstrating, for example, that he is immersed in 'gay culture', lives in a stable gay relationship, and is healthy (which is to say, not liable to contract AIDS through risky behaviour), or else have his asylum claim denied.

What the institutions of immigration control find more difficult to conceptualize is the person whose sexuality—and for that matter, sexual identity—is fluid or not settled or simply complicated in ways that make categorization difficult. Consider, for example, the case of Mexican immi-grants who regarded themselves as 'homosocial'—because they had 'sexual encounters [with] other non-gay-identified men' as well as with women, but who redefined themselves as 'gay on moving to the United States'.[87] In some such cases, it might mean that individuals are forced to present themselves as a particular type of person in order to gain admittance. Equally, however, it might simply point to the fact that, when confronted with social, legal, and political imperatives, people choose to present themselves as one kind of person or another, adopting the identity that is most advantageous. 'On the one hand, taking homosexuality into account for immigration control implies a definition of gay identity. On the other, the objects of these policies are also subjects: their own identity is caught up in this transnational process of identification.'[88]

It is clear enough now that even as some states have become less inclined to exclude people because of their sexual orientation, so has there emerged an imperative to establish what counts as 'a good homosexual' (and so, 'a good immigrant').[89] The purpose of drawing attention to this, however, is not simply to decry the existence of prejudice and its workings in the deliberations of political authorities but to reinforce a broader point about immigration control. That control involves an exercise of power that does not simply determine who may or may not enter a society but works to shape and define the identities of the people within it.[90] Not all of those affected, whether directly or indirectly, will feel the weight of the implication equally, for experiencing the shaping and transforming of one's identity might for some be welcomed as a form of growth and personal development even as for others it is experienced as a burden. In very significant ways, immigration control is about determining which are the good identities; and not all identities are equal.

## Equality and Freedom

Many of those who worry about the impact of immigration express the concern that an influx of foreigners brings with it a risk that the fundamental values of the society or nation will be tested, eroded, or even undermined entirely. This is surely what lies behind fears, in the liberal democratic west in particular, of immigrants who are racially or culturally different—whether they come from the wrong parts of Europe, or from Asia or Africa or Central and South America. To treat all would-be immigrants equally, it appears, would be nothing more than folly, for the arrival (in sufficient numbers) of people whose commitment to, or capacity to appreciate and respect, those values can only weaken the hold of those fundamental ideas about how one should live and how a society should be governed. To the extent that it remains unchecked, immigration poses an existential threat, for in undermining fundamental values it chips away at a people's very identity and makes social solidarity precarious.

The argument advanced in this chapter (and in this book more generally) does not doubt that the movement of people brings with it serious challenges or assume that immigration is risk-free, either for those who move or for those who find their surroundings changed by the arrival of visitors, sojourners, or settlers. The point, however, is that the greater danger that has been overlooked is the threat to some important values posed by immigration *control*. People fearful of the harm that might come from the arrival of outsiders have overlooked the harm they might be doing, through their efforts of control, to their own institutions and to themselves. Immigration control inescapably involves creating laws, policies, and procedures that tend to violate norms of equality in general and the ideal of equality before the law in particular. The more vigorously the goal of control is pursued, the heavier the price that will have to be paid.

Immigration control is not unique in this regard. The search for control is dangerous in many other circumstances. One reason for this, as Hayek in particular argued in his critique of central planning, is that human beings are, on the whole, recalcitrant creatures who will resist efforts to confine them and look for ways around obstacles put in their path. Control will engender resistance, which will in turn call for redoubled efforts of control—and all the more so if the rewards of resistance are worth the risk of sanction. People cannot be moved around like pieces on a chessboard as 'the man of system' might have us believe.[91] But there is a deeper reason still why control is dangerous, and again a reason to which Hayek draws our gaze. Greater control can only be achieved, ultimately, not by rules or laws or policies of enforcement but by effecting a deeper transformation of people's thinking. To be effective, control must not be resisted but embraced—if not by everyone, then at least by enough that those who are reluctant to accept it are too indifferent or fearful to put up a fight. What is needed is not a remaking of laws but a reconstruction of consciousness.

When it comes to immigration, the most important tool of control is to persuade the population that it is warranted to treat some people—outsiders—differently: to treat them as less than equals. Those who do not *belong* may have some rights, but not the same rights or as many rights as those who do. On the face of it this may look like an innocuous move, for surely there is no harm in saying that those who are foreign to us are not our equals—or at

least, not within our territory. But this is where the difficulties begin, for as
we have seen, not everyone who is foreign is foreign to the same degree or
in the same way, or indeed foreign by nature as opposed to 'foreign' because
we (or some) have so declared in order to secure an advantage. Boundaries
between people and between nations are neither fixed nor immutable. To try
to distinguish sharply between the claims of those on one side and those on
the other is to court trouble—or injustice. Even after the distinction has been
drawn, however, the difficulties will not go away, for those on the inside do
not thereby lose their connections with those on the other side of the divide
(whether that divide is the boundary of the nation or the rule differentiating
the standing of one person from that of another within the same territory).
People continue to relate to one another, whether as family, or as friends, or
as colleagues, or as employers and employees, or as teachers and students,
and even as buyers and sellers. Greater efforts still will have to be made to
persuade them that some people just do not belong. At this point, those putting the case will cast around for criteria upon which the base the distinction.
History suggests that they will use whatever comes to hand—nationality,
religion, race, or some combination of these and other identifiers that look
like they might do the trick. And the trick is to convince enough people that
some people may legitimately be treated unequally because they do not
belong. The risk this carries, in the first instance, is that a heavy burden will
be borne by many 'insiders', who will see others to whom they are close, or
upon whom they depend, treated unequally in ways that harm them all. But
it also brings the further risk that when the demand to draw the distinction
between insiders and outsiders grows so great, the institutions protecting
against arbitrariness and injustice will themselves be compromised in order
to serve that end. At worst, this means the rule of law becomes subordinated
to the end of social control.

Two things might be said in response to this concern. The first is that it
is exaggerated: western liberal democracies remain robust, and what better
evidence is there of this than the constant clamour of people to enter them?
The second is that the risk is worth taking, and perhaps the price is worth
paying, for there are gains to be made by the effort of control, and there is
much to be lost by failing to control. Is equality, and the freedom it makes
possible, really that important? Or do different considerations entirely
matter more: considerations of economy, culture, and the self-determination
of a state or nation? These are the challenges we need now to consider.

# 5

# Economy

They called for workers, but people are coming.
—MAX FRISCH, FOREWORD TO ALEXANDER J. SEILER, *SIAMO
ITALIANI—DIE ITALIENER. GESPRÄCHE MIT ITALIENISCHEN
ARBEITERN IN DER SCHWEIZ*

If you torture the data long enough, nature will always confess.
—RONALD COASE, *ESSAYS ON ECONOMICS AND ECONOMISTS*

Economic control is not merely control of a sector of human life which
can be separated from the rest; it is the control of the means for all our
ends. And whoever has sole control of the means must also determine
which ends are to be served, which values are to be rated higher and
which lower, in short, what men should believe and strive for.
—FRIEDRICH HAYEK, *THE ROAD TO SERFDOM*

## Economic Questions

Immigration control might well bring with it risks of all kinds, including risks
to freedom, equality, and the rule of law. Yet all policies have their costs, so
it ought to be asked what is gained by taking the risk, or bearing the costs,
of immigration management. The most obvious and widely advanced arguments in favour of controlling—and limiting—immigration are economic
ones: uncontrolled immigration, it is alleged, threatens a society's economic
wellbeing, and only a properly regulated immigration process will ensure

that losses do not exceed gains or, worse, that the immigrants do not destroy the host economy altogether. The purpose of this chapter is to consider such a response: that the price of immigration control—the diminution of freedom and equality and the dereliction of the rule of law—is worth paying because the economic gains are so considerable. The argument this chapter defends is that these gains are illusory. But showing this is no straightforward matter.

While it might seem clear that an appeal to science and the empirical evidence will give us a firm foothold from which to tackle the vexing question of how to respond to the worry that immigration control means a loss of freedom, in reality the economics of immigration is treacherous terrain. Numerous studies proclaim, and indeed offer to demonstrate, that immigration is economically beneficial—particularly in the short term, but especially in the long run.[1] Yet sceptical voices are everywhere, suggesting that the economic consequences of immigration are not benign and often entirely malignant.[2] When contentious political decisions hang in the balance, science often turns out to be an unreliable friend, capable of turning out equally convincingly for prosecution and defence alike.[3]

Even before scientific investigation can begin, however, there are conceptual and theoretical questions that need to be addressed but which have no obvious, clear, or determinate answers. The most pressing of these is the question of how to identify the agent or agents whose gains or losses need to be considered. If immigration control is to be defended because the economic benefits it brings are great enough to offset the losses (of all sorts) it threatens, *who* gains? Or loses? This is a very much under-theorized aspect of the immigration question.

Under-theorized though it may be, however, it is not a question that has gone unanswered, and behind the most common answers are advocates who are anything but under-motivated. It is worth taking some time to dwell upon this, if only to make clear at the outset that the economic questions that must be explored more carefully matter ultimately only because they bear on deeper ethical questions about individual wellbeing and the consequences of economic transformation on human welfare. In this regard, the debate about immigration has to be seen in the context of the concern in some western democracies about the plight of the industrial working classes and, to some extent, of the rural poor, in the face of the changes wrought by the economic forces of globalization. The mobility of labour has to be seen as a part of a more general phenomenon: a highly competitive global market in which the mobility of all factors of production can quickly lead to those industries and communities that are unable to adapt to changes, or the pace of change, being left behind as more nimble enterprises prosper. Of course history is full of episodes of this kind, whether one considers the matter from the perspective of the grand narrative and points, say, to the Industrial Revolution, or simply recognizes that from time to time technological advance or the discovery of new alternatives will make some endeavours suddenly profitable and render others more or less pointless—as happened with the American whaling industry, for example.[4] But even if such developments are commonplace, they are disruptive of people's lives, and the consequences may be personal tragedy as well as social division, both within communities and between groups and classes more generally.

Recent scholarship and popular commentary have seen a flurry of work describing and analysing these disruptions. Some of it has tackled the more ambitious question of why contemporary western societies seem to be 'coming apart', and look for explanations for class division, material inequality, declining social mobility, and the emergence of populist or anti-elite social and political movements.[5] Other works have tracked, documented, and sought to bring to life the personal and human impact of economic and social change on individuals and communities.[6] While not all these works have identified immigration as a factor that is a part of the trouble, many raise the question and suggest that the movement of people has some role to play in explaining the problems—or at least the discontents—evident in western democracies, and speculate about whether stricter immigration controls might not alleviate at least some of the harms they have suffered.[7] According to some of the narratives, however, immigration is economically harmful to a society and its victims are the most vulnerable members of the national community.

Whether or not this is so is thus the question that must be examined here, not because it is an interesting technical puzzle for economic theorists, nor because what matters is the health of some abstraction called 'the economy'. The question matters because what is at stake is the wellbeing of individuals and communities—of immigrants and natives alike.

This chapter begins, then, by reviewing the economic arguments advanced for controlling (and particularly, limiting) immigration, noting along the way where the claims made are controversial, and assessing the seriousness of the economic concerns.[8] It then turns to consider the immediate economic costs of efforts to control immigration, before the next part addresses the indirect economic consequences of immigration control. In all of this, the prevailing assumption of economic analysis is that the impact of immigration on the welfare of the natives of immigrant-receiving countries is the most important or relevant consideration. The final part of the chapter turns to consider this assumption more carefully. There are two aspects to it—one a temporal judgment about the generation of natives whose interests are most important, and the second a conceptual judgment about the identity of the collective whose interests are at stake. An examination of this matter will clarify the nature of the economic arguments about immigration and immigration control, and open the way for a fuller consideration in chapters 6 and 7 of some of the other reasons advanced in defence of immigration control.

## The Economic Case for Immigration Control

The economic argument for limiting and controlling immigration has several aspects. Advocates of immigration restrictions are concerned about the impact of immigration on the overall wellbeing of the receiving society. This means that they are concerned about the economic effects of immigration on 1) the native population in general, 2) particular groups within that population, and 3) the workings of the state as an organization or collective entity. They are therefore concerned about the *aggregate* effects of immigration, its *distributional* consequences, and its *institutional* implications. The general claim is that there are significant economic costs to immigration that is inadequately restricted and controlled, and that all too often the gains from immigration are shared by a favoured segment of society while the burdens are borne by others less fortunate. We should consider these in turn, beginning with the arguments for restricting immigration because of its negative aggregate effects.

### AGGREGATIVE CONCERNS

It is rare for anyone to argue for an end to immigration altogether. The economic case for restricting immigration is therefore most commonly an argument for managing rather than eliminating it—though generally this means managing it downwards and selecting particular types of people.[9] The most prominent economic arguments for restricting immigration are about the impact of immigration on the domestic labour market. Though concerns have been raised about the effects of immigration on the preservation of social capital, or on the protection of the urban as well as the natural environment, it is the labour market effects that are the most significant economic issue.

This economic case against immigration in the popular literature is put very sharply by Peter Brimelow with regard to immigration to America. He argues that: 'On balance, current mass immigration contributes essentially nothing to native-born Americans in aggregate'; 'counting transfer payments, mass immigration is probably a loss for the native-born'; and 'mass immigration does cause a substantial redistribution of income among the native-born—basically from labour to capital'.[10] Mark Krikorian is similarly critical (again, referring specifically to immigration to the United States), writing: 'while immigration certainly increases the size of our economy, it subverts the widely shared economic goals of a modern society: a large middle-class open to all, working in high-wage, knowledge-intensive, and capital-intensive jobs exhibiting growing labour productivity and avoiding too skewed a distribution of income'.[11] Moreover, he argues, mass immigration is 'an impediment to the long-term competitiveness of industries that use cheap immigrant labour'[12] by slowing down innovation (to replace labour) and reducing productivity.[13] Such arguments are not advanced only by conservative writers. Philip Cafaro has put the 'progressive' case for reducing immigration and emphasized that keeping the labour supply down is essential to maintaining high wages—especially for the poorer classes. The basic principle, for Cafaro, quoting Paul Samuelson, is simple: 'Limitation of the supply of any grade of labor relative to all other productive factors can be expected to raise its wage rate; an increase in supply will, other things being equal, tend to depress wage rates.' Recent history, he suggests, 'has proven this notion correct'.[14] Let us look more closely then at these concerns.

The Cafaro analysis appears to commit the 'lump of labour' fallacy in failing to appreciate the nature of labour, the need to differentiate carefully among its various kinds and the different consequences of its movement.[15] While he is able to appeal to the authority of Paul Samuelson, it is not clear how seriously he has taken the *ceteris paribus* clause in the line he quotes. The more substantial theoretical and empirical support for the concerns of immigration economics sceptics comes from the work of George J. Borjas, who also quotes Samuelson to the effect that an increase in supply will, *other things being equal*, tend to depress wages. On the question of the overall contribution of immigration to economic growth in general or the welfare of natives in particular, Borjas suggests not that it amounts to nothing but simply that it amounts to very little. We should look more closely at Borjas's analysis, which considers (and questions) the gains from immigration to native workers, to a country, and to the world as a whole. On the first two of these three considerations, Borjas's view is plain: 'A central lesson of economic theory is that the net gains from immigration depend directly on its distributional impact: the greater the loss in wages suffered by native workers, the greater gains to the receiving country.'[16] Those gains themselves he finds to be negligible, though they come at a significant cost in the form of losses incurred by some (the least well off) to benefit others (the already better off). We shall return to the distributional question later in this chapter, but the general claim about the paucity of economic gains deserves more careful examination.

Assume a very simple model of an economy with two inputs, capital and labour, and further assume that the workforce is made up of natives (who own all the capital, the supply of which does not change with the price or is, as economists put it, 'perfectly inelastic') and immigrants (whose skills are such that they are perfect substitutes for natives). Assume also that the supplies of both natives and immigrants are unaffected by price. What would be the impact of an increase in immigration, assuming this equilibrium with homogeneous labour? Borjas's contention is that, using a standard Cobb-Douglas[17] production function that calculates the likely output of the deployment of capital and labour, we can see that the economic gain from the increase in available labour will never be more than negligible.[18] In the case of the United States, the immigration surplus in recent years has been around 0.24 per cent of GDP—which means that 'in 2013 the entire stock of foreign-born persons in the United States added around $35 billion to the fruits accruing to natives in a $15 trillion economy'.[19] Though this result is an extrapolation from a formal model rather than an empirical finding, Borjas's point is that it is not possible *in principle* to do much better: 'It is mathematically impossible to manipulate the canonical model of the competitive labor market so as to yield a high net gain from immigration to the United States, even after immigration has increased the labour supply by 15 percent.'[20] Try though we might to modify the assumptions of the model, and to add the complexity implicit in simulations that take into account the heterogeneity of labour, or the different elasticities of the supply of capital, the immigration surplus remains small. Thus, Borjas concludes that the implications of the homogeneous labour model hold as a reliable generalisation: 'The net gains from immigration (and *even* from high-skill immigration) to an economy as large as the United States cannot be numerically substantial, *as long as* the analysis remains within the confines of the canonical model of a competitive labour market.'[21]

Borjas is also sceptical about the claims that the free movement of labour would result in very substantial gains in wealth and income across the globe and would make significant inroads into the problem of world poverty. On this occasion, he does not doubt that in principle a removal of restrictions on migration that resulted in the flow of workers from low-wage to high-wage regions would lead to a large global immigration surplus.[22] Indeed, his own calculations showed the possibility, in principle, of a 28.1-trillion-dollar increase in global GDP in 2013 were the world's borders open—even after the moving costs of migrant workers were taken into consideration.[23] He further notes that such gains 'would accrue *each year* after the restrictions were removed', so that in less than a generation the accumulated gains in global wealth could near a quadrillion dollars.[24] Nevertheless, Borjas remains sceptical about claims regarding the likely magnitude of gains from the removal of immigration restrictions because the assumptions underlying such calculations are suspect, and unrecognized or unacknowledged by open-border advocates.[25] Crucially, proponents of free movement fail to notice the significance of the number of people who would have to move for such gains to be made. For the trillions of dollars in gains they foresee, literally billions of people would have to move. For the estimated 28.1-trillion-dollar gain, approximately 2.6 billion workers (or 5.6 billion people if family dependents were included) would have to migrate from the poor global south to the wealthy global north.[26]

In the end, Borjas is critical of the claims of those predicting substantial economic gains from the elimination of immigration barriers for two main reasons. First, the possibility of enormous global economic gains is undercut by the sheer unlikelihood of significant numbers of people moving. In the end, 'large wage differences across regions can persist for a very long time simply because *many people choose not to move*'.[27] People stay put because the costs of moving are often high, both financially and psychically. 'For example, if the entire developed world were to allow immigration at *triple* the current rate in the United States, *it would still take 500 years for all the movers to move*.'[28] Second, Borjas thinks that it is highly unlikely that very high levels of immigration will not reduce the advantages that the high-productivity countries enjoy and which attract immigrants in the first place. Immigrants bring with them cultural attitudes that will lead to institutional transformation. Should this, for example, cut the productive advantage of the global north by, say, half, the 28.1-trillion-dollar windfall would turn into a trillion-dollar loss.[29] While there is no way to be certain of what would be the effect of mass movement on productivity, the advocates have taken the rosy view by assuming that productivity levels in the immigrant-receiving countries would remain the same.

As a leading figure in immigration economics, Borjas commands respect, and his work is widely cited not only by popular advocates of immigration control but also by academic scholars, who acknowledge the thoroughness and sophistication of his research. Nonetheless, it is not clear that Borjas's analysis can withstand critical scrutiny, or that his most important conclusions serve the cause of immigration restriction.[30] We should consider this matter more closely, beginning with his conclusions about the aggregate effects of mass immigration, before turning to his views about the distributional and institutional implications in the sections of this chapter that follow.

One thing that should be noted at the very outset, however, is that nothing in Borjas's work calls for—or implies any great economic aggregate advantage is to be gained by—the reduction of immigration or that any great aggregate loss is likely to be incurred by an increase. In this regard, his conclusions are broadly in line with the general thrust of the literature of economics. Evidence pointing to losses endured by immigrant-welcoming societies suggests, at worst, modest losses overall, while evidence pointing to gains suggests only modest gains. Borjas himself thinks that, at least in the United States, 'the economic impact of immigration, *on average*, is at best a wash'.[31] This is important because, while it brings into question the claims of those who see massive economic gains coming from immigration, it also undercuts the arguments of those who think immigration brings with it significant economic losses. On the evidence considered by one of the leading labour economists of this generation—one who is generally critical of arguments for greater freedom of movement—the case for immigration control cannot rest on claims about its aggregate economic advantages, domestically or globally.

This point is doubly reinforced, however, by a closer examination of Borjas's analysis, which itself makes very particular, and in some cases, questionable, assumptions about the terms under which the aggregate economic impact of immigration should be measured.

Let us begin with the claim that the global benefits of immigration have been exaggerated. One of the reasons for this, Borjas maintains, is that economists have failed to acknowledge how much global gains depend on the movement of large numbers—literally billions—of people, both as workers and as their dependents, when such a development is wildly improbable. Now, if massive immigration flows are indeed so improbable, it would be odd to put a strong case for restricting immigration. Indeed, if people are so unlikely to move, what would be the point of creating large expensive bureaucracies and building walls to prevent them from doing so? Most immigration sceptics tend to think that the challenge is to find ways of reducing immigration when too many want to move.

The problem with making any judgment about the likelihood of high or low immigration in the wake of a reduction of barriers to movement is that preferences for movement are themselves shaped and further complicated by the degree to which immigration is restricted, and by the forms those restrictions take. For example, if some barriers were removed such that potential workers with job offers could enter a country freely, but spouses without current job offers could not (or could not seek work on entering), there might be a significant influx of seasonal workers who would gladly come to work for four months in the year, but a limited movement of families. If a job offer were not a condition of entry, more might move as families, but many might still opt for seasonal work so that family life is not disrupted. Were movement freer still, even more might opt to work as transients or sojourners rather than as immigrants. Survey evidence suggests that there remains in the world a substantial demand for immigration—particularly from poorer to richer parts of the world.[32] There are hundreds of millions of people who would like to immigrate, and most of them want a life in the developed west; though Borjas is surely right to suggest that, were all immigration barriers removed overnight we would not see the billions looking to move that some immigration sceptics fear.[33]

Those who move, on the whole, improve their own economic circumstances, raise the overall economic wellbeing of the receiving society, and contribute to the rise in global income and wealth (including that of the societies from which they emigrated). Nothing that Borjas writes contradicts this. The debate in this instance is only about the *magnitude* of the economic gains from labour mobility. Are those gains as small as Borjas suggests? The answer to this question turns on the assumptions one makes about the impact immigration has on productivity and growth. If one assumes, as Borjas does, that returns to scale are constant rather than increasing, that technology is fixed rather than responsive and evolving, that capital supplies are inelastic, and that immigrant workers are more or less interchangeable with natives, then it does indeed become very difficult, if not impossible, to imagine anything but very limited gains from an increase in the size of the labour force. The first and last of these assumptions in particular should be brought into question.

The assumption of constant returns to scale is one that dominated economic theory from the early nineteenth century (shaped in good measure
by the trade theory developed by David Ricardo) well into the twentieth.
Despite the fact that the classical model of economic growth developed
by Adam Smith in *The Wealth of Nations* implicitly relied upon a model of
increasing returns in asserting that the gains from trade were due in part to
the specialization made possible by the expansion of the exchange nexus—by
the size of the market[34]—it took until the 1980s and 90s for the 'return of
increasing returns'.[35] Since then, however, growth theory has been dominated by models that consider the effects of human capital externalities, the
diversity of skills, specialization, market integration, and the gains from a
rising number of scientists and engineers—thus allowing for the possibility
of increasing returns to scale.[36] Much recent work on immigration economics also takes increasing returns into account. Borjas is perfectly correct
to say that within the canonical model of a competitive labour market no
significant gains from immigration are achievable; but the problem here
lies with the use of this model, which is incapable of taking account the
many ways in which there can be gains from exchange. One thing it under-
appreciates is the gains from specialization that is the result of an increase
in the size of the labour force. Such gains are the product of the increase in
the extent of the market. Even immigrant labour that is merely a *substitute*[37]
for native labour has the capacity to extend the market, at the very least by
adding more producers and consumers, but also by shifting resources from
non-market to market employment (if only, for example, by some people
working harder!).[38]

Exactly to what extent immigration adds to economic growth is difficult
to determine with precision and the empirical evidence brought to bear
on this question suggests that assessments vary. On the whole, however,
the economic consequences of immigration are benign, both for receiving
societies and the world generally, if growth is desirable and the measure is
the increase in total wealth and income. This is even more clearly the case
if one adopts the Solow model, which is the canonical model for assessing
economic growth.[39] This is not to say, however, that the effects are uniformly
positive—people move for a variety of reasons, and not always in the right
direction from the point of view of an economist.[40] Nor does everyone necessarily gain from a rise in economic growth—a point that Borjas has been at
pains to emphasize. We should turn, then, to the matter of the distributional
consequences of immigration.

## DISTRIBUTIVE CONCERNS

The people who most clearly gain from immigration are the immigrants themselves. Provided they can do so voluntarily (and are not trafficked and enslaved), people move because it is to their advantage—though, to be sure, things can turn out badly for some. The gains enjoyed by the poor who move from the less prosperous parts of the world to the wealthier countries are especially notable, since they usually not only mean improvements in the living standards of the immigrants themselves but also lead to increases in income for many who receive remittances from friends and relatives now living and working abroad. An important distributive consequence of immigration can be an increase in the wealth and income of the poorer parts of the world relative to the richer. This does not mean that there must be a *transfer* of wealth or income from the global rich to the global poor. To the extent that immigrants improve their standards of living through work or trade, they acquire their wealth through exchange and therefore leave their employers or customers better off. The remittances they send home do not diminish the wealth of the countries to which they have moved compared to what that wealth might have been had they never moved. Immigration might change the balance of global wealth and income, but only because the gains to the global poor are greater, relatively speaking, than those enjoyed by the global rich. Viewed in this light, the distributive consequences of immigration look entirely benign—at least, insofar as the reduction of global poverty and the movement towards global equality are considered to be highly desirable outcomes.

But there is more to the distributive question than this. While both parties must gain in any voluntary economic exchange, third parties need not. Many critics of immigration are sceptical of its value (even if only to some degree) because the gains enjoyed by some come at the expense of others—and indeed others they consider to have (ethically) better claims to enjoy the benefits of economic exchange than immigrants. The case for restricting immigration, for critics like George Borjas, is that most of the gains from immigration are captured by immigrants, their employers and the wealthy more generally, to the disadvantage of natives who compete unsuccessfully in the labour market and enjoy a negligible share of the benefits immigration might bring to society as a whole.

Borjas is not the only critic of immigration to have voiced this concern. Stephen Macedo considers this to be one of the dilemmas facing US immigration policy: high levels of immigration by poor and low-skilled workers from Mexico and elsewhere in Central America and the Caribbean may worsen the standing of poorer American citizens.[41] Paul Krugman expresses a similar concern, noting that poor Mexicans coming to the United States drive down the wages of the American poor but add little to national wealth or income.[42] Conservatives and progressives, liberals and socialists, and nationalists of all stripes have seen merit in the complaint that, whatever good it might bring (and not all are agreed that it does), immigration harms the native poor—most noticeably when immigrants outcompete natives in the labour market. There is a broad consensus among economists that immigrants may sometimes have a negative impact *to some degree* on native wages and on native employment.[43] What is less certain is the extent of that impact. In the United Kingdom, the evidence suggests no discernible overall effect on native wages or employment.[44] Borjas finds the impact upon both wages and employment in the American case to be more significant than do others, with the differences resting ultimately upon disputes about methodologies for calculating numerical values.

All that said, there is clearly very little evidence of a dramatic overall decline in native wages or employment because of immigration. According to the most recent major study in the United States, wages declined as a result of the current stock of immigrant labour (about 16.5 per cent of the population) by about 5.2 per cent, while generating an immigration surplus of about 54.2 billion dollars and so increasing overall national income by about 0.31 per cent.[45] The distributional fallout, from the natives' perspective, has an impact in two different ways. First, it means a decline in the wages of two kinds of groups: the previous generation of immigrants, and natives with comparably low skills or educational attainments (for the most part, high-school dropouts). Second, it could mean (as suggested by the US case), a substantial transfer of wealth or income from labour to capital. Though the percentages here are small, these distributional consequences are matters of serious concern in the eyes of economists like Borjas, as well as to immigration sceptics more generally. We should therefore look more closely at these concerns.

Let us turn first to the claim, made most clearly by Borjas, that the gains from immigration tend to be captured by the immigrants themselves, and that a very small share of it goes to the native population. In *We Wanted Workers*, Borjas points out that in the United States in 2015, in an 18-trillion-dollar economy, the immigrant share of the workforce (16.3 per cent) did indeed generate a 2.1-trillion-dollar increase in GDP. However, he argues, 'the immigrants themselves get paid about 98 percent of this increase'.[46] Very little of the gain, he continues, 'trickles down to natives'.[47] This is also Peter Brimelow's complaint, as noted earlier.

What is ignored in this analysis, however, is the gains enjoyed by those who bought and consumed the goods or services produced by those immigrants. It is entirely unremarkable that immigrants should gain substantially in expending their labour—why else would they work? Yet it is no less obvious that those for whom these immigrants labour gain more from the exchange than they forgo—why else would they buy? The 'consumer surplus' is by far the greater indicator of the gains enjoyed by natives.[48] (In everyday terms, Borjas's claim seems to be that if an immigrant is paid fifty dollars for mowing my lawn and fifty dollars is therefore added to GDP, there is no gain to natives because all of that fifty-dollar increase is going to the immigrant in wages. But I've had my lawn mowed, and to me that was worth more than fifty dollars—making me a happier and richer native.) It would be difficult to imagine a situation in which immigrants truly captured nearly all the gains from exchange—unless they were simply forbidden to work and lived on charity—just as it would be hard to find a situation in which they did not enjoy a substantial return for their labour—unless they were slaves. The idea that immigrants capture most of the gains from the wealth they generate is not a significant concern because it is simply untrue.

Let us turn, then, to the question of the impact of immigration on wages and employment among low-skilled or less educated natives. Even if the empirical evidence suggests that immigrants have little or no impact on wages, this may be because, thanks to the existence of immigration restrictions, most immigrants move only in response to existing demand for labour rather than for exogenous reasons. Consequently, they do not shift the supply curve outwards and thereby reduce real wages—except in the very short term. However, in a world with fewer or no immigration restrictions, it would be possible for free movement to have an exogenous impact on the supply of labour, increasing the number of available workers and therefore reducing real wages for natives in the short to medium term. Surely this should be a matter of greater concern?

The best way to consider this concern is probably to look at it under the aspect of John Rawls's Difference Principle, which is a part of the second of his two principles of justice.[49] In Rawls's view, provided the commitment to protect the basic liberties continues to be given priority, a just society ought to arrange its institutions to improve the conditions of its least advantaged members. A just society is one in which the least advantaged socio-economic

TABLE 5. Rawls's Difference Principle and the Best Society for the Least Advantaged

| Society | Least advantaged | Better advantaged | Most advantaged |
| --- | --- | --- | --- |
| A | 10,000 | 10,000 | 10,000 |
| B | 12,000 | 60,000 | 90,000 |
| C | 30,000 | 50,000 | 100,000 |
| D | 25,000 | 100,000 | 500,000 |

group or class is as well off as is possible without infringing the basic liberties of anyone. Imagine, then, the hypothetical distributive alternatives in table 5 (the numbers identifying annual money-income in dollars or pounds or euros or rupees).

According to the Rawlsian view, Society C is what we should aim for. From this point of view, there would be good reason to move from Society A to Society B; even better reason to move from Society B to Society C; but no justification for moving from Society C to Society D. Our concern should be the economic wellbeing of the poorest or least advantaged in our society, and our aim should be to raise that to as high a level as possible, even if it means significantly reducing the economic wellbeing of the better advantaged or the most advantaged. The question now is whether this view of what is ethically defensible in assessing the economic justice of a society can supply us with some guidance in thinking about what to do about the impact of immigration on the employment and wage prospects of native workers.[50]

Although Rawls's view has not passed without criticism, let us take it as given that this interpretation of the Difference Principle describes a desirable outcome from the perspective of economic justice. Does this give us sufficient reason to think that economic policy should aim to raise the wages of the least advantaged natives, and that immigration control is the appropriate measure for achieving this end?

We should note at the outset that a not insignificant problem that needs to be addressed is exactly what is meant by 'natives'. This is, as we have already seen in chapter 2, a complex question. A native could be defined as someone not foreign-born, or as a non-foreign-born citizen, or as a citizen (foreign-born or naturalized), or as a legally permanent resident. In some understandings of the term native, every immigrant is a potential future native; in others no immigrant could ever become a native, even if he or she becomes a naturalized citizen. In the UK, a British citizen who has resided abroad for more than a year and returns the live in Britain is both a native by virtue of citizenship and an immigrant in the statistical measures used to calculate net migration rates. If the point is to protect the wages of the least well-paid natives, it matters who counts as a native.[51] (It might also matter whether we count households resulting from intermarriage between natives and immigrants as one or the other.[52]) But leaving these complexities aside, it is not clear that a concern for the least advantaged natives is well served by immigration controls whose purpose (if only in part) is to raise poor native wages.

First, a general reduction in immigration numbers, whether achieved by a lowering of net migration targets or further restriction on eligibility to work, may do little to improve the conditions of the least advantaged natives if it results in a decline in the number of immigrants whose labour is *complementary to* rather than a *substitute for* native labour. Natives harmed would include those whose employers are firms that depend upon skilled foreign workers or face domestic shortages of skilled labour.

Second, it cannot be assumed that a general reduction of labour supply will lead to a rise in wages in all industries—since the ability of firms to compete with others will depend on their overall costs, the availability of substitutes for their products, and the attractiveness of mechanisation as a substitute for labour, among other factors. In the end, what will be decisive is the individual worker's marginal productivity, and a mere reduction in the supply of labour will do little or nothing to affect that. Indeed, a reduction in the labour supply may in some circumstances reduce native income and employment.[53]

Third, and consequently, to the extent that a reduction of the labour supply does lead to a rise in wages, there is no reason to think that the least skilled natives will benefit unless they possess the skills or proclivities to take on the work that becomes available. A frequently cited example here is the case of agricultural labour in the United States, which relies substantially on Mexican workers. Though the work of crop-picking is not highly skilled, it is difficult to attract 'natives' to apply for these jobs, and harder still to find natives who are willing to stay the course, since the work is physically demanding. There may be a number of reasons for this. Even at higher wages, the opportunity costs for natives considering such jobs may just be too high. The seasonal nature of the work is a further disincentive, since it might take time away from job searching while offering inadequate reward or security. An absence of cheap labour from Mexico might raise agricultural wages in the United States, but still not sufficiently to attract native labour because farms too have to keep their costs down in order to compete with other producers, both domestic and foreign.

A similar example can be drawn from the United Kingdom, where the price of agricultural labour has fallen because of the influx of eastern European workers able to move freely within the European Union. The post-Brexit withdrawal of those workers might see a rise in native agricultural wages, but not beyond the point at which those farming enterprises cease to be competitive in a global market for agricultural produce. It remains to be seen whether the loss of European workers results in higher wages for UK farm workers, or in greater mechanization, or in a decline in agricultural enterprises as industries relocate to other countries, or close altogether.

Now, it could be argued here that the elimination of low-paid labour is itself a desirable goal. The move towards a high-wage-high-productivity economy might be an appropriate goal of government policy. Mark Krikorian puts the point in his analysis of the impact of mass immigration on innovation.[54] The superabundance of cheap labour, he argues, harms the future competitiveness of industries where immigrants are most heavily concentrated because it discourages those industries from making efforts to increase the productivity of labour. Capital will only be substituted for labour when the price of labour rises, and mass immigration makes this unnecessary and thus less likely to happen. At the extreme, we might see the 'de-adoption' of labour-saving technology—for example, as factories stop using automation technology when immigration drives down the price of labour. What we see here, Krikorian observes, is a pure example 'of the conflict between mass immigration and the goals of a modern society'.[55] To put the point more sharply, he quips: 'Without a change in [U.S.] immigration policy, we run the risk of future observers noting that "Japan got robots while America got Mexicans".'[56]

Though the analysis here, as far as it goes, appears plausible, the evidence suggests otherwise. Immigration, on the whole, boosts rather than slows innovation.[57] Indeed, the more diverse the immigrant population the higher the rates of innovation—though this observation has to be qualified by considering differences across sectors (manufacturing, service) and between high- and low-skill immigrants.[58] At the very least, however, the evidence cautions against seeing immigration as generally likely to work against innovation.

The larger question still remains: is immigration control a good, leave aside the best, way of addressing the interests of the least advantaged? The availability of cheap labour will undoubtedly lead employers sometimes to consider declining innovative alternatives, just as rising labour costs will surely provoke them to cast about for less expensive substitutes. But it is hard to see why it is in the immediate interest of native workers that immigrant labour be replaced by new technologies—particularly if such technologies eliminate low-wage labour generally, thus harming immigrants and natives alike.

Nor is it evident that immigrant labour cannot also create its own paths to innovation and higher productivity. If we return to the analysis offered by James Buchanan of the sources of increasing returns to scale, the key insight is that the growth in productivity comes from the expansion of the market, which brings with it the greater possibility of specialization, and in that process, innovation. In this regard, the Japanese strategy of building robots instead of importing immigrants may help explain why by 2015 it had endured two decades of little to no economic growth.[59] Japan's policies of strict limits to immigration and the importation of foreign labour have, in combination with such other factors as an ageing population, led to a shrinking workforce and shortages of labour not only in high-skill industries but also in lower-paid service professions, including childcare. The shortage of these workers has had the further effect of reducing the participation of professional women in the workforce, contributing to further losses in economic productivity. But more than this, many have argued that the low level of immigration has also deprived Japan of the entrepreneurial drive that immigrants bring.[60] None of this is to suggest that immigration is a panacea for all labour market ills, or that single country experiences are sufficient for making reliable broader generalizations. It does, however, show that limiting or restricting immigration is not certain, or even especially likely, to spur innovation and productivity growth. Recognizing this may be why in 2018 Japan's government decided to drastically revise its immigration policy to allow more foreign workers into the country[61]—and why, even before that, it had begun to increase immigration surreptitiously.[62]

To return to the more general point of this discussion, if the concern in question is the wellbeing of the least advantaged in society, immigration control is an uncertain, indeed clumsy, tool with which to address the problem. While immigration restrictions will undoubtedly bring benefits to some, they will also no less certainly harm others among the worst off in society. Even a more carefully tailored immigration policy designed to meet particular economic needs while protecting sectors of the native population may not be able to avoid the pitfalls that accompany a more general strategy of limiting immigrant numbers. A part of the reason for this is that, as Borjas himself has emphasized, immigrants are people and not just factors of production—and they will not be controlled entirely. They will have their own goals and aspirations; but these will also change in response to economic conditions, personal and political circumstances, and chance encounters with people or opportunities that cannot be predicted. The same holds for natives, whose own circumstances and preferences may change in unexpected ways.

The question to which this brings us is how to think about the nature of an economy (or more to the point, a society), and the labour market that is one of its elements. To borrow an analogy from David Brooks,[63] a society is less like a lake with fixed boundaries than a river. It's a mistake to think of it as a body of water that can be closed off so that no more fish enter, leaving more food for the fish already there. A river might be running high or running low, and its course, along with the volume and flow of water, is likely to vary with the circumstances. Interventions to shape its effects might distort that course, but those effects too will vary. Thus, an intervention to reduce the number of workers entering a country does not affect everyone uniformly by simply raising wages across the entire lake or pool of labour but leads to shortages in some areas even as others experience a glut.[64] Proposals simply to reduce the volume of immigration in the interests of native workers might help some workers but also harm others. Proposals to manage the labour flow run up against the problem that demand is unpredictable, shaped as it is by not just by a variety of domestic factors but by the push and pull of economic and political forces well beyond a country's borders.

Here it ought to be noted that one very important reason why immigrant labour is more likely to flow to where there is demand is that immigrants are, by their very nature, more mobile than natives. Having left their countries in search of work, they move unencumbered by such burdens as mortgages, spouses with employment commitments, children in school, and welfare entitlements that might afford them the opportunity to search for jobs only in specific areas. Natives may not be able to move so readily across the country to where employment—or higher-waged work—is available. And indeed, the evidence indicates that recent immigrants are more likely to move, while older immigrants are less mobile.[65]

But what then of those who are the 'victims' of competition from immigrant labour? In the American case, these tend to be predominantly a class of people with low educational attainments—high-school dropouts, to simplify matters. Borjas is right to say that 'the economic, social, and political consequences of pursuing policies that harm the most disadvantaged Americans are ignored at our peril', and that it is 'short-sighted to dismiss the wage effect of immigration on low-skill workers by arguing that few workers are affected in this fashion'.[66] Nonetheless, this does not imply that controlling immigration is the best, or even a particularly good, way of addressing the issue. For one thing, it would be odd to single out categories of people on the basis of how they are affected by some particular economic phenomenon in order to justify addressing their plights. Some people would have done better had we not removed certain import tariffs, others would have done better had we not reduced defence spending, yet others would have fared better had we not imposed environmental regulations. Particularly when the groups affected are small, it would be odd to make policy hostage to their interests, even if those interests ought to be considered and addressed.[67] A more sensible alternative would be to find ways to compensate those who might lose out when changes that are generally advantageous leave them behind. In the end, there is nothing special about immigration as a source of harm to some, and while social policy should address the condition of the least advantaged, its concern should be all disadvantaged, and the remedies it proposes not of a form that causes significant harms to others. In this regard, what some economists call 'keyhole solutions'[68] might be a better bet than a more sweeping policy of restricting immigration. This suggestion acquires even greater force to the extent that immigration control might actually exacerbate rather than remedy the social problems in question.

All that said, however, there remains the broader concern that immigration has a deleterious effect on society by contributing to—perhaps even dramatically increasing the extent of—the general level of *inequality*. This is perhaps the worry implicit in Borjas's charge that the most significant consequence of immigration is the wealth transfer that ensues, from workers to firms, or from labour to capital. Borjas makes this argument with respect to global equality as well as domestic equality within the developed west (and the United States in particular). A move towards a world of open borders would ultimately bring about a world in which '*wages are equalized:* workers who initially have high wages end up earning less, and workers who initially have low wages end up earning more'.[69] He estimates that that the earnings of the wealthy north's workforce would drop by about 40 per cent, while workers from the poorer south would more than double. More significantly, he notes, 'the income of capitalists worldwide will increase almost 60 percent'.[70] Open borders, in short, create very large gains for southern workers and capitalists, but 'Northern workers simply do not benefit from the New World Order'.[71] Within the United States, in the current world of controlled borders but significant immigration, Borjas argues, the 5.2 per cent reduction in native wages estimated by the National Academy of Sciences report on immigration translates into a wealth transfer of about half a trillion dollars from native workers to firms.[72]

The questions we have to ask here are what all this means, and whether we should be concerned. Let us begin by taking a close look at the claims Borjas advances, to get a more precise understanding of their meaning. First, there is the claim that after wages are equalized (in the borderless world to come), workers who initially have high wages end up earning less, while those who initially have low wages end up earning more. What needs clarifying here is what is to be understood by 'earning less' and 'earning more'. Assuming that the equalization of wages takes time—indeed, a considerable amount of time since, as Borjas noted earlier, there is a limit to the pace at which migration can move even when barriers to movement are removed—it is unlikely that the wages in question that fall are the actual, absolute, wages of workers now as viewed, say, a generation into the future. Not only will many people have changed jobs, or retired from the workforce, but many jobs themselves will have disappeared, to be replaced by new types of employment. Nonetheless, it is perfectly possible that many actual jobs remain more or less what they were and simply attract a lower wage (and find takers because the remaining alternatives are even less attractive), particularly if a country (or a world economy) has sunk into depression and economic stagnation for a generation.

A more likely story, however, which is surely what Borjas is driving at, is that the *general wage level* will fall in the countries of the developed north. This is certainly possible and has happened with wage levels throughout human history. In recent times, in the United States for example, wage levels have fallen for a variety of reasons, but the underlying reason has sometimes been a rise in the supply of labour relative to the level of demand. Between 1970 and 1980 the general wage level fell as the United States saw a 30 per cent increase in the size of the labour force. Since 1979, according to some analyses, American wage levels have been stagnant,[73] though that general statement masks rises and falls in the course of those four decades as well as differences within different percentiles of the wage range—since incomes have risen for the top ten per cent and fallen for those that the bottom end of the scale. A substantial increase in the size of the labour force as a result of an upsurge of immigration could well bring about a fall in the general wage level. Is this a matter about which we should be concerned—and concerned sufficiently to address it through immigration policy?

For a fall in the general wage level to be a matter of concern that demands addressing through immigration control the following would have to be true. First, a fall in the wage level would have to be harmful to society generally, and to the most vulnerable members of society in particular. Second, it would have to be possible to raise the general wage level without causing further harm. Third, immigration control would have to be the best way, or at least a vital part of any effort, to alleviate the problem of falling wage levels. None of these is necessarily or always—or even generally—true. Let us consider these matters in turn.

First, a fall in the general level of wages can without doubt harm some people—most notably, those who suffer a loss of income without offsetting compensations. But there are many other things to consider before concluding that this is harmful to society more generally, or even to the least advantaged. One of the most significant causes of falls in wage levels in the twentieth century was the entry of women into the workforce. In the 1970s, for example, female participation in the labour market in the United States rose from 42 to 52 per cent which, combined with the postwar baby boom, saw the labour force increase by 30 per cent in a decade and real hourly earnings fall by 2.3 per cent.[74] While a decline of this sort is not inconsequential, it need not mean a loss for the most vulnerable in society. The opportunity to enter the labour force was clearly a benefit to many women for a variety of reasons, including economic ones. For others, the additional earnings brought in by a second job-holder (whether part- or full-time) would have lifted total family income and perhaps improved the wellbeing of some of the least advantaged. The entry of more women into the workforce would also have meant more talent and enterprise to expand the size of the market and made possible further gains from specialization and the division of labour.[75]

Whether or not a decline in the general wage level is desirable also depends significantly on economic circumstances and the broader conditions causing wages to fall. Indeed, falling wages may reflect a flexibility in the labour market that operates to limit unemployment and to make it possible for firms to survive in unfavourable economic circumstances. One modern historical illustration is worth considering. This is the history of reforms carried out by the Australian Labor governments in the 1980s to address the deteriorating economic conditions brought about, in part, by rigidities in the labour market. While the reforms were successful, the short-term consequence was a significant decline in the general level of real wages, which lowered living standards for many even as it strengthened the long-term national and international competitiveness of Australian firms.[76] Too high a general wage level may be a disadvantage, just as a low or declining wage level would erode earnings for many even as it makes firms more robust and perhaps reduces unemployment.

This returns us to the second issue: whether it is possible to raise the general wage level without causing (too much) harm. In this case, it would surely depend on the circumstances and the measures taken. Removing unneeded regulatory obstacles, eradicating privileges for favoured interests, and generally taking steps to improve the efficiency of an economy, might raise wages by increasing the productivity of labour. But it is not clear that measures taken simply to raise wages will be successful, or that they will not result in unwanted side-effects. Engineering a reduction in the supply of labour might raise the general wage level, but at the cost of job losses in industries that cut back on production for a lack of workers, or the elimination of some industries altogether, or an increase in the volume of illegal or black-market activity.

We come, then, to the third question—whether immigration management is a good way of trying to control the labour supply and lift wages. Once again, it is not obvious that a reduction in immigration would prove a successful strategy for achieving even such a limited goal. Consider the current concerns about wage stagnation in the United States over the past generation. Among the most significant factors accounting for this is the dramatic expansion of Chinese manufacturing—including in the production of high-quality industrial goods.[77] Though there has been no absolute decline in the volume of American manufacturing, the world has seen a substantial rise in the quantity of products brought to market. Regardless of where they are produced, an increase in the supply of goods will exert downward pressure on the prices of similar manufactures or their substitutes, eat into the profit margins of competing firms, and lower the demand for labour whose productivity has not risen to meet the challenge. A reduction in immigration to a country whose firms are challenged by cheap manufactures worldwide may do little or nothing to boost wages. Unless the productivity of labour increases, there might be little point in firms raising wages—particularly in the face of competitive pressure to further reduce prices. Indeed, rising production costs fuelled by an increase in the price of labour might have other adverse consequences—in the case of the United States, either encouraging American firms to relocate abroad, or discouraging other firms from starting up in or moving to America.

To put the same point in another way, how would it be different if, instead of moving, would-be immigrants stayed at home but managed nonetheless to improve dramatically their own labour productivity, drawing on the resources of the world? Their wages would rise as they produced more. If they sold their wares on the international market because they produced goods in demand, they would reduce the demand for the same goods in northern, former immigrant-destination, countries. That would lower the wages of people in northern firms. What is doing the work of reducing some wages and increasing others is not the moving but the rising productivity of some labour. If so, the only way to keep northern wages high would be to prevent southern workers from improving their own productivity and supplying the world's markets with their own goods. This might be accomplished by erecting higher tariff barriers, subsidizing domestic industries, or using other measures to restrict trade; but the negative consequences of a trade war might be too high a price to pay for the very limited wage gains to some workers resulting from controls to reduce immigration.

What, however, of Borjas's contention that increased immigration brings with it a transfer of wealth from labour to capital? Recall that the two claims are that there would be a gain from mass migration to southern workers and to capitalists generally, and that there would be a loss to northern workers. Within the United States, he said, native workers have already in effect written a cheque for half a trillion dollars to their employers—such have been the gains to American capital. Can this really be the case? And if it can (or has been), should it be a cause for alarm?

To answer the first of these two questions, we need to look more closely at the exact nature of the claim. By a transfer[78] of wealth or (a share of) income Borjas could mean that one distinct group of people suffer a loss of wealth or income as individuals while another group, as a consequence, enjoys a comparable increase in their individual economic gains. Such statements as the following suggest this. Borjas writes: 'Those who compete with immigrants are effectively sending billions and billions of dollars annually to those who use immigrants.'[79] He also says: 'yes, immigrants created an additional $54 billion worth of new wealth, but a by-product of that creation was a *wealth transfer* of half a trillion dollars' (emphasis added).[80] Yet it cannot be that some people are literally transferring their money to others—voluntarily or otherwise—over and above the exchanges involved in the buying and selling of labour, since each individual worker, from year to year, simply experiences an increase or decrease in income depending on the hours worked and the wages offered. There is no other 'transfer' involved, any more than a shopkeeper who loses market share to a new competitor could say that there was a 'transfer' of income from him to his rival. It might be fine to say that there is a transfer in some metaphorical or figurative sense; but the terminology is misleading—if not entirely tendentious—insofar as it suggests that there is something ethically questionable happening.

Borjas could, on the other hand, mean by the transfer of wealth or income simply that, as a consequence of immigration, there has been or would be a change in the balance of the returns accruing to different factors of production—labour and capital. If this is what he means, it is odd to speak of it as a 'transfer'—again, unless the term is used purely figuratively. At any given time where will be some balance between the returns to capital and the returns to labour, and that balance would surely shift between any two time periods selected for comparison. Even to speak in these terms, however, is misleading. *Labour* and *capital* have no natural existence. These terms are purely heuristic devices whose purpose is to address certain abstract and theoretical questions of economics.[81]

This brings us, then, to the question of why it should matter if there were such a shift or 'transfer'. One reason might be that such a change would imply a redistribution of income for consumption from the poor to the wealthy. This seems unlikely, but also untroubling, for a number of reasons. First, in the American case, the shift in the balance of returns from labour to capital in the order of half a trillion dollars does not look significant in the context of an 18-trillion-dollar economy. Second, it does not look like such a change is a shift from consumption by the poor to (more) consumption by the rich, since some part of what accrues to capital will be reinvested rather than consumed by shareholders spending their dividends.[82] Third, the strengthening of the position of firms, even if it comes about through a lowering of wages, has its advantages not only for the owners of capital but also for workers themselves. This is in part because financially robust firms are better able to endure and expand, but also because the most likely avenue through which workers' wages will rise (or employment be assured) in the longer term is the increase in the productivity of labour—which is a function in large part of the capital (whether in the form of technology or education and training, to identify just a couple of examples) to which labour has access. There is a trade-off to be made between (present) consumption and investment for (future) consumption. While it would make no sense to starve today to save for a feast one will never be able to enjoy, there is no obvious way to identify the correct balance to be struck.

The upshot of all this is that, while it may be true that immigration does have distributive consequences, it is not clear that these are entirely negative for natives. To the extent that they are negative, given the positive economic benefits of immigration, there is no reason to think that a concern for the least advantaged in society is best addressed by measures to control immigration. If there are economic reasons to control immigration, we shall have to look elsewhere.

## INSTITUTIONAL CONCERNS

Another prominent set of economic arguments in favour of immigration control centres on the worry that, despite whatever gains might come from flexible labour markets, and the ready availability of cheap as well as skilled labour, immigrants threaten to undermine the economic wellbeing of destination societies in more fundamental ways. Foreign entry to a society, on this view, should be restricted because too great an influx of outsiders might change or erode the traditions or practices that made the society prosperous in the first place. People from poor countries are poor often not because their countries lack resources but because their economic and political systems are ramshackle. But if they move to prosperous countries carrying attitudes or convictions that lead to the breakdown of the economic and political systems of their new societies, everyone loses. Democracies with generous welfare systems might be particularly vulnerable if large numbers of poor immigrants become voters and vote themselves more benefits. The golden goose is killed by foreigners pressuring it for more eggs. When the poor especially move to rich countries, what will be equalized is not just wages but institutions, as successful nations import from unsuccessful ones not only labour but also bad attitudes, bad ideas, and bad practices.[83]

A closer look at this issue requires an examination of several different aspects of the institutional anxiety. There are four main areas of concern: the fiscal impact of an influx of immigrants, the consequences for the provision of public goods and care for the environment, the effect on behavioural norms and the subsequent effects on economic life, and the potential transformation of legal and political institutions. We should consider these different worries in turn.

The fiscal issue arises because immigrants, however much they might bring with them the advantages of cheap or skilled labour, will also impose liabilities upon the societies in which they settle. Are immigrants liabilities or assets? Immigration may be costly because of the strain greater numbers place on public facilities, from beaches, parks, and public highways, to sewerage services and pollution controls. These effects may be exacerbated when such goods are publicly controlled and under-priced. But before we begin to discuss this, we have to address the question of how the costs are to be measured. When publicly owned facilities are under-priced (or not priced at all) it is very difficult to establish the value of the goods and services consumed by immigrants. But it is also difficult to work out the cost of immigration without determining how to calculate the value of returns to public assets. Should one consider the returns on the investments made by earlier generations (which exist in the form of roads, public buildings, police and fire stations, for example)? If such facilities were financed by earlier generations and the returns are now passed on to current taxpayers in the form of lower tax rates, all members of the present generation benefit. Immigrants coming into such an arrangement are then sharing in a boon that would otherwise have been available only to natives. On the other hand, one might regard these facilities as if they were financed by a bond issue repaid over the life of the building out of current tax revenue, which means that there is no intergenerational transfer reflected in the taxation levels. If so, immigrants paying tax would have to be regarded as contributors to the cost of construction. Which conceptual understanding should we adopt in trying to determine the costs and benefits of immigration? Indeed, what view should we take on the question of who receives the returns on earlier public investment: government employees, or politicians, or all current taxpayers, or some current taxpayers, or beneficiaries of the programmes? How these questions are answered will make an important difference to whether migrants are viewed as having a favourable or unfavourable effect on the rest of the populace with regard to any given facility.[84] Equally, of course, one would have to consider the extent to which migrants incur liabilities, say by acquiring an obligation to pay taxes needed to repay public debt.[85]

It should immediately be clear that making an overall judgment about whether immigrants are liabilities or assets depends on how one responds to questions whose answers must embody some kinds of normative judgment. In the end, the exercise might simply be not worth pursuing because any conclusion reached will be dependent on calculations resting on assumptions whose validity is not easy to establish and that are simply not widely shared. It may be for this reason that discussion of the fiscal implications of immigration has tended to centre on the impact of immigrants on current public expenditure.

Here, the objection to immigration (and the argument for immigration control) is that immigrants cost more in government expenditure than they contribute to tax revenues. Once again, however, the problem is how to measure the fiscal impact in question. There are two main accounting methods, but each has its weaknesses as well as its strengths.[86] The first is the *static accounting method*, under which the difference between immigrant taxes and other contributions (credits) and fiscal transfers to immigrants (debits) is calculated over a single fiscal year. The advantage of this method is its simplicity, but the drawback is that takes no account of longer-run considerations, including the effects of the life-cycles of immigrants, or indeed the indirect effects of immigrants on native wages and employment. The alternative to the static method is *dynamic modelling*, which takes into account the age profiles of immigrants as well as the impact of their descendants. But the two main forms of dynamic modelling—net transfer profile-based projections, and the generational accounting method—require making estimates about such things as fiscal policy, debt/GDP ratios, the real interest rate, the level of benefits paid to immigrants, taxes paid by immigrants, costs of education, the likelihood of return migration by immigrants and their descendants, as well as a host of other factors. Yet again, the answers to questions about the economic impact of immigration will depend on assumptions whose validity will be contested.

All this said, however, such measurement exercises have been carried out on numerous occasions. Unsurprisingly, in some accounts, immigration is shown to be slightly beneficial in fiscal terms, while in others it is shown to be slightly costly. The National Academies' Immigration Report discussed earlier found that in the short run immigrants imposed a fiscal burden on the United States but in the long run the conclusions were less clear because the answers depended on the assumptions adopted. George Borjas, in his reading of the National Academies' report on immigration, is candid about what implications can be drawn from this: *none*. 'Assumptions matter, and different assumptions lead to wildly different answers. . . . *All estimates of the long-run fiscal impact are useless!*'[87] If there is an economic argument to be made in favour of immigration control, it will not be one that leans heavily on an analysis of the fiscal impact of immigrants in destination societies.[88]

There is, however, a slightly different fiscal issue, which is the problem—not unusual in federal systems such as the United States—that the fiscal burden falls disproportionately on states or provinces rather than on the national government. While the central government might make gains through taxation, state and local governments end up footing the bills as the ones who are supplying the public services—from schools to hospitals to road repairs—whose costs cannot be covered by local taxation. This, however, might not suffice to establish a strong case against immigration rather than an argument for revising the burden sharing among government agencies and different governments more generally. This would be an ongoing issue regardless of the level of immigration, since demographic changes as well as internal population movements will necessitate a continual renegotiation of fiscal arrangements across any nation with multiple jurisdictions.

A different concern is not so much about the financial burdens immigrants impose as the pressures they exert on the rest of the population who are competing for the use of public goods. Here the issue is less such non-excludable goods as national defence (whose costs a larger population would actually help defray) than *congestible* goods such as housing, public services (from health to transport to schools) and public spaces, and welfare. Immigrants who settle in cities worsen overcrowded living conditions, while those who move to the less densely populated parts of the country contribute to urban sprawl and the erosion of the natural environment. For some critics, large-scale immigration works against the development of sensible population policies that are needed to address environmental concerns both at the national and the global level.

With regard to the issue of shortages in public services it is not evident that immigration *per se* is the problem—or that the matter would be resolved or made more tractable if immigration were reduced. If immigrants do not worsen the fiscal condition of the state, the tax revenues generated should be sufficient to fund the services needed. The issue here is one of management, though this is not to deny that in the short term an influx of people to a jurisdiction might create shortages and put pressure on facilities until supply is increased.

One particular concern that needs to be addressed directly is that immigrants strain the welfare resources of a society. Here the worry is not only that a sharp increase in immigration might put pressure on public welfare services but that the availability of welfare would inevitably draw in people looking to move in order to be able to live (or live better) off public funds. Milton Friedman famously pointed out that one could not have a welfare state and an open immigration policy—one or the other had to give.[89] The evidence, however, suggests that this concern is exaggerated for at least two reasons. The first is that it is inconsistent with the motivations of the vast majority of immigrants. Borjas is right to recognize the many disincentives to immigrate; but the implication of this has been that those who do decide to do so tend to be people who are young and enterprising and looking to work. This does not pose a serious fiscal problem—particularly in the long term. Second, there is no reason when accepting immigrants also to grant them eligibility for welfare services—and indeed, many states require a waiting period of several years before newly arrived immigrants are able to take advantage of certain public resources.[90]

While immigrant consumption of public resources is not a real concern, however, it cannot be denied that an increase in immigration will contribute to population growth, which will have an effect on both the rural and the urban landscape—and on the natural environment more generally. For some critics of immigration, it is population policy that is the issue. Mark Krikorian, for example, argues that mass migration (which he describes as the current policy of the American government), 'by artificially adding tens of millions of people to the population', undermines a number of objectives that citizens of the modern United States wish to pursue. These include 'less-dense living, environmental stewardship, and historic preservation'.[91] There is a trade-off to be made: 'either enjoy the modern, spacious, suburban, automobile-based lifestyle that most people aspire to, and kiss those environmental amenities good-bye, or on the other hand, preserve those amenities by living increasingly cramped, uncomfortable, primitive lives, with more and more draconian government regulation of behaviour'.[92]

A similar stance is taken by Philip Cafaro, who argues for a drastic reduction in immigration to the United States. Environmental stewardship, in his view, requires an end not only to world population growth but also the curtailing of mass migration. Krikorian worries that population growth will lead to a decline in American living standards as economic growth ceases to keep up with the rise in the number of people. Cafaro, however, is sceptical about growth and advances an ideal of a low-population low-growth green economy in which urban sprawl is reversed, more land is restored to its former condition as wilderness, consumption goes down, and the human footprint on the planet becomes smaller and less and less evident to the other creatures that inhabit it.[93] These views differ insofar as one wants to see a stable population so that economic growth will enable everyone to consume at least as much if not more, while the other wants a falling population as a part of a movement to change the way people live, but both see immigration control as the means to achieve this. Krikorian's pro-growth view rests on the claim that this is what the American people want, while Cafaro's anti-growth view is grounded in a view that only by reducing numbers can Americans engage in the kind of environmental stewardship that is morally required.[94]

A full consideration these two writers' stances would require a more extensive analysis of a broad range of economic and scientific claims made in their books, but the very contrast between their positions brings out a noteworthy difficulty with the environmental argument for immigration control.

Though Krikorian has asserted that the American public has expressed a preference for a particular kind of world and lifestyle, the Cafaro view offers evidence that there also exists a very different vision of the ideal world the country should be embracing. It does not look like too much can be claimed about the way in which people actually would prefer to live, since tastes vary considerably—and not just among critics of immigration. The history of urbanization shows a steady shift of the world's populations to cities (2008 being commonly acknowledged as the turning point by which more than half of humanity were city-dwellers), with migration one of the three drivers of change—the other two being natural increase and the re-classification of population centres.[95] Migration to cities is both internal and international.[96] It would not do to suggest that any of this shows that people prefer urban life, since the reasons for moving or staying put are too various—and many of our preferences are endogenous, reflecting our propensity to like better what we have grown accustomed to. Some might move to a city reluctantly to find employment, just as others cannot wait to get away from the tedium of small-town life. But there is nothing either to show that there is any great appetite to arrest the drift to the cities, or that cities will somehow cease to attract people for whom employment, as well as the range of goods and communities that urban agglomerations offer, make the opportunity cost of rural life too high to bear.

To the extent that environmentalists like Cafaro are concerned that the growth of the planet's human population is straining the carrying capacity of the earth, the argument for restricting immigration looks odd. As societies become wealthier, so do their birth-rates decline, and thus any movement of the poor to wealthy countries promises to reduce global populations as more people opt to have smaller families.[97] But here Cafaro offers an unusual argument for reducing immigration to the United States. The problem with the American way of life is that it is too wedded to consumption and bringing more people to the United States would have the negative consequence of adding to the number of high-level consumers in the world—thereby placing even greater strain on the planetary ecosystem. An unremarked-upon implication of this view is that, in the interests of ecological responsibility, it would be justifiable not only to restrict immigration but also to work to ensure that the poorest parts of the world do not see any appreciable rise in their standard of living—at least until global levels of consumption have been reduced, either by population decrease or a fall in levels of consumption in America, and the developed world more generally. Still, this argument might work (assuming one accepted the premises) if it could plausibly be accepted that America, and the world's richer countries generally, were ready to reduce their populations and also reduce their standards of living. However, if such reductions are in fact highly unlikely, it might be more sensible to increase immigration to the developed world as a way of reducing world population growth, so that even if there will be more heavy consumers, there will also be fewer consumers overall.[98]

A different kind of ecological concern raised by critics of immigration has to do less with the impact of (additional) humans on the natural world than with the consequences of bringing foreigners into the delicate socioeconomic environment that has enabled a society to survive and prosper. Here the argument is that immigration threatens to undermine, or at least diminish, a society by allowing its norms and traditions to be eroded as newcomers bring with them their own beliefs and practices, which suppress and eventually replace the successful ways of the host population.

For a closer look at this argument we should turn once again to Borjas, who raises it in *We Wanted Workers*. Drawing on the work of Acemoglu and Robinson that attempts to explain global inequality, he notes that some nations succeed while others fail because of differences in social and political institutions.[99] Like Paul Collier, whose work we will consider more closely in the next chapter, Borjas thinks that 'one reason poor countries are poor is that they are short of effective organizations', and that 'migrants are essentially escaping from countries with dysfunctional social models'.[100] If we are to see economic gains from immigration, both Borjas and Collier think, 'people must be able to move to the industrialised economies without importing the institutions, the dysfunctional social models, the political preferences, and the culture and norms that led to poor economic conditions in the sending countries in the first place'.[101] And indeed Borjas considers it 'inconceivable . . . that the North's institutional, social and political fabric would remain intact after the entry of billions of new persons'.[102] For this reason he maintains that: 'Advocating policy shifts that lead to massive migration flows or that rearrange the world order—such as the adoption of open borders—without being able to fully predict or even to understand the eventual impact of that rearrangement seems premature and irresponsible.'[103]

There are a number of problems with this analysis. Let us put to one side the inconsistency between the argument that open borders would lead to billions moving and disrupting destination societies and Borjas's earlier argument that billions are extremely unlikely to move. If people are so reluctant to immigrate, open borders would lead to no such movement and the problems imagined would never eventuate.[104] But perhaps the problem of institutional importation and corruption is likely even with much smaller numbers—with the movement of millions rather than billions. The problem here, however, is that there is no explanation as to why this is likely to prove damaging. It is certainly true that the fortunes of nations can decline—even precipitously, if we consider cases like Argentina, which was once of the most prosperous countries in the world at the start of the twentieth century but, through successive generations of misguided policies, turned into one of the poorest among the western democracies.[105] An influx of foreign workers is not necessary for economic decline. Nor is it sufficient. And just as there are no examples of economic decline resulting from mass migration, there are plenty of cases of countries prospering in the face of large-scale immigration.

A part of the reason for this may be that, with immigration in the past, the movement of people has been gradual enough that the destination society was able to absorb them without losing its own ethos. Institutions remained intact because immigrants were effectively forced to assimilate, leaving their bad habits behind. Yet we do have an example of massive immigration overnight, of people from a poor and economically backward state to a rich western welfare state. On 3 October 1990 the 16 million citizens of the former German Democratic Republic became fully a part of a reunified Germany at the end of a process of merging with the 63 million members of the former Federal Republic of Germany. After forty-one years of communist rule, East Germany was not only poor in resources and income but also burdened with a dysfunctional economic and political system and a population that had grown up in a society in which the habits of western liberal capitalist democratic citizenship were frowned upon and actively discouraged.[106] West Germany effectively absorbed what was widely considered to be a failed economic system, with large debts and a crumbling infrastructure. Over the first twenty years after reunification, Germany transferred 1.9 trillion dollars to the east to rebuild its society—spending in effect 100 billion dollars a year. Though the east remains noticeably poorer than the west, and it would not do to say that reunification has come without problems that remain unresolved a generation later, the point here is that the result was not the collapse of Germany or the dereliction of its economic system.[107] Indeed, Germany as a whole has flourished to become the most prosperous of the European economies as well as continuing to be a stable liberal democracy.[108]

In many ways this 'immigration' of Germans was more of a challenge to the new Germany than has been, say, the movement of a comparable number of Mexicans to the United States over the past fifty years. The fiscal impact of Mexican immigration, even by the most unfavourable of measures, does not begin to approach 100 billion dollars for that entire period, let alone for a year. The German experience has been more of a challenge than the 2.53 million net immigrants that the UK absorbed in the period of highest immigration in its history, between 2001 and 2011. Germany's experience is even more striking when one considers that in this period immigrants continued to enter the country from other parts of the world, so that by 2014 Germany had more than nine million foreign-born residents, and as a part of the Schengen region its borders were also open to all people already in the EU, Switzerland and Norway (though not to the UK population).[109] In spite of all this, there is little evidence to suggest that Germany's economic institutions have weakened or become dysfunctional—even though substantial numbers of the people who have become a part of that society hailed from dysfunctional economies such as East Germany or the dysfunctional societies such as the war-torn ones from which millions of asylum seekers moved.[110] If anything, the recent immigration history of Germany supplies a striking illustration of the capacity of wealthy capitalist democracies to absorb relatively poor immigrants in large numbers in very short order.

The greatest challenge Germany has faced in absorbing the population from the east is perhaps managing the social or cultural integration of people whose ways of thinking were at odds with, or even hostile to, the ideas of the capitalist west. To a significant extent, erstwhile East Germans feel like second-class citizens even after decades of reunification and some continue to identify with their former nation.[111] What is not in evidence, however, is any transformation of behavioural norms across the country as a whole that might adversely affect economic life. To be sure, there are political issues arising out of the social transformation reunification has wrought, but these do not speak to the economic objections to immigration.

The German example suggests that we can dispose fairly quickly of the fourth concern about the institutional impact of immigration: that it might undermine the political and legal structures that are the foundation of economic stability. Though such an undermining is possible in principle, there is no evidence that it is a serious concern. The immigration experience of modern Germany suggests that robust legal and political institutions can remain strong in the face of sudden and massive migration, even if it would be too much to claim that such movements of people will have no consequences for domestic politics. We shall return to this question and address it more fully in chapter 6.

## The Economic Costs of Immigration Control

While the economic costs of immigration have been thoroughly explored and frequently invoked in discussions of the broader question of borders and human movement, relatively little attention has been paid to the matter of the costs of immigration *control*. It is important that this side of the ledger be examined. Controlling immigration requires controlling people, and that is always a resource-intensive endeavour—not least because we are, if nothing else, a recalcitrant species, one of whose instincts is kick against obstacles put in our way and to pursue with heightened relish those things that are forbidden. If the omnipotent Author of All Creation could not by the force of His command prevent two naked innocents free of want from plucking and eating the fruit of the Tree of Knowledge, what hope is there of humans controlling the actions of millions of their fellows even after an enormous expenditure of energy and treasure?

We should consider the economic costs of immigration control under several different aspects. Most straightforwardly, we need to examine the *direct* costs of immigration control, since the management of human movement and the monitoring of behaviour within a society involves the establishment of complex and expensive regulatory frameworks. However, there are also *indirect* costs to consider, both because of the *immediate* economic side-effects of immigration control and the *long-term institutional* consequences that bear on economic activity in a society.

### DIRECT COSTS OF IMMIGRATION CONTROL

To return to the point made at the beginning of this book, immigration control is a matter not simply of controlling movement across national borders but of managing a domestic and international population to ensure that people behave in ways that are consistent with the aims and objectives of governments and their agencies. This makes it difficult to account fully for the economic costs of controlling immigration, since these encompass—along with the expenses incurred by governments in policing national borders—the costs borne by governments in the regulation and monitoring of all aspects of civil society, from business enterprises to public service providers (including education, transport, and healthcare, to name a few examples) to private institutions (such as universities, seminaries, and charities). On top of this must be added the costs borne by the regulated and monitored firms, institutions, and organizations which have not only to comply with regulations but also to demonstrate that they have endeavoured to do so. (The opportunity costs of compliance might be high, but the risks of compliance failure can be higher still.)

Though a comprehensive treatment of the direct economic costs of immigration control is beyond the scope of this inquiry, the matter is worth some treatment, if only to give us our bearings on the broader economic issues at stake. We might begin by considering the fiscal burden immigration management brings when the objective is mere border control. In the United States, the resources devoted to policing its frontiers have increased steadily, and since the passage of the 1986 Immigration Reform and Control Act the American government has spent 263 billion dollars on immigration enforcement.[112] This includes the cost of border security and interior enforcement. The cost of the former is reflected in expenditures on staffing and resources needed at and between United States ports of entry, while the cost of the latter is the result of staffing and resourcing the Immigration and Customs Enforcement (ICE) agency, whose purpose is to apprehend, detain, and deport non-citizens. Over the 2012 fiscal year alone the Obama administration spent nearly eighteen billion dollars on immigration enforcement, or about four billion dollars more than on all other federal law enforcement agencies combined.[113] By 2016 there were more than 49,000 agents working on border security and interior enforcement.

The European Border and Coast Guard Agency, launched by the European Union on 6 October 2016 as the successor to Frontex,[114] has a budget that reached 420 million euros annually in 2020.[115] Its role is primarily one of controlling the external borders of the Schengen Area by facilitating coordination among member states for that purpose—though each state would also retain responsibility for control of its own borders. The UK Border Force (since 2012, a separate agency from the UK Border Authority), for example, had a budget of 558 million pounds in 2018–19 for controlling the borders of the United Kingdom.

Looking beyond the United States and Europe, Australia in 2016–17 spent 1.1 billion Australian dollars on the processing of Irregular Maritime Arrivals (IMAs)—most of that on the offshore detention of asylum seekers. Its expenditures on other aspects of border control are indicated by the budgets of its major agencies: the Australian Customs and Border Protection Service has an annual budget of 1.4 billion Australian dollars and employs over 5,000 staff, though it is also responsible for revenue collection as a customs agency; and the Australian Immigration and Border Protection Service operates with a budget of 4.6 billion Australian dollars, employing over 8,400 staff.

Immigration control is expensive. Yet numbers alone do not always reveal enough, since the cost of any expenditure must be judged not simply by the price but by what is gained and what is forgone. We should look then at the indirect and less visible costs of immigration control to gain a better appreciation of its value.

## INDIRECT COSTS OF IMMIGRATION CONTROL

There are two types of indirect costs of immigration control. One is the various advantages forgone by the imposition of immigration restrictions. The second is the range of positive harms generated by these measures. Let us consider these in turn.

The most obvious indirect economic cost of immigration control is that incurred by businesses or employers who have to forgo opportunities they could only pursue if they had the right people to engage. Of course, in large societies in which labour is plentiful other alternatives might generally be available. Nonetheless, at the margin, it will make a difference if some potential employees are priced out of the labour market because of the compliance costs of hiring them, or others excluded from consideration altogether because they hold the wrong nationality.

Take the case of the seventeen thousand 'curry houses' in the UK, 90 per cent of which are owned by British Bangladeshis who employ about one hundred thousand people and contribute about 4 billion pounds in taxes. While the first immigrants who set up these enterprises also worked in them, the following generations have been less willing to enter the family businesses, which have become more and more reliant on imported chefs. But after April 2016 restaurants were required to pay a fee of 2,000 pounds for importing skilled labour and comply with work permit regulations imposing a salary minimum of 29,750 pounds—costs that were simply not realistic for most restaurant owners. A predicted consequence of this was the closure of a third of all curry houses over the following decade.[116]

The point here is not that immigration control creates hungry Britons (whether directly or indirectly). It is rather that there are unintended, unwanted, and often unanticipated costs to that control. There is little dispute that organizations everywhere—both public and private—depend to some degree on foreign labour. Even the European Union, for all its unapologetic commitment to controlling its external borders, worries that it faces the prospect of imminent labour shortages given its declining population and ageing workforce.[117]

The economic advantages forgone by immigration controls should not, however, be measured only by the immediate losses sustained by those unable to find workers, or the unemployment that might result from enterprises having to close altogether because deprived of access to particular kinds of expertise, or even by the gains that failed to materialize for those who might otherwise have benefited from more or better or cheaper goods that could have been produced. The greater loss still is the forgone product of the extension of the market in the broadest sense—the market here understood as that process in which individuals and groups compete, collaborate and cooperate, and in so doing discover new things.[118] When women began to enter the labour market in large numbers, twentieth-century western democracies saw a decline in national wage levels, even though women were more poorly paid because of restrictive legislation and discrimination by employers as well because of differences in experience and skill. The gains to society, however, were considerable not merely because of rising family incomes or any increases in national wealth but because everyone could now gain from the expansion of the pool of talent and imagination. The loss incurred by controlling and limiting immigration is not simply a loss of cheap, or even of skilled, labour but a loss of creative energy. One important indicator of this is the predominance of immigrants among the entrepreneurs who set up new and highly successful businesses. Overall, immigrants are more likely than native-born populations to establish business enterprises—in all parts of the western world.[119]

But it is not necessary to look to the examples of immigrants whose contribution is to generate great fortunes, or even new businesses, to see the economic gains forgone by controlling immigration.[120] Consider the case of Saroo, the young boy lost in the streets of Calcutta and adopted by an Australian family, who eventually found his mother in India after he reached manhood. This is the story of the 2016 movie, *Lion*. Imagine now that Saroo is able to bring his mother to Australia. She quits her job carrying rocks in exchange for helping her son at home and looking after her grandchildren—enabling both their parents to work full-time. Without earning a wage, or displacing any Australian workers (since Saroo and his wife would not have hired a nanny but instead split the childcare duties between them, perhaps with one of them giving up full-time work), Saroo's mother has increased the volume and productivity of labour in Australia by enabling her son and daughter-in-law to use their own creative abilities to a greater extent, improved the quality of her own life as well as the lives of her children and wider family—and possibly helped raise the level of wages for rock labourers in India.

None of this is to suggest that immigration does not come with economic costs of its own. But if the case for controlling immigration is to be made on the basis of a cost-benefit analysis, the direct and indirect costs of limiting immigration need to be entered into the equation.

What also need to be considered are the indirect costs incurred through the positive harms generated by immigration control. We noted earlier the use of 'golden goose arguments' to defend immigration control. Restricting immigration has been defended on the grounds that successful societies tend to attract foreigners who, either by sheer weight of numbers or in virtue of their not embracing the right values, undermine the institutions that sustain their success. There are also arguments that immigrants entering labour markets or even business diminish the opportunities of native workers and enterprises. The other side of this, however, is the danger that the effort to limit competition from immigrants will strengthen tendencies towards rent-seeking. In any capitalist economy, individuals and enterprises alike are always tempted to enhance their competitive advantages not only by improving the quality of their offerings but also by hobbling their rivals. Those looking to secure privileges or special protections are more likely to succeed if the case is built on the need to defend the claims of natives against the intrusions of foreigners—even (or perhaps, particularly) when the real source of competition is fellow citizens. One obvious way to steal a march on a local competitor is to complain that its business is sustained by immigrant labour. Whenever the notion that enterprises need protection from competition is upheld, rent-seeking by particular interests is given further encouragement.

The reason this is a matter for concern, ultimately, is the corrupting effect of control. It is not simply that controlling immigration limits the extent of the market and discourages the division of labour. It is that it encourages individuals and enterprises to operate in the economic realm not as competitors within a framework of rules but as rivals whose best bet is to rig the rules to their advantage. Now it would not do to overstate this, if only because persistent effort by businesses to change the rules of the game is undeniably a feature of any capitalist economy.[121] Eliminating or even reducing immigration control is not going to alter this fundamental fact. Nonetheless, it is important to recognize that this is an aspect of the corruption that immigration control encourages.

This point holds even more strongly if we consider the indirect effects of immigration controls to the extent that they shape not only the behaviour of individuals and firms in the marketplace but also the way in which the institutions of governance function. The apparatus of immigration control involves a complex and extensive network of officials, government agencies, lawyers, courts, detention centres, prisons (both public and private), international organizations, and business enterprises that serve or cooperate with government to enforce regulations or punish or deport (both citizens and aliens). For those who operate in this network there is much at stake: jobs, promotions, livelihoods. When one asks the ever-pertinent question, 'cui bono?',[122] the answer is plain, even if complex: many people benefit from immigration control and have an interest in sustaining, or even extending, it. The most obvious example of this is the prison system, whose beneficiaries include prison officer unions (and of course, their members),[123] private prison corporations, and (notably in the United States) the towns that think they depend for their livelihood on the building and expansion of correctional facilities.[124] Immigration control is not the only driver of the growth of prisons,[125] but as the imperative to manage migration has become more urgent, so has the involvement of prison systems become more extensive.

The corrupting effect of this is evident not purely in the amount of money that pours into immigration enforcement. The sums involved are considerable when they are made known, though it remains the case that much of this is concealed. For example, in the United States the actual financial burden of the criminalization of immigration violations is obscure because many of the operations funded are not explicit items in the federal budget and not subject to systematic oversight.[126] But no less importantly, the opportunity to make money has led to aggressive marketing and lobbying by the prison industry to invest in public-private partnerships. Private prison consultants have emerged to broker such partnerships that 'technically place the financial risk of building these speculative facilities on the backs of bondholders but in reality put it on the backs of local communities'.[127] The expansion of detention facilities has been sold to communities as an economic benefit even though, in reality, the promised gains are as illusory as those thought to derive from the building of correctional facilities generally.

That said, it bears noting that a full account of the corrupting effects of the growth of detention regimes will need to acknowledge the subtler and more complex aspects of the economic relationships that are thereby established. One would need to consider the range of entities trying to profit from detention by looking at contracts and subcontracts related to the working of such incarceration facilities. It would also be necessary to identify the additional ways in which money is made on detention.[128] In the case of many detention centres, money is made from the detainees by employing their labour (at rates much below minimum wage) and by not providing them with goods and services they need or desire, so that they are forced to purchase them at inflated prices (and so, if they do not have funds sent to them by friends or relatives outside, to work at exploitative wages). The profiting institutions include not only governments but also private companies.[129] The issue here is not simply the unfair treatment of detainees—including the misidentified citizens among their ranks—but the economic distortions and questionable practices encouraged by these institutions of immigration control.[130]

The indirect costs of immigration control are considerable, although for the most part they are well hidden and do not figure in calculations of the economic pros and cons of immigration. It is worth bearing in mind, however, that to some extent the costs of control are not subject to monetary calculation any more than are the benefits of immigration. Leaving aside the problem of measuring the impact of, for example, the restriction of liberty on detainees,[131] it is not easy to put a price on the harm done to an open society by the systematic promotion of practices that are condoned only because they are little known, or carefully and deliberately concealed.[132]

## The Economics of (Intergenerational) Identity

Between 1800 and 1950 American life expectancy rose from under 40 years to close to 70, and by 2012 was approaching 80. People in some countries live even longer, and even among the poorest nations in the world the chances of reaching a ripe old age are higher and rising. But an ageing population also brings with it problems of all kinds. Diseases rarely encountered in centuries past have become more common, and the cost of care for the elderly has risen. Dementia and Alzheimer's disease take their toll not only on those marked by these conditions but also upon the families and loved ones who care for them. With the proportion of healthcare budgets increasingly devoted to those in the last years (and indeed, in the last *year*) of life, the fiscal burden of longevity is becoming more and more apparent. Living long and prospering has its advantages, but it has its costs.

But imagine that our response to this was to reason that what was needed was a reduction of the human lifespan. Suppose that we thought about it in the following way:

> The problems that come with having a lot of old people are substantial and growing. The costs look unlikely to decline. And the generational transfer of income seems nothing if not unfair. Reducing the number of

older people by, say, denying them access to healthcare after a certain age, reducing expenditure on medical research that would prolong life, encouraging the resort to voluntary euthanasia, weakening the restrictions on involuntary euthanasia, and generally making old age less desirable than death (by creating a 'hostile environment' for the elderly) is not just sensible but morally required. We should discourage people from living too long.

For most people, myself included, this sort of reasoning would appear thoroughly confused, if not wholly repugnant. It responds to the problems that arise from the discovery of a great good by trying to destroy that good. Most people are likely to consider someone who thought this way to have failed to think clearly, or rationally—or morally. And yet, this is precisely how many people think about immigration.

If there is an overriding reason for this it seems likely that people are motivated by two considerations. One is a concern for the worst-off members of society—or, more simply, the poor. The welfare of the poor is the worry that lies behind the argument about the distributive consequences of immigration that we discussed earlier in this chapter. A second, very different, consideration is the impact of immigration not on the poor, or any particular segment of society, but on the society or country itself—looking at it now and into the future. What would too much immigration mean for the future of America, or Europe, or Australia? The first is a concern for particular persons—people within the nation. The second concern, however, is not so clear.

We might grasp this better by noting a possible inconsistency between the two concerns. It is widely agreed that in the long run immigration brings economic advantages to the extent that it raises the wealth and income of a society. The critics of this argument, however, point out that the gains are bought at the expense of the poor: the well-to-do improve their standards of living but the poorest in society find themselves competing with new immigrants for everything from jobs to public goods and services and end up with a slightly lower level of wellbeing. We examined this argument in an earlier section of this chapter. What has gone unremarked, however, is that if the solution is to limit immigration to protect the interests of the present poor *vis-à-vis* those of the present rich, this also means protecting the present poor from the future poor—who would, by hypothesis, be better off if there had been more immigration in the past. Why, one might ask, should the interests of the present poor of a nation be preferred to its future poor?

No satisfactory answer has been offered to this question, if only because no answer has been offered at all.

This may be because in debates about immigration and immigration control two kinds of concerns compete for attention. The first is the wellbeing of actual persons and the second is the condition of something more abstract: a society, or a culture, or a nation. We should turn, then, to an examination of the latter concern in the two chapters that follow.

# 6

# Culture

The issue is not, as some people appear to imagine, one of being nice to the immigrants or strangers in our midst, however diverse their race or culture. The issue is one of numbers, now and especially in the future.

—ENOCH POWELL, *REFLECTIONS OF A STATESMAN*[1]

## The Cultural Caveat

If there is a case for border control, immigration's friends and critics alike tend to see it in the 'cultural defence'. Self-described liberal nationalists like Will Kymlicka make it very plain that open borders are inconsistent with the preservation of national communities and the survival of distinct national cultures.[2] But even such advocates of open borders as Joseph Carens concede that, at least in principle: 'States have the right to restrict immigration . . . if they can show, on the basis of evidence . . . that further migration would endanger the survival of the national language and culture, and they may exercise this right of restriction . . . so long as and to the extent that the danger persists.'[3] While Carens introduces the 'cultural caveat' as a limiting case for extreme circumstances, however, many others have advanced the case for immigration controls by pointing most forcefully to the cultural question. Samuel Huntington, for example, famously argued that the imperative to control Mexican immigration to the United States was a cultural one, since the influx of significant numbers of Hispanic Catholics threatened to transform (if not undermine) America's Protestant social and political institutions.[4] And indeed governments routinely identify 'culture' as the pre-eminent reason for controlling immigration numbers and, at times, for selective admission of would-be settlers.

Does culture provide a decisive, or a significant, reason for controlling immigration; and if it does, what kinds of immigration controls are warranted, given that such controls are ultimately controls not only on would-be settlers but also (and predominantly) on citizens and residents? These questions are the focus of this chapter, whose main thesis is that the cultural defence does not establish a sufficiently strong case for limiting freedom.

The first section that follows begins with a closer look at the nature of the cultural defence to establish what are the main arguments for limiting freedom in the name of culture. The chapter then turns to examine the nature of cultural claims—to look harder at the assumptions that underpin them. This should provide the basis for a more thorough critique of the cultural defence.

## The Cultural Argument for Immigration Control

The cultural argument for restrictions on immigration is necessarily an argument for the protection or preservation of a state or national culture—although it could also in some cases be an argument for the protection of particular cultures within a state. 'While nationalism does not necessarily imply restrictions on immigration, it is clearly the case that without a sense of nationalism there would be no basis for any restrictions.'[5] In part this is because, as Paul Collier argues, 'it would be bizarre collectively to limit the entry of foreigners' if people did not feel any greater sense of identity with each other than with outsiders.[6] Yet it is not simply that people might share a sense of identity through association; no less important is the idea that the identity of the collective is tied to the territory of the state. The character of the nation, it is sometimes held, is intertwined with the character of the land. Not only is the nation entitled to the fruits of the land it has cultivated and for which it has (legitimate) responsibility, but it also has a claim to that territory by virtue of the history that it has created and the meaning that place has come to have for its people.[7]

The obvious question to ask is: how might immigration pose a danger to the culture of a society? A related question is the matter of what precisely it is that is endangered. Immigration might be a danger to culture either because of the number of immigrants becoming a part of the society or because of the cultural, economic, political or demographic composition of the intake.

The things that might be endangered include the cultural homogeneity of the society, or its historic cultural identity, or its historic cultural diversity. The cultural consequences of immigration could be regarded as dangers for two types of reasons: 1) because the consequences diminish the wellbeing or the quality of life of those who live in society—enjoyed either by the 'indigenous' population, or the immigrant population, and the combined collective of indigenous and immigrant people; or 2) because immigration itself brings about some kind of cultural loss, regardless of its impact on the wellbeing of the denizens of a society. We should examine the nature of these dangers more closely, first by looking at how they are presented by the cultural defenders of immigration controls, and then by identifying the elements of their concern.

An interesting place to start to look at the arguments of the cultural defence is with the controversial address delivered in Birmingham on 20 April 1968 by the Conservative opposition member of Parliament for Wolverhampton South West and Shadow Defence Secretary, Enoch Powell. The famous 'Rivers of Blood' speech was intended to discuss not immigration to Britain but the introduction by the Labour government of the Race Relations Act, which prohibited racial discrimination in a number of areas, notably housing.[8] Many local authorities had been denying housing to immigrant families who had not been in the country for a sufficient period and favouring citizens and long-term residents. Though the immediate subject of the speech was not immigration policy, it raised many if not all of the major concerns with which contemporary advocates of the cultural defence of immigration control are preoccupied, and proposed a reduction of the inflow of immigrants, encouragement and facilitation 'through generous assistance' of a return of migrants to their homelands (or 'other countries anxious to receive their manpower and the skills they represent'), and more careful attention to be paid to the composition of persons entering the country.

Powell had a number of worries. Pre-eminent among them was that the influx of immigrants from the British Commonwealth—with at least five thousand arriving every year under the government-sponsored voucher scheme—promised (or threatened) to transform the nature of the United Kingdom to such an extent that many Britons would no longer feel at home in their own land. These numbers in themselves were not the problem, for Britain could undoubtedly absorb and integrate different people without difficulty over time. Trouble would come rather because the families and relatives of these immigrants would themselves form communities and wish to bring more members of their groups into the country—as they would be well entitled to do as British residents and, in due course, citizens. Eventually, this would mean enough people arriving to transform the British social landscape. Immigrants would not be spread evenly across the country but concentrate in particular regions, and acquire influence by virtue of their concentration. In those areas they would compete with the established population for services and, when numerous enough, for political power.

At the heart of Powell's concern may have been the risk of what he called 'communalism'—of the emergence of a society divided along communal lines and wracked by conflict among contending groups divided by fundamental differences of outlook. This tendency would be evident, to begin with, in the pursuit by some groups of rights to maintain their own customs, so initiating the fragmentation of society. Policy encouraging such splintering was the immediate cause for alarm: 'For these dangerous and divisive elements the legislation proposed in the Race Relations Bill is the very pabulum they need to flourish. Here is the means of showing that the immigrant communities can organise to consolidate their members, to agitate and campaign against their fellow citizens, and to overawe and dominate the rest with the legal weapons which the ignorant and the ill-informed have provided.'[9] Before the century's end, he thought, the United Kingdom would become like the United States, though without the excuse that it was burdened by the legacy of the past that was slavery, since Britain's race problem would be one of its own immediate making. Though he did not suggest that British streets would be turned into 'rivers of blood', his allusion to the prophecy offered by the priestess in Virgil's *Aeneid* indicated subtly but clearly his fear that the blending of peoples in any political order would always bring with it tension, conflict, and violence.[10]

It is customary now to dismiss Powell as a racist. Even in his own time his Conservative peers repudiated him, and after his Birmingham speech he was removed from his position in the shadow cabinet. Yet what is striking is how much his arguments are in fact early versions of those advanced by contemporary cultural defenders of immigration controls. To see this, we might usefully begin with Paul Collier's influential defence of controlled immigration, since he takes the trouble explicitly to dismiss (and excoriate) Enoch Powell in the course of making his own argument for restricting freedom of movement.[11]

In Collier's view, 'nations are important and legitimate moral units'.[12] Would-be immigrants are attracted to successful nations. The preservation of these units is important, so the impact of immigration is important to the extent that it might threaten that success.[13] On the whole, the economic impact of immigration he considers to be of limited significance, since the economic effects are 'usually modest'.[14] It is to the social effects that we must turn our attention. This is not to suggest that social and economic effects are unrelated or can always be clearly separated. The fact that the economic consequences of immigration might be more deleterious for some groups is both a social and an economic matter. Our focus, nonetheless, should be on the social consequences. Indeed, immigration control, argues Collier, should be understood as an 'increasingly important tool of social policy for all high-income societies'.[15]

The reason we need to be mindful of the social consequences of immigration, according to Collier, is that the wellbeing of society depends substantially on the possibility of trust and cooperation within and among groups. The existence within society of diverse groups, some of whom are 'culturally distant', lowers trust and cooperation not only between groups but also, more importantly, within the 'indigenous' groups. This is particularly so when immigrants are slow or reluctant to absorb the indigenous culture. Without immigration controls, however, there is a tendency towards greater migration from groups that are culturally distant. This is so, in Collier's analysis, because groups that are culturally proximate to the indigenous population assimilate while those that are culturally distant form diaspora communities, and diaspora attract more immigrants. In his words: 'for a given income gap between countries of origin and a host country, *the sustained migration rate will be greater the more culturally diverse is the country of origin from the host country*'.[16] The implication of this is that immigration must be reduced for cultural reasons. Collier puts this point very plainly:

> a message of this book has been that cultures matter. Culture is what separates diasporas from the indigenous, and some cultures are more distant from the culture of the indigenous population than others. The more distant the culture is, the slower will be the rate of absorption of its diaspora, and also slower will be the sustainable rate of migration.[17]

There is little if anything in Collier's analysis or argument that distinguishes his view from Enoch Powell's. Both argue in favour of a substantial reduction of immigrant inflow, the encouragement of repatriation where possible,[18] and greater attention to the cultural origin of potential settlers. The grounds are identical: migrants of different cultural backgrounds settling in excessively large numbers will create conflict and instability. Though Collier tries to distance himself from Powell by insisting that it is no part

of his argument that this kind of immigration will lead to intergroup violence, and describes the Conservative MP's raising 'the spectre of "rivers of
blood" flowing from violence between immigrants and the indigenous' as
no more than 'deluded melodrama', the fact is that Powell made precisely
the points Collier has.[19] His warning was not of inevitable and impending
violence but of a decline in social cooperation, the loss of identity for many
people who might become minorities in their own country, and the rise of
communalism. His solutions are precisely the ones Collier offers. Collier's
contribution to the defence of this view has been to lend the weight of (poor)
social science to the analysis.[20]

At the heart of the cultural defence of immigration controls is the worry
that diversity and the rapid transformation of society through an influx of
new settlers will inflict not so much economic damage as cultural harm.
There are a number of ways in which the host society might be culturally
weakened.[21]

The first and most obvious way would be through the arrival of carriers
of a bad or harmful culture. This might be because some cultures are bad
in themselves, or because some cultures are bad because unsuited to other
peoples, whose own traditions or ways of life are somehow incompatible
with them.

The second way in which it might be harmed is through the dilution of the
culture as large numbers of people joining a society with no commitment to
its particular traditions leads to the erosion of those traditions either because
indigenous populations are drawn away from them or a new form of public
culture comes to dominate and crowd out older ways. This might be a harm
either because some people, while willing to do so, are unable to adapt to the
changes that immigration brings; because others become alienated as they
see their once familiar surrounds changing and resent having to adapt; or
because the change is experienced as a loss, including by those who simply
lament the passing of a once distinctive way of life even as they also adapt
successfully to the new society.

The third way in which a society might be harmed is by the impact of
the diversity immigration could bring, on particular minorities within society, who could find themselves struggling for recognition among a greater
number of minorities. An influx of immigrants from different parts of the
world into Canada might result in a society of many ethnic groups vying for
recognition to the extent that minorities like the Québécois or various native
peoples find themselves no longer considered special groups but simply
numbered among the throng of ethnic identities competing for attention.

Immigration has produced this kind of disaffection in Australia and New Zealand to the extent that Aborigines and Maoris have complained that the creation of multicultural societies effectively relegates them from their positions as special minorities to the status of minorities among minorities.

The fourth way immigration might be harmful, in particular to a liberal egalitarian society, is through the influx of people whose cultural traditions are illiberal, and particularly if they are unsympathetic or hostile to equality for women. Admitting such groups and then granting the groups equal standing with others might not only perpetuate the subordination of women in the immigrant minority communities but also slow, halt, or reverse the progress towards greater equality between the sexes in the society as a whole.

The fifth way in which society might be harmed is through the emergence of intergroup conflict if newcomers form distinctive communities and identities of their own, either because the host society is unwilling to integrate them, or they are reluctant or incapable of integrating. The absence of such integration need not necessarily result in conflict, since different groups can coexist peacefully; but it is possible for differences to lead to hostility. This is perhaps what Powell most feared would be the outcome of movement of people from the Commonwealth—the countries of the former British Empire—to the United Kingdom.

All of these concerns appear in one form or another in the arguments of advocates of immigration controls, and also in the analyses of those who are more uncertain about the proper response to immigration as a phenomenon of the modern world.[22] To understand the nature of these concerns, and also to assess their significance, we need to look more deeply into the presuppositions that underpin them.

## The Value of Culture

If cultural loss and cultural transformation are serious concerns the obvious question to ask is: why? Though the answer seems to be straightforwardly that they lead to harms of the sort described above, it needs to be made clear who exactly is enduring the harm or the loss. Here matters become more complicated and less obvious. Leaving to one side for the moment the problem of defining or specifying a culture, there are two ways in which a culture might have value. In the first instance, it might be of value because it serves the interests of those who live in it and thereby sustain it. In the second, it might be held to have value regardless of whether it serves the interests of its members—perhaps because it embodies or exemplifies something that is valuable in itself, meaning that it can be appreciated by the world, which would be the poorer without it.

To think about the value of a culture in the first way is to advance what might be called a *collective conception* of the value of a culture. According to this understanding, a culture is valuable to the extent that it provides some benefit or advantage to the members of the collective who sustain it. What a culture might provide its members with could include practical benefits, such as the skills and knowledge it transmits through education, including an understanding of their environment and of the wider world that enables them to survive and flourish. It might also provide its members with more intangible but no less important benefits such as the sense of identity and belonging that comes with being a part of a cultural community or a tradition. To defend the protection or preservation of a culture on the collective conception is to do so on the grounds that a culture serves its members in a way that other traditions or arrangements might not.

To think about the value of a culture in the second way is to advance what might be called a *corporate conception* of the value of a culture. According to this understanding, a culture is important because it embodies values regardless of whether those values coincide with the interests of their members. On this view, at least some cultures can have value not (only) because they serve their members well but because by their continued existence they make possible the persistence into the future of values that ought not to be lost.[23]

In the *collective conception* a culture has value to the extent that it serves the interests of the people who sustain it. The worth of the culture depends on its capacity to serve their interests, and the more people it has, whose interests it successfully serves, the more valuable it is—and the more worthy it is of protection. However, on this conception of the value of culture, it is also quite possible for the people who sustain that culture to change, and in so doing to transform the content or character of their culture. Indeed, a society containing a diversity of people, some of whose interests conflict, may well find its nature changing with the times. But there can be no conflict between the interests of the people and the interest in preserving the value of the culture, for the worth of the culture nothing more than its value to the people who sustain it. The interests of any individual member of a culture cannot be trumped by the value of the culture.

In the *corporate conception*, on the other hand, the culture matters not simply because it serves the interests of its members. The culture itself is the bearer of value, and it is quite possible for the value of the culture to conflict with the interests of individual members. If, for example, the culture is regarded embodying a particular kind of value, on the *corporate conception* there may be grounds for preserving that culture—and perhaps an imperative to do so—even if that conflicts with the self-declared interests of individual members who no longer wish to live by those cultural traditions. The value of the culture thus lies not merely, or perhaps not at all, in its value to its members but in its value to the world. At the extreme, this view suggests that the value of the culture trumps the interests of the individuals who comprise it—some of whom may want to dissent from its traditions or abandon them altogether (say, by emigrating). Protecting the culture here would mean protecting it against anyone who might undermine it, including its own members. (This view is not as far-fetched as it might appear. People who, in the name of preserving a cultural identity, deny their members freedom to dissent, or exit, from the community, and insist that outsiders have no right to intervene to uphold the freedom of individuals to abandon their cultural traditions, may be asserting a *corporate conception* of culture.)

Advocates of the cultural defence of immigration controls appeal to both conceptions of the value of culture in order to make their case. What needs closer examination, however, is the implications of appealing to one conception of the value of culture or the other. In the *collective conception* of the value of culture, it really does not matter what culture is in place, as long as the culture in question serves the needs and interests of its members. From a liberal egalitarian perspective, what matters is that everyone has access to the goods that only culture can supply, assuming that everyone needs such goods at least to some degree—for everyone needs a sense of identity and a feeling of belonging somewhere. But on this understanding, it should not be a concern if culture is transformed (whether by an influx of immigrants or by any other mechanism), provided the members of the culture continue to survive and prosper as they adapt to the changes that transformation wrings. The main worry would not be that immigration transforms society but that it transforms it too quickly so that the people are unable to adapt to cultural change. This was a fate met by many indigenous peoples in societies overrun by settlers[24] or conquered by foreign powers intent on imposing new and unfamiliar norms.[25] The interesting question here is whether the risk of rapid cultural transformation comes from the sheer number of immigrants, or is more likely to be the product of improperly selective migration—with too many immigrants coming from socially or culturally distant groups.

In the *corporate conception* of the value of culture, however, cultural loss matters regardless of whether it is a matter of indifference to the people in the society that once sustained it. If a culture disappears, even if because its bearers lose interest in sustaining it, or intermarry with other peoples, or move away, something is lost to the world. Indeed there may be a loss even if no one values the culture, for there is at least the possibility that sometime in the future someone will. This was the thought that animated Raphael Lemkin when he coined the term 'genocide' to identify a particular kind of destruction in the wake of the Holocaust (which he, as a Polish Jew, had narrowly survived). 'The idea of a nation signifies constructive cooperation and original contributions, based on genuine traditions, genuine culture, and a well-developed national psychology. The destruction of a nation, therefore, results in the loss of its future contributions to the world.'[26]

This sentiment is echoed among some advocates of the cultural argument for immigration controls. Paul Collier, for example, notes that while utilitarians and libertarians might not much care if poor societies were emptied out, others are not so sanguine. Supposing Mali emptied and ceased to exist; for libertarians and utilitarians, he notes, Malians can now reinvent themselves elsewhere and live much better. 'If Angola were to become predominantly Chinese, or England to become predominantly Bangladeshi, the change of identity would be of no consequence: individuals are free to adopt any identity they choose. But most people would be uneasy with such consequences.'[27] Just as we do not want to see species become extinct, even when we are unlikely ever to see them, so do we not want cultures to become extinct. 'It is not a satisfactory solution to Malian poverty if its people should all become prosperous elsewhere. Similarly, were Angola to become an extension of China, or England an extension of Bangladesh, it would be a terrible loss to global cultures.'[28] As Charles Taylor observes, what matters to the Québécois is not simply that they prosper separately but that they persist as a people: they care about 'la survivance'—survival through indefinite future generations.[29]

## Making Sense of the Cultural Defence of Immigration Control

Given these two possible understandings the value of culture and the harm of cultural transformation or loss, what now are we to make of the cultural defence of immigration controls as having a legitimate purpose in protecting culture and averting its destruction? If we take the *collective conception* of the value of culture, the immediate issue that has to be addressed is how it is that immigration poses a threat to culture. Is it the volume of immigration or its composition or some combination of the two?

Now the first thing to note is that general conclusions that hold universally may not be possible because not all states are the same: they differ in size and cultural composition—not to mention wealth, economic organization, and political stability. We might also note that some states are dominated by traditional cultures while others are predominantly modern or cosmopolitan societies—even if they contain within them significant cultural minorities. Immigration will surely impact different societies differently. What kinds of states are likely to be culturally vulnerable, and what are the likely sources of that vulnerability? States that are small in geographic size and population, and culturally homogeneous (and traditional) might be particularly vulnerable. Large, wealthy, cosmopolitan states seem least likely to be vulnerable to cultural harm. Consider the case of the United Arab Emirates which, with one of the world's highest net migration rates of 21.71 per cent and an expatriate population that makes up 87 per cent of its 8 million people, is a striking example of a country dominated numerically by immigrants. It remains predominantly Muslim but ethnically half the country is from South Asia, and its expatriate population includes a significant percentage of Christians and Hindus. Despite the native population being such a small minority, the UAE's wealth and non-democratic political system have enabled it to keep its indigenous cultural norms. To the extent that the country has been transformed since independence in 1971, change might be attributed as much to modernization as to massive immigration. At the other extreme, Japan has for many years had a net migration rate of zero yet seen its society transformed culturally, becoming a much more westernized society than has any Middle Eastern one. It may be difficult to establish precisely the cultural effects of immigration when other factors play a part in the process of social change.

Let me focus in the first instance on the case of immigration to countries of the developed western democracies. In the analysis offered by writers like Paul Collier, the concern is that the source of cultural transformation and disruption is the arrival of a significant number of migrants joining diaspora communities that do not properly integrate into the host country. When multicultural policies further encourage immigrants to form tight-knit communities that sustain their culture of origin, this creates a deeper disparity between the diaspora communities and the indigenous population, who are less bonded in exclusive social networks.[30] This argument fits with two of the problems raised by Enoch Powell: the alienation of the indigenous population, who find immigrants given advantages to enable them to maintain strong social networks while they are denied that opportunity; and the risk of communal conflict as resentment grows.

If this analysis is correct, to the extent that immigration policy is the only option being considered to address the problem, the implication must be that selective immigration is needed. This would mean reducing the intake of immigrants from culturally distant groups, and particularly those groups that already have substantial populations in the host society. Simply reducing the numbers of immigrants overall would not address the alleged problem, since the tendency of diaspora communities to attract migrants would still mean a continuation of the process of building exclusive migrant networks. The trouble here is that countries of the liberal democratic west are neither willing nor able to pursue group selective immigration policies explicitly and systematically. In part this is because it would run counter to their egalitarian traditions and a public philosophy that repudiates racial discrimination.[31] It is also inconsistent with a number of UN Conventions to which they are signatories. This has not prevented many countries looking to discriminate covertly,[32] but it limits their capacity to pick and choose immigrants. This effort is further compromised by governments' commitments to uphold the principle of family reunification—which further fosters the growth of diaspora communities.

There is another aspect to this dilemma. The argument from national identity confronts the following problem. If the advocates of immigration restrictions wish to do so on the basis of a thin conception of the cultural distinctiveness of national identity—one which sees that identity as given by little more than a shared language and commitment to democratic institutions—the tendency of immigrants to assimilate suggests that there is little reason to limit either the numbers or source of people coming to settle. A thin conception of identity is difficult to undermine. On the other hand, if advocates of restrictive immigration adopt a thick or robust notion of national identity, it will be difficult to operate any policy that was not grounded in some form of racial, ethnic, religious, or broadly cultural profiling—which would be difficult in the case of most countries, since they are already internally diverse.[33]

Can the problems raised by the *collective conception* of the value of culture be resolved by a non-selective reduction in the numbers of immigrants, or by other ways of controlling immigration? If the society in question does already have a thick traditional culture or is highly homogeneous culturally, it might make a difference if immigration were reduced.[34] This is most likely in small societies that are easily changed or even transformed by an influx of diverse people. If it were it a liberal democracy it would make the public culture thinner and either more cosmopolitan or less grounded in shared substantive beliefs, perhaps with different groups coexisting but none dominating or shaping the political ethics of the state. (In non-democratic states like the UAE, immigration by diverse minorities might make a negligible difference since they can play only a limited role in the politics of the society.) There may therefore be a case for small traditional, non-cosmopolitan societies restricting immigration to protect their citizens from the culturally transformative effects of rapid mass migration. Tibet might have had a case on the *collective conception* of the value of culture before it was forced to accept Chinese settlers sent there by its conquerors.[35] Larger, wealthier, and more cosmopolitan countries, however, would have much less of a case for limiting immigration on cultural grounds since there is little prospect that even a large influx of people would transform the society in the short term. At most, the country might see the development of pockets of traditional society in the diaspora communities of which Collier writes and about which Powell was so concerned.

What, however, of the worry Collier raises about the impact of the growth of diaspora communities on social cooperation? According to his analysis, the problem is that there comes with increased immigration from poorer countries a decline not only in cooperation between communities but also in cooperative behaviour among people in the indigenous population. This could be worrying for at least two reasons: first, a divided society might be less willing to support institutions of social cooperation, particularly if they involve the redistribution of resources through the welfare state; second, a decline in levels of cooperation or trust might produce a fragmented society in which different groups contend and compete with one another for a larger share of the social pie.

If these are serious potential problems, however, it is not clear that substantial, non-selective, immigration is the problem rather than the solution. To begin with, it is worth noting that the empirical claim advanced by Collier and others about the impact of diversity on support for redistributive institutions is highly questionable. Though the issue may not be settled, studies by Keith Banting and Will Kymlicka suggest that there is no positive correlation between a politics of group differentiation and support for redistributive institutions.[36]

If the worry is that the existence of cultural groups will lead to political competition and conflict among the various ethnic, religious or linguistic communities into which society becomes divided, it is not clear that immigration is the source of the problem. Such is the nature of democratic politics that political parties will always try to identify—or even create—and exploit possible divisions within society in order to build up their own constituencies in the pursuit of electoral success.[37] To the extent that intergroup conflict is a possibility, it is not the mere coexistence of different communities within a single region or state that is the problem, since conflict has arisen in many ethnically homogeneous societies no less than stability has been maintained in many diverse ones.

The question of whether diversity is a danger or an asset is a vexed one. For those who see it as a positive force, substantial and non-selective immigration may be a benefit. The diversity of groups would make it difficult for any group to dominate politics, and the effects of competition and conflict could to that extent be stabilizing because it supplies a check against the most powerful elements in society—as Acton famously argued.[38]

It would not, do, however, to be overly sanguine about the politics of culture, for it is clearly one significant source of tension within society. It is no less important, however, not to assume that immigration control is the obvious, or even a likely, solution to the problems that arise out of cultural conflict.

From the perspective of the *collective conception* of the value of culture it is uncertain that immigration is as much of a harm or danger as the advocates of the cultural defence of immigration control fear. If we take the *corporate conception* of the value of culture, however, it would appear that the issue is not in fact harm to any existing society but a very different concern. The problem is not the risk of cultural conflict or the danger of immediate cultural loss but the long-term transformation or disappearance of groups and societies.

If the transformation that takes place is so slow that no harm is suffered by the inhabitants of society, who successfully adapt to the changes that take place as society evolves, either from one cultural tradition into another variant, or from a traditional culture to a cosmopolitan one, it is not evident that the loss of a culture is one that should be bemoaned. Here much depends on how one identifies and individuates cultures and recognizes one to have passed out of existence or another to have come into being. Whether one takes the relevant unit to be a geographical area or a language group or a religion or a nation or an ethnic group, all human collectivities exhibit some kind of internal diversity, change to some extent over time, and given long enough might be said to have gone out of existence because differences in degree can make for differences in kind. Identities might be given by the continuities established in historical narratives, yet such narratives are not natural but social constructions that have been embraced by particular populations—sometimes through extensive campaigns to make it so. Even if that were not the case, however, why should one regret the loss of an identity when no one alive does so?

One possible explanation is that the loss of any culture is a bad in itself. Collier seems to think this; and Raphael Lemkin certainly did when he expressed the view that the loss of a culture was a loss not merely (if at all) for the people of that culture but for the world as a whole. Yet this just does not seem plausible—or at least it does not seem likely that the loss of any culture is necessarily a loss. There are a number of possible reasons for valuing all groups in themselves, but none are plausible.

One reason is the argument from diversity: it is simply better to have a greater variety of cultures in the world because cultures are the bearers of value, and more cultures mean more value. But there are a number of objections to this position. First, if diversity is itself a good thing, there is no reason to think that the elimination of any group must mean a loss of diversity. A culture could be eliminated by being divided. When Czechoslovakia divided into Slovakia and the Czech Republic, the nation of Czechoslovakia disappeared, but two nations appeared in its stead. Second, if diversity itself were a value, cultures themselves would be improved by becoming more internally diverse; yet if some groups became more internally diverse they would lose their distinctive existing group character. Here again it has to be asked whether it makes sense to hold diversity itself to be a good. Diversity may bring some advantages, but something may also be lost. The most we could say is that there are trade-offs involved when we opt for greater or lesser diversity. There is no reason, however, to say that an absolute increase in diversity must be more desirable. Third, even if diversity is what is most desirable, this is no reason to suppose that the existing pattern of diversity is most desirable, or that the existing stock of varieties is either optimal or the minimum we require to enjoy the good life. We may have more variety than we need or are capable of appreciating, or it may be that some other combination of varieties would serve us equally well, if not better.

A different argument for valuing cultures in themselves is that only by doing so can we ensure that certain values are not lost. Every group represents a kind of value, or carries a stock of benefits which we may regret losing. The destruction of a nation, Lemkin lamented, meant the loss of its future contributions to the world. This argument is also unconvincing.

First, even if the loss of a group did mean the loss of its future contributions, the relevant benchmark for comparison is not the world exactly as it is minus that group but the world as it might be now that that group has disappeared. It is quite possible, for example, that some groups are unable to make any substantial contribution to the world because their customs and traditions serve only the narrow ends of their members. If, however, they were to be absorbed by other groups, their former members might make far better use of their talents. For example, if the Amish assimilated into American society we would lose the attraction of another community to wonder at when driving through Pennsylvania, but gain from a possibly more fruitful use of the talents of men and women whose only option till then was subsistence farming. There is no warrant for suppressing them or preventing them from perpetuating a way of life they find, and their descendants learn to find, meaningful and rewarding. But should those descendants drift away and the remnant struggle to reproduce its traditions there is no reason for the rest of the world to strive to replicate that culture.

Second, even if the loss of some value is simply a net loss, that may not in itself be cause for concern. Some losses may be so trivial that they have very little impact on most people's lives, and yet others may have no significant impact on anyone's. For example, while the loss of some species may be regretted because of its vital role in the ecosystem (and the loss of large numbers of species may be a serious matter), the loss of others may have a negligible impact. To the extent that we do not encounter this species, it may make no difference to our lives since we cannot delight in it (if it is, in fact, delightful). And its loss in the ecosystem may mean little other than that the balance of nature is mildly adjusted—benefiting certain species and disadvantaging others. Or to take a human example, if a language is lost as its speakers decline in numbers, this need not be something to be deeply regretted as a serious loss in itself—even though it may be a cause for dismay among those who wish they had learnt their mother tongue before it disappeared, and for despair on the part of the last native speaker who has no one with whom to converse.[39] The disappearance of many of these languages will have no impact on us at all. When the German explorer Alexander von Humboldt came to the village of Maypures in Venezuela, some two hundred years ago, he discovered a parrot that was the last native speaker of Atures, a language none of the villagers understood. I submit that, when the bird died, the only thing worth mourning was the dead parrot, not the dead language.

Collier has suggested that there is value to be had in simply knowing that something exists, even if one never ever comes into contact with it. One may never see a panda, but be content (and happier) knowing that it exists somewhere in the world. Yet if this psychological state rests on something so flimsy as an awareness of something's existence, it's hard to see why one might not be content just to know that something *once existed*.

Third, the disappearance of some cultures as such may be not so much a loss as a benefit. As was noted earlier, the dereliction of traditions of slavery is something in which we should rejoice rather than view as a matter of regret. Analogously, there is no reason to regret the disappearance of a species if that species is the variola virus that causes smallpox. Indeed, as I write, the world is doing its best to contain and, if possible, eliminate the coronavirus.

A final possible reason for valuing groups as such is that this is one way of preserving an important form of equality. This is the great merit of the *corporate conception* of the value of culture. Simply recognizing *individuals* as equally valuable means failing to recognize persons as equal since it means ignoring or giving less weight to the interests of persons who are members of smaller or less powerful groups. International law recognizes the sovereignty of smaller states like Tonga as equal to that of more powerful ones like Germany. If international law recognized the rights of such collectivities only in proportion to the size of their memberships, people would be treated very unequally—more unequally than they are treated now. The most that this argument establishes, however, is that there may be some merit in the convention of recognizing all nation states as equally sovereign entities. This may be useful insofar as it checks the power of the dominant states. But it is not enough to establish that groups such as states have any value in themselves, much less that they have equal value.

If immigration means that, over time, society is transformed from one kind of culture to another this is not in itself any reason for immigration control. Change is the way of the world, and cultures are necessarily unstable. To the extent that one is serious about slowing, albeit not arresting, the transformation and loss of culture, immigration control is an inadequate tool, even if one is prepared to use it vigorously enough to limit human movement more significantly than most countries are willing to consider. In a world in which it is not only human beings who are mobile but also corporations, practices, and ideas that cross borders all the time, limiting who may settle more or less permanently in one place or another seems like a rather feeble mechanism for determining the cultural shape of human societies.

## The Corporate Conception of Nations

Though the cultural case for immigration control has its limitations, the philosophical core of the argument continues to find expression in a more comprehensive theory that needs to be considered. This is the theory of self-determination. The self in this case is the nation, and its incarnation in the modern world is the state. The argument for immigration control here is that it is warranted, perhaps even vital, to protect the integrity of this particular entity. We should turn then to consider the problem of immigration by giving fuller attention to the question of the state, and the political ideal of national self-determination.

# 7

## State

Take two trays of a weighing scale: put a gram on one, and on the other, put a ton. On one side is the "I", on the other is the "WE", the One State. Isn't it clear? . . . And this is the natural path from insignificance to greatness: forget that you are a gram, and feel as though you are a millionth part of the ton.

—YEVGENY ZAMYATIN, *WE*

### Our Home, Our Family

In her maiden speech to the House of Representatives of the Australian Parliament in 1996, Pauline Hanson argued that 'if I can invite whom I want into my home, then I should have the right to have a say in who comes into my country'.[1] In criticizing Australia's immigration policy for admitting too many people, and too many Asians in particular, the newly elected independent member for Oxley was giving expression to a commonly advanced claim: the people have the right to determine who may come to their country. The same argument was made more recently in the United States by Patrick Buchanan, who wrote: 'America is our home. We decide who comes in and who does not, how large the American family becomes, whom we adopt and whence they come.'[2]

But is a country a home, or a population a family? What should be understood by the claim that I have a right to say—or have a say in—who enters my home, and does this supply an appropriate analogy for thinking about immigration control? Difficulties abound. To begin with, it is not obvious what it means, or to what extent it would be desirable, for anyone to be able to decide who to invite in and who to turn away at the door. Perhaps if one were the sole occupant of an apartment it would be a good thing to have complete authority to decide who may enter—granting that allowances might be made for fire-fighters, who should not have to wait for an owner's permission when the building is burning. If, however, the apartment is occupied by a couple, things might go better if each had some discretion to admit guests as they pleased—though it would be considerate of one to consult the other in special cases, and a bad idea for either to let a room to a tenant or host an in-law without warning. Should the apartment be occupied by a group of people, life would go a little better if each had some discretion to decide who might visit, without needing always to seek authorization from the rest of the group: it would be a less than harmonious household if each had a veto on every entry or even if a majority vote were needed to issue any invitation. This would hold more strongly still if the home in question were not an apartment but a condominium. If the entire body of owners and renters had to be consulted before anyone could visit or stay, or before a cleaner or baby-sitter could be employed, that housing complex would be a less attractive place for many; and given human nature, it is highly likely that such a requirement would be breached more often than observed. Though there are, to be sure, many housing associations that impose strict restrictions on the freedom of their residents.

Imagine now, however, that such restrictions were proposed by a neighbourhood, whose residents asserted: this is our home and we ought to have a say—and indeed, a veto—on who may or may not enter. Is this the point at which my freedom to invite in whomsoever I choose trumps your freedom to tell me who may or may not enter 'our home'—turning your right to veto my choices into a duty to mind your own business? If not, perhaps that point comes when the 'home' in question is the suburb, or the county, or the city, or the province. The further we get from the single-occupant apartment model, the less plausible does the idea of each person having a veto (or even a say) on who enters a home become—provided, that is, that we value a certain kind of freedom.

The idea that an entire country is like a 'family' is as problematic as the thought that it is like a 'home'. Families come in many shapes and sizes. When the family means, say, two parents and their children, the decision to increase its size, whether naturally or by adoption, is a matter for the members—or perhaps the adults alone. But when the family includes in-laws, aunts and uncles, and distant cousins, it is not evident that anyone's decision to procreate or adopt is a matter in which Grandma should have a say, let alone a veto—and Uncle Fester's views are perhaps best ignored.[3] Matters are further complicated when one considers that families also grow when parents divorce and re-marry, or when adult children acquire partners— often acting unilaterally to bring into the fold outsiders who may not always find their new relatives entirely welcoming. Even nuclear families range in character from the Karenins to the Simpsons to the Brady Bunch to the Addamses. Extended families could be as different (or alike) as the Kennedys and the Corleones. For thinking about immigration control, the family analogy might be even less promising than the metaphor of a country as a kind of home.[4]

Yet if a country is neither a home nor a family, what precisely is it—at least for the purpose of discussing the immigration question? This is an important issue from the perspective of many of those who want to control and limit immigration because a significant justification for doing so—perhaps one that is more important than the economic and cultural defences—is that this is something that the country or its people wants. Not only in popular discourse but also in the literature of political theory, advocates of immigration control insist on the importance of recognizing the right to exclude—and the need to control—strangers or outsiders or foreigners. What matters for these advocates is that the right to exclude be acknowledged for no other reason than that this right is itself of fundamental importance, perhaps in the same way that a family has the right to exclude outsiders from joining it or the occupants have a right to deny strangers entry into their homes. A country has a right to determine who comes in and to impose conditions of entry, whether or not others like it or agree with the reasons for their exclusion. At the heart of it all is the question of *self-determination*. Immigration control is about taking control—or taking back control when it is in danger of being lost.

This is the matter now to be considered more closely in this chapter, whose main concern is to scrutinize the arguments for immigration control grounded in claims about self-determination. The most pressing problem that has to be addressed here is how to establish who or what is the *self* whose self-determination is a matter of concern. There are two aspects to this question. The first is the problem of settling the identity of the *principal* whose self-determination is at stake. The second is the problem of identifying the *agent* who is to exercise the right of self-determination—unless, of course, the principal and the agent are one and the same. This brings us very quickly to the subject of the state. As we noted at the beginning of this book, while migration is as old as human history, immigration is a relatively modern phenomenon if we understand it as a certain kind of movement of people between different national jurisdictions controlled by states. The state is that entity which has the authority (alone or collectively with other states) to control immigration across, and immigrants within, its borders. But what exactly is this entity and whose interest(s) does it serve? In whose interest(s) does it act? Is it like a household? Or is it a family? Might it be that it is neither of these things, though writings on the state and on immigrations frequently assume it is one or the other or even both? Addressing arguments defending immigration control in the name of self-determination requires coming to a better understanding of the nature of the state and the political community.

The conclusion towards which this chapter moves is that the arguments for immigration control grounded in claims about self-determination are untenable. The most important reason why is that they rest on an implausible understanding of the state and its workings, as well as an indefensible view of political community. On occasion, they rest on a mistaken view of the nature of liberal democracy. Ultimately, this chapter hopes to show that the quest for control is at best illusory, and at worst dangerous.

To do this, the chapter begins with an account of the self-determination argument as it has been advanced not only in popular debate but also in the writings of the most important contemporary political theorists. It offers an exposition of the normative argument(s) for the right of states to exercise control over territory, as well as a reconstruction of the case for seeing the state as an expression of the identity of the people, and its decisions as reflection of the popular will. Exposition and reconstruction are followed in the succeeding sections by critical analysis of these arguments. The aim here will be to show how an understanding of the nature of the state and its relationship to society makes many of the arguments defending immigration control limited at best—if not altogether inadequate. The chapter concludes with some general observations about self-determination as a political ideal and its bearing on the immigration question.

## National Identity, Territory, and Self-determination

At the heart of all assertions of the importance of immigration control as a key element of national self-determination is the conviction that there does exist a kind of national community of people who share an identity and a territory, and whose duties to one another as members of such a community generally supersede the duties they might owe to others. While it would be going too far to suggest that every proponent of the priority of the principle of nationality must believe in 'our country, right or wrong', all consider the claims of compatriots to have not only special significance, but also an importance that warrants disregarding even the most urgent interests of outsiders.[5] Compatriots enjoy a relationship with one another they do not share with others, and this relationship generates rights and duties that, in particular circumstances, take precedence over all else. According to one formulation of the argument, they share 'associative obligations',[6] though views might differ on how these obligations are generated by association, and what precisely is the nature and extent of those obligations. Let us look more closely at the substance of this view about the nature of the national community and the various arguments in defence of its special importance.

A good place to start is the analysis offered by David Miller in his effort to explain why we should resist thinking about the world in the way that cosmopolitans[7] do. For Miller (and as we shall see later, for others who also argue for giving pre-eminence to the claims of nationality), it is important to recognize that the obligations we owe others, and the claims we can make on them, very much depend on the relationships we have—relationships, he suggests, that are 'intrinsically valuable'. It is relatively uncontroversial to suggest that we might have special duties to those who are closest to us— children, partners, parents, some other relatives, and intimate friends—but more difficult to say how far similar obligations might extend to 'relationships that are wider in scope and in particular to the type of relationship that exists between the members of a nation state'.[8] Nonetheless, such obligations do exist and are no less important.

What is the nature of the relationship between compatriots? According to Miller, it is multidimensional, but distinguishable into three broad strands. First, there is 'an economic system that produces goods and services, and ancillary systems that insure people against various risks, including that of being no longer able to contribute to and reciprocally benefit from the productive economy'.[9] Second, 'members relate to one another as citizens, participating in an elaborate political/legal scheme' that 'allows them collectively to control and shape the scheme as a whole'.[10] Third, members relate to one another as fellow nationals who 'share a broadly similar set of cultural values and a sense of belonging to a particular place', and indeed who 'think of themselves as a distinct community of people with historical roots that exists as one such community among others'.[11] This form of association, Miller suggests, is intrinsically valuable because it enables people to coexist in terms of justice, and to exercise some degree of control over the future direction of their association: 'they can achieve, within practical limits, both distributive justice and collective freedom'.[12]

Not everyone who thinks that there are obligations born of this sort of political association considers that national identity is of any great relevance. David Miller, however, is among those who think that national identity carries with it feelings of solidarity and emotional attachment. It deepens the association 'because the political community conceives of itself as extended in time, indeed often as reaching back into antiquity', which also means that the obligations it creates 'stretch backward and forward—they can be inherited from the past and owed to future generations'.[13] And no two nations are the same:

> each contains a unique blend or mixture of cultures as a result of the various groups that have contributed to that long history. Furthermore, national identity attaches the community to a particular homeland whose special features often contribute in an important way to the identity itself, whether these are distinctive landscapes, buildings of historic significance, or sites where key events in the nation's history took place. So where citizens also share a national identity, their association has the further feature that they can explain why they belong together and why they should exercise their citizenship in this particular place.[14]

This view of the significance of nationality is the basis for concluding that citizens can expect a good deal from each other—and that what they owe outsiders is more limited. From the 'weak cosmopolitan' perspective that Miller defends, for as long as there are no human rights at stake, there is no need for citizens to assume burdensome obligations for the good of foreign nationals—including any obligation to admit them as immigrants.[15]

Of crucial importance in this view of the world is the idea of *territoriality*. The existence of a national community depends on its having a 'homeland', which should be understood as an area over which it exercises 'territorial jurisdiction'. In the modern world, for thinkers like Miller, territorial rights are held by states, which represent the people who have the right to occupy a tract of territory.[16] What is essential, however, is that the people themselves have the right to occupy the territory in question.[17] Territorial rights cannot be established by a state 'expelling most of the rightful occupants of a region and replacing them with its own subjects', even if after that a majority of the population support the state.[18] (Though, clearly, innumerable states have operated in precisely this way.[19])

But how is the right of occupancy then established in the first place? For Miller, the simplest case is that of the group of people who settle on unoccupied land and reside on it continuously—thereby establishing 'unchallengeable' title.[20] But sometimes things are more complicated, since the 'movement and mingling of populations over the course of history gives rise to disputes over the identity of "the people" who are entitled to establish jurisdiction'.[21] Miller himself defends a nationalist theory that that 'vests rights of occupation primarily in groups with shared national identities that over time have transformed the land at stake, typically endowing it with both material and symbolic value'.[22] It is worth noting how deep and powerful is the bond this creates, according to Miller, not only among the founders of a society but also among their descendants. In an earlier work, *On Nationality*, he wrote:

> because our forefathers have toiled and spilt their blood to build and defend the nation, we who are born into it inherit an obligation to continue their work. .... This then means that, if we are going to speak of the nation as an ethical community, we are talking not merely about a community of the kind that exists between a group of contemporaries who practise mutual aid among themselves, and that would dissolve at the point at which such practise ceased; but about a community that, because it stretches back and forward across the generations, is not one that the present generation can renounce.[23]

So strong are the obligations we owe each other in virtue of our inherited membership, Miller believes, that we would be in violation of our duties should we emigrate—even though he considers it would be going too far were we to deny people the freedom to do so.[24]

David Miller is not alone in advancing this general line of argument. Margaret Moore, for example, defends a similar view about the source of obligation. Just as associative obligations might arise out of membership of families, so might they arise out of membership of political communities, 'which are intergenerational communities who are united together with a shared sense of identity'.[25] One critical question here is how to understand or identify the 'people' that make up a political community. For Moore there are three desiderata: first, the people must 'share a conception of themselves as a group', identifying with co-members 'in terms of either being engaged, or desiring to be engaged, *in a common political project*' and in being able to be 'mobilized in actions orientated towards that goal'; second, they must be capable of establishing political institutions through which to exercise

self-determination; and third, they must have a history of political cooperation such that we can 'identify objective and historically rooted bonds of
solidarity, forged by their relationships directed at political goals or within
political practices'.[26]

The third desideratum is worth dwelling upon. According to Moore, it
means that for a group to count as a people who can claim to be a political community, and be entitled to exercise collective determination over
a territory, it must be 'a group whose shared identity has been forged and
maintained by actual historical relations—such as a history of sharing a sub-
state unit or a history of political mobilization against an oppressive colonial state'.[27] There must be a high level of 'group solidarity', which should
spring from 'a valuable history of shared political association' so that, in the
end, it will be possible to see the group 'forging a shared collective world
where people's interests and lives are intertwined such that it makes sense
for members of that group to be collectively self-determining in shaping the
collective conditions of their existence'.[28]

Another contemporary political theorist who stresses the importance of
acknowledging the existence of political communities as self-determining
collectivities is Ryan Pevnick. While differing from many critics of free
movement in being a strong advocate of immigration-friendly policies,
Pevnick also argues for the importance of controlling immigration in the
name of self-determination.[29]

At the core of Pevnick's argument is an understanding of the state as a
political community, and of the political community as a 'historical project that extends across generations and into which individuals are born'.[30]
According to this view,

> the state is very largely a result of the labor and investment of the com-
> munity. The citizenry raises resources through taxation and invests those
> resources in valuable public goods: basic infrastructure, defense, estab-
> lishment and maintenance of an effective market, a system of education,
> and the like . . . these are goods that only exist as a result of the labor and
> investment of community members.[31]

Pevnick invokes Abraham Lincoln to advance the view that those members of a political community who have perished (whether on the battle-
field or from more mundane causes) bequeathed institutions to the current
generation, which is now entrusted with the task of preserving and passing
them on to the generations to come.[32] This is a view he also attributes to
Rawls, for whom, he says, 'the fundamental organizing idea of democratic

theory is that of "society as a fair system of cooperation over time, from one generation to the next".[33] His overall purpose is to develop an account of political community as an intergenerational enterprise that can also be understood as an 'associative ownership framework'.

The two aspects to this analysis are equally important. For Pevnick the political community owns its institutions and its territory, but this can only be understood as the result of an *historical* process, in which state institutions are brought into existence by a 'concerted collective effort'.[34] Recognizing the importance of self-determination depends upon appreciating both that political community is a form of collective ownership and that it is an inheritance. Ownership claims do not trump all other considerations, since owners may have substantial duties to others for all kinds of reasons. States may, for example, have duties to asylum seekers that issues of ownership cannot diminish. However, the fact that people and states have duties to help others in distress in no way casts doubts on the legitimacy of any political community, or its right to self-determination.[35] Nor, for that matter, does any defect in the state's past: the injustices committed by the state may well render it responsible for rectifying past wrongs, but they do not weaken its right of self-determination.[36]

In Pevnick's account, the state is a political community and a jurisdiction, but it is also a collective owner of all that falls within its jurisdiction. Invoking Jeremy Waldron, he argues that the state is a system of collective property, such that '"the community as a whole determines how important resources are to be used. These determinations are made on the basis of the social interest through mechanisms of collective decision-making"'.[37] Members of such a community provide each other, through their associational relationships, with a range of valuable goods, such as protection from internal and external threats, risk-protection schemes (pensions and healthcare), and facilitating programmes (such as public education). Since such goods exist only because of the 'coordinated decisions, labor, and contributions of members', these members are 'in a position to legitimately deny membership to some outsiders because this entitlement amounts to a prima facie privilege to do with it, within boundaries, what they wish'.[38]

What all these views share is an understanding of political community as having three critical dimensions: first, a common history of ancestral collective effort or struggle to create and sustain that community; second, an attachment to a land or lands; and third, a self-conscious sense of solidarity with one another—of being members who identify with one another, who belong together. To be sure, there are other theories of territorial rights and the foundation of political community.[39] But among those that emphasize the importance of the right of the political community to exclude others in the name of national self-determination, these three aspects of group identity are central. The emphasis, if we might put it pithily (not to say, colourfully), is on *blood, soil* and *belonging*. The political community in all these cases is identified with the state, which is considered to be the embodiment of the will of the populace or 'people' it encompasses, and the agent that exercises authority on its behalf. The existential justification of the state, however, is grounded in an origin story that ties a people to a territory with which they self-consciously identify, and which they see as their own.

> Breathes there the man, with soul so dead
> Who never to himself hath said,
> This is my own, my native land![40]

Let us consider these aspects of the argument for immigration control from self-determination more closely, beginning with the question of the origins of political community.

## Ancestral Voices

A people, it appears, must have a history if it is to be a people, and a state must have both if it is to count as a legitimate construction, and be recognized by everyone as such. No less importantly, at least in the eyes of some, what history has wrought creates obligations that bind future generations, who owe something to their ancestors—not just a debt of gratitude for their earlier efforts but also a duty to continue their work and preserve the edifice their forebears have bequeathed. Out of history's sound and fury comes a message: continue this work of generations, today and into the future. And the message looks all the more peremptory when it comes with the reminder that sacrifices have been made, blood has been spilt, and that the present sleeps under the shade of a tree watered by the sorrows of the past and nourished by the bodies of the dead.

In order to consider this argument, we need to look more closely at the elements that comprise it. First, there is the claim that there is a history, of a people or of a state, that can be identified, told, and held up as an objective (even if not entirely uncontested) account of the past. Second, there is the further claim that this account establishes the coherence or identity of an existing community and the right of that community to recognition as a political entity—recognition by those who lie outside the community, but also, presumably, by those within who might dispute its claims. Third, there is the claim that the existence of the historically legitimated community creates: a) obligations on the part of its members to i) sustain the community they have inherited, ii) continue the work of former generations, iii) not renounce their allegiance to their homeland; b) rights on the part of members to view their homeland as their own, and to determined who may or may not enter their territory or join their community; and c) duties on the part of outsiders, whether as individuals or as associations such as states, to recognize the existence of the political community and its right to determine who may enter its territory or join it as a member.

Let us take these claims in turn, beginning with the general presumption that there is such a thing as a history of a political community or a state or a people to which appeal can be made to settle many of the questions that arise in political life. While it might be true that every community has a history, it is certainly not true that the way to distinguish a community is by looking to its history. Even to speak of *its* history may be to beg a question that the appeal to history was meant to settle. Communities and histories are not natural kinds, or phenomena that might be uncovered by careful observation. The same is true of peoples, and even of states.[41] Identifying and distinguishing a community or a people or a state is a political matter. If every state or people has a history, that history is a construction—a myth—that is the product of someone's (or some group's) crafting and telling, selecting from the numerous facts and events to create a narrative that will serve the ends of particular persons or interests. There are no natural histories of peoples or states, but should anybody write one it would surely not serve the interests of anyone to the extent that it could only reveal the reality of their origins in our vulnerabilities and limitations (including our fears and superstitions) rather than in philosophical conviction or principle.[42]

The mythical character of national narratives has not gone unremarked, even by those who appeal to history to argue for moral significance of states. David Miller, for example, acknowledges the force of the argument that 'national identities are in an important sense fictitious because they rely on the creation of a single narrative—a national story—which is at least highly selective and in the worst case starkly at odds with the historical facts'.[43] But the significance of this may not have been fully appreciated. Indeed, the nature of the problem needs a fuller explanation.

The difficulty is not just that the myth-makers might have played fast and loose with the facts (though that is true enough, and we shall return to this). It is that even without the facts being falsified or distorted through questionable selection, there are many plausible concurrent and cross-cutting narratives that might be presented, all of which are true enough and able to capture some part of the reality of common life. Societies have not only political histories but also social ones, not only national histories but local ones, not only domestic histories but also international (and sometimes, imperial) ones. For the *Annales* school, the *longue durée* is the better approach to the study of history, with its emphasis on studying the slow development of structures—which might well straddle political boundaries—to gain an understanding the lives of people whose existence was shaped by forces that are older, deeper, and geographically broader than those identified by the mere chronicling of political events and the lives of the powerful.[44] The days and the identities of people are undoubtedly shaped by the activities of political elites and the institutions that they create or reform; but they are also what they are because of their religious affiliations, their professions, the trading relations they depend upon within and beyond the regions in which they live, and the connections they form with people who come and go as merchants, missionaries, seasonal workers, judges, showmen, and other itinerants. To suggest that there is a national history that is somehow the history that gives people their identity and is the source of their obligations looks improbable at best—except, perhaps, to those who have been raised on that myth from childhood.

It looks even less probable when one considers the extent to which national political histories are crafted and re-crafted by the victors in political contests. Political victories, at their most significant, can transform societies not only by creating or reforming institutions but by reshaping the very boundaries of a political society—some of which transformations might even consign particular polities to the dustbin of history.[45] But no less importantly, the victors and their supporters shape the narratives that follow, re-presenting the history of the country in terms that justify the course of human events, and legitimize the triumphs now heralded. Thus, the American Revolution was soon cast as a popular rising up against British rule by a people who wanted to govern themselves, even when the Patriots had the support of at most a bare majority of the White population, while the Loyalists comprised between 15 and 20 per cent, with the remainder neutral, and a good half of the colonists of European origin people who simply tried to avoid involvement in any kind of rebellion. Thomas Jefferson might have wanted the tree of liberty regularly 'watered by the blood of patriots', but it surely also thrives on a generous sprinkling from the veins of people who would rather mind their own business.[46]

It is perhaps worth remarking that even as much of modern historiography has had a state-centric focus, looking to craft national narratives in the mode of what Prasenjit Duara has called 'linear histories', there have been some attempts to examine the past without seeing it as an unfolding to the present as we now understand it.[47] But the theory of nationality seems to long for a more serviceable historical past.[48]

In his critique of the social contract theory, David Hume cautioned his contemporaries against letting 'the establishment of the *Revolution* deceive us, or make us so much in love with a philosophical origin of government'.[49] The revolution to which he referred was the Glorious (or Bloodless) Revolution. That change of regime, he reminded his readers, was brought about not by popular demand but by the machinations of political elites:

> it was only the majority of seven hundred, who determined that change for near ten millions. I doubt not, indeed, but the bulk of those ten millions acquiesced willingly in the determination: But was the matter left, in the least, to their choice? Was it not justly supposed to be, from that moment, decided, and every man punished, who refused to submit to the new sovereign? How otherwise could the matter have ever been brought to any issue or conclusion?[50]

Historical arguments, in this regard, are no better than philosophical fictions that do not deserve to be taken seriously. They will routinely be invoked by political advocates—on all sides of any debate—and it cannot be expected that a populace brought up on a diet of myth and confabulation will never fall for the arguments that confront them. But they have no place in more rigorous discussions.

From all this it should be clear that history has a very dubious role to play in the establishment of the coherence or identity of a political community. If history can be called upon to tell one story about the identity of a people, it can often be used to tell another, and very different, one.

Consider the case of the United Kingdom of Great Britain and Northern Ireland. If we told a story going back about 750 years the following might be some notable events. In 1284, after two years of war, Edward I, King of England, conquered and annexed Wales. After expelling the Jews in 1290, he invaded Scotland, turning it into a dependency in 1296. He was defeated by William Wallace in 1297 but successfully invaded Scotland again in 1298. On his death in 1307, his successor, Edward III, withdrew from Scotland, but this did not prevent continuing warfare and the Scots invaded northern England in 1318. Peace with Scotland was not concluded until the reign of

Edward III, when the Treaty of Edinburgh was signed in 1328. In 1404, Owain Glyndwr took control of Wales, declaring himself Prince, and it was not until 1409 that the Welsh surrendered again to the English. For the next two hundred years the English continued to war with the Scots, who from time to time also sided with the French, notably during the Hundred Years War. In 1542 Mary was crowned Queen of Scots and in 1559 claimed her right to the English throne, without success, and shortly after abdicating was executed by Elizabeth I for treason. But on Elizabeth's death in 1603, Mary's brother, James VI of Scotland, acceded to the English throne as James I. Ireland had been invaded and settled by the English and Scots since the twelfth century, but the English throne did not cement control until 1541. In the seventeenth century that control was extended, first by the incursions of Oliver Cromwell and then, more importantly, by the Protestant forces under William of Orange, which resulted in the settlement in Catholic Ireland of large numbers of Protestants from Scotland and England. In 1707 the Act of Union joined England and Scotland as Great Britain and in 1801 Ireland was placed under the control of the British Parliament. In 1921, Ireland was granted independence under the Anglo-Irish Treaty, but six counties remained as a part of the United Kingdom of Great Britain and Northern Ireland. In 1973 the UK joined the European Common Market and in 2016 a referendum saw the public vote for the country to leave the European Union of which the UK was now a member, only a year after Scotland voted in its own referendum to remain as a part of the United Kingdom, though with 45 per cent of its population wishing not to do so.

Out of this narrative could also be carved others, for the Irish, for the Scots, for the Welsh, and indeed for the English, as well as for those who wish to see themselves above all as British. Though a thought should also be spared for those who would like now, after Brexit, to consider themselves European. But the narrative is further complicated by the fact that Britain also ruled for some time the largest empire the world has known, with colonies on every continent, and subjects in every corner of the earth. A story might also be told, then, about a larger identity, born of unwilling membership of a club that had incorporated millions (and that insisted on everyone paying their dues). The question is, which identity matters, and which story will work best to shore it up? *Historical continuities do not imply political unities.*[51]

Political histories, especially if they are official or 'recognized' histories, are nothing more than 'just-so' stories. They are not reflections of an already existing identity but vital tools used in the construction of identities. This is surely one reason why histories are so often contested. Some Scots and Irish do not wish to be identified as British, most Tibetans probably don't want to be identified as Chinese, the Malay ruling elite do not want to consider Chinese and Indian citizens of Malaysia as *bumiputra* or indigenous despite their presence in the country for centuries, and Hindu nationalists want a history of India that presents the Muslim element as an aberration rather than a significant part of any narrative about the subcontinent. And many Catalans do not wish to see themselves as a part of Spain.[52] None of this is to express scepticism about truth or the possibility of objective inquiry. It is simply to point out that the construction of identities does not depend on objective historical inquiry, for histories are written or told to serve political ends, one of which might be the creation or the shoring up of identities. States are all too real, but national identities, peoples, and their histories are fictions.[53] There may be good reasons to recognize states or peoples or national identities, but the facts of history do not readily supply them.

All of this makes it even more difficult plausibly to maintain that the existence of a historically legitimated community generates rights and obligations. But regardless of the trouble with history, the metaphysics here is curious to say the least. How does (imputed) membership of a group engender obligations to sustain the group, continue its project(s) and never to renounce allegiance to it? Theorists such as David Miller, Margaret Moore and Ryan Pevnick are not the first to assert that rights and obligations are inherited. An early statement of this position can be found in Plato's *Crito*, in which Socrates defends his decision not to escape while awaiting execution by citing his obligation to abide by the law that has sentenced him to death. The polis that has condemned him, Socrates argues, can quite rightly say to him: 'Since you were born and nurtured, and educated too, could you say that you are not ours, both our offspring and slave, you yourself as well as your forebears?'[54] He is not 'unaware that fatherland is something more honourable than mother and father and all the other forebears, and more venerable and more holy, and more highly esteemed among gods and among human beings who are intelligent', and accepts that he 'must revere and give way to and fawn upon a fatherland more than a father when it is angry with you, and either persuade it or do whatever it bids, and keep quiet and suffer if it orders you to suffer anything, whether to be beaten or to be bound'.[55] Socrates's argument here is not like, say, Hobbes's—that we are obligated to obey the law because we are its authors—but rather a direct appeal to a proclaimed truth that we are bound by unchosen ties to a fatherland that has, in some sense, created us. But why there is such a tie that binds—or why the tie *binds*—is left unexplained.

In more modern times, a variant of this argument has been elaborated by Sir Robert Filmer in his *Patriarcha* which, in attacking the new and dangerous tenet of the natural liberty of mankind, advanced the thesis that the source of all political obligation was paternal authority, descending naturally from the authority of forefathers and traceable to the very origins of mankind.[56] 'As the father over one family, so the king, as father over many families, extends his care to preserve, feed, clothe, instruct and defend the whole commonwealth.'[57] The emergence of the modern state, and the subsequent rise of the contractual theory of political obligation—which insisted on the conventional nature of political order—brought into question the implicit assumption of two thousand years of European thought that society had its origins in the family, and that society and state were more or less inseparable.[58] Patriarchal doctrines, such as Filmer's, attempted to answer and correct 'the erroneous non-naturalism of the contractualists' and return understanding to the previously accepted belief that the source of authority and obligation lay in the family.[59]

Even so, the proponents of the patriarchal theory needed an account of how the authority of rulers was acquired, and if it was not to be from the willing agreement of the people today, it had to be from the past. They thus rejected the *conventional* or contractual theory in favour of a *genetic* one: authority would be traced back into history. But this approach brought with it problems of its own. The historiographical problem was how to identify the relevant events in the past without arbitrariness. The philosophical problem was to work out how far back in history to go, so that the stopping point was not simply arbitrary. Arguably, neither of these problems was ever satisfactorily resolved, though Filmer clearly thought (not unreasonably) that one had to go back to the very beginning, to the authority that issued from God through Adam.

The contemporary origin stories under consideration here, however, seem neither alive to the historiographical problems involved in the appeal to the authority of the past nor clear about how it is that the past authorizes—or legitimizes—anything. Filmer's story has at least a certain consistent logic, even if Locke rightly criticized it for its sheer implausibility because of its many improbable implications.[60] But the *genetic* arguments offered by Miller and Moore, for example, offer no explanation either of why some elements from the past can be invoked to establish the existence of a legitimate order or how the legitimacy of anything in the past was established in the first place to be passed on to the current generation, who are supposedly bound by their forebears to stay together and obliged to ensure that their successors inherit the same bonds.

In the end, the appeal to the voices of imagined ancestors does not get us very far: there are too many of them, there is cacophony where there needs to be clarity (if not harmony), and it is not evident why any of the cries from the past should be believed or heeded. It is especially unclear why any claims, because they invoke those ancestral mutterings, should be considered to strengthen arguments about how we should conduct our affairs now.

## This Land is Your Land, This Land is My Land

*Nobody living can ever stop me,*
*As I go walking that freedom highway.*
—WOODY GUTHRIE, 'THIS LAND IS YOUR LAND'

No less important than the appeal to history, to establish the claims of political community, is the appeal to connections shared by people with an attachment to place. Of course, there is a historical dimension to this: ties to land and territory are also deemed to have significance because settlement and development have been the work of generations. But land or territory belong to a people, so it is argued, for other reasons too: because the current generation continue to work the land (whether literally or figuratively) to make it productive, because it has sustained the economic, legal, and political institutions that make it possible for the community to prosper, and generally because a society is an ongoing scheme of social cooperation— one which, in some sense, *owns* the territory it occupies. The point is to say that there is such a thing as an independent political community—a state— whose existence is the outcome of history, but which also has a coherence because it is the work of a population that sustains it in a place it possesses and rightfully controls, and which therefore has a right to determine for itself the course of its future.

But none of this really stands up to serious scrutiny. So let us take a closer look at the arguments and assumptions underpinning these claims of political community, beginning with the idea that a society is a system of cooperation.

The best known recent statement of this idea, at least in political theory, is one put forward by John Rawls in *A Theory of Justice*, where he wrote:

Let us assume, to fix ideas, that a society is a more or less self-sufficient association of persons who in their relations to one another recognize certain rules of conduct as binding and who for the most part act in accordance with them. Suppose further that these rules specify a system of cooperation designed to advance the good of those taking part in it. Then, although society is a cooperative venture for mutual advantage, it is typically marked by conflict as well as by an identity of interests.[61]

Rawls's formulation is perhaps somewhat stylized, since his concern is to offer a philosophical definition rather than a sociological account of society, so as to defend a theory of justice in distribution within a single social order. Nonetheless, it is important because it captures the thinking implicit in defences of self-determination, which tend to rest on a view of the political community as a kind of self-sufficient association. The people who comprise this association are the ones jointly responsible for its economic productivity (or lack thereof), and the level of legal and political stability that enables it to enjoy the way of life it has. A good society, in Rawls's terms, would arrange its institutions to ensure the protection of certain basic freedoms, but also make sure that, while the least advantaged were taken care of, there were plenty of incentives for the more productive members of society to enjoy the gains generated by their talents so that the society became wealthier and better able to lift the living standards of all, and especially of the worst off.

Robert Nozick famously criticized the foundation of this argument by pointing out that it was in fact very difficult, if not impossible, to know who in any system of social cooperation was a greater contributor to the social product if that product was truly *joint*. Rawls's idea that inequalities could be justified if they gave some people an incentive to produce more foundered on the problem that if there were a joint social product it would not be possible to determine whether the additional product created by those incentivized was greater or less than the incentives they were offered.[62]

But the problem goes deeper still. The trouble is that what we have is not a single, closed, self-sufficient, system of social cooperation but a world in which cooperation takes place both within and across national boundaries. What we have, in Hayek's phrase, is an 'extended order of human cooperation'.[63] This is most obviously the case with economic activity: the international division of labour is now so complex that very little is produced that does not involve the use of materials found in many parts of the world, or the labour of people across the planet. Self-sufficiency is a matter of degree, and complete self-sufficiency in a complex society quite impossible. Trading city-states like Singapore and Hong Kong, with few natural resources of their own, are almost entirely dependent on economic cooperation with the outside world for their livelihoods; but even a large economic region such as the United States—the largest single economic unit in the world, nearly 90 per cent of whose trade takes place within its borders—still depends on the outside world for much of its economic activity, as importer, exporter, and co-producer. (Even this observation conceals many complexities. While a state like South Dakota sees imports and exports accounting for only 5.3 per cent of its GDP, 38 per cent of Michigan's GDP is an expression of import and export activity.[64]) Nor is this something entirely new, since trade is as old as recorded history. The impact of the coronavirus on the Chinese economy, and the subsequent disruption to global production when intricate supply chains were interrupted or broken, offers as clear an example as one could wish for to demonstrate that production involves cooperation across borders.

Nor is it that only economic activity takes place across national boundaries. Human cooperation has many dimensions. People find themselves in association with one another not purely because of their economic dealings but also because they have common religious attachments, share professional or recreational interests, exchange ideas, and come together to build enterprises dedicated to everything from charitable works to the protection of wildlife to the promotion of invented languages. They also make common cause politically, at the state level through international organizations, but no less importantly through Non-Government Organizations (NGOs) and activist associations such as Amnesty International. The network of human cooperation is not a patchwork of self-contained systems that engage each other as independent units but a more complex form of interaction that resembles the World Wide Web in its interconnected structure.

A society is not an ongoing scheme of social cooperation. Social cooperation is ongoing, and it takes place within and across and among societies.[65] Indeed, societies form and reform within networks of cooperation. This holds true not only for societies within states but even for states as such. States are not in themselves 'cooperative ventures' and their emergence or disappearance does not create or terminate all forms of cooperation, even though changes in some of the rules of cooperation that might result from state formation or transformation can make all kinds of cooperation more difficult (or, sometimes, easier). The secessions of Singapore from Malaysia, of Norway from Sweden, or of Slovakia from Czechoslovakia did not put a stop to cross-border trade, or bring an end to all forms of social interaction, even if many arrangements had to be revised.[66]

States are not necessary for social cooperation. The question is what difference they make. According to one line of argument, advanced in different ways by David Miller and by Ryan Pevnick, they make all the difference.

Some countries and peoples prosper while others do not, and the reasons for this have much to do with the way in which these societies have governed themselves. And certainly it is true that some countries do better than others. At the start of the twentieth century, Australia and Argentina were among the wealthiest countries in the world with comparable standards of living, but after three generations Australia was still at the top of the league table while Argentina had fallen dramatically in its economic performance. At the time of independence in 1957, Ghana and Malaysia were comparably placed as former British colonies with low standards of living, but sixty years later Malaysia was ranked twenty-seventh in GDP while Ghana was seventieth— despite the countries having similar-sized populations. How countries run their affairs surely makes a difference. Miller argues that it does, and that this has a bearing on the duties some states have to others, since those who manage their affairs badly have consequently diminished claims against those who have managed them well.[67]

Ryan Pevnick also takes the view that the success of some societies can be attributed to the collective efforts of the political community, who are entitled to benefit from the gains made.[68] A good example, he thinks, is supplied by Malaya, which became independent in 1957, and Singapore, which had been a self-governing colony since 1955. Together they formed a union when they joined with Sabah and Sarawak to create the Federation of Malaysia in 1963. Disagreements between the leaders of the two countries, however, led quickly to separation, and by 1965 Singapore was on its own. Pevnick writes: 'The country then embarked upon a project of national unification and economic development that included a renewed commitment to education, the construction of an advanced infrastructure, and the recruitment of substantial foreign investment.' Such was Singapore's success that by 2009 its per capita GDP was 49,228 dollars, while Malaysia's was little over 14,000 dollars. In Pevnick's assessment, 'the development of Singapore was a triumph and the political community that generated these gains has at least some special entitlement to them'.[69]

Yet in fact, it is quite misleading to say of Singapore that 'the country embarked' upon anything. The separation of the two states was the product of a squabble between two elites about how power should be shared. The policies pursued by Singapore were the policies favoured by its elites—and in particular, by its brilliant and far-sighted but uncompromising leader, Lee Kuan Yew—often regardless of popular support. The same could be said of Malaysia in that it was also the creation of its elites, though they were beholden, as Singapore was not, to a federation of sultanates and a divided population. In neither case can it be said that the populace must take credit—or blame—for the course of economic development. If they can, then so must the North Koreans be held responsible for their immiseration under a succession of communist regimes, the Haitians for their poverty compared with that of their island neighbours in the Dominican Republic, and the Venezuelans for their descent into wretchedness under the democratically elected but corrupt and hapless governments of Hugo Chavez and Nicolás Maduro. Institutions matter, and indeed can make an enormous difference to the welfare of a society, but they are not typically the deliberate creations of a populace, and often are the unintended results of generations of (global) social transformation. When reform (whether for better or for worse) is the result of the efforts of a political elite over a short period of time, even democratic endorsement may mean nothing more than that a narrow victory was won going against the wishes of a majority of the populace, whose preferences were not translated into political success. Had Lee Kuan Yew succeeded in becoming Prime Minister of a federation of Malaysia and Singapore, the economic history of those peoples would surely have been very different.

Societies do not control their economic welfare; or, for that matter, their political destinies. Nor do their political leaders exert such a level of command over social and economic forces, even though it remains true that there are better and worse institutions, better and worse policies, and better and worse decisions, and it is perfectly reasonable to praise or criticize them accordingly.

In the end, there is just no such thing as the 'will of the people', though the advocates of self-determination often write as though there were, and as if the state is somehow the embodiment of a collective intention. Consider the claim that the state is a historical project extending across generations. While it is true enough that states, like all human institutions, are the product of human action and interaction, they are hardly the fruit of the efforts of generations of people who could meaningfully be described as engaged, consciously or otherwise, in a shared project. To the extent that any persons are so engaged, they are members of small political elites who have fostered institutional changes for a mixture of motives, from personal ambition to financial interest to ideological fervour. The vast majority of people are carried along by events, occasionally co-opted to facilitate changes when popular support is needed, but as often simply left with no choice but to go along with the outcomes that result from the triumph of one elite or another, or the compromises contending elites strike.

A number of commonplace observations suggest how difficult it is to defend the idea of the state as a shared historical project. First, innumerable states do not survive for more than a few generations. Most of the states of Africa, the Middle East, and Southeast Asia came into existence only in the twentieth century, nearly all of them as a consequence of postwar decolonization. Very few of them have enjoyed stable political boundaries. Even Europe, the birthplace of the modern state, has seen continual re-drawings of boundaries as states have emerged, changed shape, and disappeared. At present there are in Europe fifty sovereign states, six partially recognized states, and six dependent territories, as well as two special areas of internal sovereignty.[70] In the course of its modern history Europe has encompassed hundreds of nations and city-states in the seventeenth century, and only twenty at the beginning of the twentieth. Second, very few states before the twentieth century were democracies, and there were few with mechanisms to ensure the accountability of rulers to the wishes or interests of the general population. Meaningful participation in the development of social and political institutions was limited to the elite. Even within democratic states, political structures mostly remain within elite control, though the extent of elite responsiveness has long been a subject of dispute (not only in politics but also in political science). This not to say that there may not be something to the Burkean view (that Ryan Pevnick's position resembles), since there is no doubt that traditions and institutions survive generations, or that elites looking to trample upon them ought to be viewed with suspicion. But to see in the continuity of some political institutions evidence that states are shared projects is to take matters too far.

All too often, however, states do not so much develop out of the shared concerns of local populations as exploit and transform those populations in order to suit their own interests and the ambitions of the elites that dominate the political process. There may be cases in which the state evolves organically out of civil society, but it has also frequently acted as a predator, which has tried to bring order not so much to serve the interests of society as to facilitate its own extractive activities.[71] Even if one sees state and society as mutually constitutive, it would be too much to claim that the outcome is the result of some shared concern rather than the product of contention among a range of forces and interests.

No less problematic is the account of the state as the result of the labour and investment of the community, with citizens raising resources through taxation and investing those resources in public goods, from national defence to education to the market system itself. As history, this presents a somewhat romantic vision of the place of taxation in the lives of societies. For most of human history, going back to the ninth century BCE, the main purpose of taxation was to fund military conflict. The modern European state has for much of its existence found itself struggling against a population that was highly resistant to its demands for revenue, often to finance its wars.[72] Nonetheless, the emergence of what Joseph Schumpeter famously called the 'tax state' brought about profound changes to society, reshaping not only its institutions of economic management but also its cultural norms.[73] The modern state is, in part, the creature of its own fiscal structure, which has itself transformed society, international trade, and international relations. It is simplistic to suggest that states raise revenues prompted by a civic-minded citizenry, intent on guiding it to provide public goods and services. States have fought wars of which citizens disapproved, and spent revenues on projects no one but the immediate beneficiaries of government funds have wanted. The distribution of the spoils of taxation requires a more sophisticated explanation.[74]

While it is necessary to understand that society is a system (or, better, network) of cooperation, it is important to recognize the spontaneous character of much of that process, for only some of it takes place through deliberate political organization. Pevnick writes as though the institutions of public education, healthcare provision, and pensions were political achievements, fostered and supported by an engaged citizenry. Yet all of these institutions have their origins not in political agreement but in the practical efforts of smaller communities to serve their own needs.[75] To a considerable extent, these have survived the development of state-constructed alternatives, or the interventions of state-mandated reforms. In many cases, problems with state-established schemes (for pensions, for example) has led to privatization or de-nationalization or the emergence of parallel non-state institutions. In other cases, the state has struggled unsuccessfully to suppress institutions established by communities that have resisted efforts to standardize and control them.[76] When the state has supplanted existing private institutions it has been for a mixture of reasons, from the failure of private systems, to the interests of states in acquiring control, to pressure from different groups to suppress competitors.

All of this aside, however, there is a more general puzzle about these claims about how people come to have rights to the territory they hold. What is it that generates such rights? John Locke in his *Second Treatise of Government* tried to account for how individuals could acquire the right to hold private property by suggesting that, by mixing their labour with previously unowned parts of the external world, they somehow gained an entitlement to keep what they now 'possessed' and to demand that others refrain from taking what was now 'owned'. This argument has not found favour anywhere except among a few desperate libertarians, and indeed it was ridiculed by the most famous contemporary libertarian, Robert Nozick, who compared it to claiming that I could take possession of the sea by casting into it the contents of my can of tomato juice when all I'd be doing was losing my tomato juice.[77] The idea that people come to exercise rights over territory by working and building on it is no less mysterious, and yet advocates of territorial theories keep advancing them. Margaret Moore, for example, suggests that as a reason why the Bedouin have territorial claims in areas over which they have wandered in their otherwise nomadic way of life.[78] But the alchemy here is entirely obscure. Of course, one good reason for not preventing the Bedouin from wandering these lands is that they have done so for some time and so their lives would be disrupted or destroyed if they were denied the opportunity to continue. Acts that cause injury or harm more broadly undoubtedly call for some justification. But this is not enough to establish that people, individually or collectively, somehow acquire rights and titles by their labour, let alone by mere occupation.[79]

The general point towards which all this leads is that the idea that there is such a thing as a political community that *owns* its institutions and territory is implausible. What we have in reality is much more fluid and unstable. There is no doubt that states attempt to impose greater order upon the messy and variable character of society, and assert ownership of the society they claim to keep in their trust, and promote narratives describing existing political orders in favourable terms. States require such narratives, no less than they need founding myths—such as those supplied in Locke's defence of the Revolution Settlement in 1689, or by Lincoln in the Gettysburg Address that Pevnick quotes. But these stories are significant because of the purpose they serve or the function they perform—not because they are true.

Two examples should suffice to round out the thought that there is something incongruous about the idea of a society being a self-directing collective of people working a territory to build or sustain a cooperative enterprise. If we consider the United States, that example is the history of slavery (and the economic, legal, and political marginalization or exclusion of the Black population in the decades since formal emancipation). The idea that this was self-government or self-determination must long have appeared to be little more than a cruel joke to African-Americans. If we consider Great Britain, that example is the history of empire, which saw hundreds of millions of people officially made subjects of the Crown and obligated to pay taxes, supply (military) manpower, and live under the authority of occupying forces, without having much if any involvement in their own governance, or in the course of their development. 'Is this land made for you and me?'[80]

## Consider Yourself . . . One of Us

In *A Political Theory of Territory*, Margaret Moore explains that she conceives of a 'people' as a collective agent that meets three conditions. One of these is that they are able to 'establish and maintain political institutions through which they can exercise self-determination'. Another is that they have 'a history of political cooperation together' such that we can 'identify *objective* and historically rooted bonds of solidarity, forged by their relationships directed at political goals or within political practices'.[81] In this chapter thus far, I have cast doubt on aspects of these two claims, in particular the ideas that societies are readily distinguished objective histories—which are a source of identity—and the notion that the establishment and maintenance of political institutions is suggestive of a deep social solidarity that makes self-determination possible. Moore's third condition for peoplehood, however, is that those who make up that 'collective agent' 'must share a conception of themselves as a group'—indeed, they must 'subjectively identify with co-members, in terms of either being engaged, or desiring to be engaged, *in a common political project* and they are mobilized in actions orientated towards that goal'.[82]

It is a part of Moore's last mentioned condition to which we need now to turn our attention. This is the idea that people can share a conception of themselves as a group, and that this supplies the basis for thinking about who can rightfully make a claim to self-determination. We might begin to consider this idea, first, by returning briefly to the thought that what people who form a political community share (and subjectively identify with) is a 'common political project'.

A useful way to begin would be by considering a distinction Michael Oakeshott drew between two kinds of understanding of the modern European state. One conceives of the state as a 'civil association'—a form of association in which people related to one another under the rule of law in terms that did not do more than set the conditions under which people might pursue their separate ends as members of a society that shared no collective projects and evinced no particular shared ends. The other sees the state as an 'enterprise association'—a form of association in which people related to one another as members of something more akin to a corporation, sharing a collective purpose or looking to promote a corporate goal.[83]

The most common objection levelled against Oakeshott's distinction is that it is hard to imagine any actual state operating purely as a system of non-instrumental rules of conduct, and existing as an institution that did not have policies, raise taxes, try to defend itself against enemies (both domestic and foreign), and attempt to ensure compliance with those purposes. Yet Oakeshott himself agreed: every actual state is in fact a combination of the *civil* and the *enterprise* form of association, being a mixture of formal and substantive elements, of policy and procedure. A state is not just a form of association; it also *rules*. That means that it must have legislative and judicial institutions as well as an executive capacity, and that it will pursue policies, occupy premises, impose taxes, establish and staff bureaucracies, keep records, and exhibit all the behaviours of any corporate entity. His point, therefore, is not that the idea of a civil association is the only proper or desirable form for the state to take but rather that the two aspects of the modern state exist in tension with one another. The ideal of civil association is a kind of freedom that is enjoyed when the law's premise is that the members of the state are independent and not to be conscripted by others to engage in projects and purposes that are not their own. It means that they are not dominated, for they are subject only to general rules rather than the commands of others, whether they be fellow *cives* (in Oakeshott's Latinate terminology) or figures in authority. The problem with the state as an enterprise association is that, as a *mode* of association, it cannot accept the freedom of those within its bounds to pursue their own ends should they be 'eccentric or indifferent to its purpose'.[84] Members of the enterprise state have their ends chosen for them, and if they manage to depart from them, it is because a management decision has permitted them to leave (or remain).[85] The more a state resembles an enterprise association than a civil one, the less free will its members be.

The state imagined by Margaret Moore, and also by David Miller, is one which has much more of the character of an enterprise association than of the civil association Oakeshott describes. What makes it a state is that it has a people, and those people are in some important ways bound together. The most important way in which they are joined is by their sharing in some common project or enterprise. These bonds that hold them together are strong, for they not only mean that allegiance and loyalty to the group are commanded, but also that all are obligated to work to keep the enterprise going, to help it reach certain collective goals, and not to stray from the collective purpose—unless given leave to do so by the collective. (Hence, for example, Miller's view that there is an obligation not to emigrate, even though society ought to weigh individual freedom heavily in the balance and refrain from enforcing this particular obligation.)

If the state is conceived of as a body of people united by the sharing of a common project or enterprise, however, this is a conception of association in which that participation in the enterprise is involuntary. Societies rarely are brought into the world as projects of any kind,[86] coming into existence gradually and generally by accident, as people coalesce without intending to, like puddles forming into a stream. Sometimes projects are indeed launched, but as often as not *upon* an unsuspecting population, some of whom might be carried along by the enthusiasm of their authors, even as most react with a mixture of stout resistance and indifference, or at worst, resignation. It is hard to imagine that in countries like China or the former Soviet Union, or Burma under Ne Win and the military junta, or Equatorial Guinea, or Zimbabwe, or Uzbekistan, or any one of a number of states whose governments have established major projects to shape and transform society, are anything but societies living in the grip of regimes that have very little interest in what their subjects wish or think. But even if we consider relatively free countries, it looks unlikely that the population could be described as somehow sharing a common political project, even if they might be living under institutions that are the product of the success of state-builders or reformers in the past. The creation of the United States was the result of a successful revolution of which a large minority disapproved—one that established a divided society living under a constitutional compromise that was unable to avert civil war, after which the victorious North imposed its understanding of the Union on a resentful South.[87] New Zealand was established as a British colony despite the hostility of the native Maori population, who reached a political settlement not because of any interest in participating in a nation-building project but in order to preserve their lands and separate identity. And these examples do not even begin to speak to the dozens of cases of deeply divided societies, which in many cases remain relatively peaceful only because of carefully constructed political constitutional arrangements and electoral systems that preserve a truce among groups in conflict.[88] Moore is aware of the problem of divided societies and discusses the cases of Northern Ireland, Kashmir and Kurdistan in some detail, as well as referencing some of the theoretical literature of the politics of divided societies.[89] The problem, however, is that these cases are not rare exceptions but numerous, and also undercut any claim that what makes a state is the existence of a people who are in some sense united. To be sure, in regions like Kashmir and Northern Ireland governments and other political actors have worked hard to negotiate settlements that might preserve peace and allow ordinary people to go about their business, but this bespeaks not the existence of a single people or a common project or a shared identity but the reality of the modern state as a compromise among elite groups to settle questions about who shall rule and under what arrangements.

The idea of a society or a state being made up people who share a project or projects of some kind really has to be viewed with considerable scepticism. This holds even more strongly for free societies—as forms of association that prize, at least to some degree, the opportunity to distance oneself from common goals in favour of projects shared with a selected few (or no one at all). This bring us, however, to the broader claim made by advocates of self-determination: that a society or a state is made up of people who view themselves as a group. What matters is *belonging*, or perhaps better, *belonging together*—sharing a conception of ourselves as members of a group.

Now, there is no doubt that some people do identify very strongly with their states, or with other kinds of group entities to which they are attached. What various advocates of the value and importance of self-determination have tried to suggest is that this is somehow grounded in something significant: history, or territory, or shared projects, for example. But in fact these attachments to groups, while real enough as sentiments—and often visible and even palpable in their effects—are variable, somewhat arbitrary, and explicable to a good degree by our social psychological propensity to invent group identities, attach ourselves to them, and turn others into outsiders to be viewed warily—if not with disdain and loathing. The study of 'realistic group conflict' within the field social psychology showed some time ago, largely through experimental work, that intergroup competition tended quickly to lead to greater social distance between groups and consequently to the exacerbation of in-group favouritism, feelings of solidarity and pride as well as to an increase in hostility to other groups.[90] More interestingly, however, subsequent experimental research led by Henri Tajfel showed that neither competition nor a conflict of interest were necessary for the development of group identity or hostility to other groups: the mere perception of belonging to a group was sufficient to produce in-group favouritism and discrimination against outsiders.[91] Even when there was no social interaction among the participants, so that the 'groups' were *purely cognitive entities*, these behaviours arose.[92] The fact that people might identify with others as co-members of a collective or community, then, tells us very little other than to confirm that people are ready to distinguish themselves into groups of insiders and outsiders.

The point of this is not to deny the reality or existence of the sense of belonging but to cast some doubt on its significance. The fact that people coalesce into groups does not suggest that some people naturally belong together, or even that there is a need for them to do so. It simply tells us that it is possible and indeed likely that they will do so for different, often arbitrary, and sometimes trivial, reasons. On occasion, it will be as a result of manipulation by others looking to foster the emergence of groups or identities to serve their own purposes.[93] The history of state-building is less the story of the uniting of a people in pursuit of a common goal than a tale of elite efforts to gain control over a territory and to subdue its population, first by eliminating resistance and then by inculcating a narrative that legitimizes the institutional structure created. This is easier said than done, often because competing elites might resist, and narratives also have to resonate with enough of the population in order to take hold. The European Union has tried for some time to inculcate in its populations a sense of European identity, but has failed to make much impression on people who still see their primary loyalty as belonging to their states. There is, however, nothing natural about the sense of belonging—it is simply that the EU cannot readily undo or override what the French and British and German and Italian states have accomplished over decades, or in some cases, centuries of reinforcement of the morality of national loyalty.

Different states take different views about the basis on which the people who fall under their purview are in some sense members of its political community. They distinguish differently on such questions as the basis of citizenship, the duties of citizenship, and the significance of citizenship. In the UK, citizenship is not necessary to hold voting rights in national or local elections, though EU citizens could (before Brexit) vote in local elections, while members of Commonwealth states resident in the country can still vote in all elections and, if granted Indefinite Leave to Remain in the country, may even stand for public office, including for membership of Parliament. Yet the UK also adheres firmly and exclusively to the principle of *jus sanguinis* and not *jus soli*: birth on British soil does not establish any membership rights, as it does in the United States—which nonetheless allows only citizens to stand for public office or vote in Federal elections (and in most states, to vote in local elections), and requires the President to be a birthright citizen born on American soil. These variations illustrate the larger point at stake here: belonging is not something natural or a matter of subjective feeling or a matter of chosen identity but something that is to a significant degree constructed—and constructed in different ways—by states.

## The State

The idea that immigration control is justified because it is an important tool a state may need to use, since peoples who form and sustain political communities want to be able to determine the direction of the polity, requires a much closer and more critical examination. Though this story is very much a favourite narrative—and it is completely unsurprising that governments and advocates of all sorts should find it useful—it has very little bearing on reality. To see this more fully, however, we have to turn to the matter of the nature of the state. The key point here is that immigration control is not a means of self-determination used by an existing political community, formed into a state to protect its independently given identity, but rather a part of the way in which the state creates and controls its population in order to serve its own interests.

To see this, however, we need first to understand the idea of the state and what it might mean to say that it has interests of its own. Many theories of the state, including liberal ones, present it as a form of association to which we belong, to which owe allegiance and obedience, and which we ought to recognize as embodying the will, or acting for the good, of the people of whom we are a part.[94] The agents of the state are, consequently, our agents; constrained though they may be by the institutions of governance, they are empowered to serve our collective good, for that is the purpose or point of those institutions. Cosmopolitans sometimes hold that states so empowered are capable of serving the interests of people beyond the borders of the state and are therefore well advised, and perhaps obliged, to do so. Nonetheless, they too consider the state to exist to serve the interests of particular populations in the world, including those that lie within its own borders.

Yet the state is not merely a collectivity of persons or groups of persons but something more. It is a corporate entity. This is a point well recognized in contemporary political theory, for many have observed that the modern state is a different type of creature than those kinds of political association that preceded it in Europe, and that existed elsewhere before this political form became the dominant institution of governance around the world.[95] What has not been so clearly appreciated is the implication this has for our understanding of the relationship between the state and its citizens or subjects. The general assumption has been that there is congruence between the interests of the state and the interests of those under its authority. But *encorporation*[96] changes matters in ways that need to be more closely considered. *En*corporation initiated a break between the interests of the people and the interests of their ruling institutions. It is the emergent disconnection between the interests of the state and the interests of the people that needs to be grasped. Here we return to a topic we started to consider in chapter 6 when we examined the cultural case for immigration control.

A corporation can be distinguished from other forms of collectivity by noting that, being a kind of association, with a structure of authority and a capacity for agency, it is capable of having interests of its own. Indeed, it can have interests in a way that other forms of collectivity cannot. More significantly, it can have interests that diverge from the interests of those who are members of the corporation. Corporations are groups that are distinguished from other types of group by this fact. Non-corporate groups are identified by the fact that the interests of the group and the interests of the members of the group are congruent. Some examples may help to clarify this distinction. Clubs, friendly societies, and neighbourhood associations are most readily thought of as non-corporate groups, for their purpose is simply to serve the interests of their members. Those interests need not be purely selfish interests: a conservation group may be made up of members whose interest lies in protecting the local environment and wildlife; and a political group may be made up of people whose interest is in agitating for the release of political prisoners or campaigning for electoral reform. In all of these cases, the group exists to serve the interests of the members, and has no other point. It has no interests of its own.

It is possible, however, for the group to be not simply the means for serving or securing the interests of its members but something of value in its own right. A religious tradition or an ethnic community might be valued not only because its existence serves the interests of the members but also because the group itself embodies values regarded as worth preserving. In this case, there may be a divergence between the interests of the group and the interests of at least some of its members to the extent that some individuals would do better to leave the group, though their leaving might hasten the demise of that entity. If individual members of the Ngarrindjeri tribe abandon traditional ways because they find life as non-tribal Australian citizens more fulfilling, the result might be the decline and disappearance of a culture or way of life whose existence depends on people remaining in the group and preserving its identity. Similarly, if the French-speaking natives of Québec abandoned their language and assimilated more fully into Canadian society, Québec would disappear as a distinctive linguistic or cultural entity. Thus many francophone members of that society have tried to ensure the preservation of that entity by limiting the opportunities of its members to act in ways which, while serving their individual interests, run counter to the interest of the group as a corporate entity.

It is important to notice here that the distinction between corporate and non-corporate groups or entities does not identify and separate natural kinds. It is possible for entities whose existence originates in associations among people to serve their individual interests to acquire a value over and above the interests of the members. This may sometimes be explained by the capacity of human beings to become attached, or attribute value, to forms and structures of all kinds—to the extent that those forms come to be valued, at least by some, more greatly than their own immediate, individual interests. The fact that the existence or perpetuation of the group may not be valued by all its members points to a general tension or conflict commonly found when the interests of groups are at stake. Sometimes these are conflicts between members of groups over matters of organization or policy arising out of the divergent interests of different members. But equally, it is possible for there to be conflict over whether the interests of the group as a corporate entity should take priority over the interests of the individuals who make it up. It is also worth noting that conflicts are always given expression by persons, and when the interests of an abstract entity are asserted they are asserted by particular individuals, so it is always possible that the alleged interests of the group are tied to the interests of particular persons.

The state is often presented as a kind of group established to serve the interests of its members—or at least, that is its point, even if its origins lie elsewhere. What else could the state be for? But if the state is understood as a corporate entity, rather than as a non-corporate collectivity, the state can also be understood as an entity with interests of its own. If so, how are we to understand the interests of the state, and what might those interests be? These are both conceptual questions, though the latter may also have an empirical dimension. We should turn to consider them more closely.

In order to understand what it means for the state to have interests we need first to establish what it is to have an *interest*. The only entities that can have interests are entities with the capacity for agency. To have agency is to have the capacity to make a decision whether or not to pursue some course of action. There are three possible kinds of agent: (some) non-human animals, individual humans, and some collectivities of individual humans. Plants, on this account, do not have interests—even though we can talk quite coherently about what factors or conditions are good or plants—for they are incapable of agency. It makes no sense to speak (except perhaps metaphorically) of the interests of plants. It also makes no sense to speak of the interests of inanimate objects, or landscapes, or forms of experience (like art or music) or the universe, for none of these entities can act. It might be possible that certain non-human animals can act and are, thus, capable of having interests. I propose, however, to leave aside the case of non-human animals and the possibility of their having interests.

Human individuals are the obvious example of entities with interests. To have an interest presupposes a capacity to have ends or purposes, and this capacity attaches only to entities with the capacity for agency. To say that something is in someone's interest is to say more than that thing is good for that person. It is to say that that thing serves the purposes or ends that person has (or, more controversially, *ought* to have). So, for example, to say that chicken soup is *good* for someone who is sick and malnourished is not the same as saying that eating chicken soup is in the *interest* of that person. It would not, for example, be in the interest of a devout Brahmin to consume animal products if his most important ends involve staying true to his religious commitments—even if eating chicken soup would be good to help him recover when sick. In his capacity as an agent he has interests, which are conditional upon the ends or purposes he has adopted. If his aim is to continue to live a life of religious devotion, it may not be in his interest to behave in ways that violate his convictions, even if it is in his interest to get well. Good can be absolute, but interests are always conditional.

Human individuals are not, however, the only example of entities with interests. Some forms of human collectivity are also capable of having interests and are themselves agents—entities with ends or purposes, and with the capacity to make decisions in pursuit of those ends. Not all human collectivities, however, are entities of this kind, so it is important to distinguish the different types. Humans, as I have noted, gather together in a wide variety of collectivities, ranging from families and neighbourhoods to communities and societies; from clubs and trade unions to political parties and governments. The most significant collectivity of which individuals are a part, of course, is the state. Not all of these collectivities have interests of their own. The only collectivities that can are the ones I have called associations. An entity that has no ends or purposes cannot have interests. The interests that an entity has are also tied to those ends or purposes. It would not make sense to say that something is in someone's interests if it does not relate to the ends that person has. (It is, of course, possible to say that someone has interests that do not relate to his existing ends but to ends that he ought to have, but it is doubtful that such a statement refers to the interests of that actual person rather than the interests of a possible person.)

To understand the interests of the state, then, we have to ask what are the ends or purposes of the state. By purpose here I do not mean point or function, because to the extent that the state is considered to have a function it is (at the very least) to serve the interests of its members. I mean rather to ask what are the purposes the state can have as an agent that has some ends of its own. The problem is that it is difficult to conceive of how an abstract entity can have ends, since it cannot have experiences or desires in the way that human agents can. What forms of satisfaction can an abstract entity pursue?

I suggest that the only end we can coherently attribute to an abstract entity is its own existence or perpetuation. In short: its survival. This is perhaps the primary imperative of any agent, but some agents (such as humans) might subordinate this concern to other ends they value more highly—such as flourishing in some particular way that satisfies their desires or sense of what is valuable. Abstract entities, such as corporations of any kind, cannot have desires or be motivated to fulfil them. They can only be governed by the imperative to continue to exist. The question now is, what exactly might this mean? What I'm suggesting is that implicit in the nature or logic of agency is the will to continue to exist, to operate, to function. Built into the structure of any entity with the capacity for agency is an assumption that that entity will continue to exist, and that entity will always act on that assumption. This is not to say that the internal structure of the agent will always be conducive to its survival, but to the extent that it is capable of acting it will always do so to try to overcome the obstacles, internal as well as external, to its survival.

While individual human agents or persons are capable of acting unilaterally, however, corporate agents can only act with the cooperation of human agents. There are no corporate agents without human parts. Corporate entities are therefore dependent for their survival on persons, or in the case of complex corporate entities, on groups of persons, who enable the corporation to function. At the heart of any corporate agent, therefore, is a set of relationships between that entity and the individual and other group agents—all with ends and, therefore, interests, of their own—that make it up. In any such structure, at least to the extent that it is a complex one involving many agents, there will be an elaborate set of relationships among different elements, since the overall entity will depend for its operation on the agents that comprise it, while those internal agents will also have come to depend upon the larger entity for their survival or flourishing.

The state is a complex corporate agent of this sort. Indeed it may be the most complex of all the corporate agents of which there are actual examples. The modern state is a new form of political organization. This is not to say that it bears no relation to earlier institutional structures, but it would be a mistake to think that modern states are simply larger and more complex versions of the political arrangements that were to be found in ancient Greece or medieval Europe.[97]

Even at the time of the emergence of the state in the sixteenth and seventeenth centuries, political authority existed in many forms and in different places: in the Church, in the power of noble families, in towns (and leagues of towns such as the Hansa and the Swabian League), and in the offices of the Holy Roman Empire. The conflict between the Holy Roman Empire and the Church turned out to the benefit of the monarchs of Europe, who were able take advantage of it to consolidate their own power, and further entrench it by overcoming the independent towns. This consolidation laid the foundation for the development of the state. The crucial innovation that made this development possible was the idea of the corporation as a legal person. It made possible the development of a political entity whose existence was not tied to particular persons, such as chiefs, lords or kings, or particular groups, such as clans, tribes or dynasties.

In the Europe of the end of the first millennium, political authority was nothing if not fragmented. As Charles Tilly explains: 'The emperors, kings, princes, dukes, caliphs, sultans, and other potentates of AD 990 prevailed as conquerors, tribute-takers, and rentiers, not as heads of state that durably and densely regulated life within their realms. Inside their jurisdictions, furthermore, rivals and ostensible subordinates commonly used force on behalf of their own interests while paying little attention to the interests of their nominal sovereigns. Private armies proliferated through much of the continent. Nothing like a centralized state existed anywhere in Europe.'[98] Come the start of the fifteenth century, the monarchs of Europe had begun to bring this fragmentation to an end by eliminating their competitors through military force, political alliance, and intrigue. What followed was the consolidation of royal authority by the establishment of bureaucratic structures to support the newly dominant monarchs. With it also came further centralization of political power, and the (brief) appearance of absolutist doctrines of princely authority. It was the eradication of plural centres of political authority that opened the way to the development of the state. The bureaucratic structures which arose under monarchy slowly began to liberate themselves from royal control and from society more generally, and to strengthen their own hold over society by defining its borders, gathering information about it, and establishing regular forms of taxation. Bureaucracy and taxation made possible the establishment of regular armed forces and the securing of something approaching a monopoly on the use of violence.[99]

The *en*corporation of the institutions of governance involved the incorporation of various elements of society. The entity that emerged—the state—was a structure that came to include other individual and collective agents that could contribute to the consolidation of the state's authority and so make possible its continued existence. These agents inevitably had interests of their own, but these interests would now either be pursued through the structures created by the development of the state, or be shaped by their incorporation into the state.

The state has to be understood as an institution with interests of its own, shaped ultimately by its need to do what is necessary to continue in existence. What it needs to do to survive is incorporate whatever elements of society it can to serve this end. It needs people to ensure its survival. It will survive if particular persons benefit from its survival. What it will attract are those elements that find it advantageous to be so incorporated, and over time their interests and the interests of the state will fall into alignment. The question is, what of the interests of the population at large? Does the state serve the interests of all, or only its own interests and the interests of those it has drawn into its bosom?

There are two things to note before trying to answer these questions. First, the population at large is not a fixed collectivity but one that is going to be shaped by the actions of the state. States arise out of populations, but states also create their own populations or peoples—and, indirectly, other populations.[100] Second, it is necessary to appreciate that they do so as a result of the actions of the many people who make up the state and work, directly or indirectly, to sustain it. It would be difficult to overstate the importance of this latter point. In a certain sense, a state, as an 'assemblage of power centers and capacities',[101] cannot itself exercise power, since its powers are exercised by politicians and officials operating in different parts of the state—and even key players act in ways that are constrained by rules, structures, and circumstances that limit what they can do. 'To talk of state managers, let alone the state itself, exercising power masks a complex set of social relations that extend well beyond the state system.'[102] And it says nothing of the conflicts and rivalries that exist within.

Given these two observations, it should be clear that the relationship between the state and populations is not a straightforward one. The state is not the agent of a society or a people; nor is it coextensive with society, even though it might shape or govern it. The state is a strategic actor in a world—an international society—of other similar strategic actors, all of whom operate through the interactions of the individual and group agents that comprise them. Now the complexity of the state need not be an obstacle to its acting, though it does mean that it is difficult to see it either as a mere instrument or as a single-minded overseer of society. What it is, then, is a complex actor that deploys a variety of strategies to secure the interests of those who operate it—or operate through it—and to protect its own interests in self-perpetuation. Centralization, expansion and integration are three notable strategies; *territorial exclusion* is a fourth.[103]

A number of things are worth noting here. First, these strategies were not always pursued because there was uncontested agreement about their value or because all elements of the state apparatus considered them appropriate. The centralization of authority, imperial expansion, and the incorporation and assimilation of populations were all moves that were debated by political elites and the outcomes often reflected not consensus but individual or factional political power. Territorial exclusion was a relatively recently developed state strategy, whose late emergence suggests it is hardly a vital concern of states or populations but merely a policy embarked upon in pursuit of particular political goals. Second, the consequence of any or all of these strategies might have a bearing on the size, the identity, or even the very existence of the state. Centralization might see a contraction of the state, particularly if the concentration of power in the hands of some political elites could only be accomplished by divesting the state of parts that are strongholds of competitors. Expansion might bring into the realm territories and peoples who would change the character and composition of the population, as might the integration of regions or peoples or cultures or religions. All of these strategies, depending on how they are pursued, have the capacity to be transformative of state and society both. Third, these strategies do not always work and the results they bring may be undesirable from the point of view of the architects of policy, and even destructive of the state. This may be why so many states have disappeared.

One of those strategies has been the control of the movement of people. This is a strategy that has taken many forms: the exclusion of people from a state's territory, the limiting of movement within its territory, expulsion or deportation of people from its territory, and the settling of people in other territories. Though exclusion appears to be the dominant element in this strategy, it is in fact a relatively new one—perhaps because for most of human history labour has been an asset and communities of all sorts were disposed to admit workers and reluctant to permit emigration.[104] Immigration control is a modern state strategy. But expulsion has often been used as a means of securing political ends. The expulsion on 30 July 1492 of two hundred thousand Jews from Spain is among the most famous examples, as is the later expulsion on 9 April 1609 of much of Spain's *Morisco* population by Phillip III. But this strategy has endured well into the twentieth century, for example in the forcible transfer of Germans after the Second World War.[105] As the forced migration of millions of people after the Partition of India and Pakistan reveals, however, states have not always been able to determine the outcomes of their efforts to establish territorial stability.[106]

The controlled settlement of populations has also been an important instrument for the shaping of the state and its interests, particularly for imperial powers. Britain supplies a notable example. As Vigneswaran observes, until 'the very end of the nineteenth century, the Crown exerted little interest in excluding foreigners at England's own borders, but was intensely concerned with preparing its subjects to go to the colonies, dictating how they might get there and how far they could travel into the hinterland'.[107] Migration control in this regard was *emigration* control, and its purpose was territorial expansion in the interests of the state as well as of important commercial players. For the sake of successful expansion and colonization of some parts of the world—most notably, India—it was important to send out the right types of people, even if in other regions it mattered less whether the settlers were of the 'highest' quality.[108]

The modern narrative that states need to be able to control immigration in order to preserve their distinctive territorially bound traditions, identities, and political communities bumps up awkwardly against the reality of the way in which states have generally operated for most of their histories. Until the twentieth century, many states showed little interest in immigration control as a means of asserting their political independence or their cultural integrity. When they did look to limit immigration, however, it was as often as not in order to exclude people for being poor,[109] disabled,[110] or racially undesirable. In Britain, the racial dimension became more important once colonists on the subcontinent began to face competition from Indians for senior positions in the colonial administration. The pressure on Whitehall led it to introduce measures to maintain a consistent proportion of 'Europeans' in high-ranking posts. It was from this point that the idea of a 'European heritage' as a justification of privilege began to be given greater credence.[111] One important aspect of this in practical terms was the transformation of imperial policy from one of perpetual expansion to one that distinguished a hierarchy of colonies—with the White colonies of South Africa and Australia considered to be more ready for independence. It also found expression in the eagerness of these colonies to resist non-White immigration from the backward colonies from other parts of the empire.[112] Eventually, as immigrants from colonies in Africa, the West Indies and South Asia started to enter Britain itself, race-based restrictions began to be applied to movement to the empire's homeland.[113] In the United States, race also played a major role in efforts to limit immigration, though once again the complex of political and economic motives make it difficult to regard it as stemming from a concern to preserve identity. This was less true of the American South, however, which came to regard itself as a distinctive tradition with an interest in self-determination.[114] Ironically, it also meant it favoured a form of immigration in the form of the importation of slaves. Viewed under the aspect of this historical record, the idea that the state is best regarded as a kind of keeper of traditions and defender of national identity looks decidedly improbable. The state has never done any such thing, and its adventures abroad suggest that its relationship to its populations needs to be explained by a very different narrative.

Political theorists discussing or describing the state have a tendency to look for cleaner, more philosophical, narratives than history is ready to supply. Thus even Oakeshott's theory of the modern European state, while avowedly not a general theory of the state as such, but an attempt to offer an analysis that might make sense of the development of the European political tradition over the course of only a few centuries, errs in conceiving of it in terms that makes little mention of the fact of empire, the movement of peoples, the perpetual re-drawing of boundaries, and the persistence of internecine conflict.[115] Nonetheless, my purpose here is not to disparage these efforts, or to deny the possibility that there might be something like a political—and legal—tradition that transcends the confusion of everyday life. Nor is it to suggest that there is nothing to political order but politics—the endless bickering and manoeuvring for advantage punctuated by violence and unsteady truces. A more nuanced account of a constitutional order is certainly available. The point is rather to correct the tendency to overstate the coherence of the state enterprise—indeed to see it as an enterprise— when it is really a horse of a very different colour.

In this regard, I am happy to take my cue from a legal thinker like Thomas Poole, whose study of reason of state demonstrates how a modern constitutional polity should be seen as the outcome of a complex relationship between forces internal to a society and pressures coming from without—not only because of economic circumstances but also because of legal and political ties that extend outward to other polities. Thus the development of British public law, for example, cannot be told 'as though it were an island story', even if it would be a mistake to think there was no story to tell.[116]

## Taking Back Control

For many, however, to tell the story of a state or a constitution or a society—*their* society—as the product of a mixture of chance and the influence of distant forces is to diminish that's society's significance, or its worth, or indeed its meaningfulness. It is to give up on the possibility of that society determining its future for itself. It is to relinquish control. One of the reasons advanced for controlling immigration is that it is seen as a vital aspect of 'taking back control' more generally. Internationalization is seen by many as a 'symptom . . . of the downward spiral of the nation's fortunes'.[117] The proponents of the stricter regulation of immigration regularly assert that it is necessary to 'get our country back', though even those who are less troubled by the prospect of people moving freely across national boundaries tend to think that controlling borders is a part of taking control in some larger sense.

This is an illusion. Those who are controlled are undoubtedly limited or restricted in what they can do; but this does not mean that those who exercise control are able to shape the course of events, determine the outcome of policy, or create the future for which they long. It is important not to overstate the point being made here. The argument is not that policies have no consequences, or that there are not better and worse institutions, or that political decisions do not matter. It is rather a counsel to be wary of a certain kind of promise that cannot be fulfilled. This is the promise of self-determination.

To see this we should look more closely at what such a promise might involve before turning to why it should be viewed with scepticism. One formulation of this promise is supplied by the former leader of the United Kingdom Independence Party (UKIP), Nigel Farage, who was quoted before the 2016 Brexit referendum saying: 'What is most important is who governs Britain. What is most important is that we take back control of our Parliament, our courts and borders and have the confidence to believe we can run our own country. The one thing I can guarantee is that if we vote for Brexit, we become a self-governing country. Part of that is that we regain control of our borders.'[118] A philosophical statement of this position can be found in the work of Michael Walzer, who wrote: 'the right to choose an admissions policy is more basic than any of these [other rights], for it is not merely a matter of acting in the world, exercising sovereignty, and pursuing national interests. At stake here is the shape of the community that acts in the world, exercises sovereignty, and so on. Admission and exclusion are at the core of communal independence. They suggest the deepest meaning of self-determination.'[119]

The aspiration given expression here has a number of terms that need to be distinguished. One set of terms identifies the agent whose self-determination is the *subject* of desire: the self. That self—often presented in the first person plural 'we'—is 'the country', or 'the political community', or 'the nation', or (looking beyond the passages quoted above) 'the people' or 'the state'. The other set of terms points to the *object* of self-determination: 'governing', 'taking control' (of parliaments or courts or borders), 'exercising sovereignty', 'pursuing national interests', and 'shaping the community'.

If we consider the first set of terms, denoting the self in self-determination, a number of problems immediately arise: who is the self in question, and how do we identify its wishes? In seeking an answer to the first puzzle, we might consider a number of candidates: all adult natural-born *resident* citizens; all *adult* natural-born citizens; all *natural-born* citizens (adults and minors included); all *citizens* both natural-born and naturalized; all those *eligible* for citizenship (such as people of Jewish descent living outside the country in the case of Israel, German descent in the case of Germany, or British descent in the case of the UK); all *permanent* residents; all residents of *long standing*; or all residents of a country. The class of people who might qualify as members of the self-determining political community could be shrunk further if we exclude those who hold more than one citizenship, or it could be expanded if we included, say, anyone prepared to serve in the country's armed forces. These distinctions are of more than abstract theoretical interest: the Brexit referendum of 2016 might have been decided very differently had Europeans, many of whom had lived in the UK for decades, been eligible to vote and had Commonwealth citizens living in the country as temporary visitors not been so entitled. There is no obvious or natural way to decide this question. History, as we've seen, is not much of a guide, and to appeal to it would, at the very least, beg the question. Nor is the idea that those who work and occupy are special of much help either.

An alternative might be to locate selfhood not in the population but in something less complicated: a monarch, or a parliament, or a constitution, or a territory. But these alternatives come with problems of their own. No monarch today would be inclined to declare 'l'état, c'est moi', no parliament is unaware that its legitimacy and standing rest on popular approval, no constitution is immune from disputes over its interpretation and efforts to amend it, and few territories are completely stable with entirely uncontested boundaries.

Even if we put aside these difficulties, perhaps accepting in a commonsensical way that we are roughly agreed on who the people are,[120] there remains the problem of figuring out what it is the people or the community or the nation or the country expects, prefers, or wants. Turning the various expressions of opinion in a population of thousands or millions into a statement of collective desire or popular will involves a kind of alchemy that defies rational explanation. Though victors (and indeed, the losers) in elections and referenda routinely declare that the people have spoken, they never speak in one voice. In recent referenda in Britain, 48 per cent of voters wished to *remain* in the EU, and 45 per cent of Scottish voters wished to leave the UK. Similarly, it is rare in a democratic election anywhere for a party or candidate to win more than 60 per cent of a vote. When polls reveal 60 or 70 or 80 per cent support for any policy, that also means that 40 or 30 or 20 per cent do not support it. And yet, polls themselves are uncertain measures even of popular opinion, let alone of people's deeper preferences or commitments. Thus, while the EU Commission's spring 2017 survey revealed that 70 per cent of Britons favoured free movement of all EU citizens,[121] this looks inconsistent with other polls that suggest similarly high levels of British hostility to immigration. While immigration is not the same as free movement, the different surveys suggest a complexity in people's views that makes it difficult to say what a majority prefers even on narrowly focused issues. If taking back control means giving a deciding voice to the majority of citizens it will still be difficult to figure out what that means. Polls, elections, and referenda might have some place in giving us an idea of what people think, and sometimes it may be necessary to find a decision procedure to settle questions on which agreement is not possible, but none of this is going to uncover a singular view that can be called the 'will of the people' except in some figurative sense.

In theoretical terms, however, none of this is especially surprising. As Philip Pettit has shown in his elaboration of the 'discursive dilemma', even in simple cases involving a few individuals trying to reach a common conclusion on a single-issue problem, the search for a clear majority ruling that reveals a common will can prove quite fruitless.[122]

Another alternative, however, is that self-determination means government by the people as a *sovereign* power, so that the object of that self-determination is the exercise of that power. Taking back control means taking back *sovereignty*. In the context of debates on immigration control, it means reasserting the right of a state authority to determine who may enter the country, who may participate in various ways (such as studying or taking paid employment or voting), and who may acquire temporary or permanent membership. One common way of expressing this position is to say that it is about reasserting territorial control. But it remains unclear what exactly is the relationship between sovereignty and self-determination—and territory.

Part of the difficulty stems from the problem with the notion of sovereignty itself, which has been variously defined not only by legal and political theorists but also by states pursuing different ends at different times. In the earliest modern formulation of the concept advanced by Jean Bodin in the sixteenth century, sovereignty bore no relation to territory but identified only the scope of the authority of a sovereign power over its subjects— wherever they might be.[123] Even by the time we come, nearly two hundred years later, to the work of Emer de Vattel, the most influential theorist of sovereignty in the modern period, we find very little mention of territory, and a continuing insistence on the idea that the relationship between sovereign power and subject is a juridical one, with the authority of the sovereign deriving from its character as the sole representative of the people both in domestic and international affairs.[124] Vattel's only significant discussion of territoriality appears in his rejection of the idea that states were like patrimonial kingdoms, that claimed to own the territory of the nation.[125] Sovereignty for Vattel meant being recognized as an independent state in a world of nations, all of whom enjoyed the same degree of independence—comparable to the independence free individuals enjoyed within their nations. The state, according to this very influential view, was legitimate because it drew its authority from the willingness of the people to have it act in their interests at home and abroad; but it could not abrogate its sovereignty without duly consulting the people.

Yet if we look at the way in which sovereign states operated over the course of European history from the time of Bodin until the present, we see the standard doctrines of sovereignty invoked when to the advantage of particular state actors, and ignored when inconsistent with state policy at the time. States have repeatedly ceded sovereignty and territory when it has been to their advantage, and declared sovereignty to be shareable or compatible with overlapping jurisdictions when it has suited their interests.[126] In 1803, in order to finance his wars in Europe, Napoleon sold to the United States the French-held territory of Louisiana—lands encompassing fifteen current American states and two Canadian provinces, as well as sixty thousand non-native inhabitants, none of whom were consulted by either party to the sale. (The territory had been ceded by France to Spain in 1762, and re-acquired by Napoleon in 1800 before being sold to the United States during Thomas Jefferson's presidency—despite opposition from the Federalist Party, who argued that it was unconstitutional for America to acquire territory in this way.) More recently, in 1982, the British Navy sailed to the Falkland Islands in defence of the sovereignty of the United Kingdom, which, according to Prime Minister Margaret Thatcher, had been violated by Argentina's invasion to reclaim what it held to be *its* sovereign territory. As it happened, the 1981 British Nationality Act had denied the Islanders citizenship of the United Kingdom.[127] After re-taking the territory, Britain awarded the Falkland Islanders full British citizenship under the British Nationality (Falkland Islands) Act 1983.[128]

There are in fact innumerable ways in which states have enlarged or diminished the scope of their sovereignty. One is to declare the extent of one's territory. Australia in 2001 announced a contraction of its territorial waters by passing the Migration Amendment (Excision from Migration Zone) Act, when it sought to make it more difficult for boats of asylum seekers to make landfall and so be eligible to ask for their claims to be considered.[129] This was unusual given that in recent history it has been more common for states to assert claims to extended jurisdiction. In 1945, President Harry Truman extended American jurisdiction over all resources—oil and natural gas— on the continental shelf, leading other nations to follow suit with similar declarations.[130] Another is to join with other states to create new forms of authority, as did the member states of the European Union. Yet another is to sign treaties and international agreements that, particularly once ratified, bind governments and limit their scope for action—effectively reducing sovereign power. In some circumstances, efforts to increase border control can bring with it a loss of sovereignty. Australia's case is one example, though an unusual one—it is exceedingly rare for a nation to deliberately reduce its territorial extent. But in Europe, the effort to control the external border to prevent people from entering the EU, and to determine where immigrants go should they enter (say, as asylum seekers), has made it necessary to coordinate states to follow a common policy through shared mechanisms, resulting in a loss of independent control by individual sovereign states.[131]

More generally, states limit their sovereign powers whenever they collaborate with other states. Membership of a military alliance, such as NATO, for example, may limit a nation's discretion. Subjecting itself to international regimes, for instance by signing onto the 1951 Refugee Convention, can similarly impose upon a state obligations it might rather not have.

In another sense, however, it is not clear that sovereignty is ever lost by states signing agreements from which they can withdraw. If they have bound themselves *willingly*, then the actions they take under the terms of the agreements they have made are the actions of a sovereign power. There might be no gain in sovereign power by withdrawing from certain agreements, only a loss of influence over others who might be party to the relevant treaty or convention or protocol.

In the end, however, the pursuit of self-determination through the re-assertion of sovereignty is, at best, an uncertain business. If self-determination is to mean more than the power of a political elite to shape the course of a society, it is not clear how this can be secured, since it seems merely to give some part of society the power to determine the future—and indeed, to control the present—of other parts of the political community. In fact, however it is expressed, self-determination always amounts to something less than the control of society by the whole of society. It means a loss of control on the part of many in favour of a gain to a few. To the extent that any victory is won that proclaims that certain things will be done in the name of the people, it only can only mean a loss for the many selves, both individual and collective, whose freedom to set their own courses is now limited by the power of those authorized to act in the people's name. If self-determination means giving power to others to control our selves—by regulating, monitoring, and limiting what we can do—why is this valuable? Why does it even go by the name 'self-determination'?[132]

## We

The stories told about political societies, whether by their leaders, their leading thinkers, and indeed by the led, tend to be stories about groups or communities or peoples united or bound together in ways that make them wholes—entities distinguishable from other similarly bound collectivities with altogether different identities. The similes and metaphors used to describe political society thus tend to draw attention to this boundedness. And so states are homes, or families; and territories are motherlands, fatherlands, or homelands. But these metaphors, like the stories, deceive us.

For the most part they do so by exaggerating the extent to which there is a 'we'[133] that exists: a community of interest held together by a shared past or a shared space, and governing ourselves by the laws we have inherited or made and through the leaders to whom we have freely given allegiance. To point this out is not to deny altogether the existence, or the possibility, of political community. But it is to suggest a more sceptical attitude both to the narratives and to the constructions they describe.

For one thing, political communities are formed—or 'forged'[134] as some are wont to say—less by peoples than by the leaders or elites who create them, and more often than not in order to serve their own particular interests rather than out of a disinterested concern for a previously existing body. The states that have ruled over people have been motivated predominantly by the need for labour or military manpower and the desire for revenue. The extent to which they have sought to serve the requirements of the people over whom they ruled has depended upon how much they needed them.[135] Though this is surely not the whole story.[136] For another thing, history is full of narratives of populations resisting their rulers in revolts and rebellions as well as of rulers abandoning their subjects when it was to their advantage to do so. Oceans rise, empires fall, and boundaries change, even as kings send off their battalions to remind their peoples of their love.

Cicero, in his account of the nature of a commonwealth, said that a people was an assemblage associated by a common acknowledgement of law and a community of interests, also suggesting that it could not exist without justice.[137] In pointing out that on this view Rome could *not* be a commonwealth, since it was founded on violence, theft, and injustice, St Augustine concluded that a very different definition was needed. He suggested that a people is simply 'an assemblage of reasonable beings bound together by a common agreement as to the objects of their love'.[138] What lies behind this expression is an appreciation of the arbitrary and transitory nature of human communities. They endure for different reasons, but in the end they all come and go. They exist at the confluence of different streams of people, moving in and out, across space and over the course of time, at their own distinctive paces. Any particular 'we' that comes into existence will be an assemblage of sorts, but it is an accident that should not be invested with too much significance, even if it ought not to be disparaged entirely.

# 8

# Freedom

As nightfall does not come at once, neither does oppression. In both instances, there is a twilight when everything remains seemingly unchanged. And it is in such twilight that we all must be most aware of change in the air—however slight—lest we become unwitting victims of the darkness.

—JUSTICE WILLIAM O. DOUGLAS, LETTER TO THE YOUNG LAWYERS SECTION OF THE WASHINGTON STATE BAR ASSOCIATION

Democratic peoples who have introduced liberty in the political sphere, at the same time that they increased despotism in the administrative sphere, have been led to some very strange peculiarities.

—ALEXIS DE TOCQUEVILLE, *DEMOCRACY IN AMERICA*[1]

## Abandoned Roads

In 1956, reflecting on some misunderstandings of his concerns about central planning and the allure of the idea of a rationally governed society, F. A. Hayek observed that 'the most important change which extensive government control produces is a psychological change, an alteration in the character of the people. This is necessarily a slow affair, a process which extends not over a few years but perhaps over one or two generations. The important point is that the political ideals of a people and its attitude towards authority are as much the effect as the cause of the political institutions under which it lives. This means, among other things, that even a strong tradition of political liberty is no safeguard if the danger is precisely that new institutions and policies will gradually undermine and destroy that spirit.'[2] Hayek was not the first to express this worry that people could be brought to accept or reconcile themselves to their loss of freedom—or indeed to forget that they ever had it in the first place. Alexis de Tocqueville, writing in the 1830s, thought he saw in the American republic tendencies that would erode the love of liberty, even in a society that was so imbued with the spirit of freedom from the time of its founding.[3]

We have seen how immigration controls limit freedom, not only for would-be immigrants but for the citizens and residents of an otherwise free society, and how those controls have the capacity to diminish equality and to undermine the rule of law. We have also considered the limitations of arguments that these costs are worth bearing because of the gains immigration controls bring—in the form of economic advantage, cultural preservation, and self-determination. But what does it matter if we are controlled—particularly if we are controlling ourselves? And why does the loss of freedom matter—particularly if that loss is not complete but a mere diminution? These questions are not unrelated, but to see how and to understand why any loss of freedom might be worth worrying about, we should consider these concepts and their meanings more closely. We will then be in a position better to appreciate the relationship between immigration and freedom.

## Control

What is it to be controlled, and why does it matter if we are—particularly if it is for our own good, but perhaps even more so if it is for the benefit of the many others (rather than for an exploitative few)? I shall yield to the temptation to begin a discussion of this question by quoting Proudhon's famous statement about what it means to be governed.

> To be GOVERNED is to be watched, inspected, spied upon, directed, law-driven, numbered, regulated, enrolled, indoctrinated, preached at, controlled, checked, estimated, valued, censured, commanded, by creatures who have neither the right nor the wisdom nor the virtue to do so. To be GOVERNED is to be at every operation, at every transaction noted, registered, counted, taxed, stamped, measured, numbered, assessed, licensed,

authorized, admonished, prevented, forbidden, reformed, corrected, punished. It is, under pretext of public utility, and in the name of the general interest, to be placed under contribution, drilled, fleeced, exploited, monopolized, extorted from, squeezed, hoaxed, robbed; then, at the slightest resistance, the first word of complaint, to be repressed, fined, vilified, harassed, hunted down, abused, clubbed, disarmed, bound, choked, imprisoned, judged, condemned, shot, deported, sacrificed, sold, betrayed; and to crown all, mocked, ridiculed, derided, outraged, dishonoured. That is government; that is its justice; that is its morality.[4]

Is this what it is to be controlled, and do all of these passive verbs really tell us what is wrong with that, or are they nothing more than the tendentious muttering of an anarchist? It may be one thing to be 'fleeced' or 'hoaxed' or 'abused' or 'choked' or 'shot' or 'mocked' or 'dishonoured', but still quite another to be 'authorized', 'corrected', 'disarmed' or 'judged'. Let me suggest what is at stake here by returning to the words put into the mouth of Pericles by Thucydides when the Athenian general praised the freedom of his city. Among other things, he said, the men of Athens could in 'ordinary life' go about their business, each without worrying that his neighbour was 'exercising a jealous surveillance' over him, and that in all his private relations he could enjoy a certain 'ease'. The 'ease' to which Pericles alludes is an ease of a particular kind: it comes when there is a sense of assurance that one is not under scrutiny, being watched by others looking for a misstep, and so a mere snitch away from falling into serious trouble.

To grasp what this could mean, consider the case of the East German musician and poet, Wolf Biermann, who was expatriated in 1976 after being declared a class traitor for his nonconformist attitudes and his inclination to mock the political authorities in his adopted country through his poems and songs. Biermann, like so many citizens of the German Democratic Republic (GDR), was the subject of surveillance by the Stasi or secret police, who assembled some ten thousand pages of information on him, gathered not only through direct monitoring but also through the friends and colleagues who informed on him. His experience differed from that of many of his compatriots inasmuch as he was free of government scrutiny after his expulsion. Nonetheless, it raises the question of what is troubling or disturbing about, or wrong with, such a world. One answer might be that the privacy of Biermann and others was violated, but that seems like a relatively minor harm if it is all that happened—even though we consider privacy something worth protecting. Another might be the demand for conformity itself, which seems like a denial of our individuality; but that too is surely something that should not be overstated, given that all forms of human association require their members to conform to some degree. To be sure, however, the demand for conformity within a single political society is a greater concern than in other forms of association given the difficulty of withdrawing from it and divesting oneself of that burden. We need to look elsewhere to uncover what is wrong with the kind of society Wolf Biermann came to find so unlovely—and so frightening.

One part of the answer is what it did to the relationships people were able to enjoy. To understand this, however, we should begin by recognizing that there are two ways of controlling human beings. The first is by controlling the spaces—whether physical or virtual—they can enter. This might be achieved by barriers that prevent them from moving into some places or out of others, or prohibitions that restrict their activity by the threat of sanctions should they breach the rules. The second is by more subtle exercises of power to induce people to behave in one way or another, whether by supplying positive incentives or by creating anxiety that any failure to comply would be met not only with penalties or punishment but righteous disapproval. Ultimately, what this second form of social control seeks is a transformation of consciousness. Conformity itself is not the problem for it is not intrinsically bad or undesirable. It is the capacity of social control to bring about that remaking of consciousness that is the real source of concern.

Few historical episodes give us greater understanding of the way in which institutions of social control have the capacity to bring about such a change for the worse—to produce an evil form of existence—than the case of communism. To appreciate this insight, we need not focus only on the *gulags*—the labour camps—or on the prisons or the medical clinics or other means by which populations were subjected to violence and intimidation, though the importance (and necessity) of such institutions in securing the goals of communist regimes ought not be discounted. We should turn rather to the way in which everyday life was shaped, and distorted, by the controls imposed upon citizens. The result of this was what Alain Besançon called communism's 'moral destruction', which was brought about not solely through violence but by the eroding of morality using more subtle means.

> At first, a significant portion of the population welcomes the teaching of the lie in good faith. It enters into the new morality, taking along its old moral heritage. . . . Hating the enemies of socialism, they denounce them and approve of having them robbed and killed. . . . Inadvertently,

they take part in the crime. Along the way, ignorance, misinformation, and faulty reasoning numb their faculties and they lose their intellectual and moral bearings. . . . Life . . . became grimmer, more dismal. Fear was everywhere and people had to fight to survive. The moral degradation that had been subconscious to that point now crept into consciousness. The socialist people, who had committed evil believing they were doing good, now knew what they were doing. They denounced, stole, and degraded themselves; they became evil and cowardly and they were ashamed.[5]

The moral destruction of which Besançon writes, as he goes on to explain, is not merely the loss of traditional mores, about which the old might grumble as they observe the behaviour of the young. Communism, like Nazism, set out to change not just moral rules but the very idea of the rule of morality. To achieve this end, it had to undermine the basis of morality itself, which is to be found not in the rules devised by reason (or the authorities who invoke it) but in the lives people make in their relationships—personal and private or public—with others.[6] It had to turn people into state informants on their neighbours, co-workers, friends, and families, making everyone so suspicious of one another that in the end civil society itself contracted as the realms of mutual trust shrank to the size of a kitchen.

To sustain this achievement, however, it was also necessary to go further still, for the continued working of communist society depended on a level of compliance that could be secured only by maintaining publicly the fiction that the system was working and that the faults and flaws (if they existed at all) were mere aberrations—*bugs* rather than *features*. It depended on what Alexandr Solzhenitsyn, referring to the Soviet variant of communism, called 'the lie'.[7] When Lenin and the Bolsheviks seized power they had 'the most sublime of goals: a society rebuilt without exploitation and oppression, in which humanity could at last taste true freedom'.[8] The loftiness of the goal drove the imperative to use whatever means were necessary to reach it. The lives of citizens would have to bend to that necessity, as would, inevitably, the truth. In Solzhenitsyn's Soviet Union, living 'the lie' extended to turning a blind (or blinded) eye not just to the everyday failings of a ramshackle economy but to the historical reality of the 'special camps' and the continued imprisonment and brutalization of those who fell afoul of the authorities.

What is wrong with living under the 'jealous surveillance' of one's fellows is not the inconvenience, or the heightened risk of punishment, but that to live in this way is to find oneself in a society in which something more fundamental is being—or has been—eroded. It is to live in a world in which the idea of morality has been cheapened and the importance of humanity is diminished. To learn to live under the control of others is to learn to live with the fact that yet others are also controlled and then to learn how to treat that fact as a matter of indifference. Reviewing Florian Henckel von Donnersmarck's 2006 film about the East German secret police, *The Lives of Others*, Wolf Biermann observed that it had become common years after reunification for former West Germans to strike attitudes of a kind of non-judgmental indifference to the people of the former GDR who were complicit in state crimes. In 'twisted Hamlet soliloquys', he suggests, they wonder whether they would have had the courage to oppose the totalitarian regime had they been in the place of any of its former citizens. Such a soliloquy might run as follows: 'Whether I would have been courageous in the GDR or cowardly, . . . I cannot say. And that is why I'd rather not judge these things, not to mention judging the people who—who knows—only swam with the tide or, in good faith that they were doing the right thing, collaborated with the secret police or, simply in ignorance or fear, and with great sadness in their hearts, inflicted misery on others. I'll keep out of all this.'[9] Biermann's impatience with what he called the bankruptcy and 'shabby modesty' of such 'bogus declarations' stems from the larger point he wished to make about the nature of the kind of regime he was trying to criticize. It turned people into moral cowards. To ask, at least in this instance, 'who knows what I would have done?', is to be guilty of 'a cowardly flight to what Immanuel Kant called "self-imposed immaturity"';[10] but that immaturity is precisely what marked the behaviour of those who lived under the GDR. Control doth make cowards of us all. That cowardice was expressed, in large measure, not in failing to stand up (whether openly or in secret) to an oppressive regime but in the avertings of gaze and the readiness to pretend that things (that happened to others) were not so bad—in the unwillingness to become inculpated by learning the truth.

The history of communism is so instructive because it allows us to see clearly the pathologies of the controlled society.[11] It would be a mistake, however, to take from its example only the lesson that the suppression of markets is the key to the problem, or that their liberation is a sufficient solution—important as markets might be not only for economic efficiency but also for facilitating the independence of private sources of power that makes criticism and resistance possible. Even market societies are subject to control and, as within communist ones, that control is exercised both by restricting the things people may do and by trying to shape the way people think. As is the case with totalitarian regimes, the impulse to control comes from the imperative to achieve the goals of policy; and the more likely it is that policy will meet with non-compliance or dissent, the greater is the imperative to control both what people do and how they might think. The populace will respond either by resisting or by complying—though that resistance or compliance will be a matter of degree and may vary not only in its depth but also in its extent, since some might resist while others comply. Achieving the necessary degree of compliance requires that a regime induce the populace to embrace the policy and its goals, and to be wary of dissenting—whether for fear of punishment or from anxiety that one is out of step with accepted norms. If the regime truly succeeds, however, the populace will embrace both policy and goal not simply out of fear but out of indifference or even out of a sense of right. 'To govern . . . is to structure the possible field of action of others.'[12]

Some examples would be useful here, and a good place to begin is the Australian state's policies on refugees and asylum seekers from the start of the twenty-first century. In 1975, after the end of the Vietnam War, Australia found itself a major destination for a large number of asylum seekers fearing for their safety under the new communist regime. In a short period of time, over 52,000 refugees who arrived by boat were re-settled with relatively little difficulty or public outcry.[13] It would not do to exaggerate this: Australia's long history of race-based hostility to immigration had not ended abruptly with the official abandonment of the White Australia Policy over the period between 1966 and 1972,[14] and there were plenty of voices expressing anxiety or anger over the arrival of 'boat people' from Indochina.[15] But refugee policy was a minor issue for the public, and Australian governments over the next ten years were as anxious to maintain Australia's human rights reputation[16] as they were about any public antipathy towards refugees.[17]

By 2015, however, the picture had changed very dramatically. Australia now had adopted an entirely different approach to refugees, the imperative being to 'stop the boats' and prevent asylum seekers from coming to the mainland by any other than tightly controlled official channels. The key to the new strategy was the 'Pacific solution' introduced in 2001.[18] From then onwards, asylum seekers travelling by boat would be intercepted and relocated to detention centres established on the territories of other countries in the Pacific where their claims might be assessed. The conditions under which inmates were held indefinitely were such that the policy drew widespread condemnation, with the detention centres described as making up Australia's own 'gulag archipelago'.[19] The reason for international criticism was the brutality of the living conditions under which asylum seekers were held, with reports of beatings and sexual assault commonplace. Detainees driven to despair by their circumstances resorted to violence and riot or succumbed to the pressures imposed by a sense of hopelessness by self-harming (such as by sewing up their lips with paper clips), developing serious mental illness or, ultimately, committing suicide.[20]

The point here is not to belabour the depths of the cruelty inflicted on innocent people who had committed no crimes and were, at worst, guilty of foolishness in setting out into the Pacific in barely seaworthy vessels, whether to search for opportunity or simply to escape danger.[21] What bears noting is the lengths to which successive Australian governments (and parties in opposition) would go in order to preserve a cruel and irrational policy that brought them widespread condemnation and ridicule. The cruelty of the policy was evident in the violence inflicted on detainees. The irrationality became plain once the cost of detaining asylum seekers offshore was revealed: 440,000 Australian dollars (345,000 US dollars) per person per year.[22] Condemnation came in the form of numerous reports in the international press, following criticism by humanitarian agencies.[23] Ridicule followed a leaked transcript of the telephone conversation between the newly elected American President, Donald Trump, and the then Prime Minister of Australia, Malcolm Turnbull, in which the Prime Minister tried, unsuccessfully, to explain why America should take the detainees when Australia would not.[24]

The cruelty itself is not the point here, troubling though it might be. The crucial development to note is the measures taken by successive Australian governments to sustain an exceptionally poor policy and the extent to which these efforts involved not only attempts to get around or thwart Australian legal institutions but also an effort to control the narrative that was needed to secure the support of the population. First, legislation was drafted hastily and passed quickly to ensure that the policy was put into operation with minimal scrutiny. From time to time, legislation was amended and backdated in anticipation of legal challenges to proposed actions.[25] Second, restrictions were put in place to limit independent inspections of the detention centres, and journalists were denied access. In the end, evidence of poor conditions and the abuse of detainees was smuggled out rather than brought to light as a consequence of freely conducted investigations.[26] In general, considerable efforts were taken by the government to conceal its actions and the practical working of the policy it was pursuing—calling to mind the efforts of South Africa's governments to conceal the impact of apartheid from a prying world press.[27] Third, in order to pursue a policy that required preventing asylum seekers making landfall on Australian territory, the Australian government resorted to negotiating with two regional governments and offering financial inducements to persuade them to accommodate an arrangement other governments found to be questionable. The corrupt and corrupting nature of this endeavour was widely remarked upon but generally ignored by the Australian government. Fourth, in order to pursue this course, the government had to develop and promote a certain narrative that justified its policy—one that would resonate with the Australian public, or at least with enough of the populace to make the policy electorally palatable.

The extent to which Australian government policy succeeded in shaping public opinion is difficult to assess, particularly over a highly contentious issue on which the public remains deeply divided.[28] What is less unclear is that the effort to manipulate and control the narrative was stepped up in response to criticism, and possibly also in order to reassure key political constituencies on whose support governments depend.[29] Thus, for example, governments have continued to represent asylum seekers arriving by boat as among the privileged or wealthy able to pay vast sums to 'people smugglers', who take places from more deserving refugees who have waited patiently for resettlement under the humanitarian aid programme—despite the inaccurate and misleading nature of both aspects of this official claim.[30] Successive Australian governments have also continued to insist that the policy of deterring arrivals by boat saves the lives of would-be asylum seekers without addressing the obvious and frequently made point that this may not be preventing deaths but simply ensuring that people fleeing danger come to grief sooner rather than later.

The measure of the success of the Australian government in controlling the citizenry on this question must be considered, then, not in terms of opinion poll numbers reporting levels of approval or disapproval of aspects of refugee policy, but in the way in which it has been able to *normalize* the issue. While some people might be making a fuss, drawing attention to abuses or wrongs or violations of human dignity, the whole matter has been managed well enough that it is possible to say: 'there is much to be discussed and of course opinions differ, but the government can reassure an anxious public that everything is in order and there is no cause for any concern'.

In 1976, shortly after French viewers saw the first filmed reports to appear in the west of life in a Soviet detention camp—depicting scenes of guard towers, barbed-wire fences, police dogs, and prisoners transported in trucks like animals—the journalist, K. S. Karol, asked Michel Foucault what he made of the response of the French public. That reaction had been, by Karol's account, one of relief: though the Soviet spokesmen asked about the film at first denied its authenticity, they later admitted the existence of the camp but justified it by insisting that only non-political prisoners were interned, and the French public was on the whole reassured that it was not a cause for concern since the detainees were just common criminals. Foucault, however, observed that what was striking about the Soviet claim was the assertion that 'the very existence of the camp in plain view in the middle of a city proved that there was nothing shocking about it'.[31] There was, according to the Soviet authorities, nothing to object to because the people detained were merely criminals and not political prisoners. The technique, Foucault points out, is to try to explain away the brutality by *normalizing* it. It is almost as if to say that when things are in plain view there is nothing to see. (Recall the reaction of British officials to the question of whether immigration authorities were conducting virginity tests: first to deny, then to explain away, then to justify, and then normalize.) The point of making such a move, however, is to inure the public to reality so that it might not be troubled or disturbed or provoked into action. What Solzhenitsyn called 'the lie' is not so much something people consciously believe as something they live through passive acceptance.

The Australian detention camps and the politics of their normalization provide one example of the way in which the logic of social control operates. It would be a mistake, however, to think that this case is an outlier or an exception. On the contrary, it offers only a recent (and not exceptionally dramatic) instance of the way in which states everywhere have operated to try to control their borders and their populations through the development of detention regimes. In the United States, the practice of detaining or imprisoning (suspected) unauthorized or unwanted immigrants goes back some time, particularly in the policing of the border with Mexico.[32] But there is also a significant history of refugee or asylum-seeker detention, most notably in order to control the movement of Caribbean people trying to leave Haiti and Cuba. The 'wet foot, dry foot' policy put in place under President Clinton in 1994 anticipated Australia's Pacific Solution in maintaining that asylum seekers who landed on American soil would be considered as potential refugees, while those who were intercepted and did not reach dry land would be detained offshore and returned if possible.[33] This policy has to be understood in the context of a history of immigration control that saw the creation of the world's largest detention system that is a network of prisons dubbed 'the carceral archipelago'.[34]

That term might be applied with equal justification to the system of border control, deportation, and detention established and maintained by the European Union which, for all its commitment to free movement within member states, has developed an extensive network of immigrant and asylum-seeker detention camps of its own. Though they go by different names ('removal centres' in Great Britain or 'zones d'attente' in France),[35] detention camps have grown in number across Europe. By 2009 there were 224 such camps across the EU, with forty-five in Germany, twenty in France, sixteen in Italy, thirteen in Spain, twelve in Great Britain and ten in Greece.[36] In 2011, the Migreurop network listed nearly three hundred migrant detention facilities in the twenty-seven EU states, and estimated that each year nearly six hundred thousand migrants (including EU citizens) are detained on EU territory for the purpose of 'migratory management'.[37] The period of detention ranges from a matter of days to eighteen months (not including those caught in limbo as persons denied the freedom to stay but incapable of being deported).[38]

There are few states that have not adopted the institution of the detention camp. Even Canada, which is often singled out as a country with immigrant-friendly policies, makes substantial use of the same technology of border control as its American and European counterparts, and its facilities and practices exhibit the same pathologies as those found in detention camps everywhere. On any given day, between 550 and 650 people are detained across Canada for immigration-related reasons, either in camps or in prisons (because the camps are full and the penitentiary system has been needed to deal with the overflow).[39] Nor is this a practice one that is confined to the countries of the developed west.[40] What also bears noting is the extent to which governments everywhere are reluctant to make available information about the number of detention camps in operation, their sizes, and the composition of their detainees.[41]

The point of drawing attention to the example of detention—to bring us back to the question with which this discussion began—is to enable us to see more clearly what it means to live in a controlled society. To consider this more closely we should to return to the idea Hayek put forward in *The Road to Serfdom*: that the controlled society was one whose most significant and lasting consequence was a transformation of consciousness. The transformation in question is the development of an outlook or mindset that is, in the end, indifferent to, or even able to embrace, the life of a denizen of a society in which freedom is consistently restricted, or indeed violated. The problem here is not simply that people might be complicit in the various wrongs perpetrated by authorities whose legitimacy they have helped sustain—though that might sometimes be a part of the story. It is rather that they might reach that point at which they are no longer able to recognize complicity because they are unable to recognize the wrongs committed in their name, or to see that their liberty has been lost.[42]

If this is so, then we might want to understand the nature of the controlled society by going a step past the sentiments expressed by Pericles when he identified the free society as one whose members felt a kind of 'ease', certain in the knowledge that they were not living under the suspicious gaze of their fellows. What might be even more alarming about the controlled society is that it is by rendering its members incapable of recognizing how their freedom has been diminished that such ease as they know is purchased.

## Freedom

And yet, why should we concern ourselves about freedom? Not everyone cares for freedom and it would be foolish to suggest that they do, even as it would be impertinent to tell them that they should. Though it may be hard to imagine anyone relishing the idea of being under the control of others,[43] it remains true that many things can be preferred over freedom: prosperity, piety, honour, happiness and, most obviously, love. This is not to suggest that freedom is a weird[44] preference. It is simply to recognize that a life cannot be lived meaningfully—or even coherently—if guided by only one value to the exclusion of all others; and that means that freedom is always enjoyed in a life in which other ends have a place, as well as that for some its place is lesser than it is for others.

Before we can address the question of why we should care about freedom, however, we should consider what we mean by freedom. If freedom is valuable, among the reasons for its being valuable is that it leaves us to determine for ourselves what we value, and how to pursue the various ends we come to have. As a political principle, freedom is important because it recognizes that human purposes and aspirations are diverse and accepts that people should live the lives they wish to lead, not the lives that others deem good, best, or somehow fit for them. Freedom, then, is a condition in which a particular relationship obtains between ourselves and others with respect to the various ends or purposes we have.

A person is free to the extent that she is able to pursue her ends unimpeded by others; she is freer the greater the range of opportunities she has to act and the greater the value attached to the opportunities she has; and her freedom is of value to her to the extent that she feels free. A person is also freer the more secure she is in the possession of her freedom—if she is not uncertain as to whether her freedom is about to be lost. To be free a person must *feel* free. A person who does not feel free at all attaches no value to the opportunities she has to act and is unfree.

A society is free to the extent that those who live within it (members and non-members alike) are able to pursue their ends unimpeded by others; it is more free the greater the range of opportunities they have to act and the greater the value attached to the opportunities they have; and their freedom is of value to them to the extent that they feel free. The less secure they are in the possession of their freedom, and the more unsure they are of whether that freedom is about to be lost, the less free is their society. A society is unfree if those who live within it attach no value to the opportunities they have and do not feel free.

A person, whether or not she is free, may value freedom highly, or value it little, or value it scarcely at all. Even if she values it considerably, she may rank it less highly than other things she considers more important. She might therefore be willing to forsake some (or possibly all) of her freedom for some other end. Few consider freedom to be a value whose worth is absolute or think that freedom ought never to be traded away. Many hold freedom even less dear and gladly give much of it up in the service of other goals: soldiers forsake a good deal of freedom on joining the army; priests forsake it on taking their vows; individuals give up a little of it from time to time for many reasons—to do their duty, to please others, to improve themselves, to set an example, or because they think it will make them happier. To the extent that they forsake freedom willingly they forsake less freedom since they give up some opportunities in order to gain others they value more, though sometimes this may mean contracting dramatically the scope of their freedom. (Someone who joins a monastery may still feel some longing for the many everyday pleasures he has forsaken even if the opportunity to fulfil his spiritual calling matters more to him than the numerous options he must now forgo.)

A society, composed as it is of individuals who themselves value freedom to varying degrees, may value freedom highly, or value it lightly, or value it scarcely at all. Even societies that value it greatly may value it less than other goods to the extent that their laws and institutions allow for or require that freedom be traded off from time to time in favour of other goods, such as security or welfare or equality or piety, or some combination of such goods.

They will require individuals to forsake some of their freedom to ensure that some of these other goals, collectively deemed desirable, might be met. Forsaking freedom, willingly or unwillingly, is commonplace. One important factor that distinguishes a freer society from a less free one is the extent of the freedom that is not unwillingly forsaken.

Freedom according to this view has four dimensions: scope, value, sense, and resilience. Scope refers to the range or number of opportunities an individual has to act unimpeded. Value refers to the worth of those opportunities, which can vary from the trivial (wiggling one's fingers) to the substantial (travelling where one wishes).[45] Sense refers to the individual's subjective appreciation or perception of her freedom (that is, to whether she feels free). Resilience refers to the likelihood that the freedom defined along the other dimensions will continue to exist into the future (which means that people living in fear, or with yet to be fulfilled threats to their freedom, or under arbitrary rule, are less free if there is a low probability of their freedom remaining as extensive as before).

Not all theories of freedom accept this analysis. One reason for this is that some theorists have aspired to establish a wholly 'value-free'—and so, perhaps, an *objective*—definition of freedom. Thomas Hobbes, for example, insisted that *scope* was the only matter at issue: one was free to the extent to which one could act unimpeded. The value of the options at one's disposal had no bearing on the freedom to act, any more than did the feeling one had on taking an option one did not really like. A person giving up his wallet at gunpoint might not like the available options and therefore feel unfree to do anything other than what a highwayman demands, but he is not in fact unfree to resist, any more than he is unfree when he complies. Once one goes down the path of defining freedom according to the palatability of the options, Hobbes reasoned, freedom would cease to have any independent meaning and would become a much looser term encompassing a whole range of other values—ones whose absolute and relative merits were themselves subject to dispute. But the Hobbesian view buys consistency and rigour at the expense of compatibility with other intuitions about freedom (and indeed, with everyday usage), which tend to distinguish more from less important limitations on action. More significantly still, it neglects altogether the element of the *subjective* nature of the experience of freedom. Though it would be going too far to suggest that we could be free simply because we feel free—it is quite possible to be deluded about our freedom, like a contented slave—a life that is not experienced as free cannot be regarded as free. Indeed, the Hobbesian account cannot recognize the lack of freedom even of the discontented slave if that slave actually has a wide range of options such that the scope of his freedom is considerable—and possibly even greater than that of some people who are not enslaved.[46] To be free a person has to have a range of options and those options have to include among them ones that are valuable and, crucially, *valuable to the agent.*

The risk that comes with building more into the definition of freedom than the mere absence of impediments to action is that freedom would cease to have independent standing as a value and could no longer be recognized as something that has to be weighed in the balance or traded off against other desiderata. This is why theorists of freedom are often anxious to avoid presenting 'moralized'[47] conceptions of freedom according to which freedom is not lost if the restrictions or limitations placed upon persons are justified. We want to be able to say that an imprisoned murderer who has been justly punished has lost his liberty, or that someone who is subpoenaed and required to appear in court has been forced and had his liberty curtailed even if justifiably so under the law. Nonetheless, a definition of freedom that recognized only actual (material) impediments to action as freedom-restricting would fail to recognize that freedom, as a social relation, is something that exists or is lost not merely in the physical realm but in the social world populated by conscious subjects or agents. Even Hobbes recognizes this when he maintains that liberty exists when the laws are silent but not when they prohibit actions of one kind or another.[48] (To be consistent he would have had to say that even when laws prohibit actions, individuals remain free inasmuch as they retain the option of disobeying and paying the penalty.) In the end, our freedom is something we experience in the intersubjective realm as agents rather than merely in the objective world as bodies, so among the most important restrictions on our freedom are constraints imposed on our thinking.

If all this holds true, to be free we need not merely to live with a range of options we value available to us but also to be agents of a certain kind: persons capable of thinking, assessing, and judging; of reflecting upon our circumstances; and of expressing our resentment when impeded or constrained. Very few people fail this test of agency altogether: it is hard to imagine many circumstances in which persons grow up without any capacity to judge, to reflect, or to feel the sting when prohibited—or even discouraged— from taking some desired action. It is also true, however, that not everyone is equally capable of judging, or equally interested in reflecting upon and assessing their situations, or equally bothered when constrained. Nor is everyone equally interested in or troubled by the same constraints, just as some are more sanguine than others about the future no matter what obstacles appear in their paths. Still, most of us are capable of freedom because we are able to exercise the capacity for agency.

Our freedom can be compromised, then, in either of two general ways: by actions or arrangements that impede our capacity to pursue the ends we value, or by actions or arrangements that shape or direct our thinking to accustom us to those restrictions or limitations that might otherwise have been sources of resentment. We therefore become less free when others, whether acting individually and deliberately or operating indirectly and collectively through institutions, limit or restrict us by imposing practical impediments that prevent our pursuit of ends we consider important or by prohibiting us (with the aid of promised sanctions in the event of a failure to comply) from pursuing those ends. We also become less free when others, whether acting directly, or indirectly through institutions, work to accustom us to our circumstances so that we are disinclined to view any absence of freedom as a loss.

The problem with thinking about freedom in this way is that everything turns on the judgments that have to be made about the ends people have, and the kind of world that is created, by placing some rather than other limitations upon action—or by maintaining institutions that create one kind of person rather than another. The temptation to go down the Hobbesian route is plain: thinking about freedom simply as action unimpeded by any constraint delivers us from the need to make contentious judgments about which actions are valuable or which impediments count as constraints. For Hobbes, being constrained by others is unavoidable in human society and the purpose of political institutions—and the law—is to determine which sorts of actions to permit and which to prohibit. His point, however, was never to protect or enlarge freedom but to secure other desirable ends—most notably, peace. If one doesn't particularly care for freedom, the Hobbesian definition would do very nicely.[49]

Should we wish to regard freedom as something that has some value, however, and consider that a reduction of freedom might be a loss, a different understanding is required. But such an understanding must then depend upon judgments about what ends count as worthwhile or what kinds of constraints are unacceptable. So, what is it that matters and makes for an unfree way of being? The temptation at this point is usually to look for that one decisive element that supplies the key to the problem—to find that freedom is, perhaps, a matter of being *self-directing*, or not subject to *domination* by others, or not being *coerced*, or being *independent*, or not forced to accept someone else's *arbitrary exercise of power*. Such reductionist strategies are unsatisfying, however, because they seek a simplicity that is at odds with the more complex story that needs to be told to explain what it is to be, and what is undesirable—and indeed, unlovely—about living as, an unfree being. Moreover, they place all the emphasis on the obstacles or impediments to action and so pay insufficient attention to the subjective dimension of freedom.[50]

Here a historical example might be instructive. In the years after the Prophet Muhammad conquered Medina and Mecca he established a constitution according to which non-Muslims could live freely under Muslim rule but as people of the *dhimma* or 'protected persons'. While dhimmis enjoyed full protection of rights of property and contract and could worship within their own communities as they wished, they paid additional taxes and did not have the same political rights as Muslims. They were not subject to some of the restrictions imposed upon Muslims, who were forbidden to eat pork or drink alcohol, and dhimmi communities, such as the Jewish community, were able to have their own laws and courts. Over time, dhimmi status was extended to include not only Jews, Christians, and Sabians but also other religious groups such as Zoroastrians and Hindus. It would not do to deny that the dhimmi lived as second-class citizens, for they were ruled by powers that did not recognize them as equals and did not accord them the same political rights. They were not free from coercion or domination, even as they enjoyed a measure of independence—constrained though it was by certain political realities. Their position was thus precarious, but it has to be acknowledged that although such freedom as they enjoyed was not as resilient or robustly guaranteed as they might have desired, it was something that was sustained for several hundred years under the millet system of the Ottomans. But was this freedom?

There are a number of aspects to this story. In some respects, non-Muslims clearly enjoyed less freedom than did Muslims because their political rights were limited. On the other hand, the constitutional structure that emerged was one that saw a separation of powers between rulers and the scholars (*ulama*) who were responsible for the interpretation of sharia law, making it difficult for rulers to exercise power without the support of the communities they governed. For the Jewish dhimmis, although they were not the equals of Muslims, the extent of their opportunity to practise their faith made them freer than Jews in Christian Europe (leading many to migrate particularly to Muslim Spain, which was ruled by various caliphates until the re-conquest by Christians accomplished by 1492[51]). Both Jewish and

Christian communities enjoyed a level of personal safety and security of property as well as legal autonomy and a guarantee of freedom of worship. But this was conditional on continued loyalty to Muslim rulers and payment of taxes.[52] Dhimmis were also forbidden to proselytize or display religious symbols and in parts of the Islamic world were not allowed to ride horses and camels or act in public ways that were deemed offensive to Muslims. To some extent, then, dhimmis enjoyed a substantial measure of freedom inasmuch as they were left to themselves and able to live as they wished; but at the same time, they were not equals with Muslims and enjoyed such freedom as they did only insofar as their political rulers condescended to tolerate them.

Were the dhimmis free? From the standpoint of a theory of freedom emphasizing the importance of *non-domination*, it looks like they were not—since they were subject to the power of political rulers against whom they had no political rights and were second-class citizens in the lands on which they were settled. Though they were accorded important legal protections that allowed them to live independently of the wider Muslim society, the *resilience* or robustness of that freedom would also have to be questioned since the possibility of it being taken away was always present. Furthermore, the *scope* of that freedom was limited by the number of options that were forbidden to them, again suggesting they were not free.

Nonetheless, what also needs to be weighed in the balance is the fact that for many of the dhimmi the alternatives—including ones that they had forsaken—were worse from the perspective of freedom. In the world they now inhabited they were able to govern themselves, cleave to their own traditions, and live by ethical views rejected yet tolerated by their political superiors, and above all, worship their own gods in the ways they saw as right and proper. Arguably, the freedoms they forsook were much less important to them than the ones to which they accorded most *value*. If so, it would be plausible to consider the dhimmi substantially free. Indeed, it appears as though they saw themselves to be so, even though it could not be denied that they also had to endure all kinds of restrictions.

Now, none of this is to suggest that all religious communities or individuals will see matters in this way and accord overwhelming value to religious devotion or living within their own particular traditions. The various responses of the Jews who suffered persecution and were then threatened with expulsion from fifteenth-century Spain offers a cautionary example here. Over the period leading up to the Alhambra Decree of 1492, large numbers of the Jewish population converted to Christianity, some through the forced baptisms that followed massacres of Jews in the major cities of Spain in 1391, and others in anticipation of violence. When King Ferdinand and Queen Isabella's 1492 Edict gave Jews four months to decide whether to be baptized or leave Spain, about half the Jewish population chose to stay rather than abandon their homes.[53] What does one say about the freedom of those who chose to remain in a land that required them to abandon their faith as compared to the freedom of those who moved to foreign parts that tolerated their religion but recognized them only as second-class citizens?

The point to which all of this leads is the importance of recognizing the unavoidably subjective nature of freedom—or at least acknowledging its subjective aspect. Whether or not a person (or a collective) is free turns to some degree on the extent to which they imagine themselves to be so. Even when constrained and impeded and forced to make invidious choices, people can retain a measure of freedom to the extent that they continue to regard themselves as determining for themselves what is most valuable as they work to overcome the difficulties with which they are presented by hostile others.[54] 'It is only when there is failure *even to aspire* that there is a deficit of freedom.'[55] Those who are confined or dominated or find themselves living under the perpetual threat of losing what liberty they enjoy may be to a significant degree unfree. But those who struggle against their circumstances and determine for themselves what compromises they will make to secure what they most value experience—enjoy—a freedom not available to those who are less hampered but indifferent to their fates.

To understand freedom in this way is to grasp why freedom is valuable. To be free is to be a certain kind of person, a kind of character—a particular kind of self. Having the opportunity to take advantage of options or possibilities is important to be sure. But to be free is to be a person who will take those opportunities—or resist attempts to impede or deny the effort to do so. This is not to suggest that the subjective dimension is all there is to freedom. Those who are dominated or confined are also unfree to some degree, even if less unfree than someone who is determined to overcome the obstacles in his way. An example of this may be found in the character, Uncle Tom, the hero in Harriet Beecher Stowe's novel. As a slave, he is fully aware of his lack of freedom as someone who is not only confined but also the occupant of a diminished status. Despite his friendship with a kindly master he wants his freedom not so much because he wants to enlarge the scope of the opportunities but because he wishes not to be a slave, and also because he fears that such freedom as he enjoys now might be taken away if he were to be sold. And yet, when he is sold upon the death of his first master to a much crueller owner, he reveals by refusing to beat a fellow slave that he also views himself as free, because while his body has been enslaved his soul remains his own—and the Lord's: 'I'll give ye all the work of my hands, all my time, all my strength; but my soul I won't give up to a mortal man.'[56]

Tom is not free because he is a slave. He is thus limited by all the burdens such a being must bear. Yet he is less unfree than a slave who is not only so burdened but also broken by his bondage and resigned to his fate— indifferent to the world and to the lives of others. To suffer a complete loss of freedom is to suffer the loss not only of one's opportunities but also of one's humanity.

Yet just as it is possible for a slave to retain a part of his freedom despite his enslavement, so is it also possible for people to lose a part of their freedom even as they retain many of the liberties they might enjoy as the denizens of a society in which they are able to come and go as they please to a considerable degree. In many cases it might be the result of the weakness of individuals who lack the will to assert themselves when confronted by the slightest of challenges. For this to happen to a more substantial extent, however, it is necessary that larger forces be at work in society to quell the spirits of its inhabitants. This was the concern that Tocqueville identified when he considered the danger confronting the United States which, despite its democratic institutions and traditions of freedom, he thought to be at risk of succumbing to a form of despotism. Such a despotism was unlikely to be like that of the Roman Caesars who, at their worst, exercised a violent and unchecked tyranny that 'weighed prodigiously on a few'[57] but did not extend to a great number, since 'the details of social life and of individual life ordinarily escaped [the emperor's] control'.[58] It was much more likely to a despotism of a 'more extensive and milder' sort—one that 'would degrade men without tormenting them'.[59]

What Tocqueville thought he saw in the America he had come to observe was the working of two contradictory impulses: 'the need to be led and the desire to remain free'.[60] Tormented by these two hostile passions, he noted, yet unable to destroy either one of these opposite instincts, the people worked to satisfy them both by imagining 'a unique, tutelary, omnipotent power, but elected by the citizens'.[61] The immense 'tutelary power' they created was one that had taken charge of 'assuring their enjoyment and looking after their fate', yet was at once 'absolute, detailed, regular, far-sighted and mild'.[62] Though it appeared to be a kind of paternal power, it was in fact nothing of the sort, for its purpose was not to prepare people to become adults but 'to fix them irrevocably in childhood'.[63] That power 'works willingly for [the people's] happiness; but it wants to be the unique agent for it and the sole arbiter; it attends to their security, provides for their needs, facilitates their pleasures, conducts their principle affairs, directs their industry, settles their estates, divides their inheritances'.[64] By removing from the people 'the trouble to think and the difficulty of living', the controlling power 'makes the use of free will less useful and rarer every day', and 'little by little steals from each citizen even the use of himself'.[65]

Tocqueville's concern was not the possibility of the exercise of a general tyrannical power but rather the consequences of the regular use of a milder form of power to mould the population in ways they scarcely notice. 'Subjection in small affairs manifests itself every day and makes itself felt indiscriminately by all citizens. It does not drive them to despair; but it thwarts them constantly and leads them to relinquish the use of their will [and finally to give up on themselves]. It extinguishes their spirit little by little.'[66] The great illusion from which they suffer is that the solution to the problem of how to remain free while being led can be solved if 'they combine centralization and sovereignty of the people'.[67] Being given the opportunity to choose the representatives who wield this power over them 'will not prevent them from losing little by little the ability to think, to feel and to act by themselves, and thus from falling gradually below the level of humanity'.[68]

Whether or not Tocqueville was accurate in his depiction of the United States in the nineteenth century, or prescient in his assessment of the prospects of freedom there in the years to come, his analysis of what it means to be free and what is troubling about its dereliction speaks directly to the thesis advanced in this book. To live as a free person or a free people is to live unburdened by controls that do not merely serve to diminish our opportunities but accustom us to the monitoring and regulating that numb us not only to our own loss of liberty but also to the loss of liberty in the world around us. For inescapably social beings, to become indifferent to the world around us and to the lives of others is to suffer a diminution of our humanity. To appreciate this fully, we need to understand freedom along its various dimensions.[69]

This brings us directly to one of the fundamental objections frequently levelled against the thesis of this book. So what if immigration control requires not only placing restrictions on the activities of outsiders but also the monitoring and control of citizens and residents of society more generally, since we are, after all, quite used to being regulated in all sorts of ways? And indeed, we are used to being 'at every operation, at every transaction noted, registered, counted, taxed, stamped, measured, numbered, assessed, licensed, authorized, admonished, prevented, forbidden, reformed, corrected, punished'. We are also used to seeing *others* 'hunted down, abused, clubbed, disarmed, bound, choked, imprisoned, judged, condemned, shot, deported, sacrificed, sold, betrayed'. The answer to the objection against the thesis of this book is that this attitude is perhaps itself the signal that it is time to look a little more anxiously at the freedom we have lost and the persons we have become rather than regard with indifference the losses that continue creeping in at their petty pace from day to day. Is there really no harm in an occasional 'nudge' from our masters when the aim is simply to make life a little easier and make us all a little happier?

## Immigration and Freedom

The great illusion that lies behind the ideal of immigration control is that it will restore to the people the control for which they long in the form of the exercise of sovereign power. 'There are many men today who accommodate themselves very easily to this type of compromise between administrative despotism and sovereignty of the people, and who think they have guaranteed the liberty of individuals when it is to the national power that they deliver that liberty. That is not enough for me. The nature of the master is much less important to me than the obedience.'[70] But it is difficult to imagine a world entirely without masters—political authorities—to govern us, and institutions to give shape and structure to the relations among and between rulers and ruled. What kind of regime would it be that might supply us with the structures of governance we cannot do without and yet not deprive us of too much of the freedom that is always put at risk when we are ruled? What, in other words, is a free society in a world of diverse peoples, many of whom are intent upon moving from one part of that world to another?

Tempting though it is to try to specify the key principles of such a regime, or to sketch at least in outline the institutions and structural arrangements that would make for a free society, such an enterprise is surely a forlorn one. There is no shortage of works of this kind, many full of intelligence and insight, but the truth is probably that freedom is often to be found in the most unlikely of places, or entirely absent where we think it certain to flourish. There are many different kinds of regimes that will be inclined, even if only from time to time, to show freedom a little hospitality; none that will always prove a friend. We have neither the wit nor the technology to devise an ideal regime, even for a relatively homogeneous population—assuming at least for a moment that such an enterprise could make any sense.[71] All that said, however, not every regime is equally good—or bad.

A better way to think about the question about the nature of a free society may be not so much by trying to conceive an ideal regime than to identify the parameters within which different types of societies might be identified. To that end consider, then, the kinds of societies we might imagine existing in a conceptual space along two dimensions, each of which tracks an aspect of freedom.

Along the horizontal axis we track freedom of *immigration*, from the origin at which it is prohibited altogether, with exit and entry tightly controlled and forbidden, to the other extreme at which it is no less controlled but entry or exit are required and forced upon unwilling subjects. At the centre between these extremes neither entry nor exit are controlled, being neither prohibited nor demanded, or even encouraged or discouraged. At this centre, we might say, immigration is *free*: people may come and go at will and the borders, such as they are, can be called open.

Along the vertical axis we track freedom of *integration*, from the origin at which it is prohibited altogether, with no one at liberty to live as they wish and all required keep to their stations in life whatever they may be, to the extreme at which people are no less controlled but now required to conform to a single conception of how one must live in a society that is a single integrated whole. At the centre between these extremes people are not controlled, conformity or integration being neither prohibited nor demanded, or even encouraged or discouraged. At this centre, we might say, integration is *free*: people live by their own lights and the society, such as it, can be called an open one.

The overall freedom of a society on this understanding of these two dimensions is to be gauged by the place it occupies, pinpointed at the intersection of its standards of freedom as marked along each of the two axes. The most open society on this conception of a free society is to be found at the very centre of the conceptual map that has been imagined, and represented in figure 1. The further a society moves away from the centre the less free it will turn out to be, but there is more than one direction in which to travel. Equally, a society may move more towards the centre and greater freedom along one dimension as it changes or develops, but still become less free along the other.

So, for example, if a society moves northwards from a position in the centre it heads towards norms, policies or institutions emphasizing the need

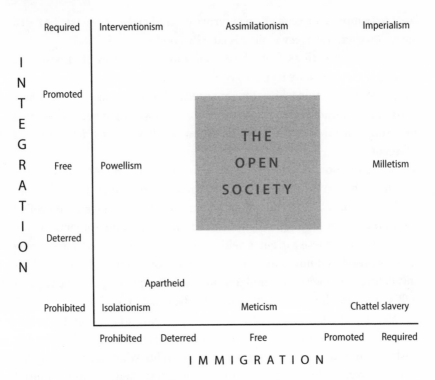

FIGURE 1. Freedom and the open society.

for greater integration and conformity on the part of its members, encouraging or even requiring them to *assimilate* to some ideal of a common set of legal, ethical, and political standards, while continuing to tolerate the entry of outsiders into its territory or jurisdiction. Should it head northwest from the centre, however, it would move toward requiring the integration and conformity of people within its control while contracting the freedom of outsiders to enter and participate in civil life within its territory or jurisdiction. At the extreme it might turn out to be a kind of regime that *intervenes* in the affairs of other societies, requiring them to conform to its demands but prohibiting outsiders from entering its realm.

If a society moves directly south from the centre it continues to be a society that is open to others entering its territory or jurisdiction, but its readiness to allow others to integrate into the society diminishes. It approaches what I have labelled *Meticism*, after the Metics of ancient Athens, who were able to work in the city but unable to secure the rights of other Athenians (and especially citizens), being forbidden to hold property or to enjoy any political rights—despite Pericles's boast that his city was open to the world.

Should it move a little to the south-southwest it would come to resemble the apartheid regime of South Africa, with immigration discouraged and would-be immigrants prohibited from integrating with others, but not so discouraged from immigrating as to deny society the benefits they might bring. Should a society move to the southwestern extreme, however, it would become a society that was entirely *isolated*, with outsiders forbidden from entering altogether and the integration of newcomers impossible because there are none. Contemporary North Korea might supply an example that falls roughly into this space—as the most closed of the closed societies we know.

If a society moves eastwards from the centre it approaches a form of *Milletism*: a term coined after the Ottoman millet system under which the communities absorbed by the empire had little choice but to accept their membership of the wider polity (with no right of secession) and pay tribute to the ruling power, but in which those communities were nonetheless free to govern themselves and individuals were free to come and go. The Roman Empire shared many of the same characteristics. The same might not be said for other imperial enterprises. Those that fall in the northeastern quadrant are *imperial* regimes that not only enforced membership but also looked to transform the societies they conquered. China in Tibet, the Soviet Union in the Baltic states, and the British in Ireland might be the most obvious examples.

If a society moves westwards from the centre it moves towards a stance labelled *Powellism*, after the famous British Conservative parliamentarian noted for his opposition to further immigration to Britain, particularly from the Asian, African, and Caribbean colonies. There is no doubt that Powell's outlook was one that favoured freedom along one dimension, as he took it as a given that all those who came to Britain would acquire the rights of British citizens and become entitled to the same public benefits as well as the same liberty to sponsor their families to come to their country. The answer to the race problem—or indeed the immigration problem more broadly—for him was not apartheid but reduced and selective immigration. This is perhaps the direction in which most western democracies anxious about immigration wish to travel.

Yet it is not simply a matter of a society deciding which way it wants to go—even if the language of 'taking back control' employed by the advocates of immigration restriction suggests it is somehow up to a society to determine for itself the direction in which it prefers to head. The conceptual map presented here identifies the spaces in which different varieties of freedom might be found, but it does not in itself reveal all the complexities and difficulties this book has sought to uncover. In real life, trade-offs cannot be reduced to a two-dimensional scale or represented by a simple matrix of options. Within the framework described here, it is not so straightforward, for example, to move from the centre towards what has been called 'Powellism', as though tighter control on immigration need have no bearing on other aspects of life, or would create no other social and political pressures. Control begets control, and necessarily so if those looking to engineer particular outcomes are determined to achieve their goals. It may not be easy, or at all possible, to move away from freedom with respect to immigration without drifting away from freedom along other dimensions—or, for that matter, paying a price in terms of other values such as equality. Pursuing a policy of reduced immigration in order to preserve cultural integrity might mean not only greater internal control through the monitoring and regulating of society but also greater selectivity in the immigrant-vetting process that amounts to treating some citizens unequally by limiting their freedom to sponsor workers or family members.

If freedom is at all our concern, it is important in the first instance to acknowledge that freedom is something that will be found in many places and under a variety of circumstances. At the same time, however, it is no less important that we recognize that it can be diminished. Most of all, it may be important to remain wary of our limited capacity to determine how much freedom we wish to retain and how much we are prepared to sacrifice for the sake of other ends (assuming we were all of the same mind in our own societies). The unintended consequences of such sacrifices are not always likely to be so evident when we decide to make them.

As an advocate of freedom I see much to commend in the thought that 'what we must aspire to in devising more free societies is less "a maximum of liberties for each compatible with equal liberty for all," and more a culture of achievement that allows a range of Selves to thrive, for the betterment of all'.[72] But I am less convinced by the suggestion that 'as social architects we must design arenas for that struggle, just as we design for coliseums and schools'.[73] If anything, a reading of history should make us wary, and indeed downright suspicious, of all proposals to construct, devise, and design our way to freedom.

The more important insight in this regard comes from Michel Foucault, who suggested that the only guarantee of freedom is freedom. He wrote:

Liberty is a *practice*. So there may, in fact, always be a certain number of projects whose aim is to modify some constraints, to loosen, or even to break them, but none of these projects can, simply by its nature, assure that people will have liberty automatically, that it will be established by the project itself. The liberty of men is never assured by the institutions and laws that are intended to guarantee them. That is why almost all of these laws and institutions are quite capable of being turned around. Not because they are ambiguous, but simply because 'liberty' is what must be exercised. . . . I think it can never be inherent in the structure of things to guarantee the exercise of freedom. The guarantee of freedom is freedom.[74]

While institutions do matter, in the end we would do better simply to resist demands for greater control over others, ourselves, and our societies more broadly, particularly when they come from advocates—not least the proponents of immigration control—claiming to speak for our interests or in our name. Though there is no reason to expect that, in the absence of concerted efforts to control our destiny, history will necessarily pull us in a more hopeful direction or lead us to a happier place, a little anarchy is surely preferable to submission to the peddlers of control in search of greater power.[75] It may be true that seldom is liberty of any kind is lost all at once but, if the history of the twentieth century tells us anything, it is surely also the case that freedom can nonetheless disappear very quickly, and not be recovered for a long, long time.

# Imagine If You Needed
# a Visa to Fall in Love

Imagine if you needed a visa to fall in love.
Would you have to make an application to the Office of
    Love Affairs?
Would you need to specify with whom you wished to fall in love?
Would you need to supply details of your past dalliances?
Would your love have to explain why other lovers wouldn't do?

Imagine that you had to take a test to fall in love.
Would you have to demonstrate how well you understood
    your love?
Would you need to show you could answer questions about
    love's history?
Would you be expected to know the sociology of love?
Would you need to know how many people have loved, how long,
    and where?

Imagine that you had to prove you were ready to fall in love.
Would you have to supply bank statements to prove you could
    afford it?
Would you need references from past lovers confirming
    your suitability?
Would you be told to promise to fall in love with one person and
    no other?
Would you have to guarantee that if love failed you would burden
    no one?

Imagine that you had to leave your love to fall in love.
That you would have to seek permission to love, from a
    distant shore.
That you would have to specify how long you proposed to love.

That you would hope eventually to enter permanently into a state
　　of love,
But could be sure only of a temporary entry permit to love, and not
　　for long.

Imagine that you could be told that your permission to love
　　had expired.
You could be told that you may no longer love the one you choose.
You could be told that without a valid love market test your case
　　is weak.
You could be told to love another, or love no one, but not love the
　　one you want.
You could be told all of this and have no say in the matter at all.

Imagine that you needed to retain a lawyer to fall in love.
That if you had limited means you would have access to legal aid
　　to help you.
But if serious would have to engage an advocate who understood
　　love's laws.
One who grasped love's connections, but also had good
　　connections.
Someone who knew how to play the game, to help you play the
　　game of love.

Imagine there comes a time when everyone laughs at how little
　　sense this makes.
When the dispensers of love visas are giggled at for how ridiculous
　　are their demands.
When lovers everywhere poke fun at official requests.
When we all laugh at the thought of anyone controlling our loves.
Try to imagine that, though it seems to be the most unimaginable
　　thing of all.

# ACKNOWLEDGEMENTS

Many people have helped me in writing this work. No one has done more than Christine Henderson, who has not only given freely of her time to discuss with me every aspect of the argument—along with every example, every quotation, and every footnote—but has read and re-read the manuscript to help me tighten its prose and make its presentation clearer. More than this, she has been a constant source of support and encouragement. This book is dedicated to her with love.

There are other debts to acknowledge. Most of the book was written while I was a member of the Department of Government at the London School of Economics and, within that, of the political theory group that was the happiest of intellectual homes for a dozen years. Friends and colleagues there who have helped me along the way include Aslan Amani, Will Bosworth, Mat Coakley, Philip Cook, Helen Coverdale, Katrin Flikschuh, Mollie Gerver, James Gledhill, Signy Gutnick-Allen, Ed Hall, Astrid Hampe-Nathaniel, Simon Hix, Hwa Young Kim, Leigh Jenco, Paul Kelly, Durukan Kuzu, Christian List, Omar McDoom, Alexandru (aka Stephan) Marcoci, Anne Phillips, Diana Popescu, Kaveh Pourvand, Yonathan Reshef, Paola Romero, Esha Senchaudhuri, David Soskice, Kai Spiekermann, Rachel Tsang, Luke Ulas, Laura Valentini, Baldwin Wong, and Lea Ypi. The Legal and Political Theory Forum was also an important home-away-from-home within the LSE and I owe a great debt to my co-organizer, Thomas Poole, as well as to various colleagues in the Law Department, including Jacco Bomhoff, Devika Hovell, Nicola Lacey, and Martin Loughlin. My students in the Lent Term 2019 class on contemporary political theory (GV316) worked through the book manuscript and offered numerous useful suggestions. Audie Edwardes in particular prompted me to address questions I had not considered—her contribution is evident in chapter 4.

I would like to make special mention of Carlo Argenton, whose doctoral dissertation, 'Liberalism Without Liberals', I supervised. It was defended successfully in 2015, shortly before he contracted an illness from which he did not recover. We lost not just a promising scholar but a wonderful friend.

This work was shared in various forms in lectures I presented as well as at seminars and workshops. I am grateful to Lea Ypi for organizing a manuscript workshop at LSE in 2017, and to the various participants who supplied me with helpful commentary on each chapter. These included Chris Bertram, Stephen Davies, Sarah Fine, Rainer Forst, Alasia Nuti, and David Owen. A similar workshop was organized by Pete Boettke at the Mercatus Center at George Mason University, and I am grateful to him as well as to the other discussants, including Sahar Akhtar, Neera Badhwar, Bryan Caplan, Dan Griswold, Arielle John, Tom Palmer, Ilya Somin, and Jeff Spinner-Halev.

More generally, I would like to thank the audiences at the Institute for Humane Studies (George Mason University), Liberty Fund, the Instituto Bruno Leoni, the Fundación Rafael del Pino, the University of California at Davis, Georgetown University, the Australian National University, Darwin College (Cambridge University), the University of Indiana, Northwestern University, Goethe Universität, the University of Edinburgh, York University, Michigan State University, University of Notre Dame, Princeton University, New York University, Oxford University, King's College London, McGill University and the University of Durham. For hosting me at these various events I would like to thank Emilio Pacheco, Douglas Den Uyl, Virgil Storr, Alberto Mingardi, Beatriz Lobatón Soriano, John Scott, Aurelian Craiutu, Jeff Isaacs, Nic Southwood, Mary Fowler, Andrew Koppelman, Richard Boyd, Thomas Kerch, Philip Cook, Kieran Oberman, Daniel Philpott, Dana Villa, Stephen Macedo, Annie Stilz, Arthur Melzer, Shikha Dalmia, David Held, Eva-Maria Nag, Mario Rizzo, Richard Epstein, Matthew Gibney, William Maley, and Humeira Iqtidar.

I would like to thank Sam Kukathas for his work on the bibliography and for chasing down numerous references. At Princeton University Press, Ben Tate has been a source of enormous encouragement as well as practical help.

In ways that are impossible to measure, this work owes a great deal to the influence of Walter Grinder, who has done so much to shape my thinking by expanding my intellectual horizons. In this regard, I am not alone.

This book was finally completed after I joined the School of Social Sciences at Singapore Management University. I am pleased to have found a welcoming home among my new friends and colleagues and am grateful for the support that has made it possible.

I wonder where I will be when my next book appears.

# NOTES

## Preface

1. I do not wish to disparage this particular philosophical enterprise. For an example of a work addressing the question of exclusion (with whose conclusions I am broadly sympathetic), see Christopher Bertram, *Do States Have the Right to Exclude Immigrants?*, Cambridge: Polity, 2018. For some other notable works in this vein see Phillip Cole, *Philosophies of Exclusion: Liberal Political Theory and Immigration*, Edinburgh: Edinburgh University Press, 2000; Michael Huemer, 'Is There a Right to Immigrate?', *Social Theory and Practice*, 36 (3), 2010, 429–61. The classic study on immigration in modern political theory is Joseph Carens's *The Ethics of Immigration*, Oxford: Oxford University Press, 2013—a wide-ranging work that takes up many topics, including a number not considered here. See also Michael Blake, *Justice, Immigration, and Mercy*, New York: Oxford University Press, 2020.

2. A good example is Robert Waldinger, *The Cross-Border Connection: Immigrants, Emigrants, and Their Homelands*, Cambridge, MA: Harvard University Press, 2015.

## Chapter 1: Panoptica

1. For important contributions to the case for open borders see, for example, Philip Legrain, *Immigrants: Your Country Needs Them*, Princeton: Princeton University Press, 2006; Alan Dowty, *Closed Borders: The Contemporary Assault on Freedom of Movement*, New Haven: Yale University Press, 1987; Teresa Hayter, *Open Borders: The Case Against Immigration Controls*, London and Ann Arbor, MI: Pluto Press, 2nd edition, 2004; Alex Sager, *Against Borders*, London and New York: Rowman and Littlefield, 2020; Joseph Carens, *The Ethics of Immigration*, Oxford: Oxford University Press, 2013; Bryan Caplan and Zach Weinersmith, *Open Borders: The Science and Ethics of Immigration*, New York: First Second, 2019. I presented arguments for open borders in 'The Case for Open Immigration', in Andrew I. Cohen and Christopher Heath Wellman (eds.), *Contemporary Debates in Applied Ethics*, Oxford: Blackwell, 2005, 207–20, and also in 'Why Open Borders?', *Ethical Perspectives*, 19 (4), 2012, 649–75. For an argument in defence of 'soft borders' see Julie Mostov, *Soft Borders: Rethinking Sovereignty and Democracy*, New York: Palgrave Macmillan, 2008.

2. Thucydides, *The History of the Peloponnesian War*, translated by Richard Crawley, London: Longman, Green and Co., 1874, 122 (italics added).

3. Ibid., 122.

4. See 'Pericles', in *Plutarch's Lives*, translated by John Dryden and revised by Arthur Hugh Clough, New York: Random House, n.d., 210. After divorcing his first wife, Pericles cohabited with Aspasia, a Milesian woman he could not marry precisely because she was foreign. After the death of his estranged son, Pericles found that he could not pass his name on to his children by Aspasia because of the laws he had himself sponsored. The irony of all this should not, however, lead us to conclude that the description of Athens offered by Thucydides's Pericles is entirely

inaccurate. At its height, imperial Athens wanted people to come in, but was jealous of granting citizenship rights; wanted workers but were wary of strangers in their midst. For a fuller discussion see Konstantinos Kapparis, 'Immigration and Citizenship Procedures in Athenian Law', *Review Internationale des droits de l'Antiquité*, 52 (2005), 71–113.

5. On this see Thomas J. Figueira, 'Xenēlasia and Social Control in Classical Sparta', *The Classical Quarterly*, New Series, 53 (1), 2003, 44–74.

6. Joseph Carens, 'Aliens and Citizens: The Case for Open Borders', in Will Kymlicka (ed.), *The Rights of Minority Cultures*, Oxford: Oxford University Press, 1995, 331–49, at 331.

7. Ibid., 331.

8. On the conceptualisation of the border in the context of concerns about security see Nazli Avdan, *Visas and Walls: Border Security in the Age of Terrorism*, Philadelphia: University of Pennsylvania Press, 2019.

9. The term 'panopticon' comes from Jeremy Bentham, who conceived of a prison designed in such a way as to enable the surveillance of the inmates by the fewest guards. The French historian and poststructuralist social theorist, Michel Foucault, drew upon Bentham's conception to argue that in modern societies surveillance is achieved less by the establishment of guards and watchtowers than by the socialization of citizens in such a way that they not only monitor each other but also internalize the norms of social control to such a degree that they are inclined to conform even when they are not under the watchful gaze of the authorities, or indeed of anyone at all. See Michel Foucault, *Discipline and Punish: The Birth of the Prison*, translated by Alan Sheridan, New York: Random House, 1995 (first published 1977). Foucault was not the first to be struck by Bentham's views here. Earlier on, the conservative thinker, Gertrude Himmelfarb, had drawn attention to the troubling side of Bentham's conception as opening up the way to promoting the idea of social control. See her 'The Haunted House of Jeremy Bentham', in Richard Herr and Harold T. Parker (eds.), *Ideas in History: Essays Presented to Louis Gottschalk by his former students*, Durham, NC: Duke University Press, 1965.

10. The US Department of Commerce records that the tourism industry in 2013 was valued at 2.8 per cent of GDP, generating 8 million jobs and $1.5 trillion in travel and tourism sales. See http://travel.trade.gov/outreachpages/download_data_table/Fast_Facts_2013.pdf (accessed 3 November 2014). The UK Tourism Alliance boasts that tourism's value to the UK could be priced at £1.26 billion or 9.6 per cent of GDP (80 per cent of which was non-domestic). See http://www.tourismalliance.com/downloads/TA_365_390.pdf (accessed 3 November 2014).

11. Observing the increase of tourists coming to the UK in 2014 the Minister for Tourism said the figures were 'fantastic', even as the government insisted that it was imperative that immigration to Britain was reduced. Minister for Tourism, Helen Grant, quoted in BBC News UK, 14 August 2014, http://www.bbc.co.uk/news/uk-28787769.

12. Although there are often complaints that immigrants become involved in illegal activities or crime, this has not led to any reduction in entry targets for visitors. Why settlers are more feared than transients is a mystery.

13. Imprisonment is most commonly used as a punishment for would-be immigrants who have re-offended by breaching immigration laws more than once. See on this Aviva Chomsky, *Undocumented: How Immigration Became Illegal*, Boston: Beacon Press, 2014.

14. Relinquishing one's membership—or extracting oneself from the embrace of one's 'owner'—is not always a straightforward matter, or even possible at all. In North Korea, for example, it is technically possible to renounce one's citizenship, but only if permission is formally granted by the People's Assembly. Several countries (Turkey and Singapore, for example) make renunciation permissible only after the completion of national service (though exceptions might be made). A recent example is the case of Kevin Kwan, author of *Crazy Rich Asians*, whose application as an American citizen to renounce Singapore citizenship was rejected (twice) because

of his failure to register for or complete his National Service. See Ewan Palmer, '"Crazy Rich Asians" Author Kevin Kwan Faces Jail for Dodging Military Service in Singapore', *Newsweek*, 22 August 2018, https://www.newsweek.com/crazy-rich-asians-author-kevin-kwan-faces-jail-dodging-military-service-1084792.

15. See Mahmoud Keshavarz and Shahram Khosravi, 'The Magic of Borders', *e-flux architecture*, 14 May 2020, 1–7.

16. *Spheres of Justice: A Defense of Pluralism and Equality*, New York: Basic Books, 1983, ch. 2.

17. *The Law of Peoples: With "The Idea of Public Reason Revisited"*, Cambridge, MA: Harvard University Press, 1999, 8–9, 38ff. The only reasons for immigrating would be either to escape injustice or flee disasters like famine. These are unlikely in a 'well-ordered society'. Rawls also asserts that the territorial space of a country is the asset of a 'people', who are entitled to protect the borders of their territory. For a critique of Rawls on this see Seyla Benhabib, 'The Law of Peoples, Distributive Justice, and Migrations', *Fordham Law Review*, 72 (5), 2004, 1761–87. For a defence see Stephen Macedo, 'What Self-Governing Peoples Owe to One Another: Universalism, Diversity and the Law of Peoples', *Fordham Law Review*, 72 (5), 2004, 1721–38.

## Chapter 2: Immigration

1. 'The myth of empire widely held in Britain through most of this period was that all those born within the empire at home or overseas were equally subjects of the crown . . . However, by the time [the British Nationality and Status of Aliens Act of 1914] was enacted, self-governing white settler societies had already taken advantage of their powers to restrict immigration.' See Marjorie Harper and Stephen Constantine, *Migration and Empire*, Oxford: Oxford University Press, 2014, 5–6.

2. See Powell, 'The UK and Immigration' (Sydney University, September 1988), in *Reflections of a Statesman: The Writings and Speeches of Enoch Powell*, selected by Rex Collings, London: Bellew, 1991, 409–15, at 410–11.

3. In these few remarks I skip very quickly over an extremely complex subject. The most comprehensive treatment of the law of nationality in the UK is *Fransman's British Nationality Law*, which runs to 1942 pages in its 3rd edition. See Laurie Fransman, *British Nationality Law*, London: Bloomsbury, 3rd edition, 2011. For an excellent discussion of the subject see Satvinder S. Juss, *Immigration, Nationality and Citizenship*, London and New York: Mansell, 1994, esp. ch. 2, 'The Growth of Immigration Controls in Britain', and 51–3 on the British Nationality Act 1948. For American nationality law see Thomas Aleinikoff, David Martin, Hiroshi Motomura, and Maryellen Fullerton, *Immigration and Nationality Laws of the United States: Selected Statues, Regulations and Forms*, n.p.: West Academic Publishing, 2016.

4. I leave to one side the finer philosophical question of whether there are *any* 'natural kinds'.

5. On this see Leslie Moch-Page, *Moving Europeans: Migration in Western Europe Since 1650*, 2nd edition, Bloomington and Indianapolis: Indiana University Press, 2003. Moch-Page notes (2ff) that not only was there a migration from rural regions to cities, particularly with the growth of industry and state bureaucracy, but also movement to and between villages, which were renewed by incoming people from the region and elsewhere.

6. The Napoleonic Inquiry of 1808–13 which attempted to establish France's manpower resources reveals the extent of the migrations of labour (both seasonal and permanent) across Europe at the time, but also shows us how little the state knew of its own geography, and how little control it exercised over that movement. See Saskia Sassen, *Guests and Aliens*, New York: The New Press, 1999, 7–32.

7. See John Torpey, *The Invention of the Passport: Surveillance, Citizenship and the State*, Cambridge: Cambridge University Press, 2000. Passports have existed for hundreds of years, but what

originated as a document that assured its holder of safe passage in foreign territory became a form of identification without which such travel became difficult if not impossible. See Valentin Groebner, *Who Are You? Identification, Deception, and Surveillance in Early Modern Europe*, New York: Zone Books, 2007; Martin Lloyd, *The Passport: The History of Man's Most Travelled Document*, Phoenix Mill: Sutton Publishing, 2003.

8. See Aviva Chomsky, *Undocumented: How Immigration Became Illegal*, Boston: Beacon Press, 2014. Chomsky's study focuses on the United States. See also Elizabeth F. Cohen, *Illegal: How America's Lawless Immigration Regime Threatens Us All*, New York: Basic Books, 2020, esp. ch. 3, 'Inventing Illegality'. Among other wealthy countries, Australia sought to control immigration earliest, passing the Immigration Restriction Act in 1901 as the first piece of legislation of the newly constituted Federal Parliament, and laying the foundation for the White Australia Policy. On this see James Jupp, *From White Australia to Woomera: The Story of Australian Immigration*, 2nd edition, Cambridge: Cambridge University Press, 2007.

9. James Hampshire draws attention to this but does not attempt to offer a theory of the (liberal) state. See Hampshire, *The Politics of Immigration*, Cambridge: Polity, 2014, 13. The matter is discussed in Sassen, *Guests and Aliens*, 135–6, where it is noted that the nineteenth-century understanding of 'immigrant' was very different from today's 'because the question of border control was less central to state sovereignty than it became with World War I'.

10. I was born a citizen of the newly independent state of Malaya. I relinquished Malaysian citizenship in 1981 to become a citizen of Australia (since neither country then permitted dual nationality) and, at the time of first writing this endnote, lived in London as an Australian national ready also to acquire British citizenship—before moving to Singapore.

11. 17 September 2019, https://www.un.org/development/desa/en/news/population /international-migrant-stock-2019.html.

12. See Michael J. Trebilcock, 'The case for a liberal immigration policy', in Warren F. Schwartz (ed.), *Justice in Immigration*, Cambridge: Cambridge University Press, 1995, 219–46, at 219.

13. George Borjas begins his study of the economics of immigration by stating: 'Nearly 215 million persons now live in a country where they were not born, so immigrants account for about 3 percent of the world's population.' Clearly he is using foreign birth as a proxy for immigrant, since many citizens of one country were born abroad and have never held any other citizenship. See Borjas, *Immigration Economics*, Cambridge MA: Harvard University Press, 2014, 1.

14. The recent history of the Baltic states—Latvia, Lithuania, and Estonia—is instructive here. Before their annexation by the Soviet Union under Stalin they contained small Russian populations. By the 1980s nearly 10 per cent of Lithuania, about a third of Latvia, and close to half of Estonia was Russian. After regaining independence in 1991, Estonia and Latvia required Russians who could not claim to be citizens on the basis of the pre-1940 citizenship laws to apply for naturalization. Many people of Russian descent who have lived most of their lives in these states now hold alien status.

15. Sikhou Camara's connections to France after 40 years of residence were substantial. He was born in Senegal when it was a French colony; his father had served in the French navy; two of his children were born in France and were working adults. See 'Retiree stripped of French citizenship over technicality', *France 24*, http://www.france24.com/en/20140214-nationality-france -citizenship-senegal-sikhou-camara/ (accessed 15 January 2015).

16. This is a particularly common practice in Australia among British-born immigrants, who are the ones least inclined to seek naturalization as citizens.

17. I quote the overly simple view I expressed in 'Immigration', in Hugh Lafollette (ed.), *The Oxford Handbook of Practical Ethics*, Oxford: Oxford University Press, 2003, 567–90, at 570.

18. In this discussion of the UK example I am drawing substantially on the analysis in Bridget Anderson and Scott Blinder, *Who Counts as a Migrant? Definitions and Consequences*,

Briefing Paper, The Migration Observatory at the University of Oxford, 10 July 2019, https://migrationobservatory.ox.ac.uk/resources/briefings/who-counts-as-a-migrant-definitions-and-their-consequences/ (accessed 24 July 2020).

19. I leave to one side the problems associated with the notion of citizenship, since it is only in the last century that its use became widespread. Australia, for example, had no citizens until the 1948 Citizenship Act. Nor did Britain.

20. See for example the case of Rigoberto Damian Calderon, born in Mexico and moved by his parents to the United States at the age of 6, but classified as an illegal immigrant 19 years later and subject to deportation, https://www.thepitchkc.com/news/article/20579544/anchor-babies-are-a-myth-as-this-soontobedeported-family-proves.

21. See also the case of the Baltic states in endnote 14 above.

22. Quoted in Anderson and Blinder, *Who Counts as a Migrant?*, 3.

23. Contrary to the claims of Migration Watch UK, http://www.migrationwatchuk.org/briefingPaper/document/95.

24. https://wayback.archive-it.org/10611/20171126022441/http://www.unesco.org/new/en/social-and-human-sciences/themes/international-migration/glossary/migrant/ (accessed 22 June 2020).

25. For a useful attempt to measure the global movement of people see Guy J. Abel and Nikola Sander, 'Quantifying Global International Migration Flows', *Science*, 343 (6178), 2014, 1520–22. See also Nikola Sander, Guy J. Abel, and Ramon Bauer, *The Global Flow of People*, for the Wittgenstein Centre for Demography and Global Human Capital, Version 1.0.19 (February 2014), http://www.global-migration.info (accessed 10 February 2015).

26. See, for example, Philip Cafaro, *How Many is Too Many?: The Progressive Argument for Reducing Immigration to the United States*, Chicago: University of Chicago Press, 2015. Cafaro asserts that most immigration to the US is legal and a relatively small part illegal, and calls for a reduction of legal immigration as well as greater enforcement to prevent illegal immigration. There is no discussion either of the definition of immigrant or of how the distinction between legal and illegal is to be drawn.

27. For an important analysis of the different kinds of 'transnational civic status', see David Owen, 'Republicanism and the Constitution of Migrant Statuses', *Critical Review in Social and Political Philosophy*, 17 (1), 2014, 90–110, esp. 95. See also Rainer Bauböck, 'Towards a Political Theory of Migrant Transnationalism', *International Migration Review*, 37 (3), 2003, 700–23.

28. For a valuable collection of essays on this subject see Cecilia Manjívar and Daniel Kanstroom (eds.), *Constructing Immigrant "Illegality": Critiques, Experiences, and Responses*, Cambridge: Cambridge University Press, 2015.

29. For a detailed analysis of this point see Hiroshi Motomura, *Immigration Outside the Law*, New York: Oxford University Press, 2014, ch. 1, and esp. 52f. The quoted remark is at 52.

30. Ibid., 25.

31. Equally, and curiously, as an Australian who moved to the UK, I was an immigrant to Britain; yet had I taken up British citizenship and moved to Poland (prior to Brexit) I would not have been an immigrant to Poland since I would have had a right of abode there as a citizen of the EU.

32. See Adrienne Yong, 'When Britain Can Deport EU Citizens—According to Law', *The Conversation*, 23 November 2017, http://theconversation.com/when-britain-can-deport-eu-citizens-according-to-the-law-86896.

33. See Demetra Kasimis, *The Perpetual Immigrant and the Limits of Athenian Democracy*, Cambridge: Cambridge University Press, 2018, ch. 1 and esp. 15–16.

34. See Susanne Hillman, 'Men with Muskets, Women with Lyres: Nationality, Citizenship, and Gender in the Writings of Madame de Staël', *Journal of the History of Ideas*, 72 (2), April 2011, 231–54.

35. See Jacqueline Babha and Sue Shutter, *Women's Movement: Women under Immigration, Nationality and Refugee Law*, Stoke-on-Trent: Trentham Books, 1994, 8. (Babha and Shutter use the term 'citizenship' rather than 'nationality', but strictly speaking citizenship only appeared as a legal category in 1948. Before then, women who married foreign men lost their status as British *subjects*. The Naturalization Act 1870 ss 10(2) and 8 established that they lost this status automatically upon marriage, but were permitted to become British again upon the husband's death—though only by application. See Fransman, *British Nationality Law*, 137.)

36. But see Ben Herzog, *Revoking Citizenship: Expatriation in America from the Colonial Era to the War on Terror*, New York and London: New York University Press, 2015.

37. For a discussion of this see Ian Haney López, *White by Law: The Legal Construction of Race*, 10th anniversary edition, New York: New York University Press, 2006, 30.

38. Torrie Hester, *Deportation: The Origins of U.S. Policy*, Philadelphia: University of Pennsylvania Press, 2017, 145.

39. See on this Dan Walsh, 'State of Origin 2015: the number that proves Queensland have had the better of eligibility wars', *Fox Sports*, 20 May 2015, https://www.foxsports.com.au/breaking-news/state-of-origin-2015-the-number-that-proves-queensland-have-had-better-of-eligibility-war/news-story/484ac53f5e39d3e0d5bdade9ea1588bd.

40. Mr Crapser was abused by his first adopted parents and abandoned by his second. He was convicted of burglary and on applying for a Green Card was told that his criminal record was enough to warrant deportation. He was 'returned' to South Korea, a country of whose language and customs he was ignorant, and left behind his American wife and three daughters. See Choe Sang-Hun, 'Deportation a "Death Sentence" to Adoptees after a Lifetime in the U.S.', *New York Times*, 2 July 2017, https://www.nytimes.com/2017/07/02/world/asia/south-korea-adoptions-phillip-clay-adam-crapser.html.

41. Australia in the late 1990s, when it was worried about the small increase of refugees, began a campaign in selected countries warning of how dangerous Australia was with its many snakes and crocodiles, and how difficult it would be for people to adapt to its permissive moral standards! This practice continues but, interestingly, now through measures that look to engage the local population in Indonesia at the moral or even theological level. In a campaign funded by the Australian Customs and Border Protection Service, and implemented by the International Organization for Migration, with the permission of the Indonesian government, an anti-smuggling message was delivered to fishermen, coastal workers, ferry operators, and local law enforcement officers in villages and ports across the islands. Aside from drawing attention to the penalties for aiding smugglers, the public information campaign that ran from 2009–10 tried to make a moral case against assisting people without proper documentation—relying on Muslim and Christian religious leaders recruited to make the case. See Anne McNevin, Antje Missbach, and Deddy Mulyana, 'The Rationalities of Migration Management: Control and Subversion in an Indonesia-Based Counter-Smuggling Campaign', *International Political Sociology*, 10 (3), 2016, 223–40.

42. See Jesse T. Richman, Gulshan A. Chatta, and David C. Earnest, 'Do non-citizens vote in U.S. elections?', *Electoral Studies*, 36 (December 2014), 149–57. Some parts of Maryland allow resident non-citizens voting rights. The general prohibition on non-citizen voting is imperfectly enforced, relying as it does on self-identification as a citizen.

43. I note that criminal punishment involving detention or imprisonment supplies a possible exception. However, imprisoned citizens do not lose all rights of participation, even though deprived of liberty; and the deprivation of some rights is temporary.

44. See Andreas Farmeir, 'Governments and Forgers: Passports in Nineteenth-Century Europe', in Jane Caplan and John Torpey (eds.), *Documenting Individual Identity: The Development of State Practices in the Modern World*, Princeton: Princeton University Press, 2001, 218–34.

45. For an illuminating study see Kamal Sadiq, *Paper Citizens: How Illegal Immigrants Acquire Citizenship in Developing Countries*, Oxford: Oxford University Press, 2009.

46. See for example Sarah Song, *Immigration and Democracy*, Oxford: Oxford University Press, 2018; Michael Blake, *Justice, Migration, and Mercy*, New York: Oxford University Press, 2020.

47. On this aspect of immigration see in particular Charles Tilly, 'Trust Networks in Transnational Migration', *Sociological Forum*, 22 (1), 2007, 1–25. For a valuable collection of essays drawing on Tilly's insights see Ernesto Casteñeda (ed.), *Immigration and Categorical Inequality: Migration to the City and the Birth of Race and Ethnicity*, New York and London: Routledge, 2018.

48. Sassen, *Guests and Aliens*, 135–7.

## Chapter 3: Control

1. In 1999 the opening of the Sangatte Refugee Centre in Calais attracted a large number of asylum seekers, prompting the French Interior Ministry to close the centre over the course of 2001 and 2002. Nonetheless, would-be immigrants and asylum seekers continued to arrive and set up makeshift camps. Though there are no satisfactory figures for the numbers involved, a large proportion of the inhabitants arrived with the intention of crossing the channel into Britain. For an early account and critical analysis see Liza Schuster, 'Asylum Seekers: Sangatte and the Tunnel', *Parliamentary Affairs* (Special Issue on Crisis Management), (2003), 56 (3), 506–22.

2. Reported in the *Telegraph*, 30 July 2015, http://www.telegraph.co.uk/news/uknews /immigration/11772410/David-Cameron-blames-Calais-crisis-on-swarm-of-migrants.html (accessed 13 August 2015).

3. All quotations above drawn from the report in the *Telegraph*, 30 July 2015.

4. Prime Minister David Cameron quoted in Hannah Jones, 'Are we going to be allowed to stay here? How government anti-immigration communications are infiltrating everyday life of British citizens', ESRC, *Mapping Immigration Controversy*, posted 14 July 2014, http:// mappingimmigrationcontroversy.com/2014/07/30/arewegoingtobeallowedtostayhere / (accessed 15 August 2015).

5. For an important study see Tom K. Wong, *Rights, Deportation, and Detention in the Age of Immigration Control*, Stanford, CA: Stanford University Press, 2015.

6. For a comprehensive examination of the nature of the border as an institution see Matthew Longo, *The Politics of Borders*, Cambridge: Cambridge University Press, 2017.

7. See story in the *Guardian*, 3 August 2015, http://www.theguardian.com/science/2015/aug /03/buzz-aldrin-travel-expenses-moon-apollo-11 (accessed 15 August 2015).

8. Authorization to travel across borders is now frequently obtained at the port of departure rather than at the port of destination.

9. A 1993 presidential directive to interdict migrant boats as far away as possible from the US mainland led to the Coast Guard intercepting Chinese vessels in the western Pacific Ocean. For a fuller account of US interdiction policy see Niels Frenzen, 'US Migrant Interdiction Practices', in Bernard Ryan and Valsamis Mitsilegas (eds.), *Extraterritorial Immigration Control: Legal Challenges*, Leiden and Boston: Martinus Nijhof, 2010, 375–96.

10. In October 2016 the French government closed the camp in Calais known as 'the Jungle', but would-be immigrants looking to move to Britain remain in large numbers, living in the forests around the city, whose port is surrounded by fences. In 2018 the then British Prime Minister, Theresa May, agreed to pay France £44.5 million to continue policing the border. See Katie Burton, 'Calais: A continuing crisis', in *Geographical*, 23 July 2018, https://geographical.co.uk/people/the -refugee-crisis/item/2846-calais-refugees.

11. http://www.telegraph.co.uk/news/uknews/immigration/11011295/Move-border-checks -back-to-Britain-say-French-politicians-amid-new-Calais-migrants-crisis.html.

12. Gina Clayton, 'The UK and Extraterritorial Immigration Control: Entry Clearance and Juxtaposed Control', in *Extraterritorial Immigration Control*, 397–431.

13. Steffen Mau, Heike Brabandt, Lena Laube, and Christof Roos, *Liberal States and the Freedom of Movement: Selective Borders, Unequal Mobility*, New York: Palgrave Macmillan, 2012, 112.

14. See Shikha Dalmia, 'How Immigration Crackdowns Screw Up American Lives', *Reason*, December 2017, http://reason.com/archives/2017/11/12/how-immigration-crackdowns-scr. See also Cassandra Burke Robertson and Irina D. Manta, 'A long-running immigration problem: the government sometimes detains and deports US citizens', 8 July 2019, https://theconversation.com/a-long-running-immigration-problem-the-government-sometimes-detains-and-deports-us-citizens-119702.

15. See Valsamis Mitsilegas, 'Immigration Control in an Era of Globalization: Deflecting Foreigners, Weakening Citizens, and Strengthening the State', *Indiana Journal of Legal Studies*, 19 (1), Winter 2012, 3–60, at 15.

16. Ibid., 17–24.

17. Ibid., 56. Mitsilegas notes that the new-found emphasis on the globalization of surveillance of movement was confirmed by the European Commission's publication of its *Commission Communication on the Global Approach to Transfers of Passenger Name Record (PNR) Data to Third Countries*, 21 September 2010.

18. Oliver Laughland, 'Australian government targets asylum seekers with graphic campaign', *Guardian*, 11 February 2014, https://www.theguardian.com/world/2014/feb/11/government-launches-new-graphic-campaign-to-deter-asylum-seekers. See also Josh Watkins, 'Bordering Borderscapes: Australia's use of humanitarian aid and border security support to immobilize asylum seekers', *Geopolitics*, 22 (4), 2017, 958–83; Josh Watkins, 'Australia's Irregular Migration Information Campaigns: Border externalization, spatial imaginaries, and extraterritorial subjugation', *Territory, Politics, Governance*, 5 (3), 2017, 282–303.

19. Kevin Sun, 'Australia is making covert propaganda videos to scare off asylum seekers', *Quartz Ideas*, 19 April 2017, https://qz.com/960950/australia-is-making-covert-propaganda-videos-to-scare-off-asylum-seekers/.

20. On what we can learn of the experience of migration from this poetry see Belgheis Alavi Jafari and Liza Schuster, 'Representations of exile in Afghan oral poetry and songs', *Crossings: Journal of Migration and Culture*, 10 (2), 2019, 183–203.

21. On this see Todd Miller, *Empire of Borders: The Expansion of the US Border Around the World*, London and New York: Verso, 2019.

22. Ibid., 7.

23. Alex Sager, 'Private Contractors, Foreign Troops, and Offshore Detention Centers: The Ethics of Externalizing Immigration Controls', *APA Newsletter: Hispanic/Latino Issues in Philosophy*, 17 (2), 2018, 11–15.

24. *The 9/11 Commission Report* (https://www.9-11commission.gov/report/911Report.pdf), 362, quoted in Miller, *Empire of Borders*, 6.

25. For a useful historical survey see John Torpey, *The Invention of the Passport: Surveillance, Citizenship and the State*, Cambridge: Cambridge University Press, 2000, 93–121. For a study of the emergence of immigration control in France, and its role in the development of identity monitoring, see Clifford Rosenberg, *Policing Paris: The origins of modern immigration control between the wars*, Ithaca, NY and London: Cornell University Press, 2006.

26. 'In the UK illegally? Go home or face arrest. Text HOME to 78070 for free advice and help with travel documents.'

27. Part of the problem was that the Home Office hotline was quickly overwhelmed with hoax calls and texts. See http://www.telegraph.co.uk/news/uknews/immigration/10417987/Home-Offices-Go-Home-immigration-vans-campaign-overwhelmed-by-hoax-texts-and-calls.html (accessed 15 August 2015).

28. On this see https://migrantsrights.org.uk/blog/2018/07/22/go-home-vans-five-years-on/.

29. See Hiroshi Motomura, *Immigration Outside the Law*, New York: Oxford University Press, 2014, 41.

30. Bridget Anderson, *Us and Them: The Dangerous Politics of Immigration Control*, Oxford: Oxford University Press, 2013, 159. This case is not unique, or even particularly unusual, but all too common—in the United States and in western Europe as well as in the UK. Recently, a friend learned that her mother was denied a visa to enter the UK from Albania because in her application she had indicated that, in addition to holidaying, she intended to visit her daughter and help her with her new baby. Though she was not to be paid for the time spent with her British-born grandchildren she would have deprived potential British nannies of work—and presumably caused her British-born son-in-law to avoid hiring professional British conversationalists to practise his Albanian.

31. For an illuminating, if troubling, case study, see Katherine Benton-Cohen, *Borderline Americans: Racial Division and Labor War in the Arizona Borderlands,* Cambridge, MA: Harvard University Press, 2009.

32. See Motomura, *Outside the Law*, 41.

33. Wong, *Rights, Deportation and Detention*, 16. See also Douglas Massey, *Categorically Unequal: The American Stratification System*, New York: Russell Sage, 2007.

34. For a fuller examination of the American case see Jacqueline Stevens, 'U.S. Government Unlawfully Detaining and Deporting U.S. Citizens as Aliens', *Virginia Journal of Social Policy and Law*, 18 (2010–2011), 606–720. See also Benjamin N. Lawrance and Jacqueline Stevens (eds.), *Citizenship in Question: Evidentiary Birthright and Statelessness*, Durham, NC and London: Duke University Press, 2017; Elizabeth F. Cohen, *Illegal: How America's Lawless Immigration Regimes Threatens Us All*, New York: Basic Books, 2020.

35. Kris Kobach, author of the controversial state-level immigration laws in Arizona (SB1070) and Alabama (HB 56), quoted in Wong, *Rights, Deportation and Detention*, 10.

36. When a professor at the London School of Economics (LSE), I note anecdotally, I was asked by another university to examine a dissertation but was then informed that it needed to see proof of my eligibility to work in the UK before it could send me the materials to read. Oddly enough, overseas examiners, who are paid similarly princely sums, are not required to prove eligibility to work in the UK and indeed usually do not possess it.

37. For example, international students in the UK, Australia, and the US are typically permitted to accept a limited amount of part-time employment.

38. For example, George and Lana Breen, from Dundee in Scotland, were informed that they were to be deported from Australia for living in the wrong suburb. They discovered they were living in the wrong zone under immigration laws when they applied for permanent residency. They received their visa under a government scheme to lure migrants to regional areas. Their appeal to the Migration Review Tribunal was unsuccessful and deportation was set for 7 March 2013. See http://www.telegraph.co.uk/news/worldnews/australiaandthepacific/australia/9884913/British-couple-to-be-deported-from-Australia-for-living-in-wrong-suburb.html.

39. Many countries offer visitors either single- or multiple-entry visas, with single-entry visas unsuitable for frequent travellers.

40. Philip Cafaro, *How Many is Too Many?: The Progressive Argument for Reducing Immigration to the United States*, Chicago: University of Chicago Press, 2015, 189.

41. Ibid., 189.

42. Ibid., 189–90.

43. Cafaro also makes this claim: ibid., 95–6.

44. Joanne Kinslor, 'New employer sanctions under the Migration Act', *Law Society Journal*, May 2013, 34–5, at 34.

45. Employers might escape civil liability if they are able to establish that they held a reasonable belief that an employee was entitled to work—perhaps because the employee supplied fraudulent documents on application for a job.

46. This would mean that not only commercial employment services but also community networks or student employment offices could be found liable for foreign workers' breaching of employment law.

47. The Howells Report precipitated the amendment. See Stephen Howells, 'Report of the 2010 Review of the *Migration Amendment (Employer Sanctions) Act 2007*', Canberra: Commonwealth of Australia, 2011, 25.

48. See for example the 'Ad-Hoc Query on Penalties and Sanctions for employing Illegal Workers', requested by the UK European Migration Network on 20 January 2014, compiled 5 March 2014, https://ec.europa.eu/home-affairs/sites/homeaffairs/files/what-we-do/networks/european_migration_network/reports/docs/ad-hoc-queries/illegal-immigration/530_emn_ahq_penalties_for_employing_illegal_workers_05march2014_wider_dissemination.pdf (accessed 24 July 2020).

49. Adam Smith, *Wealth of Nations*, Indianapolis: Liberty Fund, 1981, Volume I, Book I, Chapter X, Section C, 138.

50. Smith attacked England's poor laws for preventing people from moving from parish to parish. See *Wealth of Nations*, Volume I, Book I, Chapter X, Section C, 152.

51. David Bacon and Bill On Hing, 'The Rise and Fall of Employer Sanctions', in Julie A. Dowling and Jonathan Xavier Inda (eds.), *Governing Immigration Through Crime: A Reader*, Stanford, CA: Stanford University Press, 2013, 149–64, at 150.

52. These harms are well documented. For a comprehensive sample of the literature see Cathryn Costello and Mark Freedland (eds.), *Migrants at Work: Immigration and Vulnerability in Labour Law*, Oxford: Oxford University Press, 2014.

53. On this see Jennifer Roback, 'The Political Economy of Segregation: The Case of Segregated Streetcars', *The Journal of Economic History*, 46 (4), December 1986, 893–917. The author notes that segregation *within* carriages may have been a compromise made by companies that were under pressure to segregate *by* carriage, which would have been even more expensive.

54. Cafaro recommends reducing annual immigration to 300,000, including 100,000 family-sponsored, 150,000 refugee and asylum seeker, and 50,000 employment-based places. See *How Many is Too Many?*, 184. How these figures are justified at is a question whose answer might require a closer re-reading of the book than I have been able to undertake. In 2013, the US issued 74,859 work visas for seasonal agricultural labour alone, as well as a further 94,919 visas for other seasonal labour. It issued 311, 257 visas for intracompany transferees and a further 38, 952 visas for their spouses. In all, 1.4 million work visas were issued that year. See Daniel Costa and Jennifer Rosenbaum, 'Temporary Foreign Workers by the Numbers: New estimates by visa classification', *Economic Policy Institute*, 7 March 2017, https://www.epi.org/publication/temporary-foreign-workers-by-the-numbers-new-estimates-by-visa-classification/.

55. For a list of Canada's preferred professions, for example, see http://www.canadianimmigration.net/immigration/federal-skilled-worker-occupation-list/.

56. As most academics in the UK, Australia, Canada, and the US know, hiring internationally requires submitting a justification to immigration authorities that there is no one within the country or who already has employment rights with the relevant expertise who might fill the post instead of the foreign applicant. Yet universities look not simply to hire people who can do a particular job but to build departments or teams comprised of the best people they can find. In a global market, some of those people may be foreign; but it is highly unlikely that no one could be found domestically to do the job of teaching and producing research of a high standard. Universities must, if they are to play the game, maintain the fiction that there is *no one* domestically who is suitable.

57. Bacon and On Hing, 'The Rise and Fall of Employer Sanctions', 163.

58. For an interesting treatment of the conflict between domestic labour and employers, and the way in which it shapes immigration law, see Philip L. Martin, 'Foreign Workers in U.S. Agriculture', *In Defense of the Alien*, 20 (1997), 77–85.

59. See my 'In Praise of the Strange Virtue of People Smuggling', *Global Policy Journal*, 2013, http://www.globalpolicyjournal.com/blog/03/05/2013/praise-strange-virtue-people-smuggling. See also Javier Hidalgo, 'The Ethics of People Smuggling', *Journal of Global Ethics*, 12 (3), 2016, 311–26; Eamon Aloyo and Eugenio Cusumano, 'Morally evaluating human smuggling: the case of migration to Europe', in *Critical Review of International Social and Political Philosophy* (2018), 1–24, https://doi.org/10.1080/13698230.2018.1525118.

60. For a comprehensive study of people smuggling and the law see Anne T. Gallagher and Fiona David, *The International Law of Migrant Smuggling*, New York: Cambridge University Press, 2015.

61. http://www.ice.gov/human-smuggling-trafficking-center.

62. I do not wish to oversimplify matters here. Laws to prevent exploitation are themselves problematic, not least because they too can be captured and manipulated by the powerful, and also because their unintended consequences might be harmful to some of the most vulnerable.

63. There is, of course, the question of whether such exchanges might be harmful to third parties. This is taken up in ch. 5 on the economics of immigration.

64. See Rajika Bandhari and Peggy Blumenthal, 'Global Student Mobility and the Twenty-first Century Silk Road', in Rajika Bandhari and Peggy Blumenthal (eds.), *International Student and Global Mobility in Higher Education: National Trends and New Directions*, New York: Palgrave Macmillan, 2011, 1–24, at 1.

65. The problem, of course, is how to count students in the immigration statistics. Since students typically are people who intend to come to study and then return home—and usually are obliged to do so under the terms of their visas—they should not count as immigrants. However, given that they often come to study for longer than a single year, the duration of their stays makes them technically 'immigrants'. Whether or not they should be counted in the official statistics is a matter of political dispute. At the time of writing this, in the UK, senior members of the Conservative government were not in agreement on this question. The problem is further compounded by the unreliability of the statistical methods used for recording and counting students resident in the UK. See Steven Swinford, 'Immigration Figures under review as new checks suggest that numbers are far lower than thought', *Telegraph*, 23 August 2017: http://www.telegraph.co.uk/news/2017/08/23/immigration-figures-review-new-checks-suggest-numbers-far-lower/.

66. For example, one of my LSE students from the United States travelled home to attend a mandatory conference for scholarship holders but was not permitted to re-enter the UK because he had originally secured a single-entry visa. For attempting to enter on what he mistakenly thought was a valid visa he was also refused permission to secure another visa that year and was unable to retain his scholarship or continue his studies. (There was no visa requirement for American students entering Britain to study a decade before.) This anecdote recounts a familiar story.

67. In the UK, for example, the immigration compliance costs for the 24 Russell Group universities run to about £25 million per annum. See the report *Challenges and costs of the UK immigration system for Russell Group Universities*, 6 March 2019, https://russellgroup.ac.uk/media/5750/challenges-and-costs-of-the-uk-immigration-system-for-russell-group-universities.pdf.

68. Dean of the Faculty of Arts at Kingston University, quoted in Rachel Brooks, *The Impact of UK Immigration Policies on students and staff in further and higher education*, Report of the University and College Union (UCU), May 2015, 16. http://classonline.org.uk/docs/Impact_of_UK_immigration_policies_on_students_and_staff_in_further_and_higher_education.pdf.

69. In 2011 in the UK 450 colleges or one fifth of the further and higher education sector had their sponsorship licences revoked.

70. Rachael Pells, 'Science teacher shortage spreads, forcing government to relax immigration restrictions', *Independent*, 26 January 2016, http://www.independent.co.uk/news/education/education-news/science-teacher-shortage-government-relax-immigration-restrictions-foreign-education-department-a7547406.html. The article also reports that the government had missed its own teacher recruitment targets for the previous four years.

71. I am grateful to Dan Griswold for this example.

72. Mark Keierleber, 'Trump order could give immigration agents a foothold in US schools', *Guardian*, 22 August 2017, https://www.theguardian.com/us-news/2017/aug/22/trump-immigration-us-schools-education-undocumented-migrants.

73. Mark Keierleber, 'Sanctuary schools across America defy Trump's immigration crackdown', *Guardian*, 21 August 2017, https://www.theguardian.com/us-news/2017/aug/21/american-schools-defy-trump-immigration-crackdown.

74. One reason for this fear is the frequency of enforcement error. Another is that children with one 'undocumented' parent run the risk of being separated from families.

75. See ch. 5, 'Economy', for a fuller analysis.

76. Neil Shaw, 'Couple given 28 days to leave UK after visa denied by Home Office because they own a shop', *Daily Mirror*, 1 February 2017, http://www.mirror.co.uk/news/uk-news/couple-given-28-days-leave-9734476.

77. 'US physician may be forced to quit UK because of visa nightmare', *Guardian*, 4 August 2017, https://www.theguardian.com/uk-news/2017/aug/04/us-surgeon-may-be-forced-to-quit-uk-because-of-visa-nightmare.

78. It is not known why she had not taken out British citizenship, though it might be because Singapore does not permit dual citizenship.

79. Jen Mills, 'Woman deported from Britain after 27 year marriage', *Metro*, 27 February 2017, http://metro.co.uk/2017/02/27/woman-deported-from-britain-after-27-year-marriage-6475449/.

80. The full story is recounted in the Preface to Lawrance and Stevens (eds.), *Citizenship in Question*, ix–xiii.

81. A citizen or permanent resident needs to prove having an income of at least £18,600 to sponsor a husband or wife or civil partner, or an income of £22,400 for families with one child (and £2,400 for each additional child). The income of the sponsored spouse cannot be taken into consideration. The £18,600 threshold is the point below which a British citizen or resident becomes eligible for welfare benefits. This regulation came into effect in July 2012 and has been the subject of controversy and legal appeal. In February 2017 the Supreme Court ruled that the minimum income threshold was lawful, though it was critical of the Home Office's rules and instructions, which it said did not fully consider their legal duties to the children affected or permit alternative sources of income to be taken into account.

82. James Temperton, '40% of Britons are too poor to marry non-EU migrants,' *Wired*, 26 January 2016, http://www.wired.co.uk/article/migraton-non-eu-spouse-visa-uk.

83. On 15 February 1935 the English poet W. H. Auden married the actress Erika Mann (daughter of the novelist, Thomas Mann) to enable her to secure British citizenship in order to escape Nazi Germany. Auden was gay.

84. In the United States, to obtain a 10-year Green Card, applicants claiming marriage as grounds must submit an I-751 Petition, supplying, among other things, 'Evidence of Intimacy'. A useful guide can be found here: https://citizenpath.com/proving-a-bona-fide-marriage/.

85. The initial failure of President Trump's repeated attempts in 2017 to ban travel by Muslims from selected countries is a case in point, as Presidential Executive Orders were invalidated by a succession of federal judges.

86. Consider the case of James Mize, an American citizen by birth who married Jonathan Gregg, a naturalized American, with whom he had a daughter through a surrogate mother outside the United States. The State Department appealed to immigration law to argue that the child was not an American citizen by birth. Everything turned on the meaning of 'born' of parents, with the State Department arguing that there must be a 'blood relationship'. See Sarah Mervosh, 'Both Parents Are American. The U.S. Says Their Baby Isn't', *New York Times*, 21 May 2019, https://www.nytimes.com/2019/05/21/us/gay-couple-children-citizenship.html.

The State Department also determined in the case of twin brothers, Aiden ad Ethan Dvash-Banks, born to two married gay men through a surrogate, that only Aiden was American because conceived using sperm from his American father, but Ethan was not because his father was Israeli. What is noteworthy here is that while a federal judge ruled that this was a mistake, the State Department's response was to 'review' the ruling with a view to appealing the court's decision. See Sarah Mervosh, 'Twins Were Born to a Gay Couple. Only One Child Was Recognized as a U.S. Citizen, Until Now', *New York Times*, 22 February 2019, https://www.nytimes.com/2019/02/22/us/gay-couple-twin-sons-citizenship.html.

87. For an excellent study of the politics of immigration management see Antje Ellermann, *States Against Migrants: Deportation in Germany and the United States*, Cambridge: Cambridge University Press, 2009. With respect to the problem of policy implementation at the government agency level she observes (145–6): 'in the realm of coercive social regulation, executive capacity is a function of two key factors: first the insulation of bureaucratic agencies from the influence of elected politicians; and, second, where agencies are insulated, the partisan ideology of ministers. It is, then, all else equal, those bureaucratic agents most shielded from intervention by their legislative principals who are most likely to implement their statutory mandates in the face of organized opposition. Broad programmatic ideology has a substantial effect only where agency leaders enjoy autonomy from legislators' narrow demands; where they do not, particularistic pressures to restrain implementation will erode agencies' capacity to carry out contested policy measures.'

88. For a particularly disturbing account of the systematic misuse of power by immigration enforcement agencies, see Cohen, *Illegal*, esp. 7–44, but also throughout the book.

89. For a general treatment of the problem of risk aversion in public sector bureaucracies see Everest Turyahikayo, 'Bureaucratic Rigidity, Risk Aversion and Knowledge Generation and Utilization in the Public Sector: Reality or illusion?', *Organization Studies*, 5 (3), 2018, 9–16, esp. 13–14.

90. E. F. Kunz, 'The Refugee in Flight: Kinetic Models and Forms of Displacement', *International Migration Review*, 7 (2), 1973, 125–46.

91. See note 83 above.

92. On this see Anderson, *Us and Them*, 68–9.

93. See Catalina Amuedo-Dorantes and Esther Arenas-Arroyo, *Police Trust and Domestic Violence: Evidence from Immigration Policies*, IZA Institute of Labor Economics Discussion Paper Series, IZA DP No. 12721, October 2019, https://www.immigrationresearch.org/system/files/Police%20Trust.pdf. See also Randall Akee, 'Outdated immigration laws increase violence toward women', in *Brookings*, 30 May 2019, https://www.brookings.edu/opinions/outdated-immigration-laws-increase-violence-toward-women/.

94. On this see Helena Wray, 'The "Pure" Relationship, Sham Marriages and Immigration Control', in Joanna K. Miles, Rebecca Probert and Perveez Mody (eds.), *Marriage Rites and Rights*, Oxford and Portland, OR: Hart Publishing, 2015.

95. Rebecca Probert, Joanna Miles and Perveez Mody, 'Introduction', ibid., 4.

96. Originally named the Total Information Awareness Program. Citizen protests against the existence of such a programme led to a change of name, but not a change of substance.

97. William Cavanaugh, *Migrations of the Holy: God, State and the Political Meaning of the Church*, Cambridge: William B. Eerdmanns Publishing, 2011, 27–8.

98. Walter Lippman, quoted ibid., 28.

99. This agency no longer exists, its functions having been absorbed into the Department of Homeland Security. Deportation is now the responsibility of the Immigration and Customs Enforcement (ICE) agency within that department.

100. For a revealing and insightful account of the entire case see Leon Wildes, *John Lennon vs. the USA: The Inside Story of the Most Bitterly Contested and Influential Deportation Case in United States History*, Chicago: American Bar Association, 2016.

101. For an exposition of some of the elements of biometric identification see Btihaj Ajana, *Governing Through Biometrics: The Biopolitics of Identity*, Basingstoke: Palgrave Macmillan, 21–46. See also Jane Caplan and John Torpey (eds.), *Documenting Individual Identity*, Princeton: Princeton University Press, 2001.

102. The terminology here is problematic. As Frank Paul, the unit head of the European Commission's Large Scale Information Technology Systems, noted: they wanted all travellers to be considered as 'trusted', even though some were more trusted than others. The official terminology was revised to 'registered traveller' to identify those with travel privileges. See Gregory Feldman, *The Immigration Apparatus: Security, Labor, and Policymaking in the European Union*, Stanford, CA: Stanford University Press, 2012, 138.

103. *Paradise Lost*, IV, lines 93–4, in John Milton, *The Major Works*, edited with an introduction and notes by Stephen Orgel and Jonathan Goldberg, Oxford: Oxford University Press, 2008, 430.

104. Kevin Townsend, 'The Terrorist Justification for Mass Surveillance', *Security Week*, 1 April 2016, http://www.securityweek.com/terrorist-justification-mass-surveillance. Townsend also notes that the problem is further exacerbated by the fact that terror cells communicate often using low-tech methods, so that no amount of additional electronic surveillance would unearth more intelligence. In this article Townsend is criticizing William Hague, the former UK Foreign Secretary and Leader of the House of Commons, who argued after the 2016 terrorist attacks in Brussels that there needed to be more mass surveillance. See Hague, 'The Brussels attacks show the need to crack terrorist communications', *Telegraph*, 28 March 2016. Hague is also a former leader of the Conservative Party who wrote a book on William Pitt, in which he quotes Pitt the Younger saying: 'Necessity was the plea for every infringement of human freedom. It was the argument of tyrants; it was the creed of slaves.' See William Hague, *Pitt the Younger*, London: Harper Press, 2005, 13. It is unclear whether Mr Hague has changed his mind or lost it.

105. Didier Bigo, 'Security and Immigration: Toward a critique of the governmentality of unease', *Alternatives*, 27, 2002 (Special Issue), 63–92, at 73.

106. See the account in William Maley, *What is a Refugee?*, Brunswick and London: Scribe, 2016, 100. These communications were revealed by Wikileaks.

107. Ibid., 185.

108. In the Australian case, the conditions of the inmates of the detention camps on Nauru and Manus Island have drawn widespread condemnation both in Australia and around the world. Managing a secretive offshore facility in which women suffer from sexual violence at the hands of guards, children commit suicide, and mental health problems become endemic does not suggest an excess of concern for protective care of the exploited. For a harrowing first-hand account, see Behrouz Boochani, *No Friend but the Mountains: The True Story of an Illegally Imprisoned Refugee*, translated by Omid Tofighian, London: Picador, 2019. On Canada's immigration detention system see Stephanie J. Silverman and Peter Molnar, 'Everyday Injustices: Barriers to Access to Justice for Immigration Detainees in Canada', *Refugee Survey Quarterly*, 35 (1), 2016, 109–27. For a general study see Amy Nethery and Stephanie J. Silverman (eds.), *Immigration Detention: The migration of a policy and its human impact*, Oxford and New York: Routledge, 2015; Mary Bosworth, *Inside Immigration Detention*, Oxford: Oxford University Press, 2014.

109. Cafaro is an advocate for an expansion of employer controls and sanctions. See *How Many is Too Many?*, 189. For a contrary view worrying about 'mission creep', see Jim Harper, 'Internal Enforcement, E-Verify, and the Road to a National ID', *The Cato Journal*, 32 (1), 2012, 125–37, at 133–4.

110. On this see the Preface to Darshan Vigneswaran, *Territory, Migration and the Evolution of the International System*, Basingstoke: Palgrave Macmillan, 2013, ix–xi.

111. For a valuable account see Peter Tinti and Tuesday Reitano, *Migrant, Refugee, Smuggler, Saviour*, Oxford: Oxford University Press, 2017.

112. On this see Bigo, 'Security and Immigration'.

113. Sir Godfrey Lagden was a British civil servant who went on to serve in South Africa in the Colonial Office. He became the British Resident Commissioner in Basutoland and later Commissioner of Native Affairs in British-controlled Transvaal 1903–05.

114. Nancy L. Clark and William H. Worger, *South Africa: The rise and fall of apartheid*, 3rd edition, Oxford: Routledge, 2016, 35.

115. For some instructive works on the history of apartheid, in addition to Clark and Worger's *South Africa: The rise and fall of apartheid*, see Rodney Davenport and Christopher Saunders, *South Africa: A Modern History*, 5th edition, New York and Basingstoke: Palgrave Macmillan, 2000, esp. 375–515; Robert M. Price, *The Apartheid State in Crisis: Political Transformation in South Africa 1975–1990*, New York: Oxford University Press, 1991.

116. 'Some academics in the 1970s saw the maintenance of the migrant labour system as a centrepiece of apartheid. Migrant labour, they argued, had proved cheap for the mining industry because employers did not have to pay a wage that would support a whole urban family.' See William Beinart, *Twentieth-Century South Africa*, 2nd edition, Oxford: Oxford University Press, 2001, 156, and 155–65 more generally.

117. *The Politics of Inequality: South Africa since 1948*, New York: Praeger, 1958, 411–2.

118. Clark and Worger, *South Africa: The rise and fall of apartheid*, 22.

119. 'The state . . . faced a dilemma. Important industrialists associated themselves with the view that migrant labour inhibited productivity and that low wages constrained the growth of an internal market; they wanted a more skilled and stable workforce with lower job turnover.' See Beinart, *Twentieth-Century South Africa*, 157.

120. See Kopano Ratele, 'Sexuality as Constitutive of Whiteness in South Africa', *NORA—A Nordic Journal of Feminist and Gender Research*, 17 (3), 2009, 158–74; Michael Savage, 'The Imposition of Pass Laws on the African Population in South Africa: 1916–1984', *African Affairs*, 85 (339), 1986, 181–205.

121. Clark and Worger, *South Africa: The rise and fall of apartheid*, 40.

122. Ibid., 41.

123. Quoted in Deborah Posel, *The Making of Apartheid, 1948–61: Conflict and Compromise*, Oxford: Clarendon Press, 1991, 54–5.

124. Carter, *The Politics of Inequality*, 15.

125. See Steve Biko, *I Write What I Like: A Selection of His Writings*, edited by Aelred Stubbs, Harlow: Heinemann, 1987.

126. On this see Keith Breckenridge, 'The Book of Life: The South African Population Register and the Invention of Racial Descent, 1950–1980', *Kronos*, No. 40, 2014 (Special Issue: Paper Regimes), 225–40.

127. See Stephen Ellmann, *In A Time of Trouble: Law and Liberty in South Africa's State of Emergency*, Oxford: Clarendon Press, 1992.

128. See P. Eric Louw, *The Rise, Fall and Legacy of Apartheid*, Westport, CT: Praeger, 2004, 65.

129. For a famous account of the lengths to which the South African government went see Donald Woods, *Asking for Trouble: The autobiography of a banned journalist*, London: Penguin 1987 (first published 1980). See also the film by Richard Attenborough, *Cry Freedom*, dealing with the death of Steve Biko and the flight of Donald Woods from South Africa.

130. I am indebted to Michael Munger for drawing my attention to this history. See Jeffrey D. Grynaviski and Michael C. Munger, 'Reconstructing Racism: Transforming Racial Hierarchy from "Necessary Evil" into "Positive Good"', *Social Philosophy and Policy*, 34 (1), 2017, 144–63. For a useful set of documents and commentary see Drew Gilpin Faust (ed.), *The Ideology of Slavery: Proslavery Thought in the Antebellum South, 1830–1860*, Baton Rouge: Louisiana State University Press, 1981.

131. This is, of course, to say nothing of the impact on these societies of western foreign policy, which surely bears some responsibility for the movement of people, notably of refugees.

132. 'Thus apartheid policy in its earlier years was partly intended to ensure that many African workers remained migrant. But in·effect it was an attempt at "labour differentiation", in which established urban Africans had relatively secure rights as families, rather than a wholesale drive to extend migrancy.' Beinart, *Twentieth-Century South Africa*, 158.

## Chapter 4: Equality

1. *The Constitution of Liberty*: *The Definitive Edition*: *The Collected Works of F. A. Hayek*, ed. Ronald Hamowy. Chicago: University of Chicago Press, 2011, 148. Hayek continues: 'this extension of the principle of equality to the rules of moral and social conduct is the chief expression of what is commonly called the democratic spirit'.

2. On this see Anne Phillips, *Which Equalities Matter?*, Cambridge: Polity Press, 2004.

3. See, for example, Philip Cafaro, *How Many is Too Many? The Progressive Argument for Reducing Immigration to the United States*, Chicago: Chicago University Press, 2015, 155–6 for an explicit repudiation of racial considerations in immigration policy in an argument for dramatic reductions on immigration.

4. See Saskia Sassen, 'The de facto Transnationalizing of Immigration Policy', in Christian Joppke (ed.), *Challenge to the Nation State: Immigration in Western Europe and the United States*, Oxford: Oxford University Press, 1998, 49–86, at 49.

5. Stephen Castles, 'Twenty-First-Century Migration as a Challenge to Sociology', *Journal of Ethnic and Migration Studies*, 33 (3), 2007, 351–71 at 363.

6. Marc R. Rosenblum and Wayne A. Cornelius, 'Dimensions of Immigration Policy', in Marc R. Rosenblum and Daniel J. Tichenor (eds.), *The Oxford Handbook of the Politics of International Migration*, Oxford: Oxford University Press, 2012, 245–73, at 253.

7. It may be hard to integrate settled immigrants when their friends and relatives are deterred or prevented from migrating to join them—or denied the right even to visit.

8. The Dublin system or the Dublin Regulation, which represents the European basic understanding of border control, frequently comes into conflict with the Schengen system. On this see Martin Schain, *The Border: Policy and Politics in Europe and the United States*, Oxford: Oxford University Press, 2019, 59–61.

9. Rosenblum and Cornelius, 'Dimensions of Immigration Policy', 261. They further note: 'in general, lawmakers must choose between erring on the side of under-enforcement (permitting some illegal immigrants to remain with host states) or erring on the side of over-enforcement (in which case some legal immigrants and citizens will be caught up in the enforcement process, all host-state residents suffer a range of potential adverse effects).

10. Ibid., 261.

11. For a brief account see Carolyn Rasmussen, 'Kisch, Egon Erwin (1885–1948)', *Australian Dictionary of Biography*, Volume 15, Melbourne: Melbourne University Press, 2000. See also Kisch's own entertaining memoir: *Australian Landfall*, translated by John Fisher and Irene and Kevin Fitzgerald, London: Secker and Warburg, 1937.

12. In Australia, bills of attainder are not expressly forbidden by the Constitution, but by 1915 had been found to be unconstitutional by the High Court.

13. On the problem of deportation see Amada Armenta, *Protect, Serve, and Deport: The Rise of Policing as Immigration Enforcement*, Oakland: University of California Press, 2017; Rachel Ida Buff, *Against the Deportation Terror: Organizing for Immigrant Rights in the Twentieth Century*, Philadelphia: Temple University Press, 2018.

14. It might, of course, be cheaper simply to execute illegal immigrants. In 1978, when refugees fleeing Vietnam began to arrive in Malaysia by boat, the then Prime Minister, Dr Mahathir, promised that if they made landfall the border police would 'shoot them'. The international outcry this

provoked led him to explain that he had been misheard, and that he had only said that Malaysia would 'shoo them' away. This explanation was not widely believed given the PM's command of English and enviable diction.

15. On this see Antje Ellermann, 'The Limits of Unilateral Migration Control: Deportation and Inter-state Cooperation', *Government and Opposition*, 43 (2), 168–89.

16. Calculated by subtracting the number of emigrants from the number of immigrants to the UK.

17. More recent reports, however, suggest that the number of net immigrants may be lower than the government estimated because fewer international students remained in the country after completing their studies. See Heather Stewart, 'Exit check data raises questions over May's focus on student overstayers', *Guardian*, 24 August 2017, https://www.theguardian.com/uk-news/2017/aug/24/exit-checks-data-raises-questions-over-mays-focus-on-student-overstayers.

18. See, for example, Jonathan S. Tobin, 'Immigration and the End of the Rule of Law', *Commentary*, 22 February 2015.

19. Judith Shklar famously poured scorn on the notion, maintaining that it was more a slogan than a useful conceptual contribution to legal theory. See Shklar, 'Political Theory and the Rule of Law', in Allan C. Hutchinson and Patrick Monahan (eds.), *The Rule of Law: Ideal or Ideology*, Toronto: Carswell, 1987.

20. Fuller, *The Morality of Law*, New Haven: Yale University Press, 1964.

21. See, for example, John Finnis, *Natural Law and Natural Rights*, Oxford: Clarendon Press, 1981; Joseph Raz, *The Authority of Law*, Oxford: Oxford University Press, 1979.

22. F. A. Hayek is particularly insistent on this point. See *The Constitution of Liberty*, ch. 10 and 11.

23. For an especially helpful discussion of this point see Jeremy Waldron, 'The Concept and the Rule of Law', *Georgia Law Review*, 43 (1), 2008, 1–63. See also Waldron's entry, 'The Rule of Law', in the *Stanford Encyclopedia of Philosophy*, https://plato.stanford.edu/archives/sum2020/entries/rule-of-law/, for a more general survey of the literature on the rule of law.

24. Montesquieu, *The Spirit of the Laws*, translated and edited by Anne M. Cohler, Baser Carolyn Miller, and Harold Samuel Stone, Cambridge: Cambridge University Press, 2002.

25. Alexis de Tocqueville, *Democracy in America*, edited by Eduardo Nolla, translated from the French by James T. Schleifer, 2 Volumes, Indianapolis: Liberty Fund, 2012.

26. The Chinese Exclusion Repeal Act of 1943 repealed the 1882 act and enabled Chinese nationals resident in the US to become citizens.

27. For an account of the politics surrounding the 1965 act see Roger Daniels, *Guarding the Golden Door: American Immigration Policy and Immigrants Since 1882*, New York: Hill and Wang, 2004, 133–9.

28. On this see ibid., 224–5.

29. See Panikos Panayi, *An Immigration History of Britain: Multicultural Racism Since 1800*, London: Routledge, 2014, 308.

30. See Bridget Anderson, *Us and Them? The Dangerous Politics of Immigration Control*, Oxford: Oxford University Press, 2013, 39–41.

31. On this see Daniel S. Goldman, 'The Modern-Day Literacy Test? Felon Disenfranchisement and Race Discrimination', *Stanford Law Review*, 57 (2), 2005, 611–55.

32. In considering the case brought, the High Court of Australia found against the government, concluding that the provision of the Migration Act could not save a 'decision' that was vitiated by 'jurisdictional error', since in such a case there would be no decision at all to save. See *Plaintiff S157/2002 v The Commonwealth* (2003) 211 CLR 476. For a fuller discussion see William Maley, *What is a Refugee?*, London: Hurst, 2016, 184.

33. Catherine Dauvergne, *Making People Illegal: What Globalization Means for Migration and Law*, Cambridge: Cambridge University Press, 2009, 62.

34. According to the United National High Commission for Refugees: 'The principle of non-refoulement is the cornerstone of asylum and of international refugee law. Following from the right to seek and to enjoy in other countries asylum from persecution, as set forth in Article 14 of the Universal Declaration of Human Rights, this principle reflects the commitment of the international community to ensure to all persons the enjoyment of human rights, including the rights to life, to freedom from torture or cruel, inhuman or degrading treatment or punishment, and to liberty and security of person. These and other rights are threatened when a refugee is returned to persecution or danger.' See *UNHRC Note on the Principle of Non-Refoulement*, http://www .refworld.org/docid/438c6d972.html (accessed 29 August 2016).

35. Dauvergne, *Making People Illegal*, 58. Dauvergne adds: 'To maintain sovereignty for the purposes of, say, asserting resource rights in the Timor Sea, but not for the purposes of receiving asylum applications, is not something contemplated by international law.'

36. *Vienna Convention on the Law of Treaties*, 23 May 1969, 1155. U.N.T.S. 331, Article 31.

37. *Making People Illegal*, 58.

38. For example, states have sought to interpret the *non-refoulement* principle of the 1951 Refugee Convention *restrictively* rather within the spirit of the rule, which prohibits returning refugees to countries where they may face persecution. The United Nations High Commissioner for Refugees has suggested that the problem with the *non-refoulement* principle is not one of standards but of implementation by states. Thus the principle has been breached repeatedly. On this see Susan Kneebone (ed.), *Refugees, Asylum Seekers and the Rule of Law: Comparative Perspectives*, Cambridge: Cambridge University Press, 2009.

39. At the time of writing the US Supreme Court was hearing the case of Mr Vijayakumar Thuraissigiam, who was denied asylum after what the American Civil Liberties Union described as an 'inadequate interview that violated the requirements imposed by statute, regulations, and due process and was subsequently placed in the "expedited removal" system'. He filed a petition for a habeas corpus review of his removal order by a federal judge but was challenged by the US government on the grounds that as an asylum seeker he had no right to judicial review. Neither the Constitution nor the writ of habeas corpus supplied any guarantee of such a right. The Ninth Circuit court reversed the district court's judgment and held that the expedited removal statute violated the Suspension Clause, triggering the appeal to the Supreme Court. See ACLU, 'Department of Homeland Security v. Vijayakumar Thuraissigiam', https://www.aclu.org/cases /department-homeland-security-v-vijayakumar-thuraissigiam.

40. Since the 1994 amendments to the Migration Act 1958, the Australian Federal Court has been unable to provide a judicial remedy in migration cases even when there have been errors of law involving matters of due process, relevancy, reasonableness or proportionality. It can do little more than check to see whether an administrator had complied with the terms of the act. See Mary Crock, 'Echoes of the Old Country or Brave New Worlds? Legal Responses to Refugees and Asylum Seekers in Australia and New Zealand', *Revue Québécoise de droit international*, 14 (1), 2001, 55–89, at 69. For example, an asylum seeker's application had to be turned down because it had not been presented within the time permitted, even though the fault lay with the detention centre official who neglected to submit the documents; the court had no discretion to remedy this obvious injustice.

41. This discussion has drawn extensively from Catherine Dauvergne, *The New Politics of Immigration and the End of Settler Societies*, Cambridge: Cambridge University Press, 2016, 184–6.

42. 'The modern passport is a palpable manifestation of an idealised global order. It is a tangible link between the two main sources of modern identity: the individual and the state. It specifies a unique individual within a matrix of standardized physical categories, and it guarantees that identification with the marks and seals of a recognized nation state. It embodies both the most private and the most bureaucratically alienating of identities, being an object of intense

personal attachment even as it is a tool of global regulation and standardization. The photograph, accumulated visas, seals, and amendments further enrich it as a token of personal history even as they entrench the bearer more deeply within the file and machinery of state surveillance.' Adam M. McKeown, *Melancholy Order: Asian Migration and the Globalization of Borders*, New York: Columbia University Press, 2008, 1.

43. If we consider the two most substantial works of political theory on the immigration question, we find that although the word 'race' appears as an entry in the index, there is no discussion of the issue. There is none in Joseph Carens's *The Ethics of Immigration*, Oxford: Oxford University Press, 2013; and there is no extended examination of this matter in David Miller's *Strangers in Our Midst*, Cambridge, MA: Harvard University Press, 2016. See, however, Sarah Fine, 'Immigration and Discrimination', in Sarah Fine and Lea Ypi (eds.), *Migration and Political Theory: The Ethics of Movement and Membership*, Oxford: Oxford University Press, 2016, 125–50. See also Carens's early paper 'Nationalism and the Exclusion of Immigrants: Lessons from Australian Immigration Policy', in Matthew Gibney (ed.), *Open Borders? Closed Societies?: The Ethical and Political Issues*, Westport, CT: Greenwood Press, 1988, 41–60.

44. For a survey of recent debates on the concept of race see Gavin Evans, 'The unwelcome revival of "race science"', *Guardian*, 2 March 2018, https://www.theguardian.com/news/2018/mar/02/the-unwelcome-revival-of-race-science. For a fuller examination see Gavin Evans, *Black Brain, White Brain: Is Intelligence Skin Deep?*, London: Thistle, 2015, chs. 5–7. For a philosophical treatment of whether 'race' can be viewed as a 'natural kind' see Philip Kitcher, 'Does "Race" Have a Future?', *Philosophy and Public Affairs*, 2007, 35 (4), 293–317. For a survey of the philosophical literature see Michael James and Adam Burgos, 'Race', *Stanford Encyclopedia of Philosophy*, https://plato.stanford.edu/entries/race/ (revised 25 May 2020, accessed 1 July 2020). For a recent defence of theories of genetic racial difference see Nicholas Wade, *A Troublesome Inheritance: Genes, Race and Human History*, London: Penguin, 2017. For a systematic critique of such theories see Carl Zimmer, *She Has Her Mother's Laugh: The Powers, Perversions and Potential of Heredity*, New York: Dutton, 2018.

45. The 'Green Card Lottery' used by the United States might be one example of a randomizing system of admissions. However, it is worth noting that the first 'diversity visas' issued in 1987 were awarded on a first-come-first-served basis, favouring those who first knew about the opportunity—primarily those from Canada, Ireland, and the UK, and with the Irish getting 40 per cent of the visas. Between 1991 and 1994 the programme was amended to favour Europeans. In this period 40 per cent of visas were explicitly reserved for Irish applicants. See Anna O. Law, 'The Diversity Visa Lottery: A Cycle of Unintended Consequences in United States Immigration Policy', *Journal of American Ethnic History*, 21 (4), 2002, 3–29.

46. See Beth Lew-Williams, *The Chinese Must Go: Violence, Exclusion, and the Making of the Alien in America*, Cambridge, MA and London, Harvard University Press, 2018.

47. The classic study is Irving Abella and Harold Troper, *None is Too Many: Canada and the Jews of Europe 1933–1948*, Toronto and London: University of Toronto Press, 2013 (first published 1983).

48. On Australia's reaction to the plight of Jewish victims of the Holocaust see Suzanne Rutland, 'Australian responses to Jewish migration before and after World War II', *Australian Journal of Politics and History*, 1985, 29–48. Rutland notes, however, that the Australian public was more hostile to Jewish immigration than were governments, who were generally motivated more by humanitarian concerns. See also Suzanne D. Rutland and Sol Encel, 'No Room at the Inn: American Responses to Australian Immigration Policies, 1946–54', *Patterns of Prejudice*, 43 (5), 2009, 497–518. On the American response to Jewish migration during the Holocaust see Daniel Tichenor, *Dividing Lines: The Politics of Immigration Control in America*, Princeton: Princeton University Press, 2002, 151–67.

49. This is not to suggest that there was no awareness of the implications of the act or anxiety about the possibility of colonial subjects moving in large numbers to take up residence in Britain. On the one hand, Britain wished to shore up the idea of the unity of the empire at a time when decolonization movements were starting to be felt; on the other hand, political leaders in both major parties as well as officials in the civil service were worried about the practical consequences of legal and political equality. See Bob Carter, Marci Green, and Rick Halpern, 'Immigration policy and the racialization of migrant labour: the construction of national identities in the USA and Britain', *Ethnic and Racial Studies*, 19 (1), 1996, 135–57.

50. That preventing non-White immigration was the purpose of the bill was confirmed by the release of Cabinet papers 30 years later—revealing that the Home Secretary had recorded a memo detailing the importance of slowing Asian immigration from east Africa. See Mark Lattimer, 'When Labour Played the Racist Card', *New Statesman America*, 22 January 1999, https://www .newstatesman.com/when-labour-played-racist-card.

51. Patrial immigrants were entitled to full citizenship in Britain because they were born or adopted in the UK or were born to or adopted by parents who enjoyed patrial citizenship. Non-patrial immigrants could only be granted 'limited leave to remain' in the UK.

52. On this see, for example, Mary Bosworth, Alpa Parmar, and Yolanda Vázquez, *Race, Criminal Justice, and Migration Control*, Oxford: Oxford University Press, 2018.

53. *Hansard*, HC Deb 7 July 1948, 453, col. 411.

54. He noted in particular that with respect to the 'racially distinct and smaller countries of the Commonwealth' Britain should take pride in having 'imposed no colour bar restrictions making it difficult for them when they came here' and ensure that those who came to Britain 'found themselves as privileged in the United Kingdom as the local citizens'. See ibid., col. 403.

55. There is a substantial body of literature on the emergence of racial differentiation as a phenomenon with roots in particular interests and political imperatives in the nineteenth and twentieth centuries. See for example Marilyn Lake and Henry Reynolds, *Drawing the Colour Line: White Men's Countries and the International Challenge of Racial Equality*, Cambridge: Cambridge University Press, 2011; Theodore W. Allen, *The Invention of the White Race. Volume I: Racial Oppression and Social Control*, 2nd edition, London and New York: Verso, 2012 and *The Invention of the White Race. Volume II: The Origin of Racial Oppression in Anglo-America*, London and New York: Verso, 2012.

56. This was the Immigration Act 1924. It followed the Emergency Quota Act 1921, which restricted immigration to 3 per cent of foreign-born persons in the United States. The new act changed the formula from 3 to 2 per cent, with the calculation to be based on the 1890 rather than on the 1910 census. The act can be found here: https://loveman.sdsu.edu/docs /1924ImmigrationAct.pdf.

57. The Commission was established in 1907 by Congress to study the causes and consequences of rising immigration to the United States and its recommendations have shaped US immigration policy ever since. It produced forty-one volumes of reports and was responsible for a number of policy initiatives including the literacy test, the quota system that tied immigration to nationality, and the exclusion of Asians. According to the author of the most recent and comprehensive study of the Commission and its findings, its proposed reforms ended mass migration to the US from 1924 to 1965. See Katherine Benton-Cohen, *Inventing the Immigration Problem: The Dillingham Commission and its Legacy*, Cambridge, MA and London: Harvard University Press, 2018, 1.

58. Mae M. Ngai, *Impossible Subjects: Illegal Aliens and the Making of Modern America*, Princeton: Princeton University Press, 2005, 25.

59. Ibid., 26.

60. Ibid., 36.

61. Ibid., 37. It was not until the McCarran-Walter Act of 1952 that all racial requirements for citizenship were abolished.

62. To some extent, this question remains unsettled. Filipinos still occupy an ambiguous position in American cultural life because of their peculiar history as people colonized for 300 years by Spain and then for half a century by the United States and are routinely taken for Hispanics. See Anthony Christian Ocampo, *The Latinos of Asia: How Filipino Americans Break the Rules of Race*, Stanford, CA: Stanford University Press, 2016.

63. The Syrian case was of especial concern to Jewish people since the classification of Syrians as Asian and therefore not White (one proposal was to categorize them as Mongoloid) would mean that Jews would also be so classified. This was further complicated by the problem of determining whether Jews were members of a religious or racial category. On this issue see Eric L. Goldstein, 'Contesting the Categories: Jews and government racial classification in the United States', *Jewish History*, 19 (2005), 79–107.

64. Bhicaji Balsara was the first known Indian to be naturalized in the United States, the Circuit Court of Appeals agreeing in 1910 that as a Parsi he was a White person, unlike the Hindus. Bhagat Singh Thind was denied citizenship in 1923 because the Supreme Court ruled that Punjabis were not White.

65. It is important not to overstate the case here. Although the definition of Whiteness was contested, it would be careless to suggest that people like the Irish were not recognized as White. For a view of this kind see Noel Ignatiev, *How the Irish Became White*, London: Routledge, 1995. See, however, Philip Q. Yang and Kavitha Koshy, 'The "Becoming White Thesis" Revisited', *The Journal of Public and Professional Sociology*, 8 (1), 2016, 1–25.

66. The United States acquired what is now California, Utah, and Nevada, and portions of New Mexico, Arizona, Colorado, Texas, Oklahoma, Kansas, and Wyoming.

67. Quoted in Ngai, *Impossible Subjects*, 54. Anxiety among Anglo-Americans about the racial identity of Mexicans delayed (until 1912) the admission to statehood of Arizona and New Mexico, a third of whose population was of Mexican mixed-race descent. See Arnoldo de Leon, 'Beyond the Wall: Race and Immigration Discourse', in Sofía Espinoza Álvarez and Martin Guevara Urbina (eds.), *Immigration and the Law: Race, Citizenship, and Social Control*, Tucson: University of Arizona Press, 2018, 30–45, at 31.

68. Commenting on the legacy of the Dillingham Commission, Benton-Cohen observes: 'Even though its overt racial biases have been eliminated, the architecture built by the commission still undergirds federal immigration policy.' *Inventing the Immigration Problem*, 2.

69. Ngai, *Impossible Subjects*, 75.

70. For more on the way Mexicans came to be perceived negatively in part as a result of government immigration policy, see Ana Raquel Minian, *Undocumented Lives: The Untold Story of Mexican Immigration*, Cambridge, MA: Harvard University Press, 2018. See esp. 71–5 on the racial basis of Immigration and Naturalization Service (INS) raids on homes and workplaces, and stop and search practices, in the 1970s.

71. On this see Eyder Peralta, 'You Say You're an American, But What If You Had to Prove It Or Be Deported?', *NPR*, 22 December 2016, https://www.npr.org/sections/thetwo-way/2016/12/22/504031635/you-say-you-re-an-american-but-what-if-you-had-to-prove-it-or-be-deported; Jacqueline Stevens, When Migrants Are Treated Like Slaves', *New York Times*, 4 April 2018, https://www.nytimes.com/2018/04/04/opinion/migrants-detention-forced-labor.html.

72. On this see Vilma Ortiz and Edward Telles, 'Racial Identity and Racial Treatment of Mexican Americans', *Race and Social Problems*, 4 (1), 2012, 41–56.

73. For a survey of some of the relevant literature see Jennifer M. Chacón and Susan Bibler Coutin, 'Racialization through Enforcement', in Mary Bosworth, Alpa Parmar, and Yolanda Vázquez (eds.), *Race, Criminal Justice, and Migration Control*, Oxford: Oxford University Press,

2018, 159–75. For the UK see, for example, Robert Miles, 'The Racialization of British Politics', *Political Studies*, 38 (1990), 277–85; Shirley Joshi and Bob Carter, 'The role of Labour in the creation of racist Britain', *Race and Class*, 25 (3), 1984, 53–70.

74. Chacón and Coutin, 'Racialization through Enforcement', 161. See also John Solomos's observation of British immigration controls and their bearing on race relations: 'If the main rationalisation of the immigration controls and the race relations was the objective of producing an atmosphere for the development of "good race relations" and integration, it needs to be said that they failed to depoliticize the question of "race" as such.' John Solomos, *Black Youth, Racism, and the State: The Politics of Ideology and Policy*, Cambridge: Cambridge University Press, 1988, 41.

75. Once such norms are entrenched they are difficult to overcome. Consider the turn to the 'points system', pioneered by Canada, as a way of overcoming racial bias in admissions as well as better managing immigration. While it may have been an improvement on what operated before, it retains many of the features of the system it sought to replace—including racial bias. See on this Justin Gest, 'Points-based immigration system was meant to reduce racial bias. It doesn't', *Guardian*, 19 January 2018, https://www.theguardian.com/commentisfree/2018/jan/19/points-based -immigration-racism. Also see Helena Wray, 'The Points-based System: A Blunt Instrument', *Journal of Immigration, Asylum and Nationality Law*, 23 (2009), 231–51.

76. Chacón and Coutin, 'Racialization through Enforcement', 161.

77. Since 'virginity testing' remains widespread in a number of countries from the United States and Britain to Turkey and India, it bears noting that such an 'examination' has 'no scientific merit or clinical indication'. See the World Health Organization, *Eliminating Virginity Testing. An Interagency Statement*, 2018, https://www.who.int/reproductivehealth/publications/eliminating -virginity-testing-interagency-statement/en/.

78. Evan Smith and Marinella Marmo, *Race, Gender and the Body in British Immigration Control: Subject to Examination*, London: Palgrave Macmillan, 2014, 96.

79. Quoted ibid., 113.

80. Ibid., 87.

81. The discussion that follows is inspired by an excellent unpublished paper by my student, Audie Edwardes: 'The "Good" Homosexual: Exploring Identity Construction Through Immigration Control', submitted 25 April 2019, Department of Government, London School of Economics. It drew my attention to the way in which immigration control was used to shape sexuality, and to an important but neglected literature on the subject.

82. The 'sexual deviant' admission criterion was removed with the passage of the Immigration Act of 1990. See Connie Oxford, 'Queer Asylum: US policies and responses to sexual orientation and transgendered persecution', in Marlou Schrover and Deirdre M. Moloney (eds.), *Gender, Migration and Categorisation: Making Distinctions between Migrants in Western Countries 1945–2010*, Amsterdam: Amsterdam University Press, 127–148, at 129.

83. Article 1 A(2) of the Convention defines a refugee as someone who 'owing to well-founded fear of being persecuted for reasons of race, religion, nationality, membership of a *particular social group* or political opinion, is outside the country of his nationality and is unable or, owing to such fear, is unwilling to avail himself of the protection of that country; or who, not having a nationality and being outside the country of his former habitual residence as a result of such events, is unable or, owing to such fear, is unwilling to return to it.' (Italics added.)

84. This was decided by the Board of Immigration Appeals. See *Matter of Acosta* In Deportation Proceedings A-24159781, Decided by Board March 1, 1985: https://www.justice.gov/sites /default/files/eoir/legacy/2012/08/14/2986.pdf.

85. For an important analysis of this see Cheryl Llewellyn, 'Sex Logics: Biological Essentialism and Gender-Based Asylum Cases', *American Behavioral Scientist*, 61 (10), 2017, 1119–33.

86. This matter is explored more fully in chs. 6 and 7 below. See also Eithne Luibhéid, 'Introduction: Queering Migration and Citizenship', in Eithne Luibhéid and Lionel Cantú Jr., (eds.),

*Queer Migrations: Sexuality, U.S. Citizenship, and Border Crossings*, Minneapolis: University of Minnesota Press, 2005, ix–xlvi.

87. See H. Carrillo and J. Fontdevila, 'Border crossings and shifting sexualities among Mexican gay immigrant men: beyond monolithic conceptions', *Sexualities*, 17 (8), 2014, 919–38.

88. Eric Fassin and Manuela Salcedo, 'Becoming Gay? Immigration Policies and the Truth of Sexual Identity', *Archives of Sexual Behaviour*, 44 (2015), 1117–25, at 1117. For a more general study of the way in which immigrants respond to immigration policy to negotiate social and gender roles through cross-border marriage see Lucy Williams, *Global Marriage: Cross-Border Marriage Migration in Global Context*, Basingstoke: Palgrave Macmillan, 2010.

89. Carl F. Stychin, '"A Stranger to Its Laws": Sovereign Bodies, Global Sexualities, and Transnational Citizens', *Journal of Law and Society*, 27 (4), 2000, 601–25. See also Anna Marie Smith, 'The Imaginary Inclusion of the Assimilable "Good Homosexual": The British New Right's Representations of Sexuality and Race', *Diacritics*, 24 (2), 1994, 58–70.

90. See Sarah Hinger, 'Finding the Fundamental: Shaping Identity in Gender and Sexual Orientation Based Asylum Claims', *Columbia Journal of Gender and Law*, 19 (2), 2010, 367–408.

91. Or at least, so Adam Smith suggested. See *The Theory of Moral Sentiments*, ed. D. D. Raphael and A. L. Macfie, Indianapolis: Liberty Fund, 1976, 42.

## Chapter 5: Economy

1. See, for example, Julian Simon, *The Economics of Immigration*, Oxford: Blackwell, 1989; Lant Pritchett, *Let Their People Come: Breaking the Gridlock of Global Labor Mobility*, Washington: Center for Global Development, 2006; Michael A. Clemens, Claudio E. Montenegro, and Lant Pritchett, 'The Place Premium: Bounding the Price Equivalent of Migration Barriers', *Review of Economics and Statistics*, 101 (2), 2019, 201–13; Jonathan Portes, *What Do We Know and What Should We Do About Immigration?*, London: Sage, 2019.

2. See, for example: Peter Brimelow, *Alien Nation: Common Sense about America's Immigration Disaster*, New York: Random House, 1995; Mark Krikorian, *The New Case Against Immigration: Both Legal and Illegal*, New York: Sentinel, 2008; Anthony Browne, *Do We Need Mass Migration?: The Economic, Demographic, Environmental, Social and Developmental Arguments Against Large-scale Net Immigration to Britain*, London: Civitas, 2002; Reihan Salam, *Melting Pot or Civil War? A Son of Immigrants Makes the Case Against Open Borders*, New York: Sentinel, 2018.

3. George J. Borjas, in *We Wanted Workers: Unraveling the Immigration Narrative*, New York: W. W. Norton, 2016, suggests that the literature on immigration economics is dominated by scholars determined to demonstrate that immigration is desirable (21). He cites Paul Collier saying much the same thing in *Exodus: Immigration and Multiculturalism in the 21st Century*, London: Allen Lane, 2013. However, Tom K. Wong argues that hostility to immigration has spawned an industry dedicated to showing that immigration is a costly problem. See Tom K. Wong, *The Politics of Immigration: Partisanship, Demographic Change, and American National Identity*, New York: Oxford University Press, 2017, 13. He notes, for example, that in 1888 the American Economic Association offered a $150 prize for the best essay on 'The Evil Effects of Unrestricted Immigration'. That said, there is a relative paucity of scholarly books and papers questioning the value of immigration in *economic* terms. I searched. Even Borjas himself does not stray that far from the assessments of most economists and appears to be an outlier only in relative terms.

4. In 1846 whaling contributed enough to make it the fifth largest sector of the American economy but fifty years later it was dead, with its place in the ranks taken by manufacturing. Among the causes of its decline were the competition from cheaper (because low-waged) whaling operations in Scandinavia, and the decline in demand for whale oil as more substitutes entered the market. See Derek Thompson, 'The Spectacular Rise and Fall of U.S. Whaling: An Innovation Story', *Atlantic*, 22 February 2012, https://www.theatlantic.com/business/archive/2012/02/the

-spectacular-rise-and-fall-of-us-whaling-an-innovation-story/253355/. For a fuller history see Eric Jay Dolan, *Leviathan: The History of Whaling in America*, New York: Norton, 2008.

5. On the American side see Charles Murray, *Coming Apart: The State of White America, 1960–2010*, New York: Crown Forum, 2013. On the British see David Goodhart, *The Road to Somewhere: The New Tribes Shaping British Politics*, St Ives: Penguin, 2017. More generally see Eric Kaufmann, *White Shift: Populism, Immigration and the Future of White Majorities*, Milton Keynes: Allen Lane, 2018.

6. See, for example, Arlie Russell Hochschild, *Strangers in their Own Land: Anger and Mourning on the American Right*, New York and London: The New Press, 2016; George Packer, *The Unwinding: Thirty Years of American Decline*, London: Faber and Faber, 2014; and J. D. Vance, *Hillbilly Elegy: A Memoir of a Family and Culture in Crisis*, London: William Collins, 2016.

7. See, for example, Douglas Murray, *The Strange Death of Europe: Immigration, Identity, Islam*, London: Bloomsbury, 2017. For a social scientist's attempt to understand the emergence of working-class discontent see Justin Gest, *The New Minority: White Working Class Politics in an Age of Immigration and Inequality*, Oxford: Oxford University Press, 2016.

8. The impact of immigration is an empirical question. If all incoming immigrants for the next several years were severely disabled and incapable of working the economic gain to the society would be negative. The same would, of course, be true of the impact of a positive birth-rate if all newborns entered the world similarly disabled and incapable of ever working. The question of economic impact is one that can be sensibly addressed only by making empirically defensible assumptions about the likely capacities and behaviour of immigrants. I take it that such questions as 'what if a billion people arrived at the border?' do little to advance a serious consideration of the immigration issue. (Precisely this question has been put to me all the same, on occasion even by professional philosophers.)

9. See, for example, David Goodhart, *The British Dream: Successes and Failures of Postwar Immigration*, London: Atlantic Books, 2014, 22: 'No sensible person is opposed to immigration *tout court*. It is a matter of how many people, how quickly, how the process is managed and how it affects the national political community.'

10. Peter Brimelow, 'Economics of Immigration and the Course of the Debate since 1994', in Carol Swain (ed.), *Debating Immigration*, New York: Cambridge University Press, 2007, 157–64 at 158.

11. *The New Case Against Immigration*, 133.

12. Ibid., 134.

13. Ibid., 149–56.

14. Philip Cafaro, *How Many is Too Many?: The Progressive Argument for Reducing Immigration to the United States*, Chicago: Chicago University Press, 2015, 42. Though Cafaro suggests that his book is distinctive for offering a *progressive* case for immigration control, this is nothing new. In the early years of the Progressive movement in the United States, progressives were strongly opposed to immigration. On this see Thomas C. Leonard, *Illiberal Reformers: Race, Eugenics and American Economics in the Progressive Era*, Princeton: Princeton University Press, 2016, esp. ch. 9; Daniel J. Tichenor, *Dividing Lines: The Politics of Immigration Control in America*, Princeton: Princeton University Press, 2002, esp. ch. 5.

15. The 'lump of labour' fallacy is the idea that there is a fixed amount of work to be done, so any increase in the amount a worker produces, or the number of workers producing, reduces the number of jobs or the amount available to pay them. As Paul Krugman observes, it's an idea economists hold in low regard, but makes a comeback whenever the economy is sluggish. Krugman, 'Lumps of Labor', *New York Times*, 7 October 2003, https://www.nytimes.com/2003/10/07/opinion/lumps-of-labor.html. For a more recent critique see Jonathan Portes *What Do We Know and What Should We Do About Immigration*, ch. 1.

16. George J. Borjas, *Immigration Economics*, Cambridge, MA and London: Harvard University Press, 2014, 149.

17. The Cobb-Douglas production function, based as it was on an empirical study of the American manufacturing industry, is a linear homogeneous production function that takes into account two inputs: labour and capital. Among its weaknesses are its inability to measure industries using more than two inputs and its assumption of constant returns to scale.

18. I am drawing here on Borjas's discussion in ch. 7 of *Immigration Economics*, esp. at 150–53.

19. Ibid., 151.

20. Ibid., 151.

21. Ibid., 159. Borjas also argues that this holds true even if one works on the basis of a 'nested Constant Elasticity of Substitution (CES)' framework. Indeed, if in order to make the assumption that workers fell into more than two skill groups one reduced the dimensions of the problem (to make it numerically tractable) through the use of a nested framework, the result would be an even lower estimate of the short-run immigration surplus' (ibid., 159–61).

22. Ibid., 162–7.

23. George J. Borjas, 'Globalization and Immigration: A Review Essay', *Journal of Economic Literature*, 53 (2015), 965.

24. Borjas, *We Wanted Workers*, 39.

25. Borjas cites in particular Alex Tabarrok, 'The Case for Getting Rid of Borders—Completely', *Atlantic*, 10 October 2015; Michael A. Clemens, 'Economics and Emigration: Trillion-Dollar Bills on the Sidewalk?', *Journal of Economic Perspectives*, 25 (2011); and Michael A. Clemens, Claudio E. Montenegro, and Lant Pritchett, *The Place Premium: Wage Differences for Identical Workers across the U.S. Border*, Center for Global Development Working Paper 148, 2009.

26. Borjas, *We Wanted Workers*, 39. See also Borjas, *Immigration Economics*, 166.

27. Borjas, *Immigration Economics*, 168.

28. Borjas, *We Wanted Workers*, 42.

29. Ibid., 43–4.

30. It is important to be clear, at the very least out of fairness, that Borjas himself is not an out-and-out advocate of immigration restriction, even if he is sceptical of its benefits. We will address this matter more closely further below.

31. Borjas, *We Wanted Workers*, 197.

32. A 2012 Gallup poll found that about 640 million adults or 13 per cent of the world's population would like to move permanently to another country, and that 150 million of these most preferred the United States: http://www.gallup.com/poll/153992/150-million-adults-worldwide-migrate.aspx (accessed 10 April 2017).

33. Susan F. Martin summarises the prevailing assessment among scholars of international labour migration thus: 'it is highly likely that international labour migration will increase still further in the future, due to demographic, economic, and security trends. Migration occurs when there are economic disparities between source and receiving countries, and when individuals have the capacity to move from poorer and less secure places to wealthier and more secure countries with greater economic opportunities. These disparities are increasing, particularly with the demographic trends toward an aging, developed world and a still-growing developing one. At the same time, globalization gives more people the knowledge and resources needed to find work in other countries.' See Susan F. Martin, *International Migration: Evolving Trends from the Early Twentieth Century to the Present*, New York: Cambridge University Press, 2014, 93.

34. See James M. Buchanan and Yong J. Yoon, 'A Smithean Perspective on Increasing Returns', *Journal of the History of Economic Thought*, 22 (1), 2000, 43–8.

35. See James M. Buchanan and Yong J. Yoon (eds.), *The Return of Increasing Returns*, Ann Arbor: University of Michigan Press, 2001.

36. These points are made by David Card and Giovanni Peri in their review '*Immigration Economics* by George J. Borjas: A Review Essay', in the *Journal of Economic Literature*, 54 (4), 2016, 1333–49.

37. Immigrant labour is generally divided into two types: substitute and complementary. Immigrants whose skills are substitutes for those of natives will tend to displace natives in employment, while those whose skills are complements will tend to enhance native employment. For a brief introduction to the theory of labour market effects of immigration see Cynthia Bansak, Nicole B. Simpson, and Madeline Navodny, *The Economics of Immigration*, London and New York: Routledge, 2015, ch. 7, 153–73.

38. Buchanan and Yoon, 'A Smithean Perspective', 47.

39. For a brief discussion of the Solow model see Bansak, Simpson, and Navodny, *Economics of Immigration*, 208–10.

40. For an interesting observation on this see Paul R. Krugman, 'Increasing Returns, Monopolistic Competition and International Trade', *Journal of International Economics*, 9 (1979), 469–79, at 478. For an illuminating example illustrating the theoretical point see also Paul Krugman, 'Wrong Way Nation', *New York Times*, 24 August 2014, https://www.nytimes.com/2014/08/25 /opinion/paul-krugman-wrong-way-nation.html?_r=0.

41. Stephen Macedo, 'The Moral Dilemma of U.S. Immigration Policy: Open Borders Versus Social Justice', in Carol M. Swan (ed.), *Debating Immigration*, 2nd edition, New York: Cambridge University Press, 2018, 286–310.

42. Paul Krugman, 'Notes on Immigration', *New York Times,* 27 April 2006, https://krugman .blogs.nytimes.com/2006/03/27/notes-on-immigration/ (accessed 11 April 2017).

43. For a good international literature survey see Sari Pekkala Kerr and William R. Kerr, 'Economic Impact of Immigration: A Survey', *Finnish Economic Papers*, 24 (1), Spring 2011, 1–32.

44. Martin Ruhs and Carlos Vargas-Silva, 'Labour Market Effects of Immigration', *The Migration Observatory*, 18 February 2020, https://migrationobservatory.ox.ac.uk/resources/briefings /the-labour-market-effects-of-immigration/. This paper points to the findings of 12 studies in the UK between 2003 and 2018. The overall conclusion was that immigration had little or no effect on employment of existing workers, that when it did it had a small positive effect on those with higher education and a small negative one for those with lower, and that the impact sometimes depended on the economic cycle.

45. For the most recent research for the United States see the National Academy of Sciences report on *The Economic and Fiscal Consequences of Immigration*, https://www.nap.edu/catalog /23550/the-economic-and-fiscal-consequences-of-immigration. For Borjas's comment on the report (to which he was one among a number of contributors) see George J. Borjas, 'What Does the National Academies' Report on Immigration Really Say?', *National Review*, 22 September 2016, http://www.nationalreview.com/article/440334/national-academies-sciences-immigration -study-what-it-really-says.

46. *We Wanted Workers*, 159.

47. Ibid., 159.

48. Obviously, natives cannot gain 100 per cent of the consumer surplus generated by immigrant labour insofar as some part of what immigrants produce is consumed by other immigrants.

49. The first statement of these principles is to be found in John Rawls, *A Theory of Justice*, Oxford: Oxford University Press, 1971, 302. The final formulation and discussion of these principles is in John Rawls, *Justice as Fairness: A Restatement*, ed. Erin Kelly, Cambridge, MA: Bellnap Press of Harvard University Press, 2001, 42–3. See also the discussions of who are the least advantaged and the 'Difference Principle' 37–72.

50. For an alternative, and in many ways more compelling, theory defending an ethical focus on the least advantaged see Robert E. Goodin, *Protecting the Vulnerable: A Re-Analysis of Our Social Responsibilities*, Chicago: Chicago University Press, 1985.

51. In the UK, 12.3 per cent of the population is foreign-born. Of these, 41.6 per cent are naturalized citizens or nationals. About 7.1 per cent of the population is foreign—this figure, of course, including foreigners born in the UK who do not have UK nationality, as well as the foreign-born who have rights of residency but not nationality. In the United States, 13.1 per cent of the population is foreign-born. Of these, 49.1 per cent are naturalized American citizens. About 7 per cent of the population is foreign, having rights of residency but not nationality. All figures are from the *OECD Factbook 2015–16,* covering the years 2011–13.

52. In Europe and the UK rates of intermarriage are rising but precise figures are difficult to establish because the conceptualization of natives and immigrants is difficult. Does marriage between a first-generation immigrant with the native-born son or daughter of immigrants count as intermarriage or marriage *within* an immigrant group? See Hill Tulu and Tina Hanneman, 'Mixed marriage among immigrants and their descendants in the United Kingdom: Analysis of longitudinal data with missing information', *Population Studies: A Journal of Demography,* 73 (2), 2019, 179–96. The same problem holds for 'interracial' marriage, though that too is on the rise, the rates varying according to a number of factors including population density and history. (In Hawaiii 42 per cent of weddings are interracial while in Jackson, Mississippi, only 3 per cent are.) See Mona Chalabi, 'What's behind the rise of interracial marriage in the US?', *Guardian,* 21 February 2018, https://www.theguardian.com/lifeandstyle/2018/feb/21/whats-behind-the-rise -of-interracial-marriage-in-the-us.

53. See Andri Chassamboulli and Giovanni Peri, 'The labour market effects of reducing the number of illegal immigrants', *Review of Economic Dynamics,* 18 (4), 2015, 792–821. This paper reviewing the US and Mexican economies in 2000–2010 finds that: 'As immigrants—especially illegal ones—have a worse outside option than natives, their wages are lower. Hence, their presence reduces the labor cost of employers who, as a consequence, create more jobs per unemployed when there are more immigrants. Because of such effects our model shows increasing deportation rates and tightening border control weakens low-skilled labor markets, increasing unemployment of native low-skilled workers. Legalization, instead, decreases the unemployment rate of low-skilled natives and increases income per native.' (792).

54. Krikorian, *The New Case Against Immigration,* 149–56.

55. Ibid., 154.

56. Ibid., 156. See also Salam, *Melting Pot or Civil War?,* ch. 4: 'Jobs Robots Will Do'.

57. For a recent study see Konrad B. Buchardi, Thomas Chaney, Tarek A. Hassan, Lisa Tarquinio, and Stephen J. Terry, *Immigration, Innovation, and Growth,* National Bureau of Economic Research, Working Paper, presented 28 February 2020, https://conference.nber.org/conf_papers /f132872.pdf.

58. See Ceren Ozgen, Cornelius Peters, Annekatrin Niebuhr, Peter Nijkamp, and Jacques Poot, 'Does Cultural Diversity of Migrant Employees Affect Innovation?', *International Migration Review,* 48 (2014), 377–416; Jennifer Hunt and Marjolaine Gauthier-Loiselle, 'How Much Does Immigration Boost Innovation?', *American Economic Journal Macroeconomics,* 2 (2), 2009, 31–56.

59. https://www.usnews.com/opinion/blogs/world-report/2015/02/19/japans-economic -stagnation-is-a-cautionary-tale-for-europe.

60. https://www.theglobalist.com/japan-immigration-labor-workforce-economy/.

61. The policy came into effect in April 2019. For discussions see Emese Swarcz, 'Making Sense of Japan's New Immigration Policy', *The Diplomat,* 30 November 2018, https://thediplomat .com/2018/11/making-sense-of-japans-new-immigration-policy/; Menju Toshihiro, 'Japan's Historic Immigration Reform: A Work in Progress', *Nippon.com,* 6 February 2019, https://www.nippon .com/en/in-depth/a06004/japan's-historic-immigration-reform-a-work-in-progress.html; Alastair Gale and River Davis, 'The Great Immigration Experiment: Can a Country Let People in Without Stirring Backlash?', *Wall Street Journal,* 11 September 2019, https://www.wsj.com/articles/japans -immigration-experimentcan-it-let-people-in-without-stirring-backlash-11568213741.

62. Glenda S. Roberts, 'An Immigration Policy by *Any* Other Name: The Semantics of Immigration to Japan', *Social Science Japan Journal*, 21 (1), 2018, 89–102. The paper argues that for some time the Japanese government has increased the number of immigrants admitted but controlled the numbers by declining to use the word *imin* (immigrant) to avoid alarming the public. It has thus facilitated both long-term migration and naturalization. See also Erin Aeran Chung, *Immigration and Citizenship in Japan*, Cambridge: Cambridge University Press, 2014. The author concludes (182): 'the most remarkable feature of Japanese immigration and citizenship politics is the state's ability to uphold the façade that Japan is not a country of immigration. But it is precisely the failure to incorporate prewar immigrants and their descendants that has created the current dilemma for Japanese officials as they attempt to control another wave of immigration.'

63. 'The National Deathwish,' *New York Times*, 24 February 2017, https://www.nytimes.com/2017/02/24/opinion/the-national-death-wish.html?rref=collection%2Fcolumn%2Fdavid-brooks&action=click&contentCollection=opinion&region=stream&module=stream_unit&version=latest&contentPlacement=1&pgtype=collection&_r=0 (accessed 12 April 2017).

64. Brooks cites the example of the American construction industry which, in 2016, was experiencing an extreme shortage of labour that a rise in wages was not able to overcome. Explanations for this included the cyclical nature of the industry, preferences among workers for steadier work even at lower wages, and the aspirations of young people for other kinds of work. In short, the opportunity costs for natives were too high. Consequently, construction companies took on fewer projects, focusing on high-end homes bringing high returns rather than taking on contracts for low-cost housing.

65. See on this Alex Nowrasteh, 'Immigrants Did Not Take Your Job', *Cato At Liberty*, 2 November 2012. On declining native mobility in the United States see R. A. Washington, 'America Settles Down: A look at falling rates of migration within the American economy', *The Economist*, 5 July 2012, http://www.economist.com/blogs/freeexchange/2012/07/labour-mobility (accessed 14 April 2017).

66. *We Wanted Workers*, 144. Borjas is criticizing Bryan Caplan, who had questioned the preoccupation with the low-skilled by asking if they were the 'master race'. See Bryan Caplan, 'Are Low-Skilled Americans the Master Race?', *Library of Economics and Liberty*, 28 March 2006, http://econlog.econlib.org/archives/2006/03/are_lowskilled.html.

67. See Steven Raphael and Eugene Smolensky, 'Immigration and Poverty in the United States', *American Economic Review: Papers and Proceedings*, 99 (2), 2009, 41–4, who note at 44: 'we find little evidence of an impact of immigration on native poverty through immigrant-native labor market competition. Despite adverse wage effects on high school dropouts and small effects on the poverty rates of members of this group, the effects on native poverty rates are negligible. This latter result is largely driven by the fact that even among native-born poor households, most have at least one working adult with at least a high school education.' This is perfectly consistent with the findings of Borjas and others that immigration adversely affects the *wages* of some natives (broadly, the lower percentiles of income earners and notably high school dropouts). See George J. Borjas, Richard B. Freeman, Lawrence F. Katz, John DiNardo, and John M. Abowd, 'How Much Do Immigration and Trade Affect Labour Market Outcomes?', *Brookings Papers on Economic Activity*, 1997, No. 1, 1–90.

68. This is the idea that we address specific problems by finding narrow, targeted solutions rather than use generalized responses that might have larger, unintended and unwanted, effects. In everyday terms, the general idea is not to throw the baby out with the bathwater—or use a sledgehammer to open a peanut.

69. *We Wanted Workers*, 41.

70. Ibid., 41.

71. Ibid., 41.

72. See Borjas, 'What Does the National Academies' Report on Immigration Really Say?'. In *We Wanted Workers* (157–8) Borjas argues that the small immigration surplus of $50 billion in 2015 'conceals a large redistribution of wealth. Native workers lose $516 billion, while native-owned firms gain $566 billion', and adds that 'it follows from the same calculation that native workers are sending a half-trillion dollar check to their employers'.

73. Though this assessment should be viewed with caution. See Bruce Sacerdote, *Fifty Years of Growth in American Consumption, Income and Wages*, National Bureau of Economic Research, Working Paper 23292, March 2017, http:www.nber.org/papers/w23292. Here is the abstract of this important corrective paper: 'Despite the large increase in U.S. income inequality, consumption for families at the 25th and 50th percentiles of income has grown steadily over the time period 1960–2015. The number of cars per household with below median income has doubled since 1980 and the number of bedrooms per household has grown 10 percent despite decreases in household size. The finding of zero growth in American real wages since the 1970s is driven in part by the choice of the CPI-U as the price deflator; small biases in any price deflator compound over long periods of time. Using a different deflator such as the Personal Consumption Expenditures index (PCE) yields modest growth in real wages and in median household incomes throughout the time period. Accounting for the Hamilton (1998) and Costa (2001) estimates of CPI bias yields estimated wage growth of 1 percent per year during 1975–2015. Meaningful growth in consumption for below median income families has occurred even in a prolonged period of increasing income inequality, increasing consumption inequality and a decreasing share of national income accruing to labour.'

74. For details on women's participation in the labour force worldwide see Estaban Ortiz-Ospina and Sandra Tzvetkova, 'Working women: Key facts and trends in female labor force participation', *Our World in Data*, 16 October 2017, https://ourworldindata.org/female-labor-force-participation-key-facts.

75. For an insightful survey see Claudia Goldin, 'The Quiet Revolution that Transformed Women's Employment, Education and Family', *American Economic Association Papers and Proceedings*, 96 (2) 2006, 1–21.

76. On this see Paul Kelly, *The End of Certainty: Power, Politics and Business in Australia*, Sydney: Allen and Unwin, 1994. For a sceptical appraisal of Australian labour market deregulation, however, see Chris Briggs and John Buchanan, *Australian Labour Market Deregulation: A Critical Assessment*, Parliament of Australia Research Paper 21, 1999–2000, http://www.aph.gov.au/About_Parliament/Parliamentary_Departments/Parliamentary_Library/pubs/rp/rp9900/2000RP21#second (accessed 15 April 2017).

77. See on this David H. Autor, David Dorn, and Gordon H. Hanson, 'The China Shock: Learning from Labor-Market Adjustment to Large Changes in Trade', *Annual Review of Economics*, 8 (2016), 205–40.

78. Borjas does repeatedly use the word 'transfer', particularly in 'What Does the National Academies' Immigration Report Really Say?'.

79. Ibid.

80. Ibid.

81. Borjas would not be the first to express a concern about the shift in gains from labour to capital. Thomas Piketty, most famously, has tried to show that if the rate of return from national economic activity exceeds the rate of growth the income and wealth of the rich will grow faster than income from labour. See Thomas Piketty, *Capital in the 21st Century*, translated by Arthur Goldhammer, Cambridge, MA: Harvard University Press, 2014. Some have seen the basic hypothesis as plausible or even correct (for example, Robert Solow, 'Thomas Piketty is Right: Everything you need to know about "Capital in the Twenty-First Century"', *New Republic*, 23 April 2014, https://newrepublic.com/article/117429/capital-twenty-first-century-thomas-piketty-reviewed).

Others, however, have argued that any analysis that ignores broader institutional considerations cannot be relied upon. See Daron Acemoglu and James A. Robinson, 'The Rise and Decline of General Laws of Capitalism', *Journal of Economic Perspectives*, 29 (1), 2015, 3–28. Whatever might be the truth of the matter, it is surely too simple to try to explain a shift considering only one factor: immigration.

82. According to some economists, the problem with the rich is their propensity to save and invest rather than to consume, but I will avoid this particular topic here.

83. For a brief formal exposition of this dilemma see James M. Buchanan, 'A Two-country Parable', in Warren F. Schwartz (ed.), *Justice in Immigration*, Cambridge: Cambridge University Press, 1995, 63–6.

84. Alan O. Sykes, 'The Welfare Economics of Immigration Law: A Theoretical Survey with an Analysis of U.S. Policy', in Schwartz (ed.), *Justice in Immigration*, 158–200, at 173–5.

85. At the time of writing, the United States Federal Government debt stood at $19 trillion, of which $3.8 trillion was owed to foreign government holders of Treasury bills, notes and bonds, and $5.55 trillion was owed to other federal agencies, such as the Social Security Trust Fund—with the rest owed to other foreign and domestic investors. About half of the national debt was owed to foreign sources.

86. In the following discussion I draw mainly on Bansak, Simpson, and Navodny, *The Economics of Immigration*, 215–20.

87. Borjas, 'What Does the National Academies' Immigration Report Really Say?'

88. For a recent analysis of the fiscal impact of immigration to the UK see Christian Dustmann and Tommaso Frattini, 'The Fiscal Effects of Immigration to the UK', *The Economic Journal*, 124 (580), 2014, 593–643. In their abstract the authors summarize their findings as follows: 'Our findings indicate that, when considering the resident immigrant population in each year from 1995 to 2011, immigrants from the European Economic Area (EEA) have made a positive fiscal contribution, even during periods when the UK was running budget deficits, while non-EEA immigrants, not dissimilar to natives, have made a negative contribution. For immigrants that arrived since 2000, contributions have been positive throughout, and particularly so for immigrants from EEA countries. Notable is the strong positive contribution made by immigrants from countries that joined the EU in 2004.'

89. Friedman, 'What is America?', in *The Economics of Freedom*, Cleveland, Standard Oil Company of Ohio, 1978, 3. Given the nature of the problem, Friedman noted however, it was a good thing that there was illegal immigration from Mexico, since it benefited both Mexicans and Americans. His larger point (4) was that this case shows 'how bad laws make socially advantageous acts illegal and lead to an undermining of morality in general'.

90. I was in such a position when I moved to the UK to work at the LSE on a five-year work permit—which stated that I was ineligible for certain public funds for the duration of the visa.

91. *The New Case Against Immigration*, 189.

92. Ibid., 210–11. In Krikorian's view, this development is not one that Americans have chosen but rather one that is being foisted upon them. Americans, he claims, have indicated a preference for lower population.

93. Cafaro, *How Many is Too Many?*, chs. 5–8.

94. On the long history of failed attempts at population control (whether to increase or decrease the size of nations), see Richard Togman, *Nationalizing Sex: Fertility, Fear, and Power*, New York: Oxford University Press, 2019. Immigration control is just one of a range of methods used try to manage population size.

95. There is no common definition of 'urban' and different countries use their own. Typically a settlement of over 2,000 persons is considered urban. The geographical expansion of cities has turned what were once rural communities into parts of cities.

96. For an examination of the greater significance of immigration to *cities* rather than *states*, see Avner de-Shalit, *Cities and Immigration: Political and Moral Dilemmas in the New Era of Migration*, Oxford: Oxford University Press, 2018.

97. For an interesting speculative analysis of the implications of this see Darrell Bricker and John Ibbitson, *Empty Planet: The Shock of Global Population Decline*, London: Crown, 2019.

98. See *How Many is Too Many?*, ch. 6.

99. Daron Acemoglu and James Robinson, *Why Nations Fail: The Origins of Power, Prosperity, and Poverty,* New York: Crown, 2012.

100. Collier, *Exodus*, quoted in Borjas, *We Wanted Workers*, 43.

101. Borjas, *We Wanted Workers*, 43.

102. Ibid., 43.

103. Ibid., 49.

104. Clemens and Pritchett review the literature that purports to show that immigration restrictions would increase global growth because too much migration would see migrants from poor countries transmit low productivity to rich ones. They demonstrate that the case could only hold for very significantly higher migration. In this regard, the literature suggests that while there is not a case for 'open borders', there is a strong case for a relaxation of current restrictions on labour mobility. See Michael A. Clemens and Lant Pritchett, 'The New Economic Case for Migration Restrictions: An Assessment', *Journal of Development Economics*, 138 (2019), 153–64.

105. For a recent survey of this issue see Rok Spruk, 'The rise and fall of Argentina', *Latin American Economic Review*, 28 (16), 2019, https://doi.org/10.1186/s40503-019-0076-2.

106. For a (Marxist) analysis of the decline of the East German model see Gareth Dale, *Between State Capitalism and Globalisation: The Collapse of the East German Economy*, New York: Peter Lang, 2004. For an examination of the economic problem of East German transition, see Wendy Carlin, 'The new east German economy: Problems of transition, unification and institutional mismatch', *German Politics*, 7 (3), 1998, 14–32. For a more recent essay see Kate Connolly, 'German Reunification 25 Years On', *Guardian* 2 October 2015, https://www.theguardian.com/world/2015/oct/02/german-reunification-25-years-on-how-different-are-east-and-west-really.

107. It is important to acknowledge that an influx of immigrants of this magnitude *did* have some negative consequences for former West German workers. On this see Susanne Prantl and Alexandra Spitz-Oener, 'The Impact of Immigration on Competing Natives' Wages: Evidence from German Reunification', *Review of Economics and Statistics*, 102 (1), 2020, 79–97.

108. Though Germany had for some time officially described itself as *not* an immigration nation, this changed in 2001 when, on 4 July, an immigration commission of political party representatives, employers, unions and churches, published a report, 'Organizing Immigration—Fostering Integration', declaring the Germany *was and should be* a country of immigration. See Philip L. Martin, 'Germany: Managing Migration in the Twenty-first Century', in Wayne A. Cornelius, Takeyuki Tsuda, Philip L. Martin, and James F. Hollifield (eds.), *Controlling Immigration: A Global Perspective*, 2nd edition, Stanford, CA: Stanford University Press, 2004, 220–53, at 221.

109. It is also worth noting that there had been considerable migration of East Germans to West Germany between 1946 and 1989. Between 1989 and 1997 more than one million Germans moved from east to west following reunification. Internal migration from east to west continued through the 1990s at varying rates. On this see Frank Heiland, 'Trends in East-West German Migration from 1989 to 2002, *Demographic Research*, 11 (7), 2004, 173–194. Reunification meant absorbing the whole of the East German population not only by incorporating the territory of the former East Germany but also, by giving the entire population freedom to move, taking millions of people into the territory of the former West Germany.

110. It remains to be seen what will be the impact of the hundreds of thousands of Syrian asylum seekers who moved to Germany over a matter of months in 2015, but whatever the broader

social and cultural consequences might be, it looks unlikely that it will seriously affect an economy that has shown itself robust enough to absorb more than 25 million people in less than a generation.

111. See Dolores L. Augustine, 'The Impact of Two Reunification-Era Debates on the East German Sense of Identity', *German Studies Review*, 27 (3), 2004, 563–78.

112. This is between a quarter and a third of the current annual GDP of Mexico (depending on whose estimates one chooses—The IMF's, the World Bank's, or the UN's).

113. Marie Gottschalk, *Caught: The Prison State and the Breakdown of American Politics*, Princeton: Princeton University Press, 2016, 236.

114. Frontex, from *Frontieres Extérieures* or 'external borders', was an agency of the European Union based in Warsaw, with responsibility for policing the Schengen Area, in cooperation with the border control agencies of the Schengen member countries.

115. *Frontex Key Facts*, https://frontex.europa.eu/faq/key-facts/.

116. See Ian Trueger, 'Starved of skilled chefs, Britain is facing a chicken tikka masala crisis', *Quartz India*, 5 January 2018, https://qz.com/india/1171462/starved-of-skilled-chefs-britains-curry-restaurants-are-slowly-dying/.

117. *Determining labour shortages and the need for labour migration from third countries in the EU: Synthesis Report for the EMN Focussed Study 2015*, http://extranjeros.mitramiss.gob.es/es/redeuropeamigracion/Estudios_monograficos/ficheros/2015_2016/EN_emn_labour_shortages_synthesis__final.pdf (accessed 25 September 2019). This synthesis was produced by the European Migration Network.

118. The classic statement of this understanding of the market is F. A. Hayek's 1968 essay, 'Competition as a Discovery Procedure', in *The Collected Works of F. A. Hayek Volume 15: The Market and Other Orders,* ed. Bruce Caldwell, Chicago: University of Chicago Press, 2014, 304–13.

119. It is worth noting that, in the United States, immigrants are twice as likely to start business as the US-born population. Interestingly, refugees have an even higher rate of entrepreneurship than other immigrants. See Dan Kosten, 'Immigrants as Economic Contributors: Immigrant Entrepreneurs', *National Immigration Forum*, 11 July 2018, https://immigrationforum.org/article/immigrants-as-economic-contributors-immigrant-entrepreneurs/; Dinah Wisenberg Brin, 'Immigrants Form 25% of New U.S. Businesses, Driving Entrepreneurship in "Gateway" States', *Forbes*, 31 July 2018. The same can be said for the UK. See, for example, Sam Dumitriu, 'The role of immigrants in start-ups', *CAPX*, 11 July 2019, https://capx.co/the-vital-role-of-immigrants-in-start-up-britain/; Philip Salter, 'Half of UK's Fastest-Growing Businesses Have a Foreign-Born Founder', *Forbes*, July 11, 2019. For Canada see David Green, Huju Liu, and Yuri Ostrovsky, 'Business Ownership and Employment in Immigrant-owned Firms in Canada', *Economic Insights*, 21 March 2016, https://www150.statcan.gc.ca/n1/pub/11-626-x/11-626-x2016057-eng.htm. For Germany see 'Immigrants are bringing entrepreneurial flair to Germany', *The Economist*, 4 February 2017, https://www.economist.com/europe/2017/02/04/immigrants-are-bringing-entrepreneurial-flair-to-germany.

120. Though for a detailed account of just such a case see the autobiography of Baron Popat of Harrow: Dolar Popat, *A British Subject: How to Make it as an Immigrant in the Best Country in the World*, London: Biteback Publishing, 2019.

121. On this see G. Richard Shell, *Make the Rules or Your Rivals Will*, New York: Random House, 2004.

122. It is perhaps unsurprising how little the question 'cui bono?' (who benefits?) is asked. As Upton Sinclair observed: 'It is difficult to get a man to understand something when his salary depends upon his not understanding it.' See Sinclair, *I, Candidate for Governor: And How I Got Licked*, Berkeley: University of California Press, 1994, 109.

123. For an illuminating study see Joshua Page, *The Toughest Beat: Politics, Punishment, and the Prison Officers Union in California*, Oxford: Oxford University Press, 2011.

124. In the US, Immigration and Customs Enforcement (ICE) has promoted a tougher immigration enforcement regime as a way for local communities to raise extra revenue by contracting with the federal government to house detainees. See Gottschalk, *Caught*, 233.

125. For an account of the growth of US prisons see Gottschalk, *Caught*, ch. 3.

126. Ibid., 233.

127. Ibid., 233. Gottschalk further explains: 'Financial arrangements modeled after the lease revenue bonds . . . ensure that the bonds to build immigrant detention facilities do not need to go to before voters for approval. Local governments contract with the federal government to house detainees and then typically subcontract with a private company for a set fee to run the detention facility. If the number of detainees and the revenue streams from them fall short of expectations, the local government is still saddled with the bond payments. If it defaults, the municipality imperils its credit rating.'

128. For an important attempt to do both of these things, see D. Conlon and N. Hiemstra, 'Examining the everyday micro-economies of migrant detention in the United States', *Geographica Helvetica*, 69 (2014), 335–44.

129. Wages might be as little as 12 cents an hour, which means that some detainees may have to work for several weeks to earn enough to make a phone call—which is also charged for at 'predatory' rates by companies selling phone cards. See ibid., 340–1. Interestingly, Conlon and Hiemstra note (340) that 'among the reasons for the high costs of communication is not corporate greed per se; instead, they result from commissions paid to local and state governments'. Local governments earn millions of dollars from these commissions. In 2012, New Jersey's Essex County government, through a contract with Global Tel*Link, made $925,000 from telephone commissions.

130. For an account of the economic beneficiaries of detention in the US, from major private prison companies such as The GEO Group and CoreCivic, to the smaller for-profit companies that operate detention facilities, to the telephone, transportation, financial services, medical, food, construction, and equipment companies, to the various private equity firms who profit, see 'Immigration Detention: An American Business', *Worth Rises*, https://worthrises.org/immigration (accessed 30 September 2019). For a study of the profitability of detention in the EU see Lydie Arbogast, *Migrant Detention in the European Union: A Thriving Business*, Migreurop, July 2016, https://www.migreurop.org/IMG/pdf/migrant-detention-eu-en.pdf (accessed 30 September 2019).

131. For an account of one aspect of this see Mark Dow, *American Gulag: Inside U.S. Immigration Prisons*, Berkeley: University of California Press, 2004.

132. For a more recent and comprehensive account of immigrant detention see César Cuauhtémoc García Hernández, *Migrating to Prison: America's Obsession with Locking Up Immigrants*, New York: New Press, 2019.

## Chapter 6: Culture

1. J. Enoch Powell, *Reflections of a Statesman: The Selected Writings and Speeches of Enoch Powell*, selected by Rex Collings, London: Bellew Publishing, 1991, 386.

2. Will Kymlicka, *Politics in the Vernacular*, New York: Oxford University Press, 2001, 215. See also *Multicultural Citizenship: A Liberal Theory of Minority Rights*, Oxford: Oxford University Press, 1995. For a more recent work see Liav Orgad, *The Cultural Defense of Nations: A Liberal Theory of Majority Rights*, Oxford: Oxford University Press, 2016.

3. Carens, *The Ethics of Immigration*, Oxford: Oxford University Press, 2013, 286.

4. Samuel P. Huntington, *Who Are We? The Challenges to America's National Identity*, New York: Simon and Schuster, 2005.

5. Paul Collier, *Exodus: Immigration and Multiculturalism in the 21st Century,* London: Allen Lane, 2013, 16.

6. Ibid., 16.

7. See on this David Miller, *National Responsibility and Global Justice*, Oxford: Oxford University Press, 2007, ch. 8, and esp. 218–9.

8. See J. Enoch Powell, *Reflections of a Statesman*, 373–9.

9. Ibid., 379.

10. In his speech Powell said (ibid., 379): 'As I look ahead, I am filled with foreboding; like the Roman, I seem to see "the River Tiber foaming with much blood".' The reference is to that passage in the Aeneid when the Trojan warrior, Aeneas, consults the Sybil about the prospects of his founding the city of Rome and building an empire. Her reply to Aeneas was that she saw wars, and the river Tiber foaming with blood, suggesting that the birth of a cosmopolitan and culturally diverse political order would be violent and painful.

11. Collier refers to 'a foolish speech by a long-dead minor politician' that 'closed down British discussion of migration policy for over forty years'. See *Exodus*, 20, and also at 22 and 77. I suggest Collier is influential because he is a prominent public intellectual and a best-selling author, not because I am aware of any direct involvement he might have in advising on immigration policy.

12. Ibid., 25.

13. For an earlier exploration of this argument see James M. Buchanan, 'A Two-country Parable', in Warren F. Schwartz (ed.), *Justice in Immigration*, Cambridge: Cambridge University Press, 1995, 63–6.

14. *Exodus*, 24.

15. Ibid., 26.

16. Ibid., 91 (italics in original).

17. Ibid., 262.

18. Writing of the claims of asylum seekers in particular, Collier suggests that 'when peace is restored, people would be required to return'. The problem in both poor and high-income countries, he argues, is the 'fragility of existing cooperation'. The countries of many states lack the means to engineer a coordinated return of their diaspora citizens, but host governments of asylum-seeking migrants with the means should use their power to help. Ibid., 262.

19. Collier even offers similar arguments on the social housing question, which was the issue that first prompted Powell to address the Race Relations Bill in his Birmingham address. See ibid., 114: 'Because migrants tend to be poorer and have larger families than the indigenous population, they have atypically high needs for social housing, but meeting those needs inevitably crowds out the indigenous poor.'

20. For a charitable critique of Collier's book, see David Laitin, 'Exodus: Reflections on European Migration Policy', in Roland Hsu (ed.), *Migration and Integration: New Models for Mobility and Coexistence*, Vienna: University of Vienna Press, 2016, 86–94. For a more robust examination see Justin Sandefur and Michael Clemens, 'Let the People Go: The Problem With Strict Migration Limits', *Foreign Affairs*, January/February 2014, 152–9. Both reviews agree that Collier's analysis is unsupported by evidence other than anecdote. Sandeful and Clemens go further to point to plentiful evidence that contradicts Collier's main claims about the gains to immigrants from migration, the absence of gains to natives, the fiscal impact of immigrants on receiving countries, the impact of emigration on poor countries, and the loss of social trust that comes with accepting too many culturally different foreigners.

21. For an interesting analysis that overlaps with mine see Alex Sager, 'Culture and Immigration: A Case for Exclusion?' *Social Philosophy Today*, 23 (2007), 69–86, at 78.

22. For two recent works that exemplify the preoccupation with these concerns see David Goodhart, *The British Dream: Successes and Failures of Post-war Immigration*, London: Atlantic Books, 2013; Paul Scheffer, *Immigrant Nations*, translated from the Dutch by Liz Waters, Cambridge: Polity, 2011 (first published 2007).

23. The source of this distinction is Peter Jones, 'Group Rights and Group Oppression', *Journal of Political Philosophy*, 7 (4), 1999, 353–77, esp. 369ff.

24. See Jonathan Lear, *Radical Hope: Ethics in the Face of Cultural Devastation*, Cambridge, MA: Harvard University Press, 2006.

25. The Chinese occupation of Tibet is one recent example.

26. Raphael Lemkin, *Axis Rule in Occupied Europe*, Washington, DC: Carnegie Endowment for International Peace, 1944, 91.

27. *Exodus*, 246.

28. Ibid., 247.

29. See Charles Taylor, 'The Politics of Recognition', in *Multiculturalism: Examining the Politics of Recognition*, edited and introduced by Amy Gutmann, Princeton: Princeton University Press, 1994, 25–73, at 41, where Taylor writes: 'But where Kymlicka's interesting argument fails to recapture the actual demands made by the groups concerned—say Indian bands in Canada, or French-speaking Canadians—is with respect to their goal of survival. Kymlicka's reasoning is valid (perhaps) for existing people who find themselves trapped within a culture under pressure, and can flourish within it or not at all. But it doesn't justify measures designed to ensure survival through indefinite future generations. For the populations concerned, however, that is what is at stake. We need only think of the historical resonance of "la survivance" among French Canadians.'

30. *Exodus*, 108.

31. As David Miller points out in *National Responsibility and Global Justice*, 227–8.

32. Many countries administer 'points tests' which discriminate in favour of immigrants from a selective group of countries. On British and Swedish measures that discriminate against immigration from Turkey see Collier, *Exodus*, 262. Collier considers these measures justifiable on cultural grounds.

33. This point is made forcefully by Ryan Pevnick, *Immigration and the Constraints of Justice: Between Open Borders and Absolute Sovereignty*, Cambridge: Cambridge University Press, 2011, 133–41. For an attempt to defend immigration restrictions on such grounds see Samuel Huntington, *Who Are We?* The challenge facing Huntington, however, is that in claiming that Mexican immigration threatens the Protestant cultural identity of the United States he opens up the question of whether preserving that identity might require restricting immigration from other cultural regions.

34. David Miller notes this in observing that while it might be justified to exclude people from an association if they could disrupt the intimate relationships it protects, this reason does not readily apply to political communities, with the possible exception of confessional states in which 'the presence of unbelievers might be regarded as disruptive of the community'. *National Responsibility and Global Justice*, 211.

35. Even here, however, the problem is not easily resolved once a society has been transformed by an influx of people who have made their homes there, and whose children know nothing else. For a thoughtful discussion see Anna Stilz, *Territorial Sovereignty: A Philosophical Exploration*, Oxford: Oxford University Press, 2019, 74–8.

36. Keith Banting and Will Kymlicka (eds.), *Multiculturalism and the Welfare State: Recognition and Redistribution in Contemporary Democracies*, Oxford: Oxford University Press, 2006.

37. For an interesting study of the way in which political parties fomented inter-ethnic group competition in Australia see Raymond Sestito, *The Politics of Multiculturalism*, Sydney: Centre for Independent Studies, 1982. See also my 'Tolerating the Intolerable', *Papers on Parliament*, no. 33 (May 1999).

38. Lord Acton, 'On Nationality', in John Emerich Edward Dalberg-Acton, *Selected Writings of Lord Acton. Volume One: Essays in the History of Liberty*, ed. J. Rufus Fears, Indianapolis: Liberty Fund, 1986, 409–33.

39. Consider the case of Patrick Nudjulu, who lived on the Timor Sea coast of Australia and was one of three remaining speakers of Mati Ke. One of the other speakers did not live close by and spoke a slightly different dialect, while the other was his sister, to whom his culture forbade him to speak since puberty.

## Chapter 7: State

1. Ms Pauline Hanson, *Cth. Parliamentary Debates. House of Representatives Official Hansard No 208 1996*, 10 September 1996, 3860–63.

2. Pat Buchanan, 'Immigration: Issue of the Century', *Townhall.com*, 18 August 2015, http://townhall.com/columnists/patbuchanan/2015/08/18/immigration--issue-of-the-century -n2040032/page/full.

3. George Orwell seems to concur: 'England is not the jewelled isle of Shakespeare's much-quoted message, nor is it the inferno depicted by Dr Goebbels. More than either it resembles a family, a rather stuffy Victorian family, with not many black sheep in it but with all its cupboards bursting with skeletons. It has rich relations who have to be kowtowed to and poor relations who are horribly sat upon, and there is a deep conspiracy of silence about the source of the family income. It is a family in which the young are generally thwarted and most of the power is in the hands of irresponsible uncles and bedridden aunts. Still, it is a family. It has its private language and its common memories, and at the approach of an enemy it closes its ranks. A family with the wrong members in control—that, perhaps is as near as one can come to describing England in a phrase.' Orwell in 'England Your England', in *The Orwell Reader: Fiction, Essays and Reportage*, London: Harcourt, 1984, 249–70, at 261.

4. It is perhaps unsurprising that the paternal model of political authority has been in decline since Filmer's *Patriarcha*, though arguably vestiges remain both in theorizing about the state and in political institutions themselves. See Gordon Schochet, *The Authoritarian Family and Political Attitudes in 17th-Century England*, New Brunswick, NJ: Transaction Publishers, 1988. See also Carole Pateman, *The Sexual Contract*, Stanford, CA: Stanford University Press, 1988.

5. Many defenders of the priority of nationality might object that while they reject 'open borders', they would recognize the exceptional claims of refugees. Though that is true enough, it does not mean that they are therefore ready to say: 'restrictions on immigrants but open borders for refugees'. See my 'Are Refugees Special?', in Sarah Fine and Lea Ypi (eds.), *Migration and Political Theory: The Ethics of Movement and Membership*, Oxford: Oxford University Press, 2016, 249–68.

6. See, for example, Christopher H. Wellman, 'Immigration and Freedom of Association', *Ethics*, 119 (2009–10), 338–56, and Christopher Wellman and Phillip Cole, *Debating the Ethics of Immigration: Is There a Right to Exclude?*, New York: Oxford University Press, 2011, ch. 1.

7. On cosmopolitanism see David Miller, *National Responsibility and Global Justice*, Oxford: Oxford University Press, 2007, 23–50. For defences of cosmopolitanism in political theory see, for example, Luis Cabrera, *Political Theory of Global Justice: A Cosmopolitan Case for the World State*, London: Routledge, 2004; Kok-Chor Tan, *Justice without Borders: Cosmopolitanism, Nationalism and Patriotism*, Cambridge: Cambridge University Press, 2004; Kwame Anthony Appiah, *Cosmopolitanism: Ethics in a World of Strangers*, London: Allen Lane, 2006.

8. David Miller, *Strangers in Our Midst: The Political Philosophy of Immigration*, Cambridge, MA: Harvard University Press, 2016, 26.

9. Ibid., 26.

10. Ibid., 26.

11. Ibid., 26.

12. Ibid., 27.

13. Ibid., 27–8.

14. Ibid., 28.

15. Ibid., 37.

16. Anna Stilz also holds that only states can exercise ultimate territorial jurisdiction. See *Liberal Loyalty: Freedom, Obligation, and the State*, Princeton University Press, 2009. Cara Nine, however, argues against this, suggesting that it is not states who have jurisdiction but peoples. See *Global Justice and Territory*, Oxford: Oxford University Press, 2012, 14–15.

17. Miller, *Strangers in Our Midst*, 60.

18. Ibid., 60.

19. For example: the US, Australia, and Canada at their foundings, China in Tibet, the USSR in the Baltic states and Russia in the Ukraine, Italy during unification, France during unification, and the Roman Empire (in parts), Spain in Central and South America, the Portuguese in Brazil, the British in Ireland, Israel in the West Bank, India in Kashmir, and the list goes on.

20. Ibid., 60.

21. Ibid., 60.

22. Ibid., 60. Miller defends this view more systematically in 'Territorial Rights: Concept and Justification', *Political Studies*, 60 (2), 2012, 252–68.

23. David Miller, *On Nationality*, Oxford: Oxford University Press, 1995, 23.

24. Ibid., 42, note. It would also go against Article 13 of the Universal Declaration of Human Rights, to which the United Kingdom was one of the original signatories. That article states that: '(1) Everyone has the right to freedom of movement and residence within the borders of each state. And (2) Everyone has the right to leave any country, including his own, and to return to his country.'

25. Margaret Moore, *A Political Theory of Territory*, Oxford: Oxford University Press, 2015, 202.

26. Ibid., 50.

27. Ibid., 52.

28. Ibid., 52.

29. See Ryan Pevnick, *Immigration and the Constraints of Justice: Between Open Borders and Absolute Sovereignty*, Cambridge: Cambridge University Press, 2011.

30. Ibid., 38.

31. Ibid., 38.

32. Ibid., 39. The reference is to Lincoln's view as expressed in the Gettysburg Address.

33. Ibid., 39. Pevnick is quoting from John Rawls's *Political Liberalism*, New York: Columbia University Press, 1993, 15.

34. Pevnick, *Immigration and the Constraints of Justice*, 39.

35. Ibid., 40.

36. Ibid., 41–3.

37. Ibid., 44. See Jeremy Waldron, 'Property and Ownership', *Stanford Encyclopedia of Philosophy*, https://plato.stanford.edu/archives/sum2020/entries/property/.

38. Pevnick, *Immigration and the Constraints of Justice*, 53.

39. For an excellent survey of these see Lea Ypi, 'Territorial Rights and Exclusion', *Philosophy Compass*, 8 (3), 2013, 241–53.

40. Sir Walter Scott, 'My Native Land'. These are the opening lines of the Sixth Canto of Scott's epic poem, 'The Lay of the Last Minstrel'. The Sixth Canto is sometimes presented separately under the title 'My Native Land'. See Walter Scott, *The Lay of the Last Minstrel*, Sydney: Wentworth Press, 2016.

41. Even today there are no established criteria for statehood in international politics. There are 193 member states of the United Nations as well as two 'observer states' (Palestine and Vatican City). But there are also 11 other states whose claims to statehood are unclear, including Taiwan

(claimed by China, but which is also claimed by Taiwan), Northern Cyprus (claimed by Cyprus), Kosovo (claimed by Serbia), and South Ossetia (claimed by Georgia).

42. Much in the same way that David Hume's *Natural History of Religion*, in offering to uncover the origins of religion, could serve only to undermine the claims of theism. See *The Natural History of Religion*, Stanford, CA: Stanford University Press, 1959.

43. Miller, *Strangers in Our Midst*, 29.

44. See Michael Harsgor, 'Total History: The Annales School', *Journal of Contemporary History*, 13 (1), 1978, 1–13.

45. A partial list of modern countries rendered extinct by political events includes the following dismembered countries: Austria-Hungary (divided into Austria, Hungary and Czechoslovakia); Czechoslovakia; Gran Colombia; the Mali Federation; the Polish Lithuanian Commonwealth; the Soviet Union; the United Arab Republic; the United Kingdom of the Netherlands; the West Indies Federation; and Yugoslavia. For an interesting history of defunct states see Norman Davies, *Vanished Kingdoms: The History of Half-Forgotten Europe*, London: Penguin, 2012.

46. On loyalist numbers see Paul H. Smith, 'The American Loyalists: Notes on Their Organization and Numerical Strength', *William and Mary Quarterly*, 25 (2), April 1968, 259–77. It is exceedingly difficult to estimate the number of people who were actively for or against this (or any other) revolution, since expressions of support for any side were contingent on who was more powerful or indeed more aggressive. A plurality of the population were probably content to side with the likely victors and eager to have the matter settled so they could get back to the business of life. For a more recent study see Maya Jasanoff, *Liberty's Exiles: American Loyalists in the Revolutionary World*, New York: Vintage, 2012. For a more general study of the politics of the adoption of the American Constitution as highly contingent rather than certain, see Michael J. Klarman, *The Framers' Coup: The Making of the United States Constitution*, New York: Oxford University Press, 2016.

47. Prasenjit Duara, *Rescuing History from the Nation: Questioning Narratives of Modern China*, Chicago: University of Chicago Press, 1995.

48. This is despite attempted debunkings of nationalist narratives in the writings of such figures as Elie Kedourie, *Nationalism*, 4th expanded edition, Oxford: Blackwell, 2000; and Benedict Anderson, *Imagined Communities: Reflections on the Origin and Spread of Nationalism*, 2nd edition, London: Verso, 2016.

49. Hume, 'Of the Original Contract', in *Essays: Moral, Political, and Literary*, ed. Eugene F. Miller, Indianapolis: Liberty Fund, 1985, 472.

50. Ibid., 472–3.

51. For a bracing revisionist account of the idea of the United Kingdom, see David Edgerton, *The Rise and Fall of the British Nation: A Twentieth-Century History*, Milton Keynes: Penguin, 2019.

52. For an instructive account of the making of the border between France and Spain, see Peter Sahlins, *Boundaries: The Making of France and Spain in the Pyrenees*, Berkeley and Los Angeles: University of California Press, 1991.

53. This is not to say that identities do not matter. Since so much of in social life depends on identity, practical attention to identity questions is inescapable, even if the settling of such questions will owe more to politics than to historical truth. Consider, for example, the case of the Seminole Indians. The Seminoles were bands of Creek Indians who separated from the tribe and settled in northern Florida in the seventeenth century. They practised slavery, not only of other Indians captured in battle, but also of Africans whom they purchased or were given as gifts by the British. By the nineteenth century, however, the Black Seminole population had grown and established a strong, independent community, which actually joined with the Seminoles to resist the attempt of Americans to annex Florida. Together they fought against General Andrew Jackson in the First Seminole War (1817–18), and later in the Second Seminole War (1835–42), and

gained a measure of independence. But they were then forced to face the Creek Indians, who were intent on enslaving them, and reintegrating the Seminole Indians into Creek society. Many fled to Mexico to escape Creek slave-hunters, though a good number returned during the Civil War to work as Indian Scouts. They claim they were promised their own land in Texas in return, but in the end the War Department denied that they had land to offer, and the Bureau of Indian Affairs refused to give them land *on the grounds that they were not really Indians.* The existence of Black members of the Seminole Indians also later became a contentious issue because the sums paid to the Seminoles in compensation for dispossession would have to be further divided if Indians of African descent were included, and many Seminole Indians did not wish to acknowledge those of African descent as Seminole.

54. *Crito* 50e, in Plato and Aristophanes, *Four Texts on Socrates: Plato's Euthyphro, Apology and Crito and Aristophanes' Clouds*, translated with notes by Thomas G. West and Grace Starry West, Ithaca, NY and London: Cornell University Press, 1984, 109.

55. *Crito* 51b, 110.

56. See Robert Filmer, *Patriarcha*, in *Patriarcha and Other Writings*, ed. Johann P. Sommerville, Cambridge: Cambridge University Press, 1991 (first published 1680), esp. ch. 1, sections 6–10.

57. *Patriarcha*, 12.

58. See Schochet, *The Authoritarian Family*, 63.

59. Ibid., 55.

60. See John Locke, *First Treatise of Government*, in Locke, *Two Treatises of Government*, ed. with an introduction and notes by Peter Laslett, Cambridge: Cambridge University Press, 1988.

61. John Rawls, *A Theory of Justice*, Oxford: Oxford University Press, 1971, 4. Rawls offers a similar formulation in *Political Liberalism*. See note 33 above.

62. Nozick, *Anarchy, State and Utopia*, Oxford: Blackwell, 1974, 188–9.

63. F. A. Hayek, *The Fatal Conceit: the Errors of Socialism*, ed. William Warren Bartley III, Chicago: University of Chicago Press, 1988, 6.

64. See Mark J. Perry, 'How Much Does Your State Need Foreign Trade?', in Foundation for Economic Education, 9 March 2017 (original source: Census Bureau), https://fee.org/articles /how-much-does-your-state-need-foreign-trade/ (accessed 6 September 2017).

65. For a fuller account of what a society is see my *The Liberal Archipelago: A Theory of Diversity and Freedom*, Oxford: Oxford University Press, 2003, 77–9.

66. This is a point Margaret Moore recognizes in noting that peoples can precede the existence of and survive the collapse or disappearance of a state. See *A Political Theory of Territory*, 28.

67. See Miller, *National Responsibility and Global Justice*, esp. 68–75. See also the critique by Joseph Carens, *The Ethics of Immigration*, Oxford: Oxford University Press, 2013, 262–70.

68. Pevnick, *Immigration and the Constraints of Justice*, 115. (It is not clear how strong this claim is meant to be, but I take it that he wishes to suggest a broad general claim rather than to suggest that only on occasion can a society be held responsible for its success or failure. I discuss this issue more fully below.)

69. Ibid., 115.

70. The two special areas are the Åland Islands and Svalbard, which are special territories of Finland and Norway respectively, but have political arrangements which were settled through international agreements.

71. See for example, Leif Wenar, *Blood Oil: Tyrants, Violence, and the Rules that Run the World*, New York: Oxford University Press, 2016; James C. Scott, *Seeing Like A State: How Certain Schemes to Improve the Human Condition Have Failed*, New Haven: Yale University Press, 1999; James C. Scott, *The Art of Not Being Governed: An Anarchist History of Upland Southeast Asia*, New Haven: Yale University Press, 2010; Joel Migdal, *Strong States and Weak Societies: State-Society Relations and State Capabilities in the Third World*, Princeton: Princeton University Press, 1988; Joel

Migdal, *State in Society: Studying How States and Societies Transform and Constitute One Another*, Cambridge: Cambridge University Press, 2001; Pierre Clastres, *Society Against the State: Essays in Political Anthropology*, translated by Robert Hurley with Abe Stein, New York: Zone, 1987.

72. Aaron Wildavsky and Carolyn Webber, *A History of Taxation and Expenditure in the Western World*, New York: Simon and Schuster, 1986; David Burg, *A World History of Tax Rebellions: An Encyclopedia of Tax Rebels, Revolts, and Riots from Antiquity to the Present*, London: Routledge, 2003.

73. Joseph Schumpeter, 'The Crisis of the Tax State', in A. T. Peacock, R. Turvey, W. F. Stolper and E. Henderson (eds.) *International Economic Papers*, Volume 4, London and New York: Macmillan, 1954, 5–38 (translation of 'Die Krise des Steuerstaates', *Zeitfragen aus dem Gebiet der Sociologie*, 4 (1918), 1–71).

74. A good place to start is Margaret Levi's modern classic of Marxist analysis and rational choice theory, *Of Rule and Revenue*, Berkeley and Los Angeles: University of California Press, 1988, esp. ch. 2 on 'The Theory of Predatory Rule', and ch. 6 on 'The Introduction of the Income Tax in Eighteenth-Century Britain'.

75. James Bartholomew, *The Welfare State We're In*, 2nd revised edition, London: Biteback Publishing, 2014.

76. Here the history of state education is instructive. See, for example, E. G. West, *The State and Education*, London: Institute of Economic Affairs, 1970; Ting Hui Lee, *Chinese Schools in Peninsula Malaysia: The Struggle for Survival*, Singapore: Institute of Southeast Asian Studies, 2011; James Tooley, *The Beautiful Tree: A Personal Journey into How the World's Poorest People are Educating Themselves*, Washington: Cato Institute, 2009.

77. Nozick, *Anarchy, State and Utopia*, 174–5.

78. *A Political Theory of Territory*, 42.

79. I have offered a sketch of a theory of explaining how property claims, whether individual or collective, might arise in 'Libertarianism Without Self-ownership', *Social Philosophy and Policy*, 36 (2), 2019, 71–93.

80. This is the final line in a verse from one of the original versions of the Woody Guthrie song, 'This Land is Your Land'. The verse stood out for its scepticism, as it sang of the suffering of the people left unemployed and hungry. It was dropped later in favour of more sentimental nationalist variants.

81. Moore, *A Political Theory of Territory*, 50 (emphasis added).

82. Ibid., 50 (emphasis in original).

83. See Michael Oakeshott, *On Human Conduct*, Oxford: Oxford University Press, 1975, part 3.

84. Ibid., 316.

85. Ibid., 317.

86. There are exceptions. For example, in the early twentieth century, socialist adventurers set out from Australia to create the ideal society in Paraguay. The results were disappointing. See the account in Anne Whitehead, *Paradise Mislaid: In Search of the Australian Tribe of Paraguay*, St Lucia: University of Queensland Press, 1997.

87. Needless to say, Native Americans with their own systems of governance were not party to any of these projects; nor were African slaves.

88. There is a substantial literature on this topic. See for the most recent discussions Adrian Guelke, *Politics in Deeply Divided Societies*, Cambridge: Polity, 2012; for the classic work in this field see Arendt Lijphart, *Democracy in Plural Societies: A Comparative Exploration*, New Haven, Yale University Press, 1977.

89. *A Political Theory of Territory*, 122–8.

90. The original work here is by Muzafer Sherif, O. J. Harvey, B. Jack White, William R. Hood, and Carolyn W. Sherif, *The Robbers Cave Experiment: Intergroup Conflict and Cooperation*,

Norman: Institute of Group Relations, University of Oklahoma, 1988. For a discussion see 'Introduction', Mérove Gijsberts and Louk Hagendoorn (eds.), *Nationalism and the Exclusion of Migrants: Cross-National Comparisons*, London: Routledge, 2017, 7–8.

91. The classic work here is H. Tajfel, M. G. Billig, R. P. Bundy, and C. Flament, 'Social categorization and intergroup behaviour', *European Journal of Social Psychology*, 1 (1971), 149–78.

92. Hence the use of the term 'minimal group experiments' to describe these studies.

93. In the case of the realistic group experiments, and then the minimal group experiments, the groups were in effect created by the experimenters.

94. This is by no means universally acknowledged. Saudi Arabia's *Basic Law of Governance* states: 'Governance in the Kingdom of Saudi Arabia derives its authority from the Book of God Most High and the Sunnah of his Messenger, both of which govern this Law and all the laws of the State.' Royal Order No. (A/91) 27 Sha'ban 1412H—1 March 1992, published in *Umm al-Qura Gazette*, No. 3397.

95. For a valuable genealogical account of theorizing about the state in this period see Quentin Skinner, 'The sovereign state: a genealogy', in Hent Kalmo and Quentin Skinner (eds.), *Sovereignty in Fragments: The Past, Present and Future of a Contested Concept*, Cambridge: Cambridge University Press, 2010, 26–46. See also David Runciman, 'The Concept of the State', in Quentin Skinner and Bo Strath (eds.), *States and Citizens*, Cambridge: Cambridge University Press, 2003, 28–38.

96. I mean *en*corporation rather than *in*corporation, since the prefix 'en' denotes the bringing into existence of a condition.

97. For a critique of this tendency in modern analysis see Andreas Osiander, *Before the State: Systemic Political Change in the West from the Greeks to the French Revolution*, Oxford: Oxford University Press, 2007, esp. ch. 1.

98. Charles Tilly, *Coercion, Capital, and European States AD 990–1990*, Oxford: Blackwell, 1990, 39–40.

99. See Martin Van Creveld, *The Rise and Decline of the State*, Cambridge: Cambridge University Press, 1999, 126–88.

100. For an illuminating study of how states are created by conflicts among other states see Enze Han, *Asymmetrical Neighbors: Borderland State Building Between China and Southeast Asia*, New York: Oxford University Press, 2019.

101. Bob Jessop, *The State: Past, Present, Future*, Cambridge: Polity Press, 2016, 56.

102. Ibid., 57. It is important, however, not to overstate this or one runs the risk of ending up with a kind of structural theory that is unable to account for the possibility of agency and the exercise of power. On this see the debate between Ralph Miliband and Nicos Poulantzas. See N. Poulantzas and R. Miliband, 'The Problem of the Capitalist State', in R. Blackburn (ed.), *Ideology in Social Science: Readings in Critical Social Theory*, New York: Pantheon Books, 1972, 238–62.

103. This is an argument developed with considerable sophistication by Darshan Vigneswaran in his *Territory, Migration and the Evolution of the International System*, Basingstoke: Palgrave Macmillan, 2013, 4–5 and throughout.

104. The Soviet Union and its satellite states in the twentieth century prohibited emigration for fear of an exodus of disaffected citizens. The same is true of North Korea now. Cuba uses its prohibition of emigration to political effect, allowing some citizens to 'escape' to the United States. In the more remote past, Japan's Tokugawa Shogunate restricted emigration and trade under its policy of *sakoku*. In the nineteenth century, massive emigration of Swedish people to America provoked the disapproval of the more well-to-do Swedes, who worried both about the loss of labour and the defiance and lack of patriotism of the lower classes. See H. Arnold Barton, *A Folk Divided: Homeland Swedes and Swedish Americans, 1840–1940*, Carbondale: Southern Illinois University Press, 2006.

105. See Hugo Service, *Germans to Poles: Communism, Nationalism and Ethnic Cleansing after the Second World War*, Cambridge: Cambridge University Press, 2013.

106. On the history of Partition see Yasmin Khan, *The Great Partition: The Making of India and Pakistan*, New Haven: Yale University Press, 2017. For an interesting essay see William Dalrymple, 'The Great Divide. The Violent Legacy of Indian Partition', *The New Yorker*, 29 June 2015, https://www.newyorker.com/magazine/2015/06/29/the-great-divide-books-dalrymple.

107. *Territory, Migration and the Evolution of the International System*, 53.

108. Ibid., ch. 4, 'Expansion of the British Empire', esp. 72–3.

109. On this see Hidetaka Hirota, *Expelling the Poor: Atlantic Seaboard States and the Origins of American Immigration Policy*, New York: Oxford University Press, 2017.

110. On this see Douglas C. Baynton, *Defectives in the Land: Disability and Immigration in the Age of Eugenics*, Chicago and London: University of Chicago Press, 2016; Jennifer S. Kain, *Insanity and Immigration Control in New Zealand and Australia, 1860–1930*, London: Palgrave Macmillan, 2019.

111. This also coincided with the rise in the nineteenth of 'scientific' theories of racial hierarchy among peoples. On this see George M. Frederickson, *Racism: A Short History*, revised edition, Princeton: Princeton University Press, 2015, esp. ch. 2. The author makes the following interesting observation (68): 'The fact that pre-Darwinian scientific racism flowered in France and the United States more than in England may derive to some extent, paradoxical as it may seem, from the revolutionary legacies of nation-states premised on the equal rights of all citizens. Egalitarian norms required special reasons for exclusion. Civic nationalist ideology (operative by virtue of the egalitarian *Code Napoléon* even when France was having one of its nineteenth-century imperial or monarchical episodes) hindered legal and political acknowledgment of the hierarchy of classes and order that slowed the emergency of mass democracy in Great Britain. The one exclusionary principle that could be readily accepted by civic nationalists was biological unfitness for full citizenship.'

112. Vigneswaran, *Territory, Migration and the Evolution of the International System*, 74.

113. Ibid., 75.

114. See on this Jesse Carpenter, *The South as a Conscious Minority 1789–1861: A Study in Political Thought*, with an introduction by John McCardell, Columbia: University of South Carolina Press, 1990; George Kateb, *Lincoln's Political Thought*, Cambridge: Harvard University Press, 2015.

115. In *On Human Conduct* Oakeshott conceives of the state as a form of association marked by relations among *cives,* a term that might be translated as 'citizens', though that would be misleading to the extent that 'citizenship' did not have an established meaning throughout modern European history, and only came into use as a legal category in Britain in the twentieth century. Yet in the Europe of the past few hundred years, the population has included millions of people whose status as *cives* is obscure. Are permanent residents who do not hold citizenship *cives*? Are sojourners, or people with holiday homes, or transients *cives*? All have some kind of a legal relationship with the state, even if they do not all hold the same rights.

116. Thomas Poole, *Reason of State: Law, Prerogative and Empire*, Cambridge: Cambridge University Press, 2015, 291.

117. Ibid., 291.

118. Quoted in a local online paper, *Kent Online*, http://www.kentonline.co.uk/thanet/news/migrants-pushing-services-to-breaking-97302/ (accessed 15 August 2017).

119. Michael Walzer, *Spheres of Justice: A Defense of Pluralism and Equality*, New York: Basic Books, 1983, 61.

120. Though to be clear, this is more problematic than is often recognized. In 1993, for example, Nathan Glazer defended the terms of the 1924 National Origins Act as not racist, arguing that 'there is a difference between recognizing those who are in some sense one's own, with links to a people and a culture, and a policy based on dislike, hostility, racial antagonism'. See Glazer, 'The Closing Door', *The New Republic*, 19 (4), 1993, 15–20, at 18. Yet, as Keith Fitzgerald observes, 'Glazer does not say exactly what the difference is', and tellingly, 'assumes that the American kind would

be "European".' See Fitzgerald, *The Face of the Nation: Immigration, the State, and the National Identity*, Stanford, CA: Stanford University Press, 1996, 242.

121. As reported in the *Independent*, 2 August 2017, http://www.independent.co.uk/news /uk/politics/eu-free-movement-support-brexit-british-people-leave-european-union-survey -a7872816.html.

122. See on this Philip Pettit, 'Deliberative Democracy, the Discursive Dilemma and Republican Theory', in James Fishkin and Peter Laslett (eds.), *Philosophy, Politics and Society*, Volume 7, Cambridge University Press, Cambridge, 2003, 138–62; 'Corporate Agency–The Lesson of the Discursive Dilemma', in Marija Jankovic and Kirk Ludwig (eds.), *Routledge Companion to Collective Intentionality*, London: Routledge, 2017, 249–59. See also Christian List and Philip Pettit, *Group Agency*, Oxford: Oxford University Press, 2011.

123. Jean Bodin, *On Sovereignty: Four Chapter from the Six Books of the Commonwealth*, translated by Julian H. Franklin, Cambridge: Cambridge University Press, 1992. The absence of any mention of territory was not an oversight, since for Bodin, as for other early modern understandings, sovereignty marked a juridical relationship rather than a spatial one.

124. Emer de Vattel, *The Law of Nations, or Principles of the Law of Nature, Applied to the Conduct and Affairs of Nations and Sovereigns, With Three Early Essays on the Origins and Nature of Natural Law and on Luxury*, edited by Béla Kapossy and Richard Whatmore, Indianapolis: Liberty Fund, 2008. (*The Law of Nations* was first published in 1758.)

125. On this see Stéphane Beaulac, 'Vattel's Doctrine on Territory Transfers in International Law and the Cession of Louisiana to the United States of America', *Louisiana Law Review*, 63 (4), 2003, 1327–59.

126. On this see Lauren Benton, *A Search for Sovereignty: Law and Geography in European Empires, 1400–1900*, Cambridge: Cambridge University Press, 2010, esp. 279–99.

127. On 20 May 1982 the Prime Minister said in the House of Commons: 'Sovereignty cannot be changed by invasion. The liberty of the Falkland Islanders must be restored. For years they have been free to express their own wishes about how they want to be governed. They have had institutions of their own choosing. They have enjoyed self-determination.' See *Hansard*, HC Deb 20 May 1982, 24, col. 478.

128. For a full account of the case and its various incongruities see Laurie Fransman, *Fransman's British Nationality Law*, 3rd edition, London: Bloomsbury, 2011, ch. 12, 318–19 on the re-classification of Falkland Islands CUKCs as British citizens, and 921–23 on the present status of the dependency.

129. The act removed or excised several external territories from the Australian migration zone in the Indian Ocean. As a consequence, more asylum seekers by-passed the islands in the region and tried to reach the Australian mainland to claim asylum. In response, on 30 October 2012, the Australian government excised the entire Australian mainland.

130. Thus, for example, in 1946 Argentina claimed its shelf, while Chile, Peru, and Ecuador over the next three years asserted sovereign rights over a 200-mile zone in a bid to limit access to fish stocks by foreign fishing enterprises.

131. See the discussion in Vigneswaran, *Territory, Migration, and the Evolution of the International System*, 99–101.

132. I leave to one side the question of why any society might have a right to decide 'its' future when that means determining how people in the future should live. It might make sense to say that we have duties of stewardship to ensure that future generations do not suffer needlessly because of our decisions, but it is not clear that this gives us a right to determine how they should live.

133. When the Lone Ranger saw that he had stumbled into an Indian ambush, he said to his trusted Native American companion, 'it looks like we're surrounded, Tonto'; and Tonto replied, 'what do you mean "we", White man?'

134. When it comes to political identities, there's probably less forging than we think, and more forgery than we'd like.

135. For a comprehensive defence of this reading of history see John Ferejohn and Frances McCall Rosenbluth, *Forged Through Fire: War, Peace and the Democratic Bargain*, New York and London: Liverlight Publishing, 2017.

136. One can only speculate about what reasons lie behind China's continuing to regard Taiwan as a renegade province that it will one day reclaim, or North Korea's expressed with to reunite the Korean peninsula. Realpolitik may be one. It seems unlikely that a concern for the wellbeing of the as yet unincorporated people is another.

137. 'A commonwealth is the property of a people. But a people is not any collection of human beings brought together in any sort of way, but an assemblage of people in large numbers associated in an agreement with respect to justice and a partnership for the common good.' Cicero, *De Re Publica*, translated by Clinton W. Keyes, Loeb Classical Library, Cambridge, MA: Harvard University Press, 1928, 65.

138. St Augustine, *City of God*, translated by Marcus Dodds with an introduction by Thomas Merton, New York: Modern Library, 1993, book 19, ch. 24, 706.

## Chapter 8: Freedom

1. *Democracy in America*, ed. Eduardo Nolla, translated from the French by James T. Schleifer, 2 Volumes, Indianapolis: Liberty Fund, 2012, 1259. At the end of the original manuscript Tocqueville added: 'We tend toward liberty and toward servitude at the same time; we want to combine them, though they cannot be combined. Not able to be free, we want at least to be oppressed in the name of the people.' (1259 note w.)

2. F. A. Hayek, 'Foreword to the 1956 American edition', *The Road to Serfdom: Text and Documents: The Definitive Edition*, ed. Bruce Caldwell, Chicago: University of Chicago Press, 2007, 48.

3. See *Democracy in America*, in the epigraph at the head of this chapter. Tocqueville was not unaware of the contradictions in the American experience of freedom, not least in its long and continuing tradition of African slavery, but also in its mistreatment of the native population. On this see Christine Dunn Henderson, '"Beyond the Formidable Circle": Race and the Limits of Integration in Tocqueville's *Democracy in America*', forthcoming.

4. Pierre-Joseph Proudhon, *General Idea of the Revolution in the Nineteenth Century*, translated by John Beverly Robinson, London: Freedom Press, 1923, 293–4.

5. Besançon quote in Carl Eric Scott, 'Communist Moral Corruption and the Redemptive Power of Art', in Carl Eric Scott and F. Flagg Taylor (eds.), *Totalitarianism on Screen: The Art and Politics of the Lives of Others*, Lexington: University Press of Kentucky, 2014, 57–81, at 58.

6. This is, surely, the burden of Adam Smith's argument in *The Theory of Moral Sentiments*, ed. D. D. Raphael and A. L. Macfie, Indianapolis: Liberty Fund, 1976.

7. Solzhenitsyn was quoted saying this in 1974 after the publication of *The Gulag Archipelago*. '"In our country, the lie has become not just a moral category, but a pillar of the state," he said. "In breaking with the lie we are performing a moral act, not a political one, not one that can be punished by criminal law, but one that would immediately have an effect on our way of life."' See Christopher S. Wren, 'Solzhenitsyn calls on Russians to Reject "the lie"', *New York Times*, 22 January 1974, http://www.nytimes.com/1974/01/22/archives/solzhenitsyn-calls-on-russians-to-reject-the-lie-ready-for-anything.html.

8. T. H. Rigby, 'Mono-organizational socialism in the civil society', in Chandran Kukathas, David W. Lovell and William Maley (eds.), *The Transition from Socialism: State and Civil Society in Gorbachev's USSR*, Melbourne: Longman Cheshire, 1991, 106–22, at 111.

9. Wolf Biermann, 'The Ghosts are Leaving the Shadows', in *Totalitarianism on Screen*, 183–88, at 183.

10. Ibid., 184.

11. For a detailed and instructive overview see Anne Applebaum, *Iron Curtain: The Crushing of Eastern Europe*, London: Penguin, 2013.

12. Michel Foucault, 'The Subject and Power', *Critical Inquiry*, 8 (4), 1982, 777–95, at 790.

13. The Labor Prime Minister, Gough Whitlam, reported to be highly unsympathetic to the anti-communist Vietnamese refugees, was quoted by one of his ministers as having said on 21 April 1975 that he 'was not having hundreds of fucking Vietnamese Balts coming into this country with their hatreds against us', and that 'Vietnamese sob stories don't wring my withers'. ('Balts' here meant the immigrants to Australia from the Baltic states of Latvia, Lithuania, and Estonia, who tended to be staunchly anti-communist since their countries had been incorporated into the Soviet Union.) But while Labor's policies were not especially friendly towards refugees, Australian policy and public opinion in the 1970s were not hostile. For an account of this see Klaus Neumann, *Across the Seas: Australia's Response to Refugees: A History*, Collingwood: Black Inc., 2015.

14. For a brief history see James Jupp, *From White Australia to Woomera: The Story of Australian Immigration*, 2nd edition, Cambridge: Cambridge University Press, 2007.

15. Hostility to refugees was not new to Australia. In the period before and after the Second World War, Jewish refugees were the subject of extensive public debate. Official policy tried to limit the numbers admitted into the country and among the populace there was considerable hostility to Jewish 'reffos'. For detailed historical analysis of these episodes see the writings of Suzanne Rutland, notably the following important works: '"Are You Jewish?" Postwar Jewish Immigration to Australia, 1945–1954', *Australian Journal of Jewish Studies* 5 (2), 1991, 35–58; 'Postwar Jewish "Boat People" and Parallels with the Tampa Incident', *Austalian Journal of Jewish Studies*, 16 (2), 2002, 159–76.

16. There is an interesting parallel here with American policy in the early twentieth century when domestic pressure to restrict Chinese immigration conflicted with the government's desire to maintain friendly relations with China. On this see Beth Lew-Williams, *The Chinese Must Go: Violence, Exclusion, and the Making of the Alien in America*, Cambridge MA: Harvard University Press, 2018.

17. See Neumann, *Across the Seas*, esp. ch. 5.

18. The Pacific Solution was in place from 2001 to 2007. Although it was officially abandoned in 2008, it continued in practice under other names.

19. Julia Baird, 'Australia's Gulag Archipelago', *New York Times*, 30 August 2016, https://mobile.nytimes.com/2016/08/31/opinion/australias-gulag-archipelago.html?rref =collection%2Fcolumn%2FJulia%20Baird&action=click&contentCollection=Opinion&module =Collection&region=Marginalia&src=me&version=column&pgtype=article&_r=0&referer=.

20. For a comprehensive report see Madeline Gleeson, *Offshore: Behind the Wire on Manus and Nauru*, Sydney: University of New South Wales Press, 2016. For a contrary view, see Michael Coates, *Manus Days: The Untold Story of Manus Island*, Redland Bay: Connor Court Publishing, 2018.

21. Though the numbers vary slightly from year to year, the vast majority of detainees who were processed were deemed to have legitimate claims for asylum under the terms of the 1951 Refugee Convention, which Australia had signed and ratified. For up-to-date figures on the percentage of 'boat arrivals' successfully claiming asylum see the Australian Refugee Council website: https://www.refugeecouncil.org.au/boats-recognised-refugees/.

22. This figure comes from the Australian Coalition Government's Commission of Audit. UNICEF and the Save the Children Fund put the cost of Australia's policies at A$9.6 billion for the four years up to 2017 and estimated the cost to be A$5.6 billion for the four years to come. For a detailed analysis of the costs (and benefits) of Australia's policy see Tony Ward, *Bridging Troubled Waters*, North Melbourne: Australian Scholarly Publishing, 2017. For comparison, it costs A$300 a day to house a prisoner in a normal Australian gaol, compared to the A$1200 it costs to detain

an asylum seeker offshore. See Peter Martin, 'The appalling mathematics of offshore detention', *The Brisbane Times*, 31 August 2017, https://www.brisbanetimes.com.au/opinion/the-appalling-mathematics-of-offshore-detention-20170830-gy6ztl.html.

23. See for example: Ben Doherty, 'UN body condemns Australia for illegal detention of asylum seekers and refugees', *Guardian*, 7 July 2018, https://www.theguardian.com/world/2018/jul/08/un-body-condemns-australia-for-illegal-detention-of-asylum-seekers-and-refugees.

24. Because it would rather take a less attractive candidate who arrived by other means than accept even a Nobel Prize winner who came by boat. See Greg Miller, Julie Vitkovskaya, and Reuben Fischer-Baum, '"This deal will make me look terrible": Full transcripts of Trump's telephone calls with Mexico and Australia', *Washington Post*, 3 August 2017, https://www.washingtonpost.com/graphics/2017/politics/australia-mexico-transcripts/?utm_term=.bb0499f99074. Though President Trump was unconvinced by the explanation, he agreed to honour the undertaking made by the previous administration to take up to 1250 of those detained on Nauru and Manus Island.

25. A particularly noteworthy case is of the Bangladeshi woman—identified in Court documents as M68—who had appealed against being returned to Manus Island after removal to the Australian mainland for treatment in a complicated pregnancy. In order to ensure that the High Court could not find in her favour, the Australian government amended the Migration Act by inserting section 198AHA with retrospective effect. The High Court subsequently ruled in the government's favour, one judge noting that the plaintiff's case would have been well founded without the retrospective legislation. See Daniel Hurst and Ben Doherty, 'High Court upholds Australia's right to detain asylum seekers offshore', *Guardian*, 2 February 2016, https://www.theguardian.com/australia-news/2016/feb/03/high-court-upholds-australias-right-to-detain-asylum-seekers-offshore.

26. See Calla Wahlquist, 'Australian journalist who reported on Manus last year detained in PNG', 4 November 2017, *Guardian*, https://www.theguardian.com/australia-news/2017/nov/04/australian-journalist-who-reported-on-manus-last-year-detained-in-png.

27. See the discussion in ch. 3 above on immigration control in South Africa.

28. While numerous polls have been conducted to gauge public opinion on the refugee question, much depends on the questions asked. A 2017 poll reported that a majority of Australian citizens were concerned about the cruelty inflicted on detainees on Manus Island and Nauru, but that is hardly surprising. See Michael Gordon, 'Most agree, keeping refugees on Manus and Nauru is cruel: pollster', *Sydney Morning Herald*, 21 February 2017, https://www.smh.com.au/politics/federal/most-agree-keeping-refugees-on-manus-and-nauru-is-cruel-pollster-20170221-guhz3z.html. At the same time, a poll conducted by the Lowy Institute reported that 48 per cent of the population thought that that detainees should never be resettled in Australia, while 45 per cent thought they should. See *2017 Lowy Institute Poll*, https://www.lowyinstitute.org/publications/2017-lowy-institute-poll.

29. On this see Chandran Kukathas and William Maley, *The Last Refuge: Hard and Soft Hansonism in Contemporary Australian Politics*, St Leonards: Centre for Independent Studies, 1998.

30. It is important to note that without the aid of smugglers, a significant proportion of asylum seekers would not be able to reach official refugee camps. For some, such camps would be less reachable than the countries that would ultimately resettle them. Nor is there any assurance that they will be resettled should they reach a camp. It would be naïve to deny that asylum seekers are not at the mercy of a range of interested actors, from smugglers to officials. It would be even more naïve to think that there is a reasonable procedure on which they can rely to have their claims assessed. See William Maley, 'A New Tower of Babel? Reappraising the Architecture of Refugee Protection', in Edward Newman and Joanne van Selm (eds.), *Refugees and Forced Displacement: International Security, Human Vulnerability, and the State*, Tokyo: United Nations University Press, 2003, 306–29. The unpredictability of the process should also be noted. As Emma

Haddad observes, 'one individual in one political context will be recognized as a refugee, while a similar individual who finds herself in a different political context will fail to be recognized as a refugee'. See *The Refugee in International Society: Between Sovereigns*, Cambridge: Cambridge University Press, 2008, 213. For a study of conditions in refugee camps see Michael Agier, *Managing Undesirables: Refugee Camps and Humanitarian Government*, Cambridge: Polity, 2011. Also note that people arriving by boat would only deprive others of a place if they were found to be genuine refugees and because Australia, like many other countries, operates a quota system such that the humanitarian intake is reduced if more refugees are admitted. Without a quota system, no such displacement would occur.

31. 'The Politics of Soviet Crime', in Michel Foucault, *Foucault Live: Collected Interviews, 1961–1984*, ed. Sylvère Lotringer, South Pasadena, CA: Semiotext(e), 1996, 190–95, at 190.

32. See David C. Brotherton and Philip Kretsedemas (eds.), *Keeping out the Other: A Critical Introduction to Immigration Enforcement Today*, New York: Columbia University Press, 2008; Patrisia Macías-Rojas, *From Deportation to Prison: The Politics of Immigration Enforcement in Post-Civil Rights America*, New York: New York University Press, 2016.

33. On this, and for a more general history, see Jenna M. Lloyd and Alison Mountz, *Boats, Borders, and Bases: Race, the Cold War, and the Rise of Migration Detention in the United States*, Oakland: University of California Press, 2018, 160–4. The 'wet foot, dry foot' policy was ended by Barack Obama just before his term as President expired.

34. See ibid., particularly ch. 5: 'Safe Haven: The Creation of an Offshore Detention Archipelago'. The term 'carceral archipelago' was coined by Michel Foucault. See his *Discipline and Punish: The Birth of the Prison*, translated by Alan Sheridan, New York: Random House, 1995, 297.

35. There are other euphemisms in use. The Campsfield House facility for the detention of migrants, which in 1993 became the largest migrant detention centre in the UK, was described by the government as a 'safehouse'. Romania uses the term 'public support centres'. Turkey used the term 'guest houses' until the Committee for the Prevention of Torture recommended calling them detention centres on the grounds that those held within them were deprived of liberty.

36. Ariane Chebel d'Appollonia, *Frontiers of Fear: Immigration and Insecurity in the United States and Europe*, Ithaca, NY and London: Cornell University Press, 2012, 252.

37. See *The Hidden Face of Immigration Detention Camps in Europe* published by the campaign, Open Access Now To Detention Centres for Immigrants, launched by Migreurope and European Alternatives in collaboration with several NGOs. Open Access Now calls for unconditional access for civil society and the media to migrant camps. http://www.migreurop.org/IMG/pdf/hiddenfaceimmigrationcamps-okweb.pdf.

38. Maaike Vanderbruggen, Jerome Phelps, Nadia Sebtaoui, Andras Kovats, and Kris Pollet, *Point of no return, the futile detention of unreturnable migrants*, January 2014, http://pointofnoreturn.eu/wp-content/uploads/2014/01/PONR_report.pdf. See also Anna Lindley and Clara Della Croce, 'Migrants granted bail left trapped in British immigration detention because of nowhere to go', *The Conversation*, 8 March 2019, https://theconversation.com/migrants-granted-bail-left-trapped-in-british-immigration-detention-because-of-nowhere-to-go-110482.

39. See Harsha Walia and Proma Tagore, 'Prisoners of Passage: Immigration Detention in Canada', in Jenna M. Lloyd, Matt Mitchelson and Andrew Burridge (eds.), *Beyond Cages and Walls: Prisons, Borders, and Global Crisis*, Athens and London: University of Georgia Press, 2012, 74–90, at 76.

40. See, for example, Alexander Betts, *Survival Migration: Failed Governance and the Crisis of Displacement*, Ithaca, NY and London: Cornell University Press, 2013 for a number of African cases.

41. On this see Global Detention Project, *The Uncounted: Detention of Migrants and Asylum Seekers in Europe*, 2015, https://www.access-info.org/wp-content/uploads/DetentionReport_AIE_GDP_HighRes_17Dec15.pdf.

42. For an important examination of the notion of complicity see Chiara Lepora and Robert E. Goodin, *On Complicity and Compromise*, Oxford: Oxford University Press, 2013.

43. Though see Ogi Ogas and Sai Gaddam, *A Billion Wicked Thoughts: What the Internet Tells Us About Sexual Relationships*, New York: Penguin, 2012.

44. That is, the sole province of the Western, Educated, Industrialized, Rich, Democratic individual.

45. What counts as an opportunity to act depends on the description of the act and its meaning. A movement of one's fingers might, in one context, amount to nothing more than idle wiggling, but in another be a gesture of defiance, an attempt to communicate in signs, or an act of worship. Having an opportunity to act is not merely a matter of having the capacity for physical movement.

46. A joke about a runaway American slave brought before an Indiana court in the antebellum South is illustrative. 'Were you unhappy there?' asked the Judge. 'Oh no. I had a good life there,' replied the slave. 'Were you mistreated?' the Judge asked. 'No. Old Massa and me was the greatest friends. Fished and hunted together,' came the reply. 'Did you have good food and housing?' the Judge pressed. 'Sure enough. Ham and 'taters. Molasses. My little cabin had roses over the door,' the slave answered. 'I don't understand. Why did you run away?' asked the Judge. 'Well you Honor,' replied the slave, 'the situation is still open down there if you'd like to apply for it.' See Jonathan Hughes, *American Economic History*, 3rd edition, New York: Harper Collins, 1990, 234.

47. For a recent analysis of freedom that strives to avoid a moralized account see Christian List and Laura Valentini, 'Freedom as Independence', *Ethics*, 126 (4), 2016, 1043–74. For a critique see Ian Carter and Ronen Shnayderman, 'The Impossibility of "Freedom as Independence"', *Political Studies Review*, 17 (2), 2019, 136–46. List and Valentini's theory is an effort to address an apparent weakness in the 'republican' account of freedom developed most formidably by Philip Pettit. See Pettit, *A Theory of Freedom*, Oxford: Oxford University Press, 2001; Pettit, 'Republican Freedom: Three Axioms, Four Theorems', in Cécile Laborde and John Maynor (eds.), *Republicanism and Political Theory*, Oxford, Blackwell, 2009, 102–30. For a critique of Pettit see Ronen Shnayderman, 'Liberal vs Republican Notions of Freedom', *Political Studies*, 60 (1), 2012, 44–58.

48. Thomas Hobbes, *Leviathan*, ed. Richard Tuck, New York: Cambridge University Press, 1991, ch. 21.

49. See Chandran Kukathas, 'One Cheer for Constantinople: A Comment on Pettit and Skinner on Hobbes and Freedom', *Hobbes Studies*, 22 (2), 2009, 192–8.

50. That said, as far as analyses of freedom from the perspective of *scope* are concerned, I am most persuaded by Ian Carter, *A Measure of Freedom*, Oxford: Oxford University Press, 1999. Other notable works in this vein include Matthew Kramer, *The Quality of Freedom*, Oxford: Oxford University Press, 2003; Sebastiano Bavetta and Pietro Navarra, *The Economics of Freedom: Theory, Measurement and Policy Implications*, Cambridge: Cambridge University Press, 2012.

51. The Alhambra Decree or Edict of Granada of 31 March 1492 ordered the expulsion of Jews from Castille and Aragon, resulting in 200,000 Jews converting to Catholicism and between 40,000 and 100,000 being expelled. The edict was revoked only in 1968.

52. Non-Muslims were obliged to pay a poll tax but were exempt from the *zakat* or wealth tax that was obligatory for Muslims.

53. Estimates suggest that no more than 50,000 of a likely population of 90,000 in Castille and Aragon departed permanently. For detail see Henry Kamen, *Spain, 1469–1714: A Society in Conflict*, London: Routledge, 4th edition, 2014, 33–9.

54. I take this point to be the burden of Mariam Thalos's important work, *A Social Theory of Freedom*, New York and Abingdon: Routledge, 2016.

55. Ibid., 246.

56. See *Uncle Tom's Cabin*. Toronto: Broadview Press, 2009, ch. 36.

57. *Democracy in America*, 1247.

58. Ibid., 1246.

59. Ibid., 1248.

60. Ibid., 1255.

61. Ibid., 1255.

62. Ibid., 1250.

63. Ibid., 1250.

64. Ibid., 1250–1.

65. Ibid., 1251.

66. Ibid., 1259.

67. Ibid., 1255.

68. Ibid., 1259.

69. For a highly illuminating examination of freedom in this regard, see Sharon Krause, *Beyond Sovereignty: Reconstructing Liberal Individualism*, Chicago: Chicago University Press, 2015.

70. *Democracy in America*, 1256.

71. One notably thoughtful attempt that acknowledges and strives to accommodate the variety of ideals as well as the diversity of populations is Robert Nozick's theory of utopia in part 3 of his *Anarchy, State, and Utopia*, Oxford: Blackwell, 1974. For a critique see my 'E Pluribus Plurum, or, How to Fail to Back into a State in Spite of Really Trying', in John Meadowcroft and Ralf Bader (eds.), *The Cambridge Companion to Anarchy, State and Utopia*, Cambridge University Press 2011. For an illuminating examination of the implications of pluralism for freedom, and the unavoidability of trade-offs among values, including liberal values, see Jacob T. Levy, *Rationalism, Pluralism, and Freedom*, Oxford: Oxford University Press, 2015.

72. Thalos, *Social Theory of Freedom*, 247.

73. Ibid., 247.

74. Michel Foucault, 'Space, Knowledge, and Power', in Paul Rabinow (ed.), *The Foucault Reader*, New York: Pantheon Books, 1984, 239–56, at 245.

75. See Chandran Kukathas, 'Anarchy, Open Borders and Utopia', *IAI News: Philosophy for Our Times*, 2 February 2017, https://iainews.iai.tv/articles/anarchy-open-borders-and-utopia-auid-762.

# WORKS CITED

## Books and Articles

Abel, Guy J., and Nikola Sander. 2014. 'Quantifying Global International Migration Flows'. *Science*, 343 (6178), 1520–22.

Abella, Irving, and Harold Troper. 2013. *None is Too Many: Canada and the Jews of Europe 1933–1948*. Toronto: University of Toronto Press.

Acemoglu, Daron, and James A. Robinson. 2012. *Why Nations Fail: The Origins of Power, Prosperity, and Poverty*. New York: Crown.

———. 2019. 'The Rise and Decline of General Laws of Capitalism'. *Journal of Economic Perspectives*, 29 (1), 3–28.

Acton, John Emerich Edward Dalberg-. 1986. *Selected Writings of Lord Acton. Volume One: Essays in the History of Liberty*, edited by J. Rufus Fears. Indianapolis: Liberty Fund.

Agier, Michael. 2011. *Managing Undesirables: Refugee Camps and Humanitarian Government*. Cambridge: Polity.

Aleinikoff, Thomas, David Martin, Hiroshi Motomura and Maryellen Fullerton. 2016. *Immigration and Nationality Laws of the United States: Selected Statues, Regulations and Forms*. N.p.: West Academic Publishing.

Allen, Theodore W. 2012. *The Invention of the White Race. Volume I: Racial Oppression and Social Control*, 2nd ed. London: Verso.

———. 2012. *The Invention of the White Race. Volume II: The Origin of Racial Oppression in Anglo-America*. London: Verso.

Ajana, Btihaj. 2013. *Governing Through Biometrics: The Biopolitics of Identity*. Basingstoke: Palgrave Macmillan.

Aloyo, Eamon, and Eugenio Cusumano. 2018. 'Morally evaluating human smuggling: the case of migration to Europe'. *Critical Review of International Social and Political Philosophy*, 1–24.

Anderson, Benedict. 2016. *Imagined Communities: Reflections on the Origin and Spread of Nationalism*, 2nd ed. London: Verso.

Anderson, Bridget. 2013. *Us and Them: The Dangerous Politics of Immigration Control*. Oxford: Oxford University Press.

Appiah, Kwame Anthony. 2006. *Cosmopolitanism: Ethics in a World of Strangers*, London: Allen Lane.

Applebaum, Anne. 2013. *Iron Curtain: The Crushing of Eastern Europe*. London: Penguin.

Armenta, Amada. 2017. *Protect, Serve, and Deport: The Rise of Policing as Immigration Enforcement*. Oakland: University of California Press.

Augustine, Dolores L. 2004. 'The Impact of Two Reunification-Era Debates on the East German Sense of Identity', *German Studies Review*, 27 (3), 563–78.

Augustine, Saint. 1993. *City of God*, translated by Marcus Dodds with an introduction by Thomas Merton. New York: Modern Library.

Autor, David H., David Dorn and Gordon H. Hanson. 2016. 'The China Shock: Learning from Labor-Market Adjustment to Large Changes in Trade'. *Annual Review of Economics* (8), 205–40.

Bacon, David, and Bill On Hing. 2013. 'The Rise and Fall of Employer Sanctions'. In *Governing Immigration Through Crime: A Reader*, edited by Julie A. Dowling and Jonathan Xavier Inda, 149–64. Stanford, CA: Stanford University Press.

Bandhari, Rajika, and Peggy Blumenthal. 2011. 'Global Student Mobility and the Twenty-first Century Silk Road'. In *International Student and Global Mobility in Higher Education: National Trends and New Directions*, edited by Rajika Bandhari and Peggy Blumenthal, 1–24. New York: Palgrave Macmillan.

Bansak, Cynthia, Nicole B. Simpson and Madeline Zavodny. 2015. *The Economics of Immigration*. New York: Routledge.

Banting, Keith, and Will Kymlicka, eds. 2006. *Multiculturalism and the Welfare State: Recognition and Redistribution in Contemporary Democracies*. Oxford: Oxford University Press.

Bartholomew, James. 2014. *The Welfare State We're In*. London: Biteback Publishing.

Barton, H. Arnold. 2006. *A Folk Divided: Homeland Swedes and Swedish Americans, 1840–1940*. Carbondale: Southern Illinois University Press.

Bauböck, Rainer. 2003. 'Towards a Political Theory of Migrant Transnationalism'. *International Migration Review*, 37 (3), 700–723.

Bavetta, Sebastiano, and Pietro Navarra. 2012. *The Economics of Freedom: Theory, Measurement and Policy Implications*. Cambridge: Cambridge University Press.

Baynton, Douglas C. 2016. *Defectives in the Land: Disability and Immigration in the Age of Eugenics*. Chicago: University of Chicago Press.

Beaulac, Stéphane. 2003. 'Vattel's Doctrine on Territory Transfers in International Law and the Cession of Louisiana to the United State of America'. *Louisiana Law Review*, 63 (4), 1327–59.

Beinart, William. 2001. *Twentieth-Century South Africa*, 2nd ed. Oxford: Oxford University Press.

Benhabib, Seyla. 2004. 'The Law of Peoples, Distributive Justice, and Migrations'. *Fordham Law Review*, 72 (5), 1761–87.

Benton, Lauren. 2010. *A Search for Sovereignty: Law and Geography in European Empires, 1400–1900*. Cambridge: Cambridge University Press.

Benton-Cohen, Katherine. 2009. *Borderline Americans: Racial Division and Labor War in the Arizona Borderlands*. Cambridge, MA: Harvard University Press.

———. 2018. *Inventing the Immigration Problem: The Dillingham Commission and its Legacy*, Cambridge, MA: Harvard University Press.

Bertram, Christopher. 2018. *Do States Have the Right to Exclude Immigrants?*. Cambridge: Polity.

Betts, Alexander. 2013. *Survival Migration: Failed Governance and the Crisis of Displacement*. Ithaca, NY: Cornell University Press.

Bierce, Ambrose. 1999. *Devil's Dictionary*, with an introduction by Roy Morris, Jr. New York: Oxford University Press.

Biermann, Wolf. 2014. 'The Ghosts are Leaving the Shadows'. In *Totalitarianism on Screen: The Art and Politics of 'The Lives of Others'*, edited by Carl Eric Scott and F. Flagg Taylor, 183–88. Lexington: University Press of Kentucky.

Bigo, Didier. 2002. 'Security and Immigration: Toward a Critique of the Governmentality of Unease'. *Alternatives*, 27 (Special Issue), 63–92.

Biko, Steve. 1987. *I Write What I Like: A Selection of His Writings*, edited by Aelred Stubbs. Harlow: Heinemann.

Blake, Michael. 2020. *Justice, Immigration, and Mercy*. New York: Oxford University Press.

Bodin, Jean. 1992. *On Sovereignty: Four Chapters from the Six Books of the Commonwealth*, translated by Julian H. Franklin. Cambridge: Cambridge University Press.

Boochani, Behrouz. 2019. *No Friend but the Mountains: The True Story of an Illegally Imprisoned Refugee*, translated by Omid Tofighian. London: Picador.

Borjas, George J. 2014. *Immigration Economics*. Cambridge, MA: Harvard University Press.

———. 2015. 'Immigration and Globalization: A Review Essay'. *Journal of Economic Literature*, 53 (4), 961–74.

———. 2016. *We Wanted Workers: Unraveling the Immigration Narrative*. New York: W. W. Norton.

Borjas, George J., Richard B. Freeman, Lawrence F. Katz, John DiNardo and John M. Abowd. 1997. 'How Much Do Immigration and Trade Affect Labour Market Outcomes?'. *Brookings Papers on Economic Activity*, No. 1, 1–90.

Bosworth, Mary. 2014. *Inside Immigration Detention*. Oxford: Oxford University Press.

Bosworth, Mary, Alpa Parmar and Yolanda Vázquez. 2018. *Race, Criminal Justice, and Migration Control*. Oxford: Oxford University Press.

Breckenridge, Keith. 2014. 'The Book of Life: The South African Population Register and the Invention of Racial Descent, 1950–1980'. *Kronos*, No. 40 (Special Issue: Paper Regimes), 225–40.

Bricker, Darrell, and John Ibbitson. 2019. *Empty Planet: The Shock of Global Population Decline*, London: Crown.

Brimelow, Peter. 1995. *Alien Nation: Common Sense about America's Immigration Disaster*, New York: Random House.

———. 2007. 'Economics of Immigration and the Course of the Debate since 1994'. In *Debating Immigration*, edited by Carol Swain, 157–64. New York: Cambridge University Press.

Brotherton, David C., and Philip Kretsedemas, eds. 2008. *Keeping out the Other: A Critical Introduction to Immigration Enforcement Today*. New York: Columbia University Press.

Buchanan, James M. 1995. 'A Two-Country Parable'. In *Justice in Immigration*, edited by Warren F. Schwartz, 63–66. Cambridge: Cambridge University Press.

Buchanan, James M., and Yong J. Yoon. 2000. 'A Smithean Perspective on Increasing Returns'. *Journal of the History of Economic Thought*, 22 (1), 43–8.

Buchanan, James M., and Yong J. Yoon, eds. 1994. *The Return to Increasing Returns*. Ann Arbor: University of Michigan Press.

Buff, Rachel Ida. 2018. *Against the Deportation Terror: Organizing for Immigrant Rights in the Twentieth Century*. Philadelphia: Temple University Press.

Burg, David. 2003. *A World History of Tax Rebellions: An Encyclopedia of Tax Rebels, Revolts, and Riots from Antiquity to the Present*. London: Routledge.

Cabrera, Luis. 2004. *Political Theory of Global Justice: A Cosmopolitan Case for the World State*. London: Routledge.

Cafaro, Philip. 2015. *How Many is Too Many?: The Progressive Argument for Reducing Immigration to the United States*. Chicago: University of Chicago Press.

Caplan, Bryan, and Zach Weinersmith. 2019. *Open Borders: The Science and Ethics of Immigration*. New York: First Second.

Caplan, Jane, and John Torpey, eds. 2001. *Documenting Individual Identity: The Development of State Practices in the Modern World*. Princeton: Princeton University Press.

Card, David, and Giovanni Peri. 2016. '*Immigration Economics* by George J. Borjas: A Review Essay'. *Journal of Economic Literature*, 54 (4), 1333–49.

Carens, Joseph. 1988. 'Nationalism and the Exclusion of Immigrants: Lessons from Australian Immigration Policy'. In *Open Borders? Closed Societies?: The Ethical and Political Issues*, edited by Matthew Gibney, 41–60. New York: Greenwood Press.

———. 1995. 'Aliens and Citizens: The Case for Open Borders'. In *The Rights of Minority Cultures*, edited by Will Kymlicka, 331–49. Oxford: Oxford University Press.

———. 2013. *The Ethics of Immigration*. Oxford: Oxford University Press.

Carlin, Wendy. 1998. 'The New East German Economy: Problems of Transition, Unification and Institutional Mismatch', *German Politics*, 7 (3), 14–32.

Carpenter, Jesse. 1990. *The South as a Conscious Minority 1789–1861: A Study in Political Thought*, with an introduction by John McCardell. Columbia: University of South Carolina Press.

Carrillo, H., and J. Fontdevila. 2014. 'Border Crossings and Shifting Sexualities among Mexican Gay Immigrant Men: Beyond Monolithic Conceptions', *Sexualities*, 17 (8), 919–38.

Carter, Bob, Marci Green and Rick Halpern. 1996. 'Immigration Policy and the Racialization of Migrant Labour: The Construction of National Identities in the USA and Britain'. *Ethnic and Racial Studies*, 19 (1), 135–57.

Carter, Gwendolen Margaret. 1958. *The Politics of Inequality: South Africa since 1948*. New York: Praeger.

Carter, Ian. 1999. *A Measure of Freedom*. Oxford: Oxford University Press.

Carter, Ian, and Ronen Shnayderman. 2019. 'The Impossibility of "Freedom as Independence"'. *Political Studies Review*, 17 (2), 136–46.

Casteñeda, Ernesto, ed. 2018. *Immigration and Categorical Inequality: Migration to the City and the Birth of Race and Ethnicity*. New York: Routledge.

Cavanaugh, William. 2011. *Migrations of the Holy: God, State and the Political Meaning of the Church*. Cambridge: William B. Eerdmanns Publishing.

Chacón, Jennifer M., and Susan Bibler Coutin. 2018. 'Racialization through Enforcement'. In *Race, Criminal Justice, and Migration Control*, edited by Mary Bosworth, Alpa Parmar and Yolanda Vázquez, 159–75. Oxford: Oxford University Press.

Chassamboulli, Andri, and Giovanni Peri. 2015. 'The Labour Market Effects of Reducing the Number of Illegal Immigrants'. *Review of Economic Dynamics*, 18 (4), 792–821.

Chomsky, Aviva. 2014. *Undocumented: How Immigration Became Illegal*. Boston: Beacon Press.

Chung, Erin Aeran. 2014. *Immigration and Citizenship in Japan*. Cambridge: Cambridge University Press.

Cicero, Marcus Tullius. 1928. *De Re Publica*, translated by Clinton W. Keyes, Loeb Classical Library, Cambridge, MA: Harvard University Press.

Clark, Nancy L., and William H. Worger. 2016. *South Africa: The Rise and Fall of Apartheid*, 3rd ed. Oxford: Routledge.

Clastres, Pierre. 1987. *Society Against the State: Essays in Political Anthropology*, translated by Robert Hurley with Abe Stein. New York: Zone.

Clayton, Gina. 2010. 'The UK and Extraterritorial Immigration Control: Entry Clearance and Juxtaposed Control'. In *Extraterritorial Immigration Control: Legal Challenges*, edited by Bernard Ryan and and Valsamis Mitsilegas, 397–431. Leiden: Martinus Nijhoff Publishers.

Clemens, Michael A. 2011. 'Economics and Emigration: Trillion-Dollar Bills on the Sidewalk?'. *Journal of Economic Perspectives*, 25 (3), 83–106.

Clemens, Michael A., and Lant Pritchett. 2019. 'The New Economic Case for Migration Restrictions: An Assessment'. *Journal of Development Economics*, 138, 153–64.

Coase, Ronald H. 1995. *Essays on Economics and Economists*. Chicago: University of Chicago Press.

Coates, Michael. 2018. *Manus Days: The Untold Story of Manus Island*. Redland Bay: Connor Court Publishing.

Cohen, Elizabeth F. 2020. *Illegal: How America's Lawless Immigration Regime Threatens Us All*. New York: Basic Books.

Cole, Phillip. 2000. *Philosophies of Exclusion: Liberal Political Theory and Immigration*. Edinburgh: Edinburgh University Press.

Collier, Paul. 2013. *Exodus: Immigration and Multiculturalism in the 21st Century*. London: Allen Lane.

Conlon, D., and N. Hiemstra. 2014. 'Examining the Everyday Micro-economies of Migrant Detention in the United States'. *Geographica Helvetica*, 69, 335–44.

Costello, Cathryn, and Mark Freedland, eds. 2014. *Migrants at Work: Immigration and Vulnerability in Labour Law*. Oxford: Oxford University Press.

Dale, Gareth. 2004. *Between State Capitalism and Globalisation: The Collapse of the East German Economy*. New York: Peter Lang.

Daniels, Roger. 2004. *Guarding the Golden Door: American Immigration Policy and Immigrants Since 1882*. New York: Hill and Wang.

d'Appollonia, Ariane Chebel. 2012. *Frontiers of Fear: Immigration and Insecurity in the United States and Europe*. Ithaca, NY: Cornell University Press.

Dauvergne, Catherine. 2009. *Making People Illegal: What Globalization Means for Migration and Law*. Cambridge: Cambridge University Press.

———. 2016. *The New Politics of Immigration and the End of Settler Societies*. Cambridge: Cambridge University Press.

Davenport, Rodney, and Christopher Saunders. 2000. *South Africa: A Modern History*, 5th ed. New York: Palgrave Macmillan.

Davies, Norman. 2012. *Vanished Kingdoms: The History of Half-Forgotten Europe*. London: Penguin.

De Leon, Arnoldo. 2018. 'Beyond the Wall: Race and Immigration Discourse'. In *Immigration and the Law: Race, Citizenship, and Social Control*, edited by Sofía Espinoza Álvarez and Martin Guevara Urbina, 30–45. Tucson: University of Arizona Press.

de-Shalit, Avner. 2018. *Cities and Immigration: Political and Moral Dilemmas in the New Era of Migration*. Oxford: Oxford University Press.

Dolan, Eric Jay. 2008. *Leviathan: The History of Whaling in America*. New York: Norton.

Dow, Mark. 2004. *American Gulag: Inside U.S. Immigration Prisons*. Berkeley: University of California Press.

Dowty, Alan. 1987. *Closed Borders: The Contemporary Assault on Freedom of Movement*. New Haven: Yale University Press.

Dustmann, Christian, and Tommaso Frattini. 2014. 'The Fiscal Effects of Immigration to the UK'. *Economic Journal*, 124 (580), 593–643.

Edgerton, David. 2019. *The Rise and Fall of the British Nation: A Twentieth-Century History*, Milton Keynes: Penguin.

Edwardes, Audie. 2019. 'The "Good" Homosexual: Exploring Identity Construction through Immigration Control'. Submitted 25 April 2019, Department of Government, London School of Economics.

Ellermann, Antje. 2009. *States Against Migrants: Deportation in Germany and the United States*. Cambridge: Cambridge University Press.

Ellmann, Stephen. 1992. *In a Time of Trouble: Law and Liberty in South Africa's State of Emergency*. Oxford: Clarendon Press.

Evans, Gavin. 2015. *Black Brain, White Brain: Is Intelligence Skin Deep?*. London: Thistle.

Fahrmeir, Andreas. 2001. 'Governments and Forgers: Passports in Nineteenth-Century Europe'. In *Documenting Individual Identity: The Development of State Practices in the Modern World*, edited by Jane Caplan and John Torpey. Princeton: Princeton University Press.

Fassin, Eric, and Manuela Salcedo. 2015. 'Becoming Gay? Immigration Policies and the Truth of Sexual Identity', *Archives of Sexual Behaviour*, 44, 1117–25.

Faust, Drew Gilpin, ed. 1981. *The Ideology of Slavery: Proslavery Thought in the Antebellum South, 1830–1860*. Baton Rouge: Louisiana State University Press.

Feldman, Gregory. 2012. *The Immigration Apparatus: Security, Labor, and Policymaking in the European Union*. Stanford, CA: Stanford University Press.

Ferejohn, John, and Frances McCall Rosenbluth. 2017. *Forged Through Fire: War, Peace and the Democratic Bargain*. New York: Liveright Publishing.

Filmer, Robert. 1991. *Patriarcha*. In *Patriarcha and Other Writings*, edited by Johann P. Sommerville. Cambridge: Cambridge University Press.

Fine, Sarah. 2016. 'Immigration and Discrimination'. In *Migration and Political Theory: The Ethics of Movement and Membership,* edited by Sarah Fine and Lea Ypi. Oxford: Oxford University Press.

Fitzgerald, Keith. 1996. *The Face of the Nation: Immigration, the State, and the National Identity.* Stanford, CA: Stanford University Press.

Foucault, Michel. 1982. 'The Subject and Power'. *Critical Inquiry*, 8 (4), 777–95.

———. 1984. 'Space, Knowledge, and Power'. In *The Foucault Reader,* edited by Paul Rabinow, 239–56. New York: Pantheon Books.

———. 1995. *Discipline and Punish: The Birth of the Prison,* translated by Alan Sheridan. New York: Random House.

———. 1996. 'The Politics of Soviet Crime'. In *Foucault Live: Collected Interviews, 1961–1984,* edited by Sylvère Lotringer, 190–95. South Pasadena, CA: Semiotext(e).

Fransman, Laurie. 2011. *British Nationality Law*, 3rd ed. London: Bloomsbury.

Frederickson, George M. 2015. *Racism: A Short History,* rev. ed. Princeton: Princeton University Press.

Frenzen, Niels. 2010. 'US Migrant Interdiction Practices'. In *Extraterritorial Immigration Control: Legal Challenges,* edited by Bernard Ryan and Valsamis Mitsilegas. Leiden: Martinus Nijhof.

Friedman, Milton. 1978. 'What Is America?'. In *The Economics of Freedom.* Cleveland: Standard Oil Company of Ohio.

Galewitz, Herb, ed. 2003. *Patriotism: Quotations from Around the World.* New York: Dover.

Gallagher, Anne T., and Fiona David. 2015. *The International Law of Migrant Smuggling.* New York: Cambridge University Press, 2015.

Gest, Justin. 2016. *The New Minority: White Working Class Politics in an Age of Immigration and Inequality.* Oxford: Oxford University Press.

Gijsberts, Mérove, and Louk Hagendoorn. 2017. *Nationalism and Exclusion of Migrants: Cross-National Comparisons.* London: Routledge.

Glazer, Nathan. 1993. 'The Closing Door'. *New Republic*, 19 (4), 15–20.

Gleeson, Madeline. 2016. *Offshore: Behind the Wire on Manus and Nauru.* Sydney: University of New South Wales Press.

Goldin, Claudia. 2006. 'The Quiet Revolution that Transformed Women's Employment, Education and Family'. *American Economic Association Papers and Proceedings*, 96 (2), 1–21.

Goldman, Daniel S. 2005. 'The Modern-Day Literacy Test? Felon Disenfranchisement and Race Discrimination'. *Stanford Law Review*, 57 (2), 611–55.

Goldstein, Eric L. 2005. 'Contesting the Categories: Jews and Government Racial Classification in the United States'. *Jewish History*, 19, 79–107.

Goodhart, David. 2013. *The British Dream: Successes and Failures of Postwar Immigration.* London: Atlantic Books.

———. 2017. *The Road to Somewhere: The New Tribes Shaping British Politics.* St Ives: Penguin.

Goodin, Robert E. 1985. *Protecting the Vulnerable: A Reanalysis of Our Social Responsibilities.* Chicago: University of Chicago Press.

Gottschalk, Marie. 2016. *Caught: The Prison State and the Breakdown of American Politics.* Princeton: Princeton University Press.

Groebner, Valentin. 2007. *Who Are You? Identification, Deception, and Surveillance in Early Modern Europe.* New York: Zone Books.

Grynaviski, Jeffrey D., and Michael C. Munger. 2017. 'Reconstructing Racism: Transforming Racial Hierarchy from "Necessary Evil" into "Positive Good"'. *Social Philosophy and Policy*, 34 (1), 144–63.

Guelke, Adrian. 2012. *Politics in Deeply Divided Societies.* Cambridge: Polity.

Haddad, Emma. 2008. *The Refugee in International Society: Between Sovereigns.* Cambridge: Cambridge University Press.

Hague, William. 2005. *Pitt the Younger.* London: Harper Press.

Hampshire, James. 2014. *The Politics of Immigration.* Cambridge: Polity.

Han, Enze. 2019. *Asymmetrical Neighbors: Borderland State Building Between China and Southeast Asia*. New York: Oxford University Press.

Harper, Jim. 2012. 'Internal Enforcement, E-Verify, and the Road to National ID'. *Cato Journal*, 32 (1), 125–37.

Harper, Marjorie, and Stephen Constantine. 2014. *Migration and Empire*. Oxford: Oxford University Press.

Harsgor, Michael. 1978. 'Total History: The Annales School'. *Journal of Contemporary History*, 13 (1), 1–13.

Hayek, F. A. 1988. *The Fatal Conceit: The Errors of Socialism*, edited by William Warren Bartley III. The Collected Works of F. A. Hayek. Chicago: University of Chicago Press.

———. 2007. *The Road to Serfdom: Texts and Documents: The Definitive Edition*, edited by Bruce Caldwell. The Collected Works of F. A. Hayek. Chicago: University of Chicago Press.

———. 2011. *The Constitution of Liberty: The Definitive Edition*, edited by Ronald Hamowy. The Collected Works of F. A. Hayek. Chicago: University of Chicago Press.

Hayter, Teresa. 2004. *Open Borders: The Case against Immigration Controls*. 2nd ed. London: Pluto Press.

Heiland, Frank. 2004. 'Trends in East-West German Migration from 1989 to 2002'. *Demographic Research*, 11 (7), 173–94.

Henderson, Christine Dunn. Forthcoming. '"Beyond the Formidable Circle": Race and the Limits of Integration in Tocqueville's *Democracy in America*'.

Hernández, César Cuauhtémoc García. 2019. *Migrating to Prison: America's Obsession with Locking Up Immigrants*. New York: New Press.

Herzog, Ben. 2015. *Revoking Citizenship: Expatriation in America from the Colonial Era to the War on Terror*. New York: New York University Press.

Hester, Torrie. 2017. *Deportation: The Origins of U.S. Policy*. Philadelphia: University of Pennsylvania Press.

Hidalgo, Javier. 2016. 'The Ethics of People Smuggling'. *Journal of Global Ethics*, 12 (3), 311–26.

Hillman, Susanne. 2011. 'Men with Muskets, Women with Lyres: Nationality, Citizenship, and Gender in the Writings of Madame de Staël'. *Journal of the History of Ideas*, 72 (2), 231–54.

Himmelfarb, Gertrude. 1965. 'The Haunted House of Jeremy Bentham'. In *Ideas in History: Essays Presented to Louis Gottschalk by His Former Students*, edited by Richard Herr and Harold T. Parker. Durham, NC: Duke University Press, 1965.

Hinger, Sarah. 2010. 'Finding the Fundamental: Shaping Identity in Gender and Sexual Orientation Based Asylum Claims'. *Columbia Journal of Gender and Law*, 19 (2), 367–408.

Hirota, Hidetaka. 2017. *Expelling the Poor: Atlantic Seaboard States and the Origins of American Immigration Policy*. New York: Oxford University Press.

Hobbes, Thomas. 1991. *Leviathan*, edited by Richard Tuck. New York: Cambridge University Press.

Hochschild, Arlie Russell. 2016. *Strangers in their Own Land: Anger and Mourning on the American Right*. New York: New Press.

Howells, Stephen. 2011. 'Report of the 2010 Review of the *Migration Amendment (Employer Sanctions) Act 2007*'. Canberra: Commonwealth of Australia.

Huemer, Michael. 2010. 'Is There a Right to Immigrate?', *Social Theory and Practice*, 36 (3), 429–61.

Hughes, Jonathan. 1990. *American Economic History*, 3rd ed., New York: Harper Collins.

Hume, David. 1957. *The Natural History of Religion*. Stanford, CA: Stanford University Press.

———. 1985. *Essays: Moral, Political, and Literary*, edited by Eugene F. Miller. Indianapolis: Liberty Fund.

Hunt, Jennifer, and Marjolaine Gauthier-Loiselle. 2009. 'How Much Does Immigration Boost Innovation?'. *American Economic Journal Macroeconomics*, 2 (2), 31–56.

Huntington, Samuel P. 2005. *Who Are We? The Challenges to America's National Identity*. New York: Simon and Schuster.

Ignatiev, Noel. 1995. *How the Irish Became White*. London: Routledge.

Jafari, Belgheis Alavi, and Liza Schuster. 2019. 'Representations of Exile in Afghan Oral Poetry and Songs'. *Crossings: Journal of Migration and Culture*, 10 (2), 183–203.

Jasanoff, Maya. 2012. *Liberty's Exiles: American Loyalists in the Revolutionary World*. New York: Vintage.

Jessop, Bob. 2016. *The State: Past, Present, Future*. Cambridge: Polity Press.

Jones, Peter. 1999. 'Group Rights and Group Oppression'. *Journal of Political Philosophy*, 7 (4), 353–77.

Joshi, Shirley, and Bob Carter. 1984. 'The Role of Labour in the Creation of Racist Britain', *Race and Class*, 25 (3), 53–70.

Jupp, James. 2007. *From White Australia to Woomera: The Story of Australian Immigration*, 2nd ed. Cambridge: Cambridge University Press.

Juss, Satvinder S. 1994. *Immigration, Nationality and Citizenship*. London: Mansell.

Kafka, Franz. 2009. *The Trial*. Oxford: Oxford University Press.

Kain, Jennifer S. 2019. *Insanity and Immigration Control in New Zealand and Australia, 1860–1930*. London: Palgrave Macmillan.

Kamen, Henry. 2014. *Spain, 1469–1714: A Society in Conflict*, 4th ed. London: Routledge.

Kapparis, Konstantinos. 2005. 'Immigration and Citizenship Procedures in Athenian Law'. *Review Internationale des droits de l'Antiquité*, 52, 71–113.

Kasimis, Demetra. 2018. *The Perpetual Immigrant and the Limits of Athenian Democracy*. Cambridge: Cambridge University Press.

Kateb, George. 2015. *Lincoln's Political Thought*. Cambridge, MA: Harvard University Press.

Kaufmann, Eric. 2018. *White Shift: Populism, Immigration and the Future of White Majorities*. Milton Keynes: Allen Lane.

Kedourie, Elie. 2000. *Nationalism*, 4th expanded ed. Oxford: Blackwell.

Kelly, Paul. 1994. *The End of Certainty: Power, Politics and Business in Australia*. Sydney: Allen and Unwin.

Kerr, Sari Pekkala, and William R. Kerr. 2011. 'Economic Impact of Immigration: A Survey'. *Finnish Economic Papers*, 24 (1), 1–32.

Keshavarz, Mahmoud, and Shahram Khosravi. 2020. 'The Magic of Borders'. *e-flux Architecture*, 14 May 2020, 1–7.

Khan, Yasmin. 2017. *The Great Partition: The Making of India and Pakistan*. New Haven: Yale University Press.

Kinslor, Joanne. 2013. 'New Employer Sanctions under the Migration Act'. *Law Society Journal*, May, 34–5.

Kisch, Egon. 1937. *Australian Landfall*, translated by John Fisher and Irene and Kevin Fitzgerald. London: Secker and Warburg.

Kitcher, Philip. 2007. 'Does "Race" Have a Future?'. *Philosophy and Public Affairs*, 35 (4), 293–317.

Klarman, Michael J. 2016. *The Framers' Coup: The Making of the United States Constitution*. New York: Oxford University Press.

Kneebone, Susan, ed. 2009. *Refugees, Asylum Seekers and the Rule of Law: Comparative Perspectives*. Cambridge: Cambridge University Press.

Kramer, Matthew. 2003. *The Quality of Freedom*. Oxford: Oxford University Press.

Krause, Sharon. 2015. *Beyond Sovereignty: Reconstructing Liberal Individualism*. Chicago: University of Chicago Press.

Krikorian, Mark. 2008. *The New Case Against Immigration: Both Legal and Illegal*. New York: Sentinel.

Krugman, Paul R. 1979. 'Increasing Returns, Monopolistic Competition and International Trade'. *Journal of International Economics*, 9 (4), 469–79.

Kukathas, Chandran. 1999. 'Tolerating the Intolerable'. *Papers on Parliament*, 33, 67–81.

———. 2003. 'Immigration'. In *The Oxford Handbook of Practical Ethics*, edited by Hugh Lafollette, 567–90. Oxford: Oxford University Press.

———. 2003. *The Liberal Archipelago: A Theory of Diversity and Freedom*. Oxford: Oxford University Press.

———. 2005. 'The Case for Open Immigration'. In *Contemporary Debates in Applied Ethics*, edited by Andrew I. Cohen and Christopher Heath Wellman, 207–20. Oxford: Blackwell.

———. 2009. 'One Cheer for Constantinople: A Comment on Pettit and Skinner on Hobbes and Freedom'. *Hobbes Studies*, 22 (2), 192–8.

———. 2011. 'E Pluribus Plurum, or, How to Fail to Back into a State in Spite of Really Trying'. In *The Cambridge Companion to Anarchy, State and Utopia*, edited by John Meadowcroft and Ralph Bader. Cambridge: Cambridge University Press.

———. 2012. 'Why Open Borders?'. *Ethical Perspectives*, 19 (4), 649–75.

———. 2016. 'Are Refugees Special?'. In *Migration and Political Theory: The Ethics of Movement and Membership*, edited by Sarah Fine and Lea Ypi, 249–68. Oxford: Oxford University Press.

———. 2019. 'Libertarianism Without Self-ownership'. *Social Philosophy and Policy*, 36 (2), 2019, 71–93.

Kukathas, Chandran, and William Maley. 1998. *The Last Refuge: Hard and Soft Hansonism in Contemporary Australian Politics*. St Leonards: Centre for Independent Studies.

Kunz, E. F. 1973. 'The Refugee in Flight: Kinetic Models and Forms of Displacement'. *International Migration Review*, 7 (2), 125–46.

Kwan, Kevin. 2014. *Crazy Rich Asians*. New York: Random House.

Kymlicka, Will. 1995. *Multicultural Citizenship: A Liberal Theory of Minority Rights*. Oxford: Oxford University Press.

———. 2001. *Politics in the Vernacular*. New York: Oxford University Press.

Laitin, David. 2016. 'Exodus: Reflections on European Migration Policy'. In *Migration and Integration: New Models for Mobility and Coexistence*, edited by Roland Hsu, 86–94. Vienna: University of Vienna Press.

Lake, Marilyn, and Henry Reynolds. 2011. *Drawing the Colour Line: White Men's Countries and the International Challenge of Racial Equality*. Cambridge: Cambridge University Press.

Law, Anna O. 2002. 'The Diversity Visa Lottery: A Cycle of Unintended Consequences in United States Immigration Policy'. *Journal of American Ethnic History*, 21 (4), 3–29.

Lawrance, Benjamin Nicholas, and Jacqueline Stevens, eds. 2017. *Citizenship in Question: Evidentiary Birthright and Statelessness*. Durham, NC: Duke University Press.

Lear, Jonathan. 2006. *Radical Hope: Ethics in the Face of Cultural Devastation*. Cambridge, MA: Harvard University Press.

Lee, Ting Hui. 2011. *Chinese Schools in Peninsula Malaysia: The Struggle for Survival*, Singapore: Institute of Southeast Asian Studies.

Legrain, Philippe. 2006. *Immigrants: Your Country Needs Them*. Princeton: Princeton University Press.

Lemkin, Raphael. 1944. *Axis Rule in Occupied Europe*. Washington, DC: Carnegie Endowment for International Peace.

Lennon, John. 2000. *All We Are Saying: The Last Major Interview with John Lennon and Yoko Ono*, conducted by David Sheff, edited by G. Barry Golson. New York: St Martin's Griffin.

Leonard, Thomas C. 2016. *Illiberal Reformers: Race, Eugenics, and American Economics in the Progressive Era*. Princeton: Princeton University Press.

Lepora, Chiara, and Robert E. Goodin. 2013. *On Complicity and Compromise*. Oxford: Oxford University Press.

Levi, Margaret. 1988. *Of Rule and Revenue*. Berkeley: University of California Press.

Levy, Jacob T. 2015. *Rationalism, Pluralism, and Freedom*. Oxford: Oxford University Press.

Lew-Williams, Beth. 2018. *The Chinese Must Go: Violence, Exclusion, and the Making of the Alien in America*. Cambridge, MA: Harvard University Press.

Lijphart, Arend. 1975. *The Politics of Accommodation: Pluralism and Democracy in the Netherlands*, 2nd ed. Berkeley: University of California Press.

———. 1977. *Democracy in Plural Societies: A Comparative Exploration*. New Haven: Yale University Press.

List, Christian, and Philip Pettit. 2011. *Group Agency*. Oxford: Oxford University Press.

List, Christian, and Laura Valentini. 2016. 'Freedom as Independence'. *Ethics*, 126 (4), 1043–74.

Llewellyn, Cheryl. 2017. 'Sex Logics: Biological Essentialism and Gender-Based Asylum Cases'. *American Behavioral Scientist*, 61 (10), 1119–33.

Lloyd, Jenna M., and Alison Mountz. 2018. *Boats, Borders, and Bases: Race, the Cold War, and the Rise of Migration Detention in the United States*. Oakland: University of California Press.

Lloyd, Martin. 2003. *The Passport: The History of Man's Most Travelled Document*. Phoenix Mill: Sutton Publishing.

Locke, John. 1988. *Two Treatises of Government*, edited with an introduction and notes by Peter Laslett. Cambridge: Cambridge University Press.

Longo, Matthew. 2017. *The Politics of Borders*. Cambridge: Cambridge University Press.

López, Ian Haney. 2006. *White by Law: The Legal Construction of Race*, 10th anniversary ed. New York: New York University Press.

Louw, P. Eric. 2004. *The Rise, Fall and Legacy of Apartheid*. Westport, CT: Praeger.

Luibhéid, Eithne. 2005. 'Introduction: Queering Migration and Citizenship'. In *Queer Migrations: Sexuality, U.S. Citizenship, and Border Crossings*, edited by Eithne Luibhéid and Lionel Cantú Jr., ix–xlvi. Minneapolis: University of Minnesota Press.

Macedo, Stephen. 2004. 'What Self-Governing Peoples Owe to One Another: Universalism, Diversity and the Law of Peoples'. *Fordham Law Review*, 72 (5), 1721–38.

———. 2007. 'The Moral Dilemma of U.S. Immigration Policy: Open Borders versus Social Justice'. In *Debating Immigration*, edited by Carol M. Swain, 2nd ed., 286–310. New York: Cambridge University Press.

Machiavelli, Niccolò. 2010. *The Prince*, translated by W. K Marriott. Campbell, CA: Fast Pencil.

Macías-Rojas, Patrisia. 2016. *From Deportation to Prison: The Politics of Immigration Enforcement in Post-Civil Rights America*. New York: New York University Press.

McKeown, Adam M. 2008. *Melancholy Order: Asian Migration and the Globalization of Borders*. New York: Columbia University Press.

McNevin, Anne, Antje Missbach and Deddy Mulyana. 2016. 'The Rationalities of Migration Management: Control and Subversion in an Indonesia-Based Counter-Smuggling Campaign'. *International Political Sociology*, 10 (3), 223–40.

Maley, William. 2003. 'A New Tower of Babel? Reappraising the Architecture of Refugee Protection'. In *Refugees and Forced Displacement: International Security, Human Vulnerability, and the State*, edited by Edward Newman and Joanne van Selm, 306–29. Tokyo: United Nations University Press.

———. 2016. *What is a Refugee?*. Brunswick: Scribe.

Manjívar, Cecilia, and Daniel Kanstroom, eds. 2015. *Constructing Immigrant "Illegality": Critiques, Experiences, and Responses*, Cambridge: Cambridge University Press.

Martin, Philip L. 1997. 'Foreign Workers in U.S. Agriculture'. *In Defense of the Alien*, 20, 77–85.

———. 2004. 'Germany: Managing Migration in the Twenty-first Century.' In *Controlling Immigration: A Global Perspective*, edited by Wayne A. Cornelius, Takeyuki Tsuda, Philip L. Martin, and James F. Hollifield, 220–53. Stanford, CA: Stanford University Press.

Martin, Susan F. 2014. *International Migration: Evolving Trends from the Early Twentieth Century to the Present*. New York: Cambridge University Press.

Massey, Douglas. 2007. *Categorically Unequal: The American Stratification System*. New York: Russell Sage.

Mau, Steffen, Heike Brabandt, Lena Laube and Christof Roos. 2014. *Liberal States and the Freedom of Movement: Selective Borders, Unequal Mobility*. New York: Palgrave Macmillan.

Migdal, Joel. 1988. *Strong States and Weak Societies: State-Society Relations and State Capabilities in the Third World*. Princeton: Princeton University Press.

———. 2001. *State in Society: Studying How States and Societies Transform and Constitute One Another*. Cambridge: Cambridge University Press.

Miles, Robert. 1990. 'The Racialization of British Politics'. *Political Studies*, 38, 277–85.

Miller, David. 1995. *On Nationality*. Oxford: Oxford University Press.

———. 2007. *National Responsibility and Global Justice*. Oxford: Oxford University Press.

———. 2012. 'Territorial Rights: Concept and Justification'. *Political Studies*, 60 (2), 252–68.

———. 2016. *Strangers in Our Midst*. Cambridge, MA: Harvard University Press.

Miller, Todd. 2019. *Empire of Borders: The Expansion of the US Border Around the World*. London: Verso.

Milton, John. 2008. *The Major Works,* edited with an introduction and notes by Stephen Orgel and Jonathan Goldberg. Oxford: Oxford University Press.

Minian, Ana Raquel. 2018. *Undocumented Lives: The Untold Story of Mexican Immigration*. Cambridge, MA: Harvard University Press.

Mitsilegas, Valsamis. 2012. 'Immigration Control in an Era of Globalization: Deflecting Foreigners, Weakening Citizens, and Strengthening the State'. *Indiana Journal of Legal Studies*, 19 (1), 3–60.

Moch-Page, Leslie. 2003. *Moving Europeans: Migration in Western Europe Since 1650*, 2nd ed. Bloomington: Indiana University Press.

Montesquieu. 2002. *The Spirit of the Laws*, translated and edited by Anne M. Cohler, Baser Carolyn Miller and Harold Samuel Stone. Cambridge: Cambridge University Press.

Moore, Margaret. 2015. *A Political Theory of Territory*. Oxford: Oxford University Press.

Mostov, Julie. 2008. *Soft Borders: Rethinking Sovereignty and Democracy*. New York: Palgrave Macmillan.

Motomura, Hiroshi. 2014. *Immigration Outside the Law*. New York: Oxford University Press.

Murray, Charles. 2013. *Coming Apart: The State of White America, 1960–2010*. New York: Crown Forum.

Murray, Douglas. 2017. *The Strange Death of Europe: Immigration, Identity, Islam*. London: Bloomsbury.

Nethery, Amy, and Stephanie J. Silverman, eds. 2015. *Immigration Detention: The Migration of a Policy and Its Human Impact*. Oxford: Routledge.

Neumann, Klaus. 2015. *Across the Seas: Australia's Response to Refugees: A History*. Melbourne: Black Inc.

Ngai, Mae M. 2005. *Impossible Subjects: Illegal Aliens and the Making of Modern America*. Princeton: Princeton University Press.

Nine, Cara. 2012. *Global Justice and Territory*. Oxford: Oxford University Press.

Nozick, Robert. 1974. *Anarchy, State and Utopia*. Oxford: Blackwell.

Oakeshott, Michael. 1975. *On Human Conduct*. Oxford: Clarendon Press.

Ocampo, Anthony Christian. 2016. *The Latinos of Asia: How Filipino Americans Break the Rules of Race*. Stanford, CA: Stanford University Press.

OECD. 2016. *OECD Factbook 2015–2016: Economic, Environmental and Social Statistics*. Paris: OECD Publishing, also https://doi.org/10.1787/factbook-2015-en.

Ogas, Ogi, and Sai Gaddam. 2012. *A Billion Wicked Thoughts: What the Internet Tells Us About Sexual Relationships*. New York: Penguin.

Orgad, Liav. 2015. *The Cultural Defense of Nations: A Liberal Theory of Majority Rights*. Oxford: Oxford University Press.

Ortiz, Vilma, and Edward Telles. 2012. 'Racial Identity and Racial Treatment of Mexican Americans'. *Race and Social Problems*, 4 (1), 41–56.

Orwell, George. 1984. 'England Your England' and 'From *Nineteen Eighty-Four*'. In *The Orwell Reader: Fiction, Essays, and Reportage*, London: Harcourt, 1984.

Osiander, Andreas. 2007. *Before the State: Systemic Political Change in the West from the Greeks to the French Revolution*. Oxford: Oxford University Press.

Owen, David. 2014. 'Republicanism and the Constitution of Migrant Statuses'. *Critical Review in Social and Political Philosophy* 17 (1), 90–110.

Oxford, Connie. 2013. 'Queer Asylum: US policies and Responses to Sexual Orientation and Transgendered Persecution'. In *Gender, Migration and Categorisation: Making Distinctions between Migrants in Western Countries 1945–2010*, edited by Marlou Schrover and Deirdre M. Moloney, 127–48. Amsterdam: Amsterdam University Press.

Ozgen, Ceren, Cornelius Peters, Annekatrin Niebuhr, Peter Nijkamp and Jacques Poot. 2014. 'Does Cultural Diversity of Migrant Employees Affect Innovation?'. *International Migration Review*, 48, 377–416.

Packer, George. 2014. *The Unwinding: Thirty Years of American Decline*. London: Faber and Faber.

Page, Joshua. 2011. *The Toughest Beat: Politics, Punishment, and the Prison Officers Union in California*. Oxford: Oxford University Press.

Panayi, Panikos. 2014. *An Immigration History of Britain: Multicultural Racism Since 1800*. London: Routledge.

Pateman, Carole. 1988. *The Sexual Contract*. Stanford, CA: Stanford University Press.

Pettit, Philip. 2001. *A Theory of Freedom*. Oxford: Oxford University Press.

———. 2003. 'Deliberative Democracy, the Discursive Dilemma and Republican Theory'. In *Philosophy, Politics and Society*, Volume 7, edited by James Fishkin and Peter Laslett, 138–62. Cambridge: Cambridge University Press.

———. 2009. 'Republican Freedom: Three Axioms, Four Theorems'. In *Republicanism and Political Theory*, edited by Cécile Laborde and John Maynor, 102–30. Oxford, Blackwell.

———. 2017. 'Corporate Agency–The Lesson of the Discursive Dilemma'. In *Routledge Companion to Collective Intentionality*, edited by Marija Jankovic and Kirk Ludwig, 249–59. London: Routledge.

Pevnick, Ryan. 2011. *Immigration and the Constraints of Justice: Between Open Borders and Absolute Sovereignty*. Cambridge: Cambridge University Press.

Piketty, Thomas. 2014. *Capital in the 21st Century*, translated by Arthur Goldhammer. Cambridge, MA: Harvard University Press.

Plato and Aristophanes. 1984. *Four Texts on Socrates: Plato's Euthyphro, Apology and Crito and Aristophanes' Clouds*, translated with notes by Thomas G. West and Grace Starry West. Ithaca, NY: Cornell University Press.

Plutarch. N.d. *Plutarch's Lives*, translated by John Dryden and revised by Arthur Hugh Clough. New York: Random House.

Poole, Thomas. 2015. *Reason of State: Law, Prerogative and Empire*. Cambridge: Cambridge University Press.

Popat, Dolar. 2019. *A British Subject: How to Make It as an Immigrant in the Best Country in the World*. London: Biteback Publishing.

Portes, Jonathan. 2019. *What Do We Know and What Should We Do About Immigration?*. London: Sage.

Posel, Deborah. 1991. *The Making of Apartheid, 1948–61: Conflict and Compromise*. Oxford: Clarendon Press.

Poulantzas, N., and R. Miliband. 1972. 'The Problem of the Capitalist State'. In *Ideology in Social Science: Readings in Critical Social Theory*, edited by R. Blackburn, 238–62. New York: Pantheon Books.

Powell, J. Enoch. 1991. *Reflections of a Statesman: The Selected Writings and Speeches of Enoch Powell*, selected by Rex Collings. London: Bellew Publishing.

Prantl, Susanne, and Alexandra Spitz-Oener. 2020. 'The Impact of Immigration on Competing Natives' Wages: Evidence from German Reunification'. *Review of Economics and Statistics*, 102 (1), 79–97.

Price, Robert M. 1991. *The Apartheid State in Crisis: Political Transformation in South Africa 1975–1990*. New York: Oxford University Press.

Pritchett, Lant. 2006. *Let Their People Come: Breaking the Gridlock of Global Labor Mobility*. Washington, DC: Center for Global Development.

Proudhon, Pierre-Joseph. 1923. *General Idea of the Revolution in the Nineteenth Century*, translated by John Beverly Robinson. London: Freedom Press.

Raphael, Steven, and Eugene Smolensky. 2009. 'Immigration and Poverty in the United States.' *American Economic Review: Papers and Proceedings*, 99 (2), 41–4.

Ratele, Kopano. 2009. 'Sexuality as Constitutive of Whiteness in South Africa'. *NORA—Nordic Journal of Feminist and Gender Research*, 17 (3), 158–74.

Rawls, John. 1971. *A Theory of Justice*. Oxford: Oxford University Press.

———. 1993. *Political Liberalism*. New York: Columbia University Press.

———. 1999. *The Law of Peoples: With "The Idea of Public Reason Revisited"*. Cambridge, MA: Harvard University Press.

———. 2001. *Justice as Fairness: A Restatement*, edited by Erin Kelly. Cambridge, MA: Belknap Press of Harvard University Press.

Raz, Joseph. 1979. *The Authority of Law*. Oxford: Oxford University Press.

Richman, Jesse T., Gulshan A. Chatta and David C. Earnest. 2014. 'Do Non-citizens Vote in U.S. Elections?'. *Electoral Studies*, 36, December, 149–57.

Rigby, T. H. 1991. 'Mono-Organizational Socialism and Civil Society.' In *The Transition from Socialism: State and Civil Society in Gorbachev's USSR*, edited by Chandran Kukathas, David W. Lovell and William Maley, 106–22. Melbourne: Longman Cheshire.

Roback, Jennifer. 1986. 'The Political Economy of Segregation: The Case of Segregated Streetcars.' *Journal of Economic History*, 46 (4), 893–917.

Roberts, Glenda S. 2018. 'An Immigration Policy by *Any* Other Name: The Semantics of Immigration to Japan'. *Social Science Japan Journal*, 21 (1), 89–102.

Rosenberg, Clifford. 2006. *Policing Paris: The Origins of Modern Immigration Control Between the Wars*. Ithaca, NY: Cornell University Press.

Rosenblum, Marc R., and Wayne A. Cornelius. 2012. 'Dimensions of Immigration Policy'. In *The Oxford Handbook of the Politics of International Migration*, edited by Marc R. Rosenblum and Daniel J. Tichenor, 245–73. Oxford: Oxford University Press.

Runciman, David. 2003. 'The Concept of the State'. In *States and Citizens*, edited by Quentin Skinner and Bo Strath, 28–38. Cambridge: Cambridge University Press.

Rutland, Suzanne D. 1985. 'Australian Responses to Jewish Migration before and after World War II'. *Australian Journal of Politics and History*, 31 (1), 29–48.

———. 1991. '"Are You Jewish?": Postwar Jewish Immigration to Australia, 1945–1954'. *Australian Journal of Jewish Studies*, 5 (2), 35–58.

———. 2002. 'Postwar Jewish "Boat People" and Parallels with the Tampa Incident'. *Australian Journal of Jewish Studies*, 16 (2), 159–76.

Rutland, Suzanne D., and Sol Encel. 2009. 'No Room at the Inn: American Responses to Australian Immigration Policies, 1946–54'. *Patterns of Prejudice*, 43 (5), 497–518.

Sadiq, Kamal. 2009. *Paper Citizens: How Illegal Immigrants Acquire Citizenship in Developing Countries*. Oxford: Oxford University Press.

Sager, Alex. 2007. 'Culture and Immigration: A Case for Exclusion?'. *Social Philosophy Today*, 23, 69–86.

———. 2018. 'Private Contractors, Foreign Troops, and Offshore Detention Centers: The Ethics of Externalizing Immigration Controls'. *APA Newsletter: Hispanic/Latino Issues in Philosophy*, 17 (2), 11–15.

———. 2020. *Against Borders*. London: Rowman and Littlefield.

Salam, Reihan. 2018. *Melting Pot or Civil War?: A Son of Immigrants Makes the Case Against Open Borders*. New York: Sentinel.

Sandefur, Justin, and Michael Clemens. 2014. 'Let the People Go: The Problem with Strict Migration Limits'. *Foreign Affairs*, January/February, 152–59.

Sassen, Saskia. 1998. 'The de facto Transnationalizing of Immigration Policy'. In *Challenge to the Nation State: Immigration in Western Europe and the United States*, edited by Christin Joppke, 49–86. Oxford: Oxford University Press.

———. 1999. *Guests and Aliens*. New York: New Press.

Savage, Michael. 1986. 'The Imposition of Pass Laws on the African Population in South Africa: 1916–1984'. *African Affairs*, 85 (339), 181–205.

Schain, Martin. 2019. *The Border: Policy and Politics in Europe and the United States*. Oxford: Oxford University Press.

Scheffer, Paul. 2011. *Immigrant Nations*, translated by Liz Waters. Cambridge: Polity Press.

Schochet, Gordon. 1988. *The Authoritarian Family and Political Attitudes in 17th-Century England*. New Brunswick, NJ: Transaction Publishers.

Schumpeter, Joseph. 1918. 'Die Krise des Steuerstaates'. *Zeitfragen aus dem Gebiet der Sociologie*, 4, 1–71.

———. 1954. 'The Crisis of the Tax State'. In *International Economic Papers*, Volume 4, edited by A. T. Peacock, R. Turvey, W. F. Stolper and E Henderson, 5–38. London: Macmillan (translation of 'Die Krise des Steuerstaates').

Schuster, Liza. 2003. 'Asylum Seekers: Sangatte and the Tunnel'. *Parliamentary Affairs* (Special Issue on Crisis Management), 56 (3), 506–22.

Scott, Carl Eric. 2014. 'Communist Moral Corruption and the Redemptive Power of Art'. In *Totalitarianism on Screen: The Art and Politics of 'The Lives of Others'*, edited by Carl Eric Scott and F. Flagg Taylor, 57–81. Lexington: University Press of Kentucky.

Scott, James C. 1999. *Seeing Like a State: How Certain Schemes to Improve the Human Condition Have Failed*. New Haven: Yale University Press.

———. 2010. *The Art of Not Being Governed: An Anarchist History of Upland Southeast Asia*. New Haven: Yale University Press.

Scott, Walter. 2016. *The Lay of the Last Minstrel*. Sydney: Wentworth Press.

Seiler, Alexander J. 1965. *Siamo Italiani—Die Italiener. Gespräche mit italienischen Arbeitern in der Schweiz*. Zurich: EVZ-Verlag.

Service, Hugo. 2013. *Germans to Poles: Communism, Nationalism and Ethnic Cleansing after the Second World War*. Cambridge: Cambridge University Press.

Sestito, Raymond. 1982. *The Politics of Multiculturalism*. Sydney: Centre for Independent Studies.

Shell, G. Richard. 2004. *Make the Rules or Your Rivals Will*. New York: Random House.

Sherif, Muzafer, O. J. Harvey, B. Jack White, William R. Hood and Carolyn W. Sherif. 1988. *The Robbers Cave Experiment: Intergroup Conflict and Cooperation*. Norman: Institute of Group Relations, University of Oklahoma.

Shklar, Judith. 1987. 'Political Theory and the Rule of Law'. In *The Rule of Law: Ideal or Ideology*, edited by Allan C. Hutchinson and Patrick Monahan. Toronto: Carswell.

Shnayderman, Ronen. 2012. 'Liberal vs Republican Notions of Freedom'. *Political Studies*, 60 (1), 44–58.

Silverman, Stephanie J., and Peter Molnar. 2016. 'Everyday Injustices: Barriers to Access to Justice for Immigration Detainees in Canada'. *Refugee Survey Quarterly*, 35 (1), 109–27.

Simon, Julian. 1999. *The Economic Consequences of Immigration*. Ann Arbor: University of Michigan Press.

Sinclair, Upton. 1994. *I, Candidate for Governor: And How I Got Licked*. Berkeley: University of California Press.

Skinner, Quentin. 2010. 'The Sovereign State: A Genealogy'. In *Sovereignty in Fragments: The Past, Present and Future of a Contested Concept*, edited by Hent Kalmo and Quentin Skinner, 26–46. Cambridge: Cambridge University Press.

Smith, Adam. 1976. *The Theory of Moral Sentiments*, edited by D. D. Raphael and A. L. Macfie. Indianapolis: Liberty Fund.

———. 1981. *An Inquiry into the Nature and Causes of the Wealth of Nations*, edited by William Burton Roy Todd, Harold Campbell, and Andrew S. Skinner. Indianapolis: Liberty Fund.

Smith, Anna Marie. 1994. 'The Imaginary Inclusion of the Assimilable "Good Homosexual": The British New Right's Representations of Sexuality and Race'. *Diacritics*, 24 (2), 58–70.

Smith, Evan, and Marinella Marmo. 2014. *Race, Gender and the Body in British Immigration Control: Subject to Examination*. London: Palgrave Macmillan.

Smith, Paul. H. 1968. 'The American Loyalists: Notes on Their Organization and Numerical Strength'. *William and Mary Quarterly*, 25 (2), 259–77.

Solomos, John. 1988. *Black Youth, Racism, and the State: The Politics of Ideology and Policy*. Cambridge: Cambridge University Press.

Solzhenitsyn, Alexander. 1974. *The Gulag Archipelago, 1918–1956: An Experiment in Literary Investigation. Parts 1 and 2*. New York: Harper and Row.

Song, Sarah. 2018. *Immigration and Democracy*. Oxford: Oxford University Press.

Spruk, Rok. 2019. 'The Rise and Fall of Argentina'. *Latin American Economic Review*, 28 (16).

Stevens, Jacqueline. 2011. 'U.S. Government Unlawfully Detaining and Deporting U.S. Citizens as Aliens'. *Virginia Journal of Social Policy and Law*, 18 (3), 606–720.

Stilz, Anna. 2019. *Territorial Sovereignty: A Philosophical Exploration*. Oxford: Oxford University Press.

Stowe, Harriet Beecher. 2009. *Uncle Tom's Cabin*. Toronto: Broadview Press.

Stychin, Carl F. 2000. '"A Stranger to Its Laws": Sovereign Bodies, Global Sexualities, and Transnational Citizens'. *Journal of Law and Society*, 27 (4), 601–25.

Sykes, Alan O. 1995. 'The Welfare Economics of Immigration Law: A Theoretical Survey with an Analysis of U.S. Policy'. In *Justice in Immigration*, edited by Warren F. Schwartz, 158–200. Cambridge: Cambridge University Press.

Tajfel, Henri, Michael G. Billig, Robert P. Bundy, and Claude Flament. 1971. 'Social Categorization and Intergroup Behaviour'. *European Journal of Social Psychology*, 1 (2): 149–78.

Tan, Kok-Chor. 2004. *Justice without Borders: Cosmopolitanism, Nationalism and Patriotism*. Cambridge: Cambridge University Press.

Taylor, Charles. 1994. *Multiculturalism: Examining the Politics of Recognition*. Princeton: Princeton University Press.

Thalos, Mariam. 2016. *A Social Theory of Freedom*. New York: Routledge.

Thucydides. 1874. *The History of the Peloponnesian War*, translated by Richard Crawley, London: Longman, Green and Co.

Tichenor, Daniel. 2002. *Dividing Lines: The Politics of Immigration Control in America*. Princeton: Princeton University Press.

Tilly, Charles. 1990. *Coercion, Capital, and European States AD 990–1990*. Oxford: Blackwell.

———. 2017. 'Trust Networks in Transnational Migration'. *Sociological Forum*, 22 (1), 1–25.

Tinti, Peter, and Tuesday Reitano. 2017. *Migrant, Refugee, Smuggler, Saviour*. Oxford: Oxford University Press.

Tocqueville, Alexis de. 2012. *Democracy in America*, 2 Volumes, edited by Eduardo Nolla, translated by James T. Schleifer. Indianapolis: Liberty Fund.

Togman, Richard. 2019. *Nationalizing Sex: Fertility, Fear, and Power*. New York: Oxford University Press.

Tooley, James. 2009. *The Beautiful Tree: A Personal Journey into How the World's Poorest People Are Educating Themselves*. Washington: Cato Institute.

Torpey, John. 2000. *The Invention of the Passport: Surveillance, Citizenship and the State*. Cambridge: Cambridge University Press.

Trebilcock, Michael J. 1995. 'The Case for a Liberal Immigration Policy'. In *Justice in Immigration*, edited by Warren F. Schwartz, 219–46. Cambridge: Cambridge University Press.

Tulu, Hill, and Tina Hanneman. 2019. 'Mixed Marriage among Immigrants and Their Descendants in the United Kingdom: Analysis of Longitudinal Data with Missing Information'. *Population Studies: A Journal of Demography*, 73 (2), 179–96.

Turyahikayo, Everest. 2018. 'Bureaucratic Rigidity, Risk Aversion and Knowledge Generation and Utilization in the Public Sector: Reality or illusion?'. *Organization Studies*, 5 (3), 9–16.

Vance, J. D. 2016. *Hillbilly Elegy: A Memoir of a Family and Culture in Crisis*. London: William Collins.

Van Creveld, Martin. 1999. *The Rise and Decline of the State*. Cambridge: Cambridge University Press.

Vattel, Emer de. 2008. *The Law of Nations, or Principles of the Law of Nature, Applied to the Conduct and Affairs of Nations and Sovereigns, With Three Early Essays on the Origins and Nature of Natural Law and on Luxury*, edited by Béla Kapossy and Richard Whatmore. Indianapolis: Liberty Fund.

Vigneswaran, Darshan. 2013. *Territory, Migration and the Evolution of the International System*. Basingstoke: Palgrave Macmillan.

Wade, Nicholas. 2017. *A Troublesome Inheritance: Genes, Race and Human History*. London: Penguin.

Waldinger, Robert. 2015. *The Cross-Border Connection: Immigrants, Emigrants, and Their Homelands*. Cambridge, MA: Harvard University Press.

Waldron, Jeremy. 2008. 'The Concept and the Rule of Law'. *Georgia Law Review*, 43 (1), 1–63.

Walia, Harsha, and Proma Tagore. 2012. 'Prisoners of Passage: Immigration Detention in Canada'. In *Beyond Cages and Walls: Prisons, Borders, and Global Crisis*, edited by Jenna M. Lloyd, Matt Mitchelson, and Andrew Burridge, 74–90. Athens: University of Georgia Press.

Walzer, Michael. 1983. *Spheres of Justice: A Defense of Pluralism and Equality*. New York: Basic Books.

Ward, Tony. 2017. *Bridging Troubled Waters*. North Melbourne: Australian Scholarly Publishing.

Watkins, Josh. 2017. 'Australia's Irregular Migration Information Campaigns: Border Externalization, Spatial Imaginaries, and Extraterritorial Subjugation'. *Territory, Politics, Governance*, 5(3), 282–303.

Watkins, Josh. 2017. 'Bordering Borderscapes: Australia's Use of Humanitarian Aid and Border Security Support to Immobilize Asylum Seekers'. *Geopolitics*, 22 (4), 20, 958–83.

Wellman, Christopher Heath. 2008. 'Immigration and Freedom of Association'. *Ethics*, 119 (1), 109–41.

Wellman, Christopher Heath, and Phillip Cole. 2011. *Debating the Ethics of Immigration: Is There a Right to Exclude?*. New York: Oxford University Press.

Wenar, Leif. 2016. *Blood Oil: Tyrants, Violence, and the Rules that Run the World*. New York: Oxford University Press.

West, E. G. 1970. *The State and Education*. London: Institute of Economic Affairs.

Whitehead, Anne. 1997. *Paradise Mislaid: In Search of the Australian Tribe of Paraguay*. St Lucia: University of Queensland Press.

Wildavsky, Aaron, and Carolyn Webber. 1986. *A History of Taxation and Expenditure in the Western World*. New York: Simon and Schuster.

Wildes, Leon. 2016. *John Lennon vs. the USA: The Inside Story of the Most Bitterly Contested and Influential Deportation Case in United States History*. Chicago: American Bar Association.

Williams, Lucy. 2010. *Global Marriage: Cross-Border Marriage Migration in Global Context*. Basingstoke: Palgrave Macmillan.

Wong, Tom K. 2015. *Rights, Deportation, and Detention in the Age of Immigration Control*. Stanford, CA: Stanford University Press.

———. 2017. *The Politics of Immigration: Partisanship, Demographic Change, and American National Identity*. New York: Oxford University Press.

Woods, Donald. 1987. *Asking for Trouble: The Autobiography of a Banned Journalist*, London: Penguin.

Wray, Helena. 2009. 'The Points-based System: A Blunt Instrument'. *Journal of Immigration, Asylum and Nationality Law*, 23, 231–51.

———. 2015. 'The "Pure" Relationship, Sham Marriages and Immigration Control'. In *Marriage Rites and Rights*, edited by Joanna K. Miles, Rebecca Probert and Perveez Mody. Oxford: Hart Publishing.

Yang, Philip Q., and Kavitha Koshy. 2016. 'The "Becoming White Thesis" Revisited'. *Journal of Public and Professional Sociology*, 8(1), 1–25.

Ypi, Lea. 2013. 'Territorial Rights and Exclusion'. *Philosophy Compass*, 8 (3), 241–53.

Zimmer, Carl. 2018. *She Has Her Mother's Laugh: The Powers, Perversions and Potential of Heredity*. New York: Dutton.

Zinn, Howard. 1980. *A People's History of the United States*. New York: Harper.

## Online Sources

ACLU. 'Department of Homeland Security v. Vijayakumar Thuraissigiam'. https://www.aclu.org/cases/department-homeland-security-v-vijayakumar-thuraissigiam.

Akee, Randall. 30 May 2019. 'Outdated immigration laws increase violence toward women'. *Brookings*. https://www.brookings.edu/opinions/outdated-immigration-laws-increase-violence-toward-women/.

Amuedo-Dorantes, Catalina and Esther Arenas-Arroyo. October 2019. *Police Trust and Domestic Violence: Evidence from Immigration Policies*. IZA Institute of Labor Economics Discussion Paper Series, IZA DP No. 12721. https://www.immigrationresearch.org/system/files/Police%20Trust.pdf.

Anderson, Bridget, and Scott Blinder. 1 August 2014. *Who Counts as a Migrant? Definitions and Consequences*, Briefing Paper, The Migration Observatory at the University of Oxford. https://migrationobservatory.ox.ac.uk/resources/briefings/who-counts-as-a-migrant-definitions-and-their-consequences/.

Arbogast, Lydie. July 2016. *Migrant Detention in the European Union: A Thriving Business*. Migreurop. https://www.migreurop.org/IMG/pdf/migrant-detention-eu-en.pdf.

Australian Refugee Council. 2020. https://www.refugeecouncil.org.au/boats-recognised-refugees/.

Baird, Julia. 30 August 2016. 'Australia's Gulag Archipelago'. *New York Times*. https://www.nytimes.com/2016/08/31/opinion/australias-gulag-archipelago.html.

Barrett, David, Henry Samuel, and Tim Finan. 4 August 2014. 'Move Border Checks Back to Britain, Say French Politicians amid New Calais Migrants Crisis'. *Telegraph*. http://www.telegraph.co.uk/news/uknews/immigration/11011295/Move-border-checks-back-to-Britain-say-French-politicians-amid-new-Calais-migrants-crisis.html.

BBC. 14 August 2014. 'Tourists visiting UK in Record Numbers'. http://www.bbc.co.uk/news/uk-28787769.

Borjas, George J. 22 September 2016. What Does the National Academies' Immigration Report Really Say?'. *National Review.* http://www.nationalreview.com/article/440334/national-academies-sciences-immigration-study-what-it-really-says.

Briggs, Chris, and John Buchanan. 6 June 2000. *Australian Labour Market Deregulation: A Critical Assessment.* Parliament of Australia Research Paper 21, 1999–2000. http://www.aph.gov.au/About_Parliament/Parliamentary_Departments/Parliamentary_Library/pubs/rp/rp9900/2000RP21#second.

Brin, Dinah Wisenberg. 31 July 2018. 'Immigrants Form 25% of New U.S. Businesses, Driving Entrepreneurship in "Gateway" States'. *Forbes.* https://www.forbes.com/sites/dinahwisenberg/2018/07/31/immigrant-entrepreneurs-form-25-of-new-u-s-business-researchers/#69371d4713b6.

Brooks, David. 24 February 2017. 'The National Death Wish'. *New York Times.* https://www.nytimes.com/2017/02/24/opinion/the-national-death-wish.html.

Brooks, Rachel. May 2015. *The Impact of UK Immigration Policies on Students and Staff in Further and Higher Education.* University and College Union. http://classonline.org.uk/docs/Impact_of_UK_immigration_policies_on_students_and_staff_in_further_and_higher_education.pdf.

Buchanan, Pat. 18 August 2015. 'Immigration: Issue of the Century'. *Townhall.com.* http://townhall.com/columnists/patbuchanan/2015/08/18/immigration--issue-of-the-century-n2040032/page/full.

Buchardi, Konrad B., Thomas Chaney, Tarek A. Hassan, Lisa Tarquinio, and Stephen J. Terry. 28 February 2020. "Immigration, Innovation, and Growth." National Bureau of Economic Research Working Paper. https://conference.nber.org/conf_papers/f132872.pdf.

Burton, Katie. 23 July 2018. 'Calais: A Continuing Crisis'. *Geographical.* https://geographical.co.uk/people/the-refugee-crisis/item/2846-calais-refugees.

Caplan, Bryan. 28 March 2006. 'Are Low-Skilled Americans the Master Race?'. *Library of Economics and Liberty.* http://econlog.econlib.org/archives/2006/03/are_lowskilled.html.

Chalabi, Mona. 21 February 2018. 'What's behind the Rise of Interracial Marriage in the US?'. *Guardian.* https://www.theguardian.com/lifeandstyle/2018/feb/21/whats-behind-the-rise-of-interracial-marriage-in-the-us.

*Challenges and Costs of the UK Immigration System for Russell Group Universities.* 6 March 2019. https://russellgroup.ac.uk/media/5750/challenges-and-costs-of-the-uk-immigration-system-for-russell-group-universities.pdf.

Choe, Sang-hun. 2 July 2017. 'Deportation a "Death Sentence" to Adoptees after a Lifetime in the U.S.'. *New York Times.* https://www.nytimes.com/2017/07/02/world/asia/south-korea-adoptions-phillip-clay-adam-crapser.html.

Clemens, Michael A., Claudio E. Montenegro, and Lant Pritchett. 2009. "The Place Premium: Wage Differences for Identical Workers Across the U.S. Border." Center for Global Development Working Paper No. 148. https://doi.org/10.2139/ssrn.1211427.

Connolly, Kate. 2 October 2015. 'German Reunification 25 Years On: How Different Are East and West Really?'. *Guardian.* https://www.theguardian.com/world/2015/oct/02/german-reunification-25-years-on-how-different-are-east-and-west-really.

Costa, Daniel, and Jennifer Rosenbaum. 7 March 2017. 'Temporary Foreign Workers by the Numbers: New estimates by visa classification'. *Economic Policy Institute.* https://www.epi.org/publication/temporary-foreign-workers-by-the-numbers-new-estimates-by-visa-classification/.

Cowburn, Ashley. 2 August 2017. 'Majority of British Public Support Free Movement of Citizens Anywhere in the EU, New Survey Suggests'. *Independent*. http://www.independent.co.uk /news/uk/politics/eu-free-movement-support-brexit-british-people-leave-european-union -survey-a7872816.html.

Dalmia, Shikha. December 2017. 'How Immigration Crackdowns Screw Up American Lives'. *Reason*. http://reason.com/archives/2017/11/12/how-immigration-crackdowns-scr.

Dalrymple, William. 29 June 2015. 'The Great Divide: The Violent Legacy of Indian Partition'. *New Yorker*. https://www.newyorker.com/magazine/2015/06/29/the-great-divide-books -dalrymple.

Doherty, Ben. 7 July 2018. 'UN Body Condemns Australia for Illegal Detention of Asylum Seek- ers and Refugees'. *Guardian*. https://www.theguardian.com/world/2018/jul/08/un-body -condemns-australia-for-illegal-detention-of-asylum-seekers-and-refugees.

'Douglas's Letters Cast Light on Life'. 29 November 1987. *New York Times*. https://www.nytimes .com/1987/11/29/us/douglas-s-letters-cast-light-on-life.html.

Dumitriu, Sam. 11 July 2019. 'The Role of Immigrants in Start-ups'. *CAPX*. https://capx.co/the -vital-role-of-immigrants-in-start-up-britain/.

Evans, Gavin. 2 March 2018. 'The Unwelcome Revival of "Race Science"'. *Guardian*. https://www .theguardian.com/news/2018/mar/02/the-unwelcome-revival-of-race-science.

European Migration Network. 5 March 2014. *Ad-Hoc Query on Penalties and Sanctions for Employing Illegal Workers*. https://ec.europa.eu/home-affairs/sites/homeaffairs/files/what -we-do/networks/european_migration_network/reports/docs/ad-hoc-queries/illegal -immigration/530_emn_ahq_penalties_for_employing_illegal_workers_05march2014_wider _dissemination.pdf.

European Migration Network. 2015. *Determining Labour Shortages and the Need for Labour Migra- tion from Third Countries in the EU: Synthesis Report for the EMN Focussed Study 2015*. http:// extranjeros.mitramiss.gob.es/es/redeuropeamigracion/Estudios_monograficos/ficheros /2015_2016/EN_emn_labour_shortages_synthesis__final.pdf.

'Fast Facts: United States Travel and Tourism Industry—2013'. *International Trade Administration. National Travel and Tourism Office*. https://travel.trade.gov/outreachpages/download_data _table/Fast_Facts_2013.pdf.

Francis, Paul. 13 June 2016. 'Farage: Voters should let Britain take back control of its destiny'. *Kent Online*. http://www.kentonline.co.uk/thanet/news/migrants-pushing-services-to-breaking -97302/.

*Frontex Key Facts*. 2020. https://frontex.europa.eu/faq/key-facts/.

Gajanan, Mahita. 3 August 2015. 'Buzz Aldrin Walked on the Moon—Then Claimed $33.31 in Travel Expenses'. *Guardian*. http://www.theguardian.com/science/2015/aug/03/buzz-aldrin -travel-expenses-moon-apollo-11.

Gale, Alastair, and River Davis. 11 September 2019. 'The Great Immigration Experiment: Can a Country Let People in Without Stirring Backlash?'. *Wall Street Journal*. https://www.wsj .com/articles/japans-immigration-experimentcan-it-let-people-in-without-stirring-backlash -11568213741.

Gallup, Inc. 20 April 2012. '150 Million Adults Worldwide Would Migrate to the U.S.'. Gallup.com. http://www.gallup.com/poll/153992/150-million-adults-worldwide-migrate.aspx.

Gest, Justin. 19 January 2018. 'Points-based immigration System Was Meant to Reduce Racial Bias. It Doesn't'. *Guardian*. https://www.theguardian.com/commentisfree/2018/jan/19/points -based-immigration-racism.

Global Detention Project. 2015. *The Uncounted: Detention of Migrants and Asylum Seekers in Europe*. https://www.access-info.org/blog/2015/12/17/the-uncounted-migrant-detention -data-denounced/.

Gordon, Michael. 21 February 2017. 'Most Agree, Keeping Refugees on Manus and Nauru Is Cruel: Pollster'. *Sydney Morning Herald*. https://www.smh.com.au/politics/federal/most-agree -keeping-refugees-on-manus-and-nauru-is-cruel-pollster-20170221-guhz3z.html.

Green, David, Huju Liu and Yuri Ostrovsky. 21 March 2016. 'Business Ownership and Employment in Immigrant-owned Firms in Canada'. *Economic Insights*. https://www150.statcan.gc.ca/n1 /pub/11-626-x/11-626-x2016057-eng.htm.

Hague, William. 28 March 2016. 'The Brussels Attacks Show the Need to Crack Terrorist Com- munications'. *Telegraph*. https://www.telegraph.co.uk/opinion/2016/03/28/the-brussels -attacks-show-the-need-to-crack-terrorist-communicat/.

Hill, Amelia. 4 August 2017. 'US Physician May Be Forced to Quit UK because of Visa Nightmare'. *Guardian*. https://www.theguardian.com/uk-news/2017/aug/04/us-surgeon-may-be-forced -to-quit-uk-because-of-visa-nightmare.

Holehouse, Matthew. 30 July 2015. 'David Cameron Blames Calais Crisis on "swarm" of Migrants'. *Telegraph*. http://www.telegraph.co.uk/news/uknews/immigration/11772410/David -Cameron-blames-Calais-crisis-on-swarm-of-migrants.html.

Hope, Christopher. 31 October 2013. 'Home Office's "Go Home" Immigration Vans Campaign Overwhelmed by Hoax Texts and Calls'. *Telegraph*. http://www.telegraph.co.uk/news /uknews/immigration/10417987/Home-Offices-Go-Home-immigration-vans-campaign -overwhelmed-by-hoax-texts-and-calls.html.

Hurst, Daniel, and Ben Doherty. 2 February 2016. 'High Court Upholds Australia's Right to Detain Asylum Seekers Offshore'. *Guardian*. https://www.theguardian.com/australia-news/2016 /feb/03/high-court-upholds-australias-right-to-detain-asylum-seekers-offshore.

ICE. 29 March 2017. 'Human Smuggling and Trafficking Center'. http://www.ice.gov/human -smuggling-trafficking-center.

'Immigrants Are Bringing Entrepreneurial Flair to Germany'. 4 February 2017. *Economist*. https:// www.economist.com/europe/2017/02/04/immigrants-are-bringing-entrepreneurial-flair -to-germany.

Jaishankar, Dhruva. 19 February 2015. 'The Specter of Japan-Like Stagnation'. *U.S. News & World Report*. https://www.usnews.com/opinion/blogs/world-report/2015/02/19/japans -economic-stagnation-is-a-cautionary-tale-for-europe.

James, Michael, and Adam Burgos. Revised 25 May 2020. 'Race'. *Stanford Encyclopedia of Philoso- phy*, edited by Edward N. Zalta. https://plato.stanford.edu/entries/race/.

Jones, Hannah. 30 July 2014. 'Are We Going to Be Allowed to Stay Here? How Government Anti-immigration Communications Are Infiltrating Everyday Life of British Citizens'. ESRC. *Mapping Immigration Controversy*. https://mappingimmigrationcontroversy.com/2014/07 /30/arewegoingtobeallowedtostayhere/.

Keierleber, Mark. 21 August 2017. 'Sanctuary Schools across America Defy Trump's Immigra- tion Crackdown'. *Guardian*. https://www.theguardian.com/us-news/2017/aug/21/american -schools-defy-trump-immigration-crackdown.

———. 22 August 2017. 'Trump Order Could Give Immigration Agents a Foothold in US Schools'. *Guardian*. https://www.theguardian.com/us-news/2017/aug/22/trump-immigration-us -schools-education-undocumented-migrants.

Kosten, Dan. 11 July 2018. 'Immigrants as Economic Contributors: Immigrant Entrepreneurs', *National Immigration Forum*. https://immigrationforum.org/article/immigrants-as -economic-contributors-immigrant-entrepreneurs/.

Krugman, Paul. 7 October 2003. 'Lumps of Labor', *New York Times*. https://www.nytimes.com /2003/10/07/opinion/lumps-of-labor.html.

———. 27 April 2006. 'Notes on Immigration'. *New York Times*. https://krugman.blogs.nytimes .com/2006/03/27/notes-on-immigration/.

———. 24 August 2014. 'Wrong Way Nation'. *New York Times.* https://www.nytimes.com/2014 /08/25/opinion/paul-krugman-wrong-way-nation.html?_r=0.

Kukathas, Chandran. 2013. 'In Praise of the Strange Virtue of People Smuggling'. *Global Policy Journal.* http://www.globalpolicyjournal.com/blog/03/05/2013/praise-strange-virtue -people-smuggling.

———. 2 February 2017. 'Anarchy, Open Borders and Utopia'. *IAI News: Philosophy for Our Times.* https://iainews.iai.tv/articles/anarchy-open-borders-and-utopia-auid-762.

Lattimer, Mark. 22 January 1999. 'When Labour Played the Racist Card'. *New Statesman America.* https://www.newstatesman.com/when-labour-played-racist-card.

Laughland, Oliver. 11 February 2014. Australian Government Targets Asylum Seekers with Graphic Campaign'. *Guardian.* https://www.theguardian.com/world/2014/feb/11/government -launches-new-graphic-campaign-to-deter-asylum-seekers.

Leduc, Sarah. 14 February 2014. 'Retiree Stripped of French Citizenship over Technicality'. *France 24.* https://www.france24.com/en/20140214-nationality-france-citizenship-senegal-sikhou-camara.

Lindley, Anna, and Clara Della Croce. 8 March 2019. 'Migrants Granted Bail Left Trapped in British Immigration Detention because of Nowhere to Go'. *The Conversation.* https:// theconversation.com/migrants-granted-bail-left-trapped-in-british-immigration-detention -because-of-nowhere-to-go-110482.

Martin, Peter. 31 August 2017. 'The Appalling Mathematics of Offshore Detention'. *Brisbane Times.* https://www.brisbanetimes.com.au/opinion/the-appalling-mathematics-of-offshore -detention-20170830-gy6ztl.html.

Mervosh, Sarah. 22 February 2019. 'Twins Were Born to a Gay Couple. Only One Child Was Recognized as a U.S. Citizen, Until Now'. *New York Times.* https://www.nytimes.com/2019 /02/22/us/gay-couple-twin-sons-citizenship.html.

———. 21 May 2019. 'Both Parents Are American. The U.S. Says Their Baby Isn't'. *New York Times.* https://www.nytimes.com/2019/05/21/us/gay-couple-children-citizenship.html.

Migrant Rights Network. 22 July 2018. 'Go Home Vans—Five Years On . . .'. https://migrantsrights .org.uk/blog/2018/07/22/go-home-vans-five-years-on/.

Migration Watch UK. 17 January 2007. 'How Immigration Is Measured'. http://www .migrationwatchuk.org/briefingPaper/document/95.

Miller, Greg, Julie Vitkovskaya, and Reuben Fischer-Baum. 3 August 2017. ' "This Deal will Make Me Look Terrible": Full Transcripts of Trump's Telephone Calls with Mexico and Australia'. *Washington Post.* https://www.washingtonpost.com/graphics/2017/politics/australia-mexico -transcripts/?utm_term=.bb0499f99074.

Mills, Jen. 27 February 2017. 'Woman Deported from Britain after 27 Year Marriage'. *Metro.* http:// metro.co.uk/2017/02/27/woman-deported-from-britain-after-27-year-marriage-6475449/.

National Academies of Sciences. 21 September 2016. *The Economic and Fiscal Consequences of Immigration.* https://www.nap.edu/catalog/23550/the-economic-and-fiscal-consequences -of-immigration.

Nowrasteh, Alex. 2 November 2012. 'Immigrants Did Not Take Your Job'. *Cato At Liberty.* https:// www.cato.org/blog/immigrants-did-not-take-job.

Oliver, Alex. 21 June 2017. *2017 Lowy Institute Poll.* https://www.lowyinstitute.org/publications /2017-lowy-institute-poll.

Open Access Now to Detention Centres for Immigrants. 15 October 2014. *The Hidden Face of Immigration Detention Camps in Europe.* http://www.epim.info/wpcontent/uploads/2016 /04/The-hidden-face-of-immigration-detention-camps-in-Europe.pdf.

Ortiz-Ospina, Estaban, and Sandra Tzvetkova. 16 October 2017. 'Working women: Key facts and trends in female labor force participation', *Our World in Data.* https://ourworldindata.org /female-labor-force-participation-key-facts.

Palmer, Ewan. 22 August 2018. '"Crazy Rich Asians" Author Faces Jail for Dodging Military Service in Singapore'. *Newsweek*. https://www.newsweek.com/crazy-rich-asians-author-kevin-kwan-faces-jail-dodging-military-service-1084792.

Pells, Rachael. 26 January 2016. 'Science Teacher Shortage Spreads, Forcing Government to Relax Immigration Restrictions'. *Independent*. http://www.independent.co.uk/news/education/education-news/science-teacher-shortage-government-relax-immigration-restrictions-foreign-education-department-a7547406.html.

Pearlman, Jonathan. 21 February 2013. 'British Couple to Be Deported from Australia for Living in Wrong Suburb'. *Telegraph*. http://www.telegraph.co.uk/news/worldnews/australiaandthepacific/australia/9884913/British-couple-to-be-deported-from-Australia-for-living-in-wrong-suburb.html.

Peralta, Eyder. 22 December 2016. 'You Say You're an American, But What If You Had to Prove It or Be Deported?'. *NPR*. https://www.npr.org/sections/thetwo-way/2016/12/22/504031635/you-say-you-re-an-american-but-what-if-you-had-to-prove-it-or-be-deported.

Perry, Mark J. 9 March 2017. 'How Much Does Your State Need Foreign Trade?'. Foundation for Economic Education. Original source: Census Bureau. https://fee.org/articles/how-much-does-your-state-need-foreign-trade/.

Pflaum, Nadia. 26 January 2011. '"Anchor Babies" Are a Myth, as This Soon-to-be-deported Family Proves'. *Kansas City Pitch*. January 26, 2011. https://www.thepitchkc.com/news/article/20579544/anchor-babies-are-a-myth-as-this-soontobedeported-family-proves.

'Proving a Bona Fide Marriage on an I-751 Petition.' 10 July 2018. *CitizenPath*. https://citizenpath.com/proving-a-bona-fide-marriage/.

Robertson, Cassandra Burke, and Irina D. Manta. 8 July 2019. 'A Long-running Immigration Problem: The Government Sometimes Detains and Deports US Citizens'. https://theconversation.com/a-long-running-immigration-problem-the-government-sometimes-detains-and-deports-us-citizens-119702.

Sacerdote, Bruce. March 2017. 'Fifty Years of Growth in American Consumption, Income and Wages'. National Bureau of Economic Research Working Paper 23292. https://doi.org/10.3386/w23292.

Salter, Philip. 11 July 2019. 'Half of UK's Fastest-Growing Businesses Have a Foreign-Born Founder', *Forbes*. https://www.forbes.com/sites/philipsalter/2019/07/11/half-of-uks-fastest-growing-businesses-have-a-foreign-born-founder/.

Sander, Nikola, Guy J. Abel, and Ramon Bauer. February 2014. *The Global Flow of People*. Wittgenstein Centre for Demography and Global Human Capital. Version 1.0.19. http://www.global-migration.info/.

Shaw, Neil. 1 February 2017. 'Couple Given 28 Days to Leave UK after Visa Denied by Home Office because They Own a Shop'. *Daily Mirror*. http://www.mirror.co.uk/news/uk-news/couple-given-28-days-leave-9734476.

Solow, Robert. 23 April 2014. 'Thomas Piketty Is Right: Everything You Need to Know about *Capital in the Twenty-First Century*'. *New Republic*. https://newrepublic.com/article/117429/capital-twenty-first-century-thomas-piketty-reviewed).

Stevens, Jacqueline. 4 April 2018. 'When Migrants Are Treated Like Slaves'. *New York Times*. https://www.nytimes.com/2018/04/04/opinion/migrants-detention-forced-labor.html.

Stewart, Heather. 24 August 2017. 'Exit Check Data Raises Questions over May's Focus on Student Overstayers'. *Guardian*. https://www.theguardian.com/uk-news/2017/aug/24/exit-checks-data-raises-questions-over-mays-focus-on-student-overstayers.

Sun, Kevin. 19 April 2017. 'Australia Is Making Covert Propaganda Videos to Scare Off Asylum Seekers'. *Quartz Ideas*. https://qz.com/960950/australia-is-making-covert-propaganda-videos-to-scare-off-asylum-seekers/.

Swarcz, Emese. 30 November 2018. 'Making Sense of Japan's New Immigration Policy'. *The Diplomat*. https://thediplomat.com/2018/11/making-sense-of-japans-new-immigration -policy/.

Swinford, Steven. 23 August 2017. 'Immigration Figures under Review as New Checks Suggest That Numbers Are Far Lower Than Thought.' *Telegraph*. http://www.telegraph.co.uk/news /2017/08/23/immigration-figures-review-new-checks-suggest-numbers-far-lower/.

Tabarrok, Alex. 10 October 2015. 'The Case for Getting Rid of Borders—Completely.' *Atlantic*. https://www.theatlantic.com/business/archive/2015/10/get-rid-borders-completely /409501/.

Temperton, James. 26 January 2016. '40% of Britons Are Too Poor to Marry Non-EU Migrants'. *Wired*. http://www.wired.co.uk/article/migraton-non-eu-spouse-visa-uk.

Thompson, Derek. 22 February 2012. 'The Spectacular Rise and Fall of U.S. Whaling: An Innovation Story'. *Atlantic*. https://www.theatlantic.com/business/archive/2012/02/the -spectacular-rise-and-fall-of-us-whaling-an-innovation-story/253355/.

Toshihiro, Menju. 6 February 2018. 'Japan's Historic Immigration Reform: A Work in Progress'. *Nippon.com*. https://www.nippon.com/en/in-depth/a06004/japan's-historic-immigration -reform-a-work-in-progress.html.

Tourism Alliance: The Voice of Tourism. *UK Tourism Statistics 2014*. http://www.tourismalliance .com/downloads/TA_365_390.pdf.

Townsend, Kevin. 1 April 2016. 'The Terrorist Justification for Mass Surveillance'. *Security Week*. http://www.securityweek.com/terrorist-justification-mass-surveillance.

Trueger, Ian. 5 January 2018. 'Starved of Skilled Chefs, Britain Is Facing a Chicken Tikka Masala Crisis'. *Quartz India*. https://qz.com/india/1171462/starved-of-skilled-chefs-britains-curry -restaurants-are-slowly-dying/.

UNESCO. 'Migrant/Migration'. https://wayback.archive-it.org/10611/20171126022441 /http://www.unesco.org/new/en/social-and-human-sciences/themes/international -migration/glossary/migrant/

United Nations. November 1997. 'UNHCR Note on the Principle of Non-Refoulement'. *Refworld*. http://www.refworld.org/docid/438c6d972.html.

United Nations Department of Economic and Social Affairs. 17 September 2019. 'The Number of International Migrants Reaches 272 Million, Continuing an Upward Trend in All World Regions, Says UN', https://www.un.org/development/desa/en/news/population /international-migrant-stock-2019.html.

Vanderbruggen, Maaike, Jerome Phelps, Nadia Sebtaoui, Andras Kovats, and Kris Pollet. January 2014. *Point of No Return, the Futile Detention of Unreturnable Migrants*. http:// pointofnoreturn.eu/wp-content/uploads/2014/01/PONR_report.pdf.

Waldron, Jeremy. Revised Summer 2020. 'The Rule of Law'. *Stanford Encyclopedia of Philosophy*, edited by Edward N. Zalta. https://plato.stanford.edu/archives/sum2020/entries/rule-of -law/.

———. 'Property and Ownership'. Revised Summer 2020. *The Stanford Encyclopedia of Philosophy*, edited by Edward N. Zalta. https://plato.stanford.edu/archives/sum2020/entries/property/.

Walsh, Dan. 20 May 2015. 'State of Origin 2015: The Number That Proves Queensland Have Had the Better of Eligibility Wars'. *Fox Sports*. https://www.foxsports.com.au/breaking-news /state-of-origin-2015-the-number-that-proves-queensland-have-had-better-of-eligibility-war /news-story/484ac53f5e39d3e0d5bdade9ea1588bd.

Washington, R. A. 5 July 2012. 'America Settles Down: A Look at Falling Rates of Migration within the American Economy'. *Economist*. http://www.economist.com/blogs/freeexchange/2012 /07/labour-mobility.

West, John. 18 March 2016. 'Japan's Immigration Imperative'. *The Globalist*. https://www .theglobalist.com/japan-immigration-labor-workforce-economy/.

Worth Rises. 2019. 'Immigration Detention: An American Business'. https://worthrises.org/immigration.

Wren, Christopher S. 22 January 1974. 'Solzhenitsyn Calls on Russians to Reject "the Lie"'. *New York Times*. http://www.nytimes.com/1974/01/22/archives/solzhenitsyn-calls-on-russians-to-reject-the-lie-ready-for-anything.html.

Yong, Adrienne. 23 November 2017. 'When Britain Can Deport EU Citizens—According to Law', *The Conversation*. http://theconversation.com/when-britain-can-deport-eu-citizens-according-to-the-law-86896.

Zupan, Mark. 2018. N.d. 'The General Level of Wage Rates and Why Wages Differ—Week 11—The Market for Inputs.' *Coursera*. https://www.coursera.org/learn/market-efficiency/lecture/AkNXr/the-general-level-of-wage-rates-and-why-wages-differ.

## Cases and Conventions

European Commission. 21 September 2010. *Commission Communication on the Global Approach to Transfers of Passenger Name Record (PNR) Data to Third Countries*, COM (2010) 492 final.

*Plaintiff S157/2002 v The Commonwealth* (2003) 211 CLR 476.

Saudi Arabia. *Basic Law of Governance*. Royal Order No. (A/91) 27 Sha'ban 1412H—1 March 1992. Published in *Umm al-Qura Gazette*, No. 3397.

*Vienna Convention on the Law of Treaties*, 23 May 1969. 1155. U.N.T.S. 331, Article 31.

World Health Organization. 2018. *Eliminating Virginity Testing. An Interagency Statement.* https://www.who.int/reproductivehealth/publications/eliminating-virginity-testing-interagency-statement/en/.

## Parliamentary Reports and Debates

Great Britain, Parliament, House of Commons. 1904. 'Sessional Papers'. Inventory Control Record 1, Volume 39.

Hanson, Pauline. 1996. *Cth. Parliamentary Debates. House of Representatives Official Hansard No 208 1996*, 10 September 1996, 3860–63.

*Hansard*, HC Deb 7 July 1948 453, col. 403 and 411.

*Hansard*, HC Deb 20 May 1982, 24, col. 478.

*Immigration Act 1924* (US). https://loveman.sdsu.edu/docs/1924ImmigrationAct.pdf.

*Matter of Acosta*. In Deportation Proceedings A-24159781, Decided by Board March 1, 1985. https://www.justice.gov/sites/default/files/eoir/legacy/2012/08/14/2986.pdf.

## Film

Attenborough, Richard, dir. 2006. *Cry Freedom*. Film4.

Donnesmarck, Florian Henckel von, dir. 2006. *The Lives of Others (Das Leben der Anderen)*. Buena Vista.

# INDEX

## A NOTE ON THE TYPE

This book has been composed in Adobe Text and Gotham.
Adobe Text, designed by Robert Slimbach for Adobe,
bridges the gap between fifteenth- and sixteenth-century
calligraphic and eighteenth-century Modern styles.
Gotham, inspired by New York street signs, was designed
by Tobias Frere-Jones for Hoefler & Co.